THINKING THINGS THROUGH

THINKING THINGS THROUGH

AN INTRODUCTION TO PHILOSOPHICAL ISSUES AND ACHIEVEMENTS

Clark Glymour

A Bradford Book
The MIT Press
Cambridge, Massachusetts
London, England

This book was set in Times Roman by Asco Trade Typesetting Ltd., Hong Kong, and was printed and bound in the United States of America.

First printing.

Library of Congress Cataloging-in-Publication Data

Glymour, Clark N.
  Thinking things through : an introduction to philosophical issues and achievements / Clark Glymour.
        p.   cm.
  "A Bradford book"—T.p.
  Includes bibliographical references and index.
  ISBN 0-262-07141-X
  1. Philosophy. 2. Evidence. 3. Knowledge, Theory of. 4. Philosophy of mind. I. Title.
  B74.G59   1992
  121—dc20   91-45667
                                                                               CIP

For my parents, Joseph Hiram Clark Glymour and
Virginia Roberta Lynch Glymour

CONTENTS

PREFACE

An old story about a great teacher of philosophy, Morris Raphael Cohen, goes like this. One year after the last lecture in Cohen's introductory philosophy course, a student approached and protested, "Professor Cohen, you have destroyed everything I believed in, but you have given me nothing to replace it." Cohen is said to have replied, "Sir, you will recall that one of the labors of Hercules was to clean the Augean stables. You will further recall that he was not required to refill them."

I'm with the student. People who are curious about the subject may want a historical view of philosophy, but they also may want to know what, other than that very history, philosophy has left them. In fact, the history of philosophy has informed and even helped to create broad areas of contemporary intellectual life; it seems a disservice both to students and to the subject to keep those contributions secret. The aim of this text is to provide an introduction to philosophy that shows both the historical development and modern fruition of a few central questions. The issues I consider are these:

- What is a demonstration, and why do proofs provide knowledge?
- How can we use experience to gain knowledge or to alter our beliefs in a rational way?
- What is the nature of minds and of mental events and mental states?

In our century the tradition of philosophical reflection on these questions has helped to create the subjects of cognitive psychology, computer science, artificial intelligence, mathematical logic, and the Bayesian branch of statistics. The aim of this book is to make these connections accessible to qualified students and to give enough detail to challenge the very best of them. I have selected the topics because the philosophical issues seem especially central and enduring and because many of the contemporary fields they have given rise to are open-ended and exciting. Other connections between the history of philosophy and contemporary subjects, for example the connection with modern physics, are treated much more briefly. Others are not treated at all for lack of space. I particularly regret the absence of chapters on ethics, economics, and law.

This book is meant to be used in conjunction with selections from the greats, and suggestions for both historical and contemporary readings accompany most chapters. The book is intended as an introduction, the whole of which can be read by a well-educated high school graduate who is willing to do some work. It is not, however, particularly easy. Philosophy is not easy. My experience is that much of this book can be read with profit by more advanced students interested in epistemology and metaphysics, and by those who come to philosophy after training in some other discipline. I have tried in every case to make the issues and views clear, simple, and coherent, even when that sometimes required ignoring real complexities in the philosophical tradition or ignoring alternative interpretations. I have avoided disingenuous defenses of arguments that I think unsound, even though this sometimes has the effect of slighting certain passages to which excellent scholars have devoted careers. A textbook is not the place to develop original views on contemporary issues. Nonetheless, parts of this book may interest professional philosophers for what those parts have to say about some contemporary topics. This is particularly true, I hope, of chapters 10, 11, and 13.

Especially challenging or difficult sections and chapters of the book are marked with an asterisk. They include material that I believe is essential to a real understanding of the problems, theories, and achievements that have issued from philosophical inquiry, but they require more tolerance for mathematical details than do the other parts of the book. Sometimes other chapters use concepts from sections with asterisks, and I leave it to instructors or readers to fill in any background that they omit. Each chapter is accompanied by a bibliography of suggested readings. The bibliographies are not meant to be exhaustive or even representative. Their purpose is only to provide the reader with a list of volumes that together offer an introduction to the literature on various topics.

I thank Kevin Kelly for a great deal of help in thinking about how to present the philosophical issues in historical context, for influencing my views about many topics, and for many of the illustrations. Andrea Woody read the entire manuscript in pieces and as a whole and suggested a great many improvements. She also helped to construct the bibliographies. Douglas Stalker gave me detailed and valuable comments on a first draft. Alison Kost read and commented on much of the manuscript. Martha Scheines read, revised, and proofread a preliminary draft. Alan Thwaits made especially valuable stylistic suggestions and corrected several errors. Versions of this book were used in introductory philosophy courses for three years at Carnegie-Mellon University, and I am grateful to the students who endured them.

Part I

THE IDEA OF PROOF

Chapter 1

PROOFS

INTRODUCTION

Philosophy is concerned with very general questions about the structure of the world, with how we can best acquire knowledge about the world, and with how we should act in the world. The first topic, the structure of the world, is traditionally known as *metaphysics*. The second topic, how we can acquire knowledge of the world, is traditionally called *epistemology*. The third topic, what actions and dispositions are best, is the subject of *ethics*. The first two studies, metaphysics and epistemology, inevitably go together. What one thinks about the structure of the world has a lot to do with how one thinks inquiry should proceed, and vice versa. These topics in turn involve issues about the nature of the mind, for it is the mind that knows. Considerations of ethics depend in part on our metaphysical conception of the world and ourselves, on our conception of mind, and on how we believe knowledge to be acquired.

These traditional branches of philosophy no doubt seem very abstract and vague. They may seem superfluous as well: Isn't the question of the structure of the world part of *physics*? Aren't questions about how we acquire knowledge and about our minds part of *psychology*? Indeed they are. What, then, are metaphysics and epistemology, and what are the methods by which these subjects are supposed to be pursued? How are they different from physics and psychology and other scientific subjects? Questions such as these are often evaded in introductions to philosophy, but let me try to answer them.

First, there are a lot of questions that are usually not addressed in physics or psychology or other scientific subjects but that still seem to have something to do with them. Consider the following examples:

- How can we know there are particles too small to observe?
- What constitutes a scientific explanation?
- How do we know that the process of science leads to the truth, whatever the truth may be?
- What is meant by "truth"?
- Does what is true depend on what is believed?
- How can anyone know there are other minds?
- What facts determine whether a person at one moment of time is the same person as a person at another moment of time?
- What are the limits of knowledge?
- How can anyone know whether she is following a rule?
- What is a proof?
- What does "impossible" mean?
- What is required for beliefs to be rational?
- What is the best way to conduct inquiry?
- What is a computation?

The questions have *something* to do with physics or psychology (or with mathematics or linguistics), but they aren't questions you will find addressed in textbooks on these subjects. The questions seem somehow too fundamental to be answered in the sciences; they seem to be the kind of questions that we just do not know how to answer by a planned program of observations or experiments. And yet the questions don't seem unimportant; how we answer them might lead us to conduct physics, psychology, mathematics or other scientific disciplines very differently. These are the sorts of questions particular scientific disciplines usually either ignore or else presume to answer more or less without argument. And they are a sample, a small sample, of the questions that concern philosophy.

If these questions are so vague and so general that we have no idea of how to conduct experiments or systematic observations to find their answers, what can philosophers possibly have done with them that is of any value? The philosophical tradition contains a wealth of proposed answers to fundamental questions about metaphysics and epistemology. Sometimes the answers are supported by arguments based on a variety of unsystematic observations, sometimes by reasons that ought to be quite unconvincing in themselves. The answers face the objections that they are either unclear or inconsistent, that the arguments produced for them are unsound, or that some other body of unsystematic observations conflict with them. Occasionally an answer or system of answers is worked out precisely and fully enough that it can deservedly be called a theory, and a variety of consequences of the theory can be rigorously drawn, sometimes by mathematical methods. What is the use of this sort of philosophical speculation? On occasion the tradition of attempts at philosophical answers has led to theories that seem so forceful and so fruitful that they become the foundation for entire scientific disciplines; enter our culture, our science, our politics; and guide our lives. That is the case, for example, with the discipline of computer science, created by the results of more than 2,000 years of attempts to answer one apparently trivial question: What is a demonstration, a proof? An entire branch of modern statistics, often called Bayesian statistics, arose through philosophical efforts to answer the question, What is rational belief? The theory of rational decision making, at the heart of modern economics, has the same ancestry. Contemporary cognitive science, which tries to study the human mind through computer models of human behavior and thought, is the result of joining a philosophical tradition of speculation about the structure of mind with the fruits of philosophical inquiry into the nature of proof.

So one answer to why philosophy was worth doing is simply that it was the most creative subject: rigorous philosophical speculation formed the basis for much of contemporary science; it literally created new sciences. Moreover, the role of philosophy in forming computer science, Bayesian statistics, the theory of rational decision making, and cognitive science isn't ancient history. These subjects were all informed by developments in philosophy within the last 100 years.

But if that is why philosophy *was* worth doing, why is it still worth doing? Because not everything is settled and there may be fruitful alternatives even to what has been settled. In this chapter and those that follow we will see some of the history of speculation and argument that generated a number of contemporary scientific disciplines. We will also see that there can be reasonable doubts about the foundations of some of these disciplines. And we will see a vast space of further topics that require philosophical reflection, conjecture, and argument.

FORMS OF REASONING AND SOME FUNDAMENTAL QUESTIONS

Part of the process by which we acquire knowledge is the process of reasoning. There are many ways in which we reason, or *argue* for conclusions. Some ways seem more certain and convincing than others. Some forms of reasoning seem to show that *if certain premises are assumed, then a conclusion necessarily follows*. Such reasoning claims to be *deductive*. Correct deductive arguments show that if their premises are true, their conclusions are true. Such arguments are said to be *valid*. (If an argument tries to demonstrate that a conclusion follows necessarily from certain premises but fails to do so, the argument is said to be *invalid*.) If, in addition to being valid, an argument has premises that are true, then the argument is said to be *sound*. Valid deductive arguments guarantee that if their premises are true, their conclusions are true. So if one believes the premises of a valid deductive argument, one *ought* to believe the conclusion as well. The paradigm of deductive reasoning is mathematical proofs, but deductive reasoning is not confined to the discipline of mathematics. Deductive reasoning is used in every natural science, in every social science, and in all applied sciences. In all of these subjects, the kind of deductive reasoning characteristic of mathematics has an important role, but deductive reasoning can also be found entirely outside of mathematical contexts. Whatever the subject, some assumptions may necessitate the truth of other claims, and the reasoning that reveals such necessary connections is deductive. We also find attempts at such reasoning throughout the law and in theology, economics, and everyday life.

There are many forms of reasoning that are *not* deductive. Sometimes we argue that a conclusion ought to be believed because it provides the best explanation for phenomena; sometimes we argue that a conclusion ought to be believed because of some analogy with something already known to be true; sometimes we argue from statistical samples to larger populations. These forms of reasoning are called *inductive*. In inductive reasoning, the premises or assumptions do not necessitate the conclusions.

Of the many ways in which we reason, deductive reasoning, characteristic of mathematics, has historically seemed the most fundamental, the very first thing a philosopher should try to understand. It has seemed fundamental for two reasons. First, unlike other forms of reasoning, valid deductive reasoning provides a *guarantee*: we can be certain that if the premises of such an argument are true, the conclusion is also true. In contrast, various forms of inductive reasoning may provide useful knowledge, but they do not provide a comparable guarantee that if their premises are true, then so are their conclusions. Second, the very possibility of deductive reasoning must be somehow connected with the structure of the world. For deductive reasoning is reasoning in which the assumptions, or premises, necessitate the conclusions. But how can the world and language be so structured that some claims make others necessary? What is it about the postulates of arithmetic, for example, that makes $2 + 2 = 4$ a necessary consequence of them? What is it about the world and the language in which we express the postulates of arithmetic that guarantees us that if we count 2 things in one pile and 2 in another, then the count of all things in one pile or the other is 4?

Such questions may seem trivial or bizarre or just irritating, but we will see that efforts to answer them have led to the rich structure of modern logic and mathematics, and to the entire subject of computer science. If such questions could be answered, we might obtain a deeper understanding of the the relations between our words and thoughts on the one hand and the world they are supposed to be about on the other. So some of the fundamental questions that philosophy has pursued for 2,500 years are these:

• How can we determine whether or not a piece of reasoning from premises to a conclusion is a valid deductive argument?
• How can we determine whether or not a conclusion is necessitated by a set of premises? If a conclusion is necessitated by a set of premises, how can we find a valid deductive argument that demonstrates that necessary connection?
• What features of the structure of the world, the structure of language, and the relation between words and thoughts and things make deductive reasoning possible?

To answer these questions is to provide a *theory* of deductive reasoning. Any such theory will be part metaphysics and part epistemology. It will tell us something about sorts of things there are in the world (objects? properties? relations? numbers? sets? propositions? relations of necessity? meanings?) and how we can know about them or use them to produce knowledge.

The next few chapters of this book are devoted to these questions. In the remainder of this chapter I will consider a variety of purported deductive arguments that have played an important role in one or another area of the history of thought. The examples are important for several reasons. They give us cases where want to be able to distinguish valid from invalid arguments. They also provide concepts that are important throughout the history of philosophy and that are essential to material presented later in this book. Finally, they start us on the way to analyzing the fundamental issues of how we learn about the structure of the world.

This chapter will present some examples of arguments that are good proofs, some examples of arguments that are defective but can be remedied, and some arguments that are not proofs at all. Part of what we are concerned with is to find conditions that *separate* valid deductive arguments from invalid deductive arguments. Any theory of deductive reasoning we construct should provide a way to distinguish the arguments that seem valid from the arguments that seem invalid. To get some practice for this part of the task of theory building, we will look at simple cases in which we want to form a theory that will include some examples and exclude a number of other examples. The cases we will consider first don't have to do with the idea of deductive reasoning, but they do illustrate many aspects of what a theory of deductive reasoning ought to provide: they separate the correct instances, the positive examples, of a concept from the incorrect instances, the negative examples.

Here is a very simple case. Suppose you are given this sequence of numbers: 1, 2, 5, 10, 17, 26, 37, 50, 65, 82. What is the general rule for continuing the sequence? In this case the numbers listed are positive examples to be included in a formula, and all the numbers between 1 and

---

The Socratic method

Socrates was Plato's teacher. About 399 B.C., at the age of 70, he was put to death by the citizens of Athens, ostensibly for impiety and corrupting the youth of the city but probably in fact for his political views and for the political actions of some of his students. Plato authored a series of philosophical dialogues in which Socrates is always the major figure. Socrates, as Plato depicted him, was concerned with such questions as, What is knowledge? What is virtue? His procedure for inquiring into such questions was to collect positive cases, of virtue for example, and negative cases as well. He then attempted to formulate conditions that will include all of the positive examples and none of the negative examples. If further examples were found that conflict with a proposed condition (that is, positive examples the condition does not include or negative examples the condition does include), Socrates (or other characters in Plato's dialogues) then tried a new condition. Plato's Socrates applied the method to understanding natural objects and kinds and also moral kinds, such as virtue.

Plato held that true understanding of anything, of virtue for example, requires more than a theory that includes all the positive examples of virtue and excludes all the negative examples. One must also know *why* the positive examples of virtue are positive examples, i.e., what ties them together.

82 not in the list are negative examples that should not be included. (The sequence can be generated by the formula $n^2 + 1$, for $n = 0, 1, 2, 3$, and so on.)

Let's consider a very different kind of example, one where there are again a number of positive examples and a number of negative examples. Suppose you are given the positive and negative examples of arches shown in figure 1.1. How could you state conditions that include the positive examples but exclude the negative examples? You might try something like this: "X is an arch if and only if X consists of two series of blocks, and in each series each block except the first is supported by another block of that

Positive examples

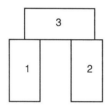

Block 1 and block 2 support block 3, and blocks 1 and 2 do not touch one another.

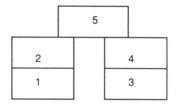

Block 1 supports block 2; block 3 supports block 4; blocks 2 and 4 support block 5; blocks 1 and 2 do not touch block 3 or block 4.

Negative examples

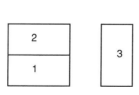

Block 1 supports block 2; blocks 1 and 2 do not touch block 3.

Blocks 1 and 2 support block 3; blocks 1 and 2 touch.

Figure 1.1
Positive and negative examples of arches

series, and no block in one series touches any block in the other series, and there is a block supported by a block in each series."

Here is still another kind of example. Artificial languages, such as programming languages or simple codes, are constructed out of vocabulary elements. A statement in such a language is a finite sequence of vocabulary elements. But not *every* sequence of vocabulary elements will make sense in the language. In BASIC or Pascal you can't just write down any sequence of symbols and have a well-formed statement. The same is true in natural languages, such as English. Not just any string of words in English makes an English sentence. Suppose you learned that the examples in table 1.1 are positive and negative examples of well-formed sequences in some unknown code, and suppose you also knew that there are an infinite number of other well-formed sequences in the code. What do you guess is the condition for a well-formed sequence in this code? Can you find a general condition that includes all of the positive examples and none of the negative examples?

Table 1.1
Sequences in a code

Positive examples (well formed)	Negative examples (not well formed)
AA	AAAA
BB	BBBB
AABB	BBBBAA
AAABB	AABBBB
BBAA	AAAAAA
BBAAA	BBBBBB
BBAABB	AAAAAAAABB
BBAABBB	BBAAAAAAAA
AABBB	AAAAAAAAA
AABBAAA	BBBBBBBBB
AAABBAAA	
AAABBBAAA	
AAA	
BBB	
AAAAA	
BBBBB	
A	
B	

For several reasons the philosophical problem with which we are concerned is more difficult than any of these examples. We want a theory that will separate valid deductive arguments from deductive arguments that are not valid. The problem is intrinsically difficult because the forms of deductive argument are very complex. It is also difficult because we are not always sure whether or not to count specific arguments as valid. And finally, this philosophical problem is intrinsically more difficult because we not only want a theory that will separate valid demonstrations from invalid ones, we also want to know *why* and *how* valid demonstrations ensure that if their premises are true then necessarily their conclusions are true.

In keeping with the Socratic method, the first thing to do in trying to understand the nature of demonstration is to collect a few examples. The histories of philosophy, science, mathematics, and religion are filled with arguments that claim to be proofs of their conclusions. Unfortunately, the arguments don't come labeled "valid" or "invalid," and we must decide for ourselves, after examination, whether an argument is good, bad, or good enough to be reformulated into a valid argument. We will next consider a series of examples of simple arguments from geometry, theology, metaphysics, and set theory. The point of the examples is always to move toward an understanding of the three questions above.

GEOMETRY

Euclid's geometry is still studied in secondary schools, although not always in the form in which he developed it. Euclid developed geometry as an *axiomatic system*. After a sequence of definitions, Euclid's *Elements* gives a sequence of assumptions. Some of these have nothing to do with geometry in particular. Euclid calls them "common notions." Others have specifically geometrical content. Euclid calls them "postulates." The theorems of geometry are deduced from the common notions and the postulates. Euclid's aim is that his assumptions will be sufficient to necessitate, or as we now say, *entail*, all the truths of geometry. We aspire for *completeness*. This means that every question about geometry expressible in Euclid's terms can be answered by his assumptions if only the proof of the answer can be found. Some of Euclid's definitions, common notions, postulates, and the first proposition he proves from them are given below:

Plato and Euclid

Plato, who died about 347 B.C., is recognized as the first systematic Western philosopher. During the height of the Athenian empire Plato directed a school, the Academy, devoted to both mathematics and philosophy. No study of philosophy was possible in the Academy without a study of mathematics. The principal mathematical subject was geometry, although arithmetic and other mathematical subjects were also studied. It seems likely that textbooks on geometry were produced in Plato's Academy and that these texts attempted to systematize the subject and derive geometrical theorems from simpler assumptions (the Greeks called the simple parts of a thing its *elements*). Euclid studied in the Academy around 300 B.C., and his book, *The Elements*, is thought to be derived from earlier texts of the school. Euclid later established his own mathematical school in Alexandria, Egypt.

Definitions

1. A point is that which has no part.
2. A line is breadthless length.
3. The extremities of a line are points.
4. A straight line is a line that lies evenly with the points on itself.
5. A surface is that which has length and breadth only.
6. The extremities of a surface are lines.
7. A plane surface is a surface that lies evenly with the straight lines on itself.
8. A plane angle is the inclination to one another of two lines in a plane that meet one another and do not lie in a straight line.
9. And when the lines containing the angle are straight, the angle is called rectilinear.
10. When a straight line set up on a straight line makes the adjacent angles equal to one another, each of the equal angles is right, and the straight line standing on the other is called a perpendicular to that on which it stands.
11. An obtuse angle is an angle greater than a right angle.
12. An acute angle is an angle less than a right angle.
13. A boundary is that which is an extremity of anything.
14. A figure is that which is contained by any boundary or boundaries.
15. A circle is a plane figure contained by one line such that all the straight lines falling upon it from one point among those lying within the figure are equal to one another.

16. And the point is called the center of the circle.

⋮

19. Rectilinear figures are those contained by straight lines, trilateral figures being those contained by three.

20. Of trilateral figures, an equilateral triangle is that which has its three sides equal.

⋮

23. Parallel straight lines are straight lines that, being in the same plane and being produced indefinitely in both directions, do not meet one another in either direction.

Common notions

1. Things that are equal to the same thing are also equal to one another.
2. If equals be added to equals, the wholes are equal.
3. If equals be subtracted from equals, the remainders are equal.
4. Things which coincide with one another are equal to one another.
5. The whole is greater than the part.

Postulates

1. It is possible to draw a straight line from any point to any point.
2. It is possible to produce a finite straight line continuously in a straight line.
3. It is possible to describe a circle with any center and distance.
4. All right angles are equal to one another.
5. If a straight line falling on two straight lines make the interior angles on the same side less than two right angles, the two straight lines, if produced indefinitely, meet on the side of the angles less than the two right angles.

Proposition 1   For every straight-line segment, there exists an equilateral triangle having that line segment as one side.

Proof   Let AB be the given finite straight line. Thus it is required to construct an equilateral triangle on the straight line AB. Let circle BCD be drawn with center A and distance AB (postulate 3). Again, let circle ACE be drawn with center B and distance BA (postulate 3). And from point C, at which the circles cut one another, to points A, B, let the straight lines CA, CB be joined (postulate 1). (see figure 1.2.) Now since point A is the center of the circle CDB, AC is equal to AB. Again, since point B is the center of circle CAE, BC is equal to BA. But CA was also proved equal to AB. Therefore, each of the straight lines CA, CB is equal to AB. And

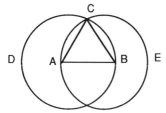

Figure 1.2

things that are equal to the same thing are also equal to one another (common notion 1). Therefore, *CA* is also equal to *CB*. Therefore, the three straight lines *CA*, *AB*, *BC* are equal to one another. Therefore, triangle *ABC* is equilateral, and it has been constructed on the given straight line *AB*.[1] Q.E.D.

Lest we forget, the central philosophical questions we have about Euclid's proposition concern whether or not his assumptions do in fact *necessitate* that for any line segment there exists an equilateral triangle having that segment as a side, and if they do necessitate this proposition, why and how the necessitation occurs. We will not even begin to consider theories that attempt to answer this question until the next chapter. For the present, note some things about Euclid's proof of his first proposition.

• The proof is like a short essay in which one sentence follows another in sequence.
• Each sentence of the proof is *justified* either by preceding sentences of the proof or by the definitions, postulates, or common notions.
• The conclusion to be proved is stated in the last sentence of the proof.
• The proposition proved is logically quite complex. It asserts that for *every* line segment *L*, there exists an object *T* that is an equilateral triangle, and that *T* and *L* stand in a particular *relation*, namely that the equilateral triangle *T* has line segment *L* as one side.
• Euclid actually claims to prove something stronger. What he claims to prove is that *if* his postulates are understood to guarantee a method for finding a line segment connecting any two points (as with a ruler) and a method for constructing a circle of any specified radius (as with a compass), then there is a *procedure* that will actually construct an equilateral triangle having any given line segment as one side. Euclid's proof that such triangles exist is *constructive*. It shows they exist by giving a general procedure, or *algorithm*, for constructing them.

• The proof comes with a picture (figure 1.2). The picture illustrates the idea of the proof and makes the sentences in the proof easier to understand. Yet the picture itself does not seem to be part of the argument for the proposition, only a way of making the argument more easily understood.

Before we leave Euclid (although we will consider him and this very proof again in the later chapters), I should note some important features of his definitions. Some of the definitions define geometrical notions, such as "point" and "line," that are used in the propositions of Euclid's geometry. These notions are defined *in terms of* other notions that the reader is supposed to understand already. Definition 1 says, "A point is that which has no part." Unless we have a prior understanding of "part" that is mathematically exact (which is not very likely), this definition can be of no use in Euclid's proofs. Why is it there? Presumably to aid our intuitions in reading the subsequent propositions and proofs. Most of Euclid's definitions are like this; they define a geometrical notion in terms of some other undefined notions. (In fact, there are quite a few undefined notions used in the definitions.) But some of Euclid's definitions define geometric notions at least partly in terms of other *geometric* notions. Thus definition 15, the definition of a circle, defines circles in terms of the notions of figure, boundary, line, equality of straight lines, and incidence ("falling upon") of a straight line and a line.

We have seen in Euclid's system and his first proposition something that is *almost* a demonstration of a conclusion from premises. We have also seen that his argument has a special structure, different, for example, from the structure a poem might have, and that it contains features designed as psychological aids to the reader. We have also seen that it is hopeless to try to define every term but that it is not in the least pointless to try to give informal explanations of the meanings of technical terms used in an argument.

Study Questions

1. List the undefined terms that occur in Euclid's definitions.

2. The key idea in Euclid's proof is to use point C, where the circle centered at A and the circle centered at B intersect, as the third vertex (besides A and B) of an equilateral triangle. Does anything in Euclid's axioms guarantee that the circle centered on A and the circle centered on B intersect?

3. Describe an imaginary world in which proposition 1 is *false*. (Hint: Imagine a space that has only one dimension.) Which of Euclid's postulates, if any, are also false in this world?

4. Are there contexts in which a proof consists of nothing more than a picture? Consider questions about whether or not a plane surface can be completely covered by tiles of a fixed shape, hexagons or pentagons, for example.

5. One of the aims of Euclid's formulation of geometry seems to have been to derive all of geometry from assumptions that are very simple and whose truth seems self-evident. Do any of Euclid's five postulates seem less simple and less self-evident that the others? Why?

GOD AND SAINT ANSELM

From the first centuries after Christ until the seventeenth century, most civilized Europeans believed in nothing so firmly as the existence of God. Despite the scarcity of doubters, Christian intellectuals still sought proofs of God's existence and wrote arguments against real or imagined atheists. Some of these attempts at demonstrations of the existence of God are still presented in religious schools nowadays, even though most logicians regard them as simple fallacies. However, at least one of the medieval proofs of the existence of God, Saint Anselm's (1033–1109), is still of some logical interest. Let's consider it.

Anselm gave his proof of the existence of God in several forms. Two versions of the argument are given in the following passage:

And so, O Lord, since thou givest understanding to faith, give me to understand—as far as thou knowest it to be good for me—that thou dost exist, as we believe, and that thou art what we believe thee to be. Now we believe that thou art a being than which none greater can be thought. Or can it be that there is no such being since "the fool hath said in his heart, 'There is no God'" [Psalms 14:1; 53:1]. But when this same fool hears what I am saying—"A being than which none greater can be thought"—he understands what he hears, and what he understands is in his understanding, even if he does not understand that it exists. For it is one thing for an object to be in the understanding, and another thing to understand that it exists. When a painter considers beforehand what he is going to paint, he has it in his understanding, but he does not suppose that what he has not yet painted already exists. But when he has painted it, he both has it in his understanding and understands that what he has now produced exists. Even the fool, then, must be convinced that a being than which none greater can be thought exists at least in his understanding, since when he hears this he understands it, and whatever is understood is in the understanding. But clearly that than which a greater cannot be thought cannot exist in the understanding alone. For if it is actually in the understanding alone, it can be thought of as existing also in reality, and this is greater. Therefore, if that than which a greater cannot be thought is in the understanding alone, this same thing than which a greater cannot be thought is that than which a greater can be thought. But obviously this is impossible. Without doubt, therefore, there exists, both in the understanding and in reality, something than which a greater cannot be thought.

God cannot be thought of as nonexistent. And certainly it exists so truly that it cannot be thought of as nonexistent. For something can be thought of as existing, which cannot be thought of as not existing, and this is greater than that which can be thought of as not existing. Thus if that than which a greater cannot be thought can be thought of as not existing, this very thing than which a greater cannot be thought is *not* that than which a greater cannot be thought. But this is contradictory. So, then, there truly is a being than which a greater cannot be thought—so truly that it cannot even be thought of as not existing.[2]

Anselm's argument in the second paragraph just cited might be outlined in the following way:

Premise 1: A being that cannot be thought of as not existing is greater than a being that can be thought of as not existing.

Therefore, if God can be thought of as not existing, then a greater being that cannot be thought of as not existing can be thought of.

Premise 2: God is the being than which nothing greater can be thought of.

Conclusion: God cannot be thought of as not existing.

The sentence in the reconstruction beginning with "Therefore" does not really follow from premise 1. It requires the further assumption, which Anselm clearly believed but did not state, that it is possible to think of a being than which nothing greater can be conceived or thought of.

The argument of the first paragraph seems slightly different, and more complicated. I outline it as follows:

Premise 1: We can conceive of a being than which none greater can be conceived.

Premise 2: Whatever is conceived exists in the understanding of the conceiver.

Premise 3: That which exists in the understanding of a conceiver and also exists in reality is greater than an otherwise similar thing that exists only in the understanding of a conceiver.

Therefore, a being conceived, than which none greater can be conceived, must exist in reality as well as in the understanding.

Premise 4: God is a being than which none greater can be conceived.

Conclusion: God exists in reality.

The arguments seem very different from Euclid's proof. Anselm's presentation is not axiomatic. There is no system of definitions and postulates. In some other respects, however, Anselm's arguments have similarities to Euclid's geometric proof. Note the following about Anselm's arguments:

• Anselm's arguments are meant to be demonstrations of their conclusions from perfectly uncontroversial premises. The arguments aim to show that the truth of the premises necessitates the truth of the conclusions.

• In the first argument, the discussion of the painter and the painting is not essential to the proof. Anselm includes the discussion of a painter and painting to help the reader understand what he, Anselm, means by distinguishing between an object existing in the understanding and understanding that an object exists. The painter discussion therefore plays a role in Anselm's proof much like the role played by the drawing in Euclid's proof: it is there to help the reader see what is going on, but it is not essential to the argument.

• Like Euclid's proof, Anselm's arguments can be viewed as little essays in which, if we discount explanatory remarks and digressions, each claim is intended to follow either from previous claims or from claims that every reader will accept.

Study Questions

1. Anselm seems to have thought that his arguments establish that there is one and *only one* being than which none greater can be conceived. But his premises do not appear to necessitate that conclusion; we could consistently suppose that there are many distinct beings each of which is such that none greater can be conceived. What plausible premises might Anselm add that would ensure that at most one being is such that none greater can be conceived?

2. One famous objection to Anselm's argument is this: If Anselm's argument were valid, then by the same form of reasoning, we could prove that a perfect island exists. But the island than which none greater can be conceived does not exist in reality. Therefore, something must be wrong with Anselm's proof of the existence of God. Give an explicit argument that follows the form of Anselm's and leads to the conclusion that there exists an island than which none greater can be conceived. Is the objection a good one? Has Anselm any plausible reply?

3. Giving a convincing counterexample to an argument shows that either the premises of the argument are false or the premises do not necessitate the truth of the conclusion. But the "perfect island" objection does not show specifically what is wrong with Anselm's argument. Try to explain specifically what is wrong with your proof that there exists a perfect island.

GOD AND SAINT THOMAS

Let me add another example to our collection of demonstrations. The most famous proofs of the existence of God are due to Saint Thomas Aquinas (ca. 1225–1274). Aquinas gave five proofs, which are sometimes referred to as the "five ways." They are presented in relatively concise form in his *Summa Theologica*. Four of the five arguments have essentially the same form, and the fifth is particularly obscure. I will consider only the first argument. In reading the argument, you must bear in mind that Aquinas had a very different picture of the physical universe than ours, and he assumed that his readers would fully share his picture. That picture derives from Aristotle. According to the picture Aquinas derived from Aristotelian physics, objects do not move unless acted on by another object. Further, Aristotle distinguished between the properties an object *actually* has and the properties it has the *potential* to have. Any change in an object consists in the object coming actually to have properties that it previously had only potentially.

In translation Aquinas's argument is as follows:

The existence of God can be proved in five ways.

The first and most manifest way is the argument from motion. It is certain, and evident to our senses, that in the world some things are in motion. Now whatever

---

Aquinas and Aristotle

Aristotle was a student of Plato's. After Plato's death, Aristotle left Athens and subsequently became tutor to Alexander of Macedonia, later Alexander the Great. When Alexander conquered Greece, Aristotle returned to Athens and opened his own school. With the collapse of the Macedonian empire, Aristotle had to flee Athens, and he died a year later. During his life he wrote extensively on logic, scientific method and philosophy of science, metaphysics, physics, biology, cosmology, rhetoric, ethics and other topics. Saint Thomas Aquinas helped to make Aristotle's philosophy acceptable to Christian Europe in the late Middle Ages. Writing in the thirteenth century, Aquinas gave Christianized versions of Aristotle's cosmology, physics, and metaphysics. The result of the efforts of Aquinas and others was to integrate Aristotelian thought into the doctrines of the Roman Catholic Church in the late Middle Ages. Aristotle's doctrines also became central in the teachings of the first universities, which began in Europe during the thirteenth century. The tradition of Christian Aristotelian thought that extends from the Middle Ages to the seventeenth century is known as *scholasticism*.

is moved is moved by another, for nothing can be moved except it is in potentiality to that towards which it is moved; whereas a thing moves inasmuch as it is in actuality. For motion is nothing else than the reduction of something from potentiality to actuality. But nothing can be reduced from potentiality to actuality, except by something in a state of actuality. Thus that which is actually hot, as fire, makes wood, which is potentially hot, to be actually hot, and thereby moves and changes it. Now it is not possible that the same thing should be at once in actuality and potentiality in the same respect, but only in different respects. For what is actually hot cannot simultaneously be potentially hot; but it is simultaneously potentially cold. It is therefore impossible that in the same respect and in the same way a thing should be both mover and moved, i.e., that it should move itself. Therefore, whatever is moved must be moved by another. If that by which it is moved be itself moved, then this also must needs be moved by another, and that by another again. But this cannot go to infinity, because then there would be no first mover, and, consequently, no other mover, seeing that subsequent movers move only inasmuch as they are moved by the first mover; as the staff moves only because it is moved by the hand. Therefore it is necessary to arrive at a first mover, moved by no other; and this everyone understands to be God.[3]

Aquinas's attempted demonstration again shares many of the features of Euclid's and Anselm's arguments. From premises that are supposed, at the time, to be uncontroversial, a conclusion is intended to follow necessarily. The argument is again a little essay, with claims succeeding one another in a logical sequence. The example of heat is another illustration, like Anselm's painter and Euclid's diagram, intended to further the reader's understanding, but it is not an essential part of the argument.

Aquinas's argument illustrates that a proof (or attempted proof) may have another proof contained within it. Thus the remarks about potentiality and actuality are designed to serve as an argument for the conclusion that nothing moves itself, and that conclusion in turn serves as a premise in the argument for the existence of an unmoved mover.

Neglecting Aquinas's remarks about potentiality, which serve as a subargument for premise 2, we can outline the argument in the following way:

Premise 1: Some things move.

Premise 2: Anything that moves does so because of something else.

Therefore, if whatever moves something itself moves, it must be moved by a third thing.

Therefore, if there were an infinite sequence of movers, there would be no first mover, and hence no movers at all.

Therefore, there cannot be an infinite sequence of movers.

Conclusion: There is a first, unmoved mover.

One way to show that the premises of the argument do not necessitate Aquinas's conclusion is to imagine some way in which the premises of the argument could be true and the conclusion could at the same time be false. With this argument, that is easy to do. We can imagine that if object *A* moves object *B*, object *B* moves object *A*. In that case no third object would be required to explain the motion of *B*. We can also imagine an infinite chain of objects in which the first object is moved by the second, the second by the third, the third by the fourth, and so on forever. Neither of these imaginary circumstances is self-contradictory (although Aquinas would certainly have denied their possibility). So we can criticize Aquinas's argument on at least two counts:

• The first "therefore" doesn't follow. The two premises are consistent with the assumption that if one thing moves another, then the second, and not any third thing, moves the first.

• The second "therefore" doesn't follow. We can consistently imagine an infinite sequence of movers without there being an endpoint, a "first mover," just as we can consistently imagine the infinite sequence of positive and negative integers in which there is no first number.

Study Questions

1. If we ignore other difficulties with Aquinas's argument, would it show that there is one and only one unmoved mover?

2. Why should the fact that we can *imagine* circumstances in which the premises of the argument are true and the conclusion is false tell against the value of the proposed proof? Does the fact that we can imagine such circumstances show that the premises do not necessitate the conclusion? If we could *not* consistently imagine circumstances in which the premises were true and the conclusion false, would that show that the premises *do* necessitate the conclusion? Why or why not?

3. Read the following argument, also from Saint Thomas. Outline the argument (follow the examples in this chapter). Explain why the premises do not necessitate the conclusion. (When Saint Thomas uses the term "efficient cause," he is using an idea of Aristotle's. You will not misunderstand the passage if you simply read the term as meaning "cause." By "ultimate cause" of an effect, Aquinas means the cause that is nearest in time to the effect.)

The second way [to prove the existence of God] is from the nature of efficient cause. In the world of sensible things we find there is an order of efficient causes. There is no case known (neither is it, indeed, possible) in which a thing is found to be the efficient cause of itself; for so it would be prior to itself, which is impossible. Now in efficient causes it is not possible to go on to infinity, because in all efficient causes following in order, the first is the cause of the intermediate cause, and the intermediate is the cause of the ultimate cause, whether intermediate cause be several, or one only. Now to take away the cause is to take away the effect. Therefore, if there be no first cause among efficient causes, there will be no ultimate nor any intermediate cause. But if in efficient causes it is possible to go on to infinity, there will be no first efficient cause, neither will there be an ultimate effect, nor any intermediate efficient causes; all of which is plainly false. Therefore it is necessary to admit a first efficient cause, to which everyone gives the name of God.[4]

INFINITY

Evidently, Aquinas had trouble thinking through the meaning of infinity. He wasn't alone, and the history of reasoning about infinity offers other examples for our collection. Paradoxes and puzzles about the infinite are very ancient, predating even Plato's writings. Some ancient puzzles about motion are attributed to Zeno of Elea, who lived in the fifth century before Christ. Some of Zeno's paradoxes involve subtle difficulties about the notion of infinity that were only resolved by mathematicians in the nineteenth century. In each case the paradox appears to be a proof of something absurd. One of Zeno's paradoxes, known as the Achilles paradox, is very simple.

Suppose Achilles races a tortoise. Let the tortoise travel with speed s. The tortoise is permitted to travel a certain distance d before Achilles begins the race. In order to catch the tortoise, Achilles must first travel distance d, which will require time $t(d)$. In that time the tortoise will have moved a distance $s \times t(d)$. To catch the tortoise after reaching point d, Achilles must first reach point $d + (s \times t(d))$ from point d. That will take Achilles an amount of time equal to $t(s \times t(d))$. In that time the tortoise will have moved a further distance $s \times t(s \times t(d))$. If we continue in this way, it always requires a finite time for Achilles to move from where he is at a moment to where the tortoise is at that same moment. In that amount of time, while Achilles is catching up to where the tortoise *was*, the tortoise will have moved a further distance. The motions generate the sequence pictured in figure 1.3. So there is no moment at which Achilles will catch the tortoise.

Zeno's argument looks like a deductive proof, but since the conclusion is false, we know that either some assumption of the argument must be false or there must be a fallacy hidden somewhere in the argument. Since the premises are apparently banal, it seems that there must be a fallacy: the premises don't necessitate the conclusion. Zeno's argument points out that corresponding to Achilles' motion and the motion of the tortoise, there is an infinite series of distances between Achilles and the tortoise. No distance in this series is zero, but as the series goes on, the distances between Achilles and the tortoise get smaller and smaller. There is a

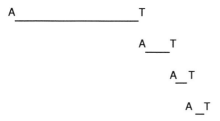

Figure 1.3
Achilles and the tortoise. A = Achilles, T = the tortoise, and the lines = the distance remaining between Achilles and the tortoise.

corresponding infinite sequence of temporal intervals in which each interval in the sequence represents the time it takes for Achilles to run from the place where he is at one moment to the place where the tortoise is at that same moment. Zeno concludes from this that Achilles cannot catch the tortoise, and this is where the fallacy lies. We are familiar with infinite sequences of positive quantities that add up to a finite quantity. The decimal expansion of the fraction 1/3, for example, is equal to 0.3 + 0.03 + 0.003 + 0.0003 + $\cdots$, where the sequence continues forever. With the help of modern mathematics, we would say that the sequence of distances between Achilles and the tortoise converges to zero and the *sum* of the sequence of temporal intervals is some finite number. That sum, whatever it is, represents the time required for Achilles to catch the tortoise.

The concept of infinity also created problems for later philosophical writers interested in the properties of God. Benedict Spinoza was a seventeenth century *pantheist*; he held that God consists of everything there is. Individual minds and bodies are, in Spinoza's terms, *modes* of God's existence.

Spinoza was troubled by the following objection to his view:

We showed that apart from God no substance can be or can be conceived; and hence we deduced that extended substance is one of God's infinite attributes.

However, for a fuller explanation, I will refute my opponents' arguments, which all come down to this. First, they think that corporeal substance, insofar as it is substance, is made up of of parts, and therefore they deny that it can be infinite, and consequently that it can pertain to God. This they illustrate with many examples, of which I will take one or two. They say that if corporeal substance is infinite, suppose it to be divided into two parts. Each of these parts will be either finite or infinite. If the former, then the infinite is made up of two finite parts, which

---

Spinoza and Euclid

Spinoza (1632–1677) was the child of Spanish Jews who had moved to Holland to avoid religious persecution. He himself was ostracized from the Jewish community for his opinions about God. Spinoza earned his living as a lens grinder, but he was well known to his intellectually prominent contemporaries and was offered university positions, which he refused.

Spinoza's major work, *The Ethics*, develops a view of nature in which there is a single substance, God. Most remarkable to a modern reader, Spinoza's *Ethics* is presented in the same format as Euclid's *Elements*. There are definitions, postulates, propositions, and proofs, or at least attempted proofs. In putting his theological views in this form, Spinoza exemplified the view, common among the great intellects of his time, that reasoning about metaphysical and epistemological questions should be rigorously scientific, and Euclid's geometry represented, even then, the ideal deductive science.

---

is absurd. If the latter, then there is than an infinite twice as great as another infinite, which is also absurd.[5]

Spinoza was unsure whether or not this argument is valid. He responded, rather implausibly, that even though everything corporeal is an attribute of God, God does not have *parts*.

The argument Spinoza must address has a special form. It sets out to prove something, in this case that God is not corporeal. It proceeds by assuming the *denial* of what is to be proved. That is, it proceeds by assuming that God *is* corporeal. From that assumption, perhaps with the aid of other assumptions that are thought to be obvious, the argument then tries to establish something thought to be *false*. The idea is that if the denial of a claim necessitates something false, then the claim itself must be true. This form of argument is known as *reductio ad absurdum* (reduction to the absurd), or more briefly, as a *reductio* argument.

We can outline the argument of Spinoza's opponents in the following way:

Assumption: God is corporeal.

Premise: Whatever is corporeal can be divided into two parts.

Premise: God is infinite.

Hence, an infinity can be divided into parts.

Premise: Every part is either infinite or finite.

Premise: The whole is the union of its parts.

Hence, either an infinity is the union of two finite parts, which is impossible, or an infinity is the union of two lesser infinities, which is also impossible.

Conclusion: the assumption is false, i.e., God is not corporeal.

We can see that the argument is invalid, and for several different reasons, all having to do with the next to last sentence, beginning "Hence." First and most simply, the last step before the conclusion omits a possible case: the infinity might be divided into two parts, one of which is finite and the other infinite. Second, an infinite collection of objects *can* be divided into two subcollections, each of which is infinite. The integers, for example, consist of all negative integers together with all nonnegative integers. The set of all negative integers is infinite, and the set of all nonnegative integers is also infinite.

INFINITY AND CARDINALITY*

Spinoza's argument does raise an interesting and fundamental question about the infinite: Can one infinity be larger than another infinity? In the nineteenth century this question engendered a number of simple proofs that created a revolution in our understanding of infinity, and since the question touches on an issue that runs through the history of philosophy, it is worth considering some of the relevant ideas and arguments here.

What do we mean when we say that one set or collection is *larger* than another? Consider the two collections below:

$\{A, B, C, D\}$

$\{X, Y, Z, U, V\}$

Clearly, the second set is bigger that the first set, but what makes it so? One answer is this: If we try to match each member of the first set with a unique member of the second set, we can do so. For example, we can match A with X, B with Y, C with Z, and D with U. But if we try to match each member of the second set with a unique member of the first set, we run out of distinct things. For example, we can match X with A, Y with B, Z with C, and U with D. But then we still have V left over; whatever member of the first set we choose to match with V, that member will already have been matched with X, Y, Z, or U. We say that there is a *one-to-one mapping* from the first set into the second set, but there is no one-to-one mapping from the second set into the first.

I will take this as our definition of "larger than" for sets:

Definition Set K is *larger than* set L if and only if there is a one-to-one mapping relating each member of L to a distinct member of K but there is no one-to-one mapping relating each member of K to a distinct member of L.

Continuing with this idea, we can say what it means for two sets to be of the *same size*. Two sets are of the same size if the first is *not* larger than the second and also the second is *not* larger than the first. When neither of two sets is larger than the other in this sense, we say they have the same *cardinality*.

Definition Any two sets K, L have the same *cardinality* if and only if there is a one-to-one mapping relating each member of K to a distinct member of L and there is a one-to-one mapping relating each member of L to a distinct member of K.

For finite sets, the notion of cardinality is just our ordinary notion of the size of a set. All sets with 4 members have the same cardinality, all sets with 5 members have the same cardinality, sets with 5 members are larger than sets with 4 members, and so on.

An obvious property of finite sets is this: If K and L are finite sets and if K is a *proper subset* of L (that is, every member of K is a member of L but some member of L is not a member of K), then L is larger than K. The set $\{X, Y, Z\}$, for example, is larger than the set $\{X, Y\}$. Infinite sets behave differently. *An infinite set can have the same cardinality as one of its proper subsets.* Consider an example, the set of positive integers, and a proper subset of it, the set of even positive integers. There is a one-to-one correspondence that takes every positive integer to a distinct even positive integer, and the same correspondence viewed in the other direction takes every even positive integer to a distinct positive integer:

1 2 3 4 5 6 7 8 9 10 ...

$\updownarrow$ $\updownarrow$ $\updownarrow$ $\updownarrow$ $\updownarrow$ $\updownarrow$ $\updownarrow$ $\updownarrow$ $\updownarrow$ $\updownarrow$

2 4 6 8 10 12 14 16 18 20 ...

The rule of correspondence is that each positive integer n is mapped to the even positive integer $2n$. So the set of positive integers has the same cardinality as the set of even positive integers. You can also easily show that the set of positive integers has the same cardinality as the set of odd positive integers, and also the same cardinality as the set of all integers, whether positive, zero, or negative. All of these distinct infinite sets have the same size.

The property of having the same cardinality as a proper subset of itself neatly separates the finite from the infinite. Finite sets can't have that property, whereas every infinite set will have it for some of its proper subsets. The distinction is sometimes used to define the notion of an infinite set:

Definition   A set is infinite if and only if it can be put into one-to-one correspondence with a proper subset of itself.

Now an obvious question raised by Spinoza's argument is this: Are some infinities larger than other infinities? In view of the considerations we have just discussed, we can understand that question in the following way: Are there two infinite sets that cannot be put into one-to-one correspondence with one another? In the nineteenth century, Georg Cantor (1845–1918) proved that there are. I will consider simple versions of two of his proofs. One concerns the number of subsets of any set. It is easy to see that any finite set has more distinct subsets that it has members. The set $\{A\}$, for example, has only one member, but it has two distinct subsets, namely itself and the empty set. The set $\{A, B\}$ has two members, but it has four distinct subsets. Given any finite set S with n members, we can count the distinct subsets of n in the following way. Imagine forming an arbitrary subset U of S. For any member of S there are two choices: either the member is in U or it isn't in U. To determine U, we have to make that choice for each of the n members of S, so we have n choices, each with 2 options. Every distinct way of making the choices results in a distinct subset of S, so there are 2^n distinct subsets. And for all n, 2^n is greater than n. Cantor extends the conclusion to sets with infinite cardinality:

Cantor's first theorem   For any set K, the set, denoted $\mathfrak{P}(K)$, whose members are all subsets of K is larger than K.

Proof   Suppose the theorem is false. Then there is some set W such that the set $\mathfrak{P}(W)$ of all subsets of W is not larger than W. So $\mathfrak{P}(W)$ can be put into a one-to-one correspondence with W, i.e., for every member of $\mathfrak{P}(W)$ there will be a corresponding distinct member of W. Let g denote such a correspondence or mapping. So g maps the set of all subsets of W, $\mathfrak{P}(W)$, one-to-one into W. Let g^{-1} denote the *inverse* of g. The inverse mapping g^{-1} maps members of W to subsets of W, and for all subsets S of W, $g^{-1}(g(s)) = S$. If K is any subset of W, then K is a member of $\mathfrak{P}(W)$, and so g puts K into correspondence with some member of W, which I denote by $g(K)$. Then the following subset of W, which I will call R, must exist: $R = \{x$ in W such that $x \notin g^{-1}(x)\}$. Remember that because g is a one-to-one correspondence, for each x there can be only one set S such that $x = g(S)$.

Now consider R as defined. R is a subset of W, so R is a member of $\mathfrak{P}(W)$. So g, which I have assumed to exist, puts R in correspondence with some member $g(R)$ of W. Every member of W is either a member of R or not a member of R. Hence $g(R)$ is either a member of R or not a member of R. Suppose that $g(R)$ is a member of R. Then since R is the set of all members x of W such that x is not a member of $g^{-1}(x)$, it must be the case that $g(R)$ is a member of W, which is not a member of R. So if $g(R)$ is a member of R, then $g(R)$ is not a member of R, which is a contradiction. Hence $g(R)$ cannot be a member of R. But if $g(R)$ is *not* a member of R, then since R is the set of all members x of W such that $x \notin g^{-1}(x)$, it follows that $g(R)$ is a member of R (because $g(R)$ satisfies the necessary and sufficient condition for being a member of R).

Hence the assumption entails that there exist a set whose existence implies a contradiction. Since a contradiction must be false, the assumption must be false. Q.E.D.

The proof of Cantor's first theorem is more complex than any of those we have considered previously. It is a reductio argument; that is, the theorem is proved by assuming its denial and deducing a contradiction. It has as an immediate corollary the result that there are infinite sets of different size.

Cantor gave a particular example of two infinite sets one of which is larger than the other. His example does not consider a set and the corresponding set of all subsets of that set. Instead, it concerns the natural numbers 0, 1, 2, 3, ... and the set of all functions defined on the natural numbers. Cantor proved that the set of all functions taking natural numbers as arguments and having natural numbers as values is larger than the set of all natural numbers itself. To understand his argument we need a few definitions.

Definition A *function of one argument* is any set of ordered pairs of objects such that for all a, b, c, if $\langle a, b \rangle$ and $\langle a, c \rangle$ are both in the set, then $b = c$. Equivalently, a function is a set of ordered pairs in which there are no two ordered pairs with the same first member but different second members.

Definition Two functions are one and the same if they are the same set of ordered pairs. The set of first members of ordered pairs in a function is called the *domain* of the function, while the set of all second members of ordered pairs in a function is called the *range* of the function.

Definition A function is *one-to-one* if and only if for all a, b, and c, if $\langle a, b \rangle$ and $\langle c, b \rangle$ are in the function, then $a = c$.

Definition A *function on the natural numbers* is a set of ordered pairs whose domain is the natural numbers and whose range is contained in the set of natural numbers.

Cantor's second theorem The set F of all functions on the natural numbers is larger than the set N of all natural numbers.

Proof Suppose that the proposition is false. Then we can form a one-to-one correspondence between the natural numbers and the functions in F so that each function in F is assigned a number and no two functions in F are assigned the same number. So let the functions in F be denoted by $w_1(x), w_2(x), \ldots$ Consider an infinite table in which each row is infinitely long and there are infinitely many rows. The ith row lists in order the values of the ith function for $x = 1$, $x = 2$, and so on. Such a table is illustrated in figure 1.4.

I will show that there is a function z on the natural numbers that is not in this table. I define z as follows: Make $z(1)$, the value of z for the number 1, equal to any value different from $w_1(1)$ (for example, $z = w_1(1) + 1$). Make $z(2)$ equal to any value different from $w_2(2)$. And for every number k, make $z(k)$ equal to a value different from $w_k(k)$. I thereby alter the diagonal of the table in figure 1.4 to form a new counterdiagonal.

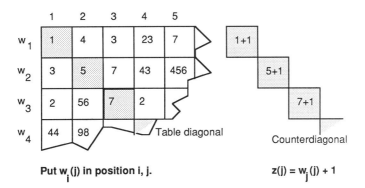

Figure 1.4
Cantor's diagonalization argument

Then for every function w_i in the table, the value of z differs from that function for some argument. Hence z is a function on the natural numbers that is not in the table. But since the table contains the supposed enumeration of the functions in F, z is not in F, which is a contradiction. Since we cannot consistently suppose that the proposition is false, it is true. Q.E.D.

Study Questions

1. Prove that it follows from Cantor's first theorem that there are two infinite sets of different size.

2. Cantor's second theorem is called a *diagonalization* argument because it can be depicted as involving a change in a diagonal. Can you picture what is going on in Cantor's first theorem as also involving diagonal? (Hint: Think of a table with a list of the members of W along the top and a list of the members of $\mathfrak{P}(W)$ along the left-hand side. In each square, enter a 1 if the member of $\mathfrak{P}(W)$ for that row has the member of W for that column as its value according to the assumed one-to-one correspondence g. Otherwise, enter 0 in the square. Now explain what the argument in the proof of Cantor's first theorem amounts to in terms of this table.)

3. What is the point of the picture in the proof of Cantor's second theorem?

4. Give a proof that there cannot exist a barber who shaves all and only those who do not shave themselves. (Hint: The argument is a simplified version of the proof strategy used for Cantor's first theorem.) Can your proof be viewed as a diagonalization argument?

CONCLUSION

I began with a set of questions that I have not yet answered:

1. How can we determine whether or not a piece of reasoning from premises to a conclusion is a valid deductive argument?
2. How can we determine whether or not a conclusion is necessitated by a set of premises? If a conclusion is necessitated by a set of premises, how can we find a valid deductive argument that demonstrates that necessary connection?
3. What features of the structure of the world, the structure of language, and the relation between words and thoughts and things make deductive reasoning possible?

My initial approach to these questions has been Socratic: I have sought for examples of arguments that present valid demonstrations and arguments that fail to demonstrate their conclusions. In each example a set of assumptions, it is claimed, necessitate a conclusion. Sometimes this claim is not correct, but it still seems plausible that the argument could be revised so that the premises do necessitate the conclusion. Thus Euclid's proof of his first proposition fails to show that the two circles he constructs intersect, and for that reason his postulates and common notions do not necessitate the first proposition. But it seems plausible that we could add axioms to Euclid's postulates so that the resulting system would permit us to deduce proposition 1. Modern reformulations of Euclid's theory do just that. On the other hand, some attempts at proof just seem to involve fundamental mistakes of reasoning. Other attempts at proof may leave us uncertain. Thus after reading and thinking about Anselm's proof of the existence of God, many people are left uncertain as to whether or not the proof is valid. (Of course, the proof could be valid—which means that *if* the premises of the argument are true, then necessarily the conclusion is true—even though the premises of the argument are in fact false.)

I have yet to formulate a theory that will agree with, and in some sense explain, our judgment about which demonstrations are valid and which are not. In the next chapter we will consider the first such theory ever formulated, Aristotle's theory of the syllogism.

Review Questions

1. Why is deductive reasoning often thought to be the first kind of reasoning that philosophy should try to understand?

2. What are three fundamental questions about deductive reasoning?

3. Explain what we want a theory of deductive reasoning to accomplish.

4. Why is finding a good theory of deductive reasoning more difficult than finding conditions that will include the positive and exclude the negative examples in the coding problem, the series problem, and the arch problem?

5. What is the Socratic method?

6. What features are common to the good deductive arguments considered in this chapter?

7. What is the role of the illustrations that accompany some of the arguments given in this chapter?

8. What was Aquinas's relation to Aristotle?

Further Reading

This bibliography contains some sources for further information on the people and issues discussed in this chapter. It is by no means complete. Many other relevant books and essays are available in any good college or university library.

Anselm and the ontological argument

Anselm. *St. Anselm's Proslogion with a Reply on Behalf of the Fool by Gaunilo and the Author's Reply to Gaunilo.* Oxford: Oxford University Press, 1965.

Barnes, Jonathan. *The Ontological Argument.* New York: St. Martin's Press, 1972.

Brecher, Robert. *Anselm's Argument: The Logic of Divine Existence.* Brookfield, Vt.: Gower, 1985.

Eadmer, D. *The Life of St. Anselm, Archbishop of Cantebury.* Oxford: Oxford University Press, 1972.

Hartshorne, Charles. *Anselm's Discovery: A Re-examination of the Ontological Proof for God's Existence.* La Salle, Ill.: Open Court, 1965.

Henry, Desmond Paul. *The Logic of Saint Anselm.* Oxford: Oxford University Press, 1967.

Hick, John. *The Existence of God.* New York: Macmillan, 1969.

Hick, John, and Arthur McGill, ed. *The Many-Faced Argument: Recent Studies on the Ontological Argument for the Existence of God.* New York: Macmillan, 1967.

Plantinga, Alvin. *The Ontological Argument from St. Anselm to Contemporary Philosophers.* London: Macmillan, 1968.

Schufreider, Gregory. *An Introduction to Anselm's Argument.* Philadelphia: Temple University Press, 1978.

Aquinas

Gilson, Etienne. *The Philosophy of St. Thomas Aquinas.* Freeport, N.Y.: Books for Libraries Press, 1971.

Kenny, Anthony. *Aquinas: A Collection of Critical Essays.* London: Macmillan, 1970.

Kenny, Anthony. *The Five Ways: St. Thomas Aquinas' Proofs of God's Existence.* New York: Schocken Books, 1969.

Leff, Gordon. *Medieval Thought: St. Augustine to Ockham.* Chicago: Quadrangle Books, 1960.

Martin, Christopher, ed. *The Philosophy of Thomas Aquinas: Introductory Readings.* London: Routledge, 1988.

Owen, Joseph, and John R. Catan, eds. *St. Thomas Aquinas on the Existence of God: Collected Papers of Joseph Owen.* Albany, N.Y.: State University of New York Press, 1980.

Pegis, Anton Charles, ed. *Basic Writings of Thomas Aquinas.* New York: Random House, 1945.

Pegis, Anton Charles. *Saint Thomas and the Greeks.* Milwaukee: Marquette University Press, 1939.

Artificial intelligence and concept learning

Bruner, Jerome Seymour, and Jacqueline Goonow. *A Study of Thinking*. New York: Wiley, 1956.

Hunt, Earl B. *Concept Learning: An Information Processing Problem*. Huntington, N.Y.: R. E. Krieger, 1974.

Winston, Patrick Henry. *Artificial Intelligence*. Reading, Mass.: Addison-Wesley, 1984.

Winston, Patrick Henry, and Richard Henry Brown, eds. *Artificial Intelligence: An MIT Perspective*. Vol. 1. Cambridge: MIT Press, 1979.

Cantor

Dauben, Joseph Warren. *Georg Cantor: His Mathematics and the Philosophy of the Infinite*. Princeton: Princeton University Press, 1990.

Purkert, Walter. *Georg Cantor, 1845–1918*. Boston: Birkhauser, 1987.

Tiles, Mary. *The Philosophy of Set Theory: An Historical Introduction to Cantor's Paradise*. New York: B. Blackwell, 1989.

Euclid and geometry

Bold, Benjamin. *Famous Problems of Mathematics: A History of Constructions with Straight Edge and Compasses*. New York: Van Nostrand Reinhold Co., 1969.

Collidge, Julian Lowell. *A History of Geometrical Methods*. Oxford: Oxford University Press, 1940.

Euclid. *The Thirteen Books of Euclid's Elements*. 2nd ed. Vols. 1 and 2. Trans. Thomas Heath. New York: Dover Publications, 1956.

Heath, Thomas. *A History of Greek Mathematics*. Oxford: Oxford University Press, 1921.

Hilbert, David. *Foundations of Geometry*. La Salle, Ill.: Open Court, 1971.

Knorr, Wilbur Richard. *The Ancient Tradition of Geometric Problems*. Cambridge, Mass.: Birkhauser Boston, 1985.

Lanczos, Cornelius. *Space through the Ages: The Evolution of Geometrical Ideas from Pythagoras to Hilbert and Einstein*. London: Academic Press, 1970.

Van der Waerden, B. L. *Geometry and Algebra in Ancient Civilizations*. New York: Springer-Verlag, 1983.

Infinity

Bolzano, Bernard. *Paradoxes of the Infinite*. New Haven: Yale University Press, 1950.

Hallet, Michael. *Cantorian Set Theory and Limitation of Size*. Oxford: Oxford University Press, 1984.

Kretzmann, Norman, ed. *Infinity and Continuity in Ancient and Medieval Thought.* Ithaca: Cornell University Press, 1982.

Sondheimer, E. H., and Alan Rogerson. *Numbers and the Infinite: A Historical Account of Mathematical Concepts.* New York: Cambridge University Press, 1981.

Socratic method

Santas, Gerasimos Xenophon. *Socrates' Philosophy in Plato's Early Dialogues.* London: Routledge and Kegan Paul, 1979.

Seeskin, Kenneth. *Dialogue and Discovery: A Study in Socratic Method.* Albany, N.Y.: State University of New York Press, 1987.

Spinoza

Allison, Henry E. *Benedict de Spinoza: An Introduction.* New Haven: Yale University Press, 1987.

Curley, Edwin, ed. *The Collected Works of Spinoza.* Princeton, N.J.: Princeton University Press, 1985.

Donagan, Alan. *Spinoza.* Chicago: University of Chicago Press, 1989.

Grene, Marjorie, and Debra Nails, eds. *Spinoza and the Sciences.* Boston: D. Reidel, 1986.

Hampshire, Stuart. *Spinoza.* Harmondsworth, England: Penguin Books, 1962.

Kennington, Richard, ed. *The Philosophy of Baruch Spinoza.* Washington, D.C.: Catholic University Press, 1980.

Scruton, Roger. *Spinoza.* New York: Oxford University Press, 1986.

Spinoza, Baruch. *The Ethics and Selected Letters.* Trans. Samuel Shirley. Indianapolis: Hackett Publishing Co., 1982.

Zeno and the paradoxes

Grunbaum, Adolf. *Modern Science and Zeno's Paradoxes.* Middletown, Conn.: Wesleyan University Press, 1967.

Hasse, H., and H. Scholz. *Zeno and the Discovery of Incommensurables in Greek Mathematics.* New York: Arno Press, 1976.

Salmon, Wesley, ed. *Zeno's Paradoxes.* Indianapolis, Ind.: Bobbs-Merrill, 1970.

Chapter 2

ARISTOTLE'S THEORY OF DEMONSTRATION AND PROOF

ARISTOTLE AND GREEK SCIENCE

In the fourth century before Christ the entire human population consisted of perhaps 130 million people. Mediterranean civilization was spread around the coast of Greece and the Greek islands and in areas of modern Italy, Turkey, Syria, Lebanon, Israel, and northern Egypt. Most travel of any distance was by open boat with one or two square rigged sails and oarsmen. Such ships carried the produce of one region to another; they also carried soldiers for the almost perpetual wars of the area.

What was known around 400 B.C.? A wide variety of practical arts, including metal production and metal working sophisticated enough to make good hand tools, weapons, and armor; carpentry sophisticated enough to make sea-going boats; the principles of navigation, architectural engineering, quarrying, and stone work; methods of manufacturing cloth and paper; methods of animal husbandry, fishing, and peasant agriculture.

And what about science? In mathematics, knowledge consisted principally of geometry and the theory of numbers. Many physical laws of mechanics and hydraulics were understood and used, but astronomy was the most developed subject in the physical sciences. Ancient astronomy was based on naked-eye observations of the positions of the stars and on observations using simple instruments. Astronomy developed because it was easy to make a large number of relevant observations, because the motions of the planets, moon, and sun could be studied as applications of geometry, and because astronomy was of practical use in navigation. Other scientific subjects like biology and medicine were also studied, and broad speculations about the structure of the universe and the structure of matter were common.

In this setting Aristotle developed a science of biology, a theory of cosmology, a theory of motion, and a theory of the constitution of matter. Aristotle also produced something that proved to be far more important than his scientific contributions: a theory of *how to conduct inquiry.* He provided answers to questions such as these: What is chance? What is causality? What is a scientific explanation? What is a demonstration? How can experience be used to provide knowledge? What is a proof?

Aristotle's scientific contributions were surpassed in many areas. By about A.D. 100 Ptolemy had developed a theory of the motion of the planets that was more detailed and precise than anything Aristotle suggested. Ptolemy also contributed to optics, and Arab scientists of the Middle Ages extended optical studies. Archimedes made more enduring contributions to physics than did Aristotle, and medieval Christian thinkers developed a theory of motion that improved on Aristotle's. But in contrast, Aristotle's general conception of how science is to be conducted influenced Western civilization almost until the eighteenth century. For roughly 2,300 years Aristotle's writings set the standards for scientific explanation and for deductive arguments. Aristotle's theory of scientific method deserves our attention, for it is the first fully developed account of human knowledge, and it contains the first substantial theory of proof we know of.

At the very core of Aristotle's understanding of how inquiry should be conducted is a theory of proof or deductive argument. Aristotle's logical theory, which endured until late in the nineteenth century, is still worth studying because it is comparatively easy to understand and, from a modern point of view, it is correct in special cases. (For similar reasons, introductory physics courses present Newton's dynamics, even though that theory has been superseded.) But before we turn to Aristotle's logical theory, we should consider his general conception of how science should be constructed and justified. That conception is in many ways very different from our own understanding, but in other ways it is quite modern. It is not only interesting in itself; it may also help us to understand why Aristotle thought that his theory of proof was correct and complete.

THE PLATONIC CONCEPTION OF KNOWLEDGE

Aristotle was Plato's pupil, and it is not surprising that these two great thinkers shared certain views. In particular, Plato and Aristotle shared a view about the logical structure of knowledge.

For Plato, the paradigmatic scientific question is of the form, "What is *x*?" Here *x* might be filled by some important moral characteristic, such as virtue or courage or justice, or by some description of a kind of thing found in nature, such as a human or earth or water, or even some mathematical object, such as a triangle. Plato wrote a series of dialogues in which questions of this kind are pursued. The *Meno*, for example, considers the question, What is virtue?

Plato believed that acceptable answers to such questions must have a particular form. Any acceptable answer must give a combination of features shared by all things that are *x* and by no things that are not *x*. In Plato's conception, it is quite unsatisfactory to answer the question, What is virtue? by giving a list of virtues. A proper answer to the question must specify what it is that all things in any such list share and that makes them, and nothing else, virtues.

How are we to answer such questions? How are we to come to know what is virtue, what is water, what is justice? Plato held that knowledge requires certainty. By "certainty" he did not mean simply an unalterable conviction. Someone can have an unalterable conviction whether or not what they believe is the truth. They might simply be dogmatic or stubborn or stupid. Certainty, as Plato understood it, requires not only that one have a belief but also that the belief be true and that it have been acquired by an infallible method. An infallible method is one that never leads to a false conclusion: whenever anyone comes to a conclusion by such a method, that conclusion is true.

Plato rightly concluded that experience can never provide us with the kind of certainty that he required for knowledge. No matter how carefully or thoroughly we observe or experiment, conclusions drawn from experience are not infallible. Both in science and in everyday life we sometimes drawn erroneous conclusions from our experience. Experience, Plato held, can form the basis of opinion, but not the basis of knowledge.

If we know anything, then, we cannot come to know it through experience. Plato held that we really don't ever *come* to know anything. Anything we know, we always knew. The psychological process by which someone seems to come to know something, the process that we sometimes mistake for learning from experience, is really a process of recollection, according to Plato. Examples provided by experience stimulate us to remember truths that were stamped on our souls before our birth. Recollection is infallible because nothing but truth was stamped on our souls.

That is how we know, according to Plato. But what is it that we know? We tend to think that knowledge is about the world, about the things and events and processes and relationships and causal powers in the world. Plato thought otherwise. The clearest examples of knowledge available to Plato were geometry and relations among numbers. According to Euclidean geometry, two points determine a straight-line segment, a triangle is a figure with three straight-line segments as sides, and the sum of the internal angles of a triangle equal two right angles. But any physical triangle we try to construct will be imperfect. Lines in nature aren't perfectly straight; the sum of the internal angles of the figures we make or draw aren't exactly the sum of two right angles. Plato in effect argued as follows: Since geometry is known, it must be true. Accordingly, whatever geometry is about, it must be true of its subject. But since geometry is not true of the objects of the physical world, it is not about them. So it is about something else.

Plato called the objects of knowledge *forms*. In Plato's conception, the forms aren't in the world, and they certainty are not parts, aspects, or properties of things in the world. They are quite literally not of the world. Of course, the objects and properties of this world have some relation to the forms, but the relation is obscure. Plato says that worldly things *participate* in forms. The idea, very roughly, is that earthly things are crude models of forms, the way a chalk drawing of a triangle is a crude model of a Euclidean triangle.

Aristotle shared with Plato the view that knowledge requires certainty, and also the view that what we seek to know are combinations of properties or features that make a thing an x—a man or a triangle or whatever may be the topic of inquiry. But Aristotle brought the forms down to earth, and the result was a conception of nature and of scientific inquiry that is rather different from Plato's.

ARISTOTLE'S CONCEPTION OF NATURE

In Aristotle's conception, if a thing changes, *it* acquires some new property or loses some old property. For change to be possible, there must exist something that can be identified as one and the same thing before and after the change. So what is the same before and after the change must itself be unchanged. Aristotle calls *substance* whatever endures through change and has properties attached to it. *Attributes* or *properties* are features that can attach to a substance at one time and not attach to it at other times.

Substance that has no properties and is completely unformed, Aristotle calls *prime matter*. Aristotle's conception of the fundamental stuff of the universe can be very roughly pictured as gobs of stuff enduring through time but having various attributes stuck to it at any moment. Of course, Aristotle didn't think of properties as literally stuck to substance, like notices on a bulletin board.

It is tempting to think that the world is put together in the same way that our descriptions of it are assembled. In English, as in Greek, we assemble sentences from noun phrases and verb phrases. Noun phrases typically occur as subjects in sentences. They include common nouns such as "cat," "dog," "moon," "eclipse," "tree." Verb phrases typically occur as predicates that are applied to subjects; they include verbs and verbs together with adjectives or adverbs, such as "is black," "is mean," "occurs rarely," "is deciduous." If we put subject terms together with predicate terms in the appropriate way and introduce extra grammatical words (such as "the") in the appropriate places, we get sentences:

The cat is black.
The dog is mean.
Eclipses occur rarely.
Vines are deciduous.

Aristotle thought that the fundamental distinctions in the world are indeed reflected in fundamental distinctions in language. He held, for example, that the particular objects, such as a mean dog, are constituted by *matter* and by *form*. A mean dog is matter *formed into* a dog that is mean.

We have devices in our language for turning a sentence into a new subject for a new predicate. We can say, for example:

The animal that is a cat is trained.
The mean dog is four-legged.
The deciduous vines are broad leafed.

According to Aristotle, the world has the same feature. When form is applied to matter, the combination becomes the matter or substance for the application of still other forms. When we have a black cat, for example, we have a particular object constituted by matter and form. That object can then be the matter that we cause another form to obtain. So if we train the black cat, the black cat is caused to acquire a further form; in other words, the black cat is formed into a trained black cat.

Aristotle thought of nature in terms of *hierarchies*. In particular, he thought of complex entities as built up by the application of a sequence of forms to bare, unformed matter. Suppose that there is bare matter with no form of any sort. If that bare matter is formed into something living, the result is living matter. If living matter is formed into an animal, the result is something animate. If animate matter is given canine form, the result is a dog. If instead animate matter is formed into something with a rational soul, the result is a human. We can picture the process by means of a kind of diagram.

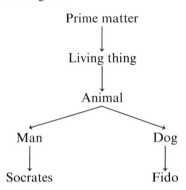

(Diagrams consisting of nodes connected by directed lines are now called *directed graphs*. If the connections are just lines and not arrows, so that the order does not matter, the diagram is simply called a *graph*.)

Another fundamental idea in Aristotle's conception of nature is the distinction between the properties that a thing has *accidentally* and the properties that a thing has *essentially*. A thing has a property accidentally if it could possibly not have had that property. It is an accidental property of a dog that it is a *trained* dog. Fido, the trained dog, would still be Fido if it had not been trained. In Aristotle's terms, it is an accidental feature of Ronald Reagan that he was elected president. Ronald Reagan would still be Ronald Reagan if he had not been elected president. Essential attributes of a thing are those features without which the thing would lose its identity. Fido is essentially a dog. Anything that is not a dog could not be Fido. Any creature that is *by nature* not furred, not four-legged, or not born of a bitch is not a dog, and hence is not Fido. These are essential properties of Fido. Similarly, Ronald Reagan is essentially a man, and anything that is not a man could not be Ronald Reagan.

For each part of nature, there is a hierarchy that includes only the essential attributes or forms of objects and ignores accidental attributes.

According to Aristotle, the goal of science is to find the structure of the appropriate hierarchy for any subject, whether it is astronomy, biology, or cosmology.

Aristotle thought that natural processes have natural ends or purposes. An acorn does not have leaves or roots or bark, but it has the *potential* to acquire leaves and roots and bark, and in the natural course of things, it will come to be an oak tree that *actually* has those features. A human infant does not have language or reason, but it has the potential to acquire both, and in the natural course of things, it will do so. Aristotle thought of all natural processes in the same way; each has an end, and in the natural course of things, that end will be achieved.

Aristotle's conception of nature involves a conception of causality different from our own. Consider questions such as "Why does the sun give warmth?" or "Why does water boil when heated?" or "Why do stars twinkle?" or "Why are vines deciduous?" These questions are requests for causal explanations. Often causal questions are about how something came to be or how it came to be a certain way. In Aristotle's view, there is not just one sort of answer to be given to these questions; there are four different sorts, corresponding to four different senses of "cause." Each question asks about an object or kind of object and about an attribute of that object or objects of that kind.

An object has a specific attribute just in case the object is obtained by imposing a specific form on an appropriate substance. So one sort of cause is the form of the object responsible for the attribute, and another sort of cause is the matter on which the form is imposed. The first is called the *formal cause*, and the second is called the *material cause*. Aristotle tended to think of formal causes as internal principles of development in natural objects, as whatever it is, aside from matter, that determines that acorns grow up to be oak trees rather than hemlock trees, for example.

For an attribute to be acquired by a thing, some action must take place to impose a further form on matter. An acorn doesn't become a oak tree unless it is covered with earth in a place where rain and sun fall. A block of marble does not become a statue of Venus without the action of a chisel. For Aristotle, the *efficient cause* of a thing possessing a certain attribute is the process by which the matter of the thing acquires the appropriate form. Efficient causes are the kinds of events or processes that we nowadays think of as causes.

According to Aristotle, natural processes have purposes or ends, just as human activities have purposes. The qualities and attributes that things take on in the normal course of events are attributes they have *so that* these purposes or ends will be achieved. One aspect of the explanation of why the sun gives warmth, for example, is the purpose or goal of that state of affairs. One might hold, for example, that the sun gives warmth *so that* life can endure on earth. Aristotle did not mean, of course, that the sun deliberately intends or plans to make life prosper on earth. The plan is nature's, not the sun's. Whatever it is *for the purpose of which* an object has an attribute, Aristotle calls the *final cause* of the thing's having the attribute.

The doctrine of four causes forms one of the centerpieces of Aristotle's conception of science. Scientific inquiry is an attempt to answer "why" questions. When such questions are about why something comes to be, they are ambiguous, according to Aristotle: their meaning depends on whether one is asking for the material, efficient, final, or formal cause.

Aristotle's conception of causality and his conception of scientific explanation as the statement and demonstration of causes formed a framework for understanding scientific inquiry that lasted until the eighteenth century. Together with his theory of proof, these conceptions make up an important part of the background against which modern philosophy was formed. I will return to them again in the next chapter when I describe seventeenth-century approaches to the idea of a proof, and I will consider them yet again in later chapters when I take up the subject of inductive inference.

Study Questions

1. Does the sentence "Sam and Suzy love one another" consist of a predicate applied to a subject? What about the sentence "Equals added to equals are equal"?

2. Biological taxonomy describes hierarchies of species, genera, and so on. Do such classifications exemplify Aristotle's conception of nature?

3. Use your own judgement to determine which of the following attributes of water are essential properties of water and which are accidental properties of water.

- It covers most of the surface of the earth.
- It is composed of molecules having two atoms of hydrogen and one atom of oxygen.
- It can be obtained from wells.
- It boils at 100 degrees centigrade at one atmosphere pressure.
- It is sold in bottles by Perrier.
- It is sometimes drunk with scotch.
- It is of two kinds, salt and fresh.

4. What do you suppose are the four Aristotelian causes that explain why mammals give milk?

ARISTOTLE'S CONCEPTION OF SCIENCE

Aristotle thought that the science of any subject should constitute a system of knowledge claims. Fundamental claims, or axioms, could be used to deduce less fundamental claims. The scientific explanation of a general fact about the world consists in a valid deductive argument that has a description of that general fact as its conclusion and has true, fundamental claims as its premises. Different sciences might have quite different axiomatic systems; there is one theory for biology, another for the constitution of matter, another for astronomy, and so on. These diverse theories may share certain fundamental assumptions, but they will also have postulates that are peculiar to their respective subject matters. Aristotle supposed that the axioms of a scientific subject would be divided more or less as Euclid divided his axioms into common notions and postulates of a peculiarly geometric character.

Aristotle's conception of scientific explanation can be illustrated with a simple example.

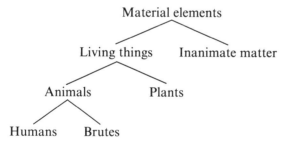

Each link in this picture corresponds to a general truth about the generation of humans:

- All humans are animals.
- All animals are living things.
- All living things are composed of matter.

Further, each of these sentences predicates something essential of its subject. It is not an accidental feature of humans that they are animals, nor is it an accidental feature of animals that they are living things, nor is it an accidental feature of living things that they are material. Next observe that each point in the illustration represents a kind of thing obtained by imposing additional form on the matter that is the kind of thing at the point above it. Thus, in Aristotle's terms, living things result from imposing a *nutritive soul* upon elemental matter. Imposing an animate soul upon a living thing results in an animal, and so on. Finally, the imposition of a form upon matter is brought about by a characteristic kind of efficient cause. Thus the form of a nutritive soul is imposed upon matter by mixing the elements (for Aristotle, these were earth, air, fire, and water) in the proper proportions.

What can be *demonstrated* from this simple theory? An Aristotelian demonstration might go like the following:

All humans are animals.
All animals are living things.
Therefore, all humans are living things.

All humans are living things.
All living things are composed of matter.
Therefore, all humans are composed of matter.

This is not a very subtle or elaborate deduction, and Aristotle clearly intended that scientific demonstration should include more intricate argu-

---

The axiomatic method

The idea that a good scientific theory should constitute a system in which less fundamental claims can be deduced from more fundamental claims is not so foreign to modern science. We still have something of that conception in modern physics. Newton's dynamics was originally formulated by Newton as an axiomatic system. The theory of relativity and the theory of quantum mechanics have been formulated as axiomatic systems. Non-Euclidean geometries have been developed as axiomatic theories. In contemporary psychology, theories about how to measure psychological properties have been formulated as axiomatic systems. In economics and statistics, theories of rational decision making are often expressed axiomatically.

Theories are sometimes *first* formulated as axiomatic systems. More often, axiomatic presentations are given when there is an understanding of the theory but that understanding needs to be clarified and made rigorous. Axiomatic presentations may enable one to see clearly the fundamental claims of a theory and to examine how other claims of the system can be validly deduced from them.

ments, such as those we find in Euclid's geometry. A central philosophical problem for Aristotle was therefore to give an account of the inferences that make for a valid deduction.

ARISTOTLE'S LOGIC

Aristotle's logic concerns sentences that have a simple structure consisting of a *quantifier* such as "all" or "some" or "no" (as in "none"), a subject term such as "humans" or "Socrates," and a predicate term such as "are animals" or "is not snub-nosed" or "are mortal." For example, "All humans are mortal" or "Socrates is not snub-nosed" are the kind of sentences whose logic Aristotle described.

The characteristic form of inference in Aristotle's logic is the *syllogism*, which consists of a pair of sentences that serve as *premises* and a sentence that serves as the *conclusion*. You have seen an example of syllogistic argument in the previous section. Here is another:

Syllogism 1
All humans are animals.
All animals are mortal.
Therefore, all humans are mortal.

This is a *valid syllogism. What makes it valid is that if the premises are true, then it follows necessarily that the conclusion is also true.* If the premises happen to be false in a valid syllogism, then the conclusion may be either true or false. What matters is that in every conceivable case in which the premises could be true, the conclusion would also be true.

You can see why this syllogism counts as valid by drawing some circles. (This is not a device that Aristotle used. It was first developed during the Renaissance). Suppose you introduce a circle H to represent the set of all humans, another circle A to represent the set of all animals, and a third circle M to represent the set of all mortal things. The first premise says that the set of all men is contained in the set of all animals. So put circle H *inside circle A* to represent the state of affairs required for the first premise to be true (figure 2.1). The second premise says that the set of all animals is contained in the set of all mortal things. So put circle M around circle A to represent the state of affairs required for the second premise to be true (figure 2.2). Now consider the figure drawn (2.2). To represent the state of affairs required to make both premises true, you *had* to put H inside A and A inside M. So necessarily H is inside M, which is what the conclusion asserts. What makes a syllogism valid is that in any way you represent

Figure 2.1
Premise 1 of syllogism 1

Figure 2.2
Syllogism 1

circumstances so that both of the premises are true, the conclusion is true as well.

Here is another valid syllogism:

Syllogism 2
All humans are animals.
Some humans are quiet.
Therefore, some quiet things are animals.

Represent the class of all humans by the circle H, and the class all animals by the circle A, and the class of all quiet things by the circle Q. The first premise, as before, says that H is contained in A. The second premise is different. It says that there are things that are both human and quiet. This can only be represented by having circle Q, representing the set of all quiet things, *intersect* circle H, representing the set of all humans. So every representation that makes the first two premises of the syllogism both true has Q intersecting H and H contained in A (figure 2.3). But then Q must necessarily intersect A, which is what the conclusion asserts.

By contrast the following syllogism is *not valid*, even though all its premises and its conclusion are true:

Syllogism 3
All humans are animals.
Some animals are mortal.
Therefore, all humans are mortal.

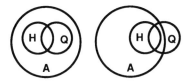

Figure 2.3
Two possibilities for syllogism 2

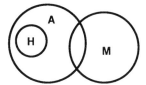

Figure 2.4
A counterexample to syllogism 3

To see that the syllogism is not valid, remember that for validity there must be *no possible way* of arranging the circles representing the sets of things that are human, *H*, animals, *A*, and mortal, *M*, so that in that representation of possible circumstances the premises are both true but the conclusion of the syllogism is false. The first premise says, as before, that *H* is included in *A*. The second premise says that circles *A* and *M* intersect. One way in which the two premises *could imaginably* be true is given in figure 2.4. In this figure *M* intersects *A*, and *H* is included in *A*, but *M* does not include any of *H*. The figure represents an imaginable circumstance in which all humans are animals, some animals are mortal, but some humans (in fact, all humans) are *immortal*. The circumstances represented are not those that obtain in our world, where in fact all humans are mortal, but they are consistently imaginable circumstances, and they show that *the truth of the premises of the syllogism do not by themselves necessitate the truth of the conclusion of the syllogism.*

That a syllogism is *valid* does not imply that its premises are true or that its conclusion is true. A valid syllogism may have false premises and a true conclusion, false premises and a false conclusion, or true premises and a true conclusion. What it may *not* have is true premises and a false conclusion. What it means for a syllogism to be valid is that if its premises were true, its conclusion would of necessity be true. So if the premises are actually true and the syllogism is valid, then the conclusion must actually be true.

Here is an example of a valid syllogism in which the premises are in fact false but the conclusion is true:

All humans are apes.
All apes have opposing thumbs.
Therefore, all humans have opposing thumbs.

Here is an example of a valid syllogism in which the premises are false and the conclusion is false:

All humans are apes.
All apes are stockbrokers.
Therefore, all humans are stockbrokers.

Aristotle realized that the validity of a syllogism has nothing to do with what the predicate terms and the subject terms *mean*, but has everything to do with what quantifiers occur in the premises and the conclusion and with where one and the same term occurs in both the premises and the conclusion. The first syllogism we considered has the following form:

All A are B.
All B are C.
Therefore, all A are C.

Any syllogism of this form will be valid, no matter what classes A, B, and C denote. A could be stars, B olives, C dragons. The following syllogism is silly, but valid.

All stars are dragons.
All dragons are olives.
Therefore, all stars are olives.

By contrast, the following form is not valid.

All A are B.
Some B are C.
Therefore, some A are C.

It is easy to see that this form of syllogistic argument is not valid by considering an example of that form in which the premises are true but the conclusion is false:

All men are mammals.
Some mammals are female.
Therefore, some men are female.

Study Questions

1. Give new examples of *valid* syllogisms with the following properties: (a) The premises are false and the conclusion is true. (b) The premises are false and the conclusion is false. (c) One premise is false, one premise is true, and the conclusion is false.

2. Give examples in *invalid* syllogisms with the following properties: (a) The premises are true and the conclusion is true. (b) The premises are false and the conclusion is true.

THE THEORY OF THE SYLLOGISM

Aristotle described fourteen valid forms of syllogistic argument. Medieval logicians gave each of them names, such as *Barbara* and *Celerant*. In Aristotle's logical theory there are four expressions, now called *quantifiers*, that can be prefixed to a subject-predicate phrase. The quantifiers are "all," "no," "some," and "not all." The traditional abbreviations for these quantifiers are respectively A, E, I, and O. By prefixing one of the quantifiers to a subject-predicate phrase, we obtain a sentence. An Aristotelian syllogism consists of three such sentences: two premises and a conclusion. (The names of the syllogisms contain a code for the quantifiers in the sentences in syllogisms of that form. The vowels in the names indicate the kind of quantifier in the second premise, the first premise, and the conclusion. Thus Darapti is a syllogism with two premises having "all" as their quantifier and a conclusion having "some" as its quantifier.)

These syllogisms are written so that the conclusion is always "(Quantifier) A are C." The term that occurs in the subject place in the conclusion (A in the examples below) is called the *minor* term. The term that occurs in the predicate place in the conclusion (C in the examples below) is called the *major* term. The term that occurs in the premises but not in the conclusion (B in the examples) is called the *middle term*.

The *form of a syllogistic argument* is determined entirely by the quantifiers attached to each sentence and by the positions of the terms in the premises. If we ignore the quantifiers for the moment, it is easy to see that there are four different patterns or *figures* (as they are called) in which the major, middle, and minor terms can be distributed (table 2.1). The valid Aristotelian syllogisms, with their medieval names, are listed in table 2.2. You may notice that the table of valid syllogisms contains no syllogisms having the pattern of figure 4. Aristotle did not include a study of syllogisms of this figure.

Table 2.1
The four figures of syllogistic arguments

Figure 1	Figure 2	Figure 3	Figure 4
A are *B*	*A* are *B*	*B* are *A*	*B* are *A*
B are *C*	*C* are *B*	*B* are *C*	*C* are *B*
A are *C*	*A* are *C*	*A* are *C*	*A* are *C*

Table 2.2
Valid Aristotelian syllogisms in the first three figures

1st figure	Barbara	Celarent	Darii	Ferio
A are *B*	All *A* are *B*	All *A* are *B*	Some *A* are *B*	Some *A* are *B*
B are *C*	All *B* are *C*	No *B* are *C*	All *B* are *C*	No *B* are *C*
A are *C*	All *A* are *C*	No *A* are *C*	Some *A* are *C*	Not all *A* are *C*
2nd figure	**Cesare**	**Camestres**	**Festino**	**Baroco**
A are *B*	All *A* are *B*	No *A* are *B*	Some *A* are *B*	Not all *A* are *B*
C are *B*	No *C* are *B*	No *C* are *B*	No *C* are *B*	All *C* are *B*
A are *C*	No *A* are *C*	No *A* are *C*	Not all *A* are *C*	Not all *A* are *C*
3rd figure	**Darapti**	**Felapton**	**Disamis**	**Datisi**
B are *A*	All *B* are *A*	All *B* are *A*	All *B* are *A*	Some *B* are *A*
B are *C*	All *B* are *C*	No *B* are *C*	Some *B* are *C*	All *B* are *C*
A are *C*	Some *A* are *C*	Not all *A* are *C*	Some *A* are *C*	Some *A* are *C*
	Bocardo	**Ferison**		
	All *B* are *A*	Some *B* are *A*		
	Not all *B* are *C*	No *B* are *C*		
	Not all *A* are *C*	Not all *A* are *C*		

There are four possible quantifiers, any of which can attach to any sentence in a syllogism of any figure. Each syllogism has three sentences, and there are four choices of quantifier for the first sentence, four choices for the second sentence, and four choices for the third sentence, and thus there are $4 \times 4 \times 4 = 64$ distinct syllogistic forms in each figure. And since there are four figures, there are 256 distinct forms of syllogistic arguments altogether. Of the 192 syllogistic forms in the first three figures, Aristotle held that only the 14 illustrated are valid. All others are invalid. How did Aristotle come to this conclusion?

Aristotle held that the valid syllogisms of the first figure are *perfect*, by which he meant that their validity is obvious and self-evident and requires no proof. Assuming this is true, it remains to show that the other syllogistic forms he gives are also valid and that other syllogistic forms in the first three figures are invalid. To show the first, Aristotle assumed certain *rules of conversion*, which are really logical rules for inferring one sentence from another. Aristotle's rules of conversion include the following:

Rule 1   From "No X are Y," infer "No Y are X."

Rule 2   From "All X are Y," infer "Some Y are X."

Rule 3   From "Some X are Y," infer "Some Y are X."

With these three rules, some of the valid syllogisms of the second and third figures can be derived from the valid syllogisms of the first figure. Aristotle's strategy is to start with the premises of a second- or third-figure syllogism and to use the rules of conversion to derive the *premises* of a first-figure perfect syllogism. If the perfect syllogism shares its conclusion with the original second- or third-figure syllogism, it follows that the original syllogism is valid (assuming the first-figure perfect syllogisms are valid and that the rules of conversion preserve truth).

For example, Cesare can be transformed into Celarent by using the first rule of conversion on the second premise. That is, from "No C are B" we infer "No B are C" by rule 1 to obtain Celarent.

Cesare	**Celarent**
All A are B	All A are B
No C are B	No B are C
No A are C	No A are C

In the same way, other valid syllogisms of the second and third figure can be converted into a syllogism of the first figure (with the same conclusion) with the rules of conversion.

How did Aristotle show that the many syllogistic forms of the second and third figures that do not occur in the table above are not valid? To answer that, we have to be clearer about what it means for an argument *form* to be valid. The syllogistic forms in the table above are not sentences, they are abstract schemes that would become sentences if genuine terms were substituted for A, B, and C. An argument is valid if and only if it is not possible for its premises to be true and its conclusion false. A *syllogistic argument form is valid provided that, however we substitute real terms for the abstract A, B, and C in the syllogistic form, if the result is a syllogism with true premises, then the resulting conclusion is also true.* So in order to show that a syllogistic form is not valid, Aristotle needed only to find examples of syllogisms of that form in which the premises are both true and the conclusion is false.

Consider the following form of syllogistic argument:

No *A* are *B*
All *B* are *C*
No *A* are *C*

Aristotle shows that this form is not valid by considering the following example:

No horse is a man.
All men are animals.
No horses are animals.

In this case it is obvious that both of the premises are true but the conclusion is false. Hence the syllogistic form is not valid.

Study Questions

1. By providing an example in which the premises are clearly true and the conclusion is clearly false, show that each of the following syllogistic forms is *invalid*:

No *A* are *B*	No *A* are *B*	No *A* are *B*
All *B* are *C*	All *B* are *C*	All *B* are *C*
No *A* are *C*	Some *A* are *C*	Not all *A* are *C*

2. Use the valid syllogistic forms of the first figure and the rules of conversion to show the validity of the form Camestres and the form Felapton.

3. Do the rules of conversion given in the text suffice to show the validity of the forms Baroco and Bocardo? Why or why not?

4. Find the valid syllogistic forms in the fourth figure.*

LIMITATIONS OF ARISTOTLE'S SYLLOGISTIC THEORY OF DEDUCTIVE ARGUMENT

Although the theory of the syllogism is an interesting and impressive theory of deductive inference, it is not comprehensive. It does not include arguments that we and Aristotle's contemporaries recognize as valid. In other respects it is *too* comprehensive: Aristotle counts as valid some arguments that we would not count as valid.

Aristotle developed his theory of the syllogism as part of a theory of scientific demonstration. One of the great ironies of intellectual history is that while geometry was the paradigmatic Greek science and Euclid lived only a generation after Aristotle, the theory of the syllogism cannot account for even the simplest demonstrations in Euclid's *Elements*. There are several reasons why.

First, the propositions of geometry are not all of a simple subject-predicate form. In fact, rather few of them are. Instead, geometrical propositions deal with *relations* among objects. Second, the propositions of geometry do not all have *just* one quantifier; they may essentially involve repeated uses of "all" and "there exists." Third, proofs require devices for referring to the same object in different ways within the same sentence. Recall from chapter 1 the content of Euclid's first proposition:

Proposition 1   For every straight line segment, there exists an equilateral triangle having that line segment as one side.

To treat this claim as the conclusion of a syllogism, Aristotle would have to treat this sentence as having a single quantifier, "all"; a subject, "straight line segment"; and a predicate, "thing for which there exists an equilateral triangle having that thing as one side." Aristotle would therefore have to interpret the conclusion of Euclid's first proof as of the form

All A are C.

That is,

All straight line segments are things for which there exists an equilateral triangle having that thing as one side.

If we look at the table of valid syllogistic forms, we see that a conclusion of this form can only be obtained from a syllogism of the form Barbara. So for Aristotle's theory of deductive argument to apply, Euclid's proof would have to provide some middle term B and axioms or subconclusions of the following forms:

All A are B

All B are C

Or more concretely,

All straight line segments are B.

All B are things for which there exists an equilateral triangle having that thing as one side.

But that is not how Euclid's proof works. Recall that if the line segment has endpoints P and Q, Euclid constructs a circle centered on P and another circle centered on Q, each having the line segment as a radius. One of his postulates says that for every point and every length, a circle centered on that point having that length as radius exists (or can be constructed). Then Euclid assumes that there is a point at which the circle centered on Q and the circle centered on P intersect one another. This point, call it S, must be the same distance from P as P is from Q, and also the same distance from Q as Q is from P. By the construction and the definition of circle, the distance from Q to P is the same as the distance from P to Q, so point S must be the same distance from Q as P is from Q. Then Euclid uses the axiom that things equal to the same thing are equal to one another to infer that the distance from S to P is the distance from P to Q. So the distances PQ, PS, and QS are all equal. Another axiom guarantees that for all pairs of points there is a line segment connecting the points, and the definition of a triangle shows that the figure thus shown to exist is a triangle.

Aristotle might let B stand for "thing with endpoints that are the centers of circles with radii equal to the distance between the points." Then Aristotle would need to show that Euclid's proof contains a syllogistic demonstration of each of the following:

All straight line segments are things with endpoints that are centers of circles with radii equal to the distance between the points.

All things for which there exists an equilateral triangle having that thing as one side are things with endpoints that are the centers of circles with radii equal to the distance between the points.

Each of these will again have to be established by means of a syllogism of the form Barbara. But however many times we compound syllogisms of the Barbara form, we will never obtain a proof that looks at all like the argument that Euclid provided.

Aristotle's theory also fails to cover several other types of arguments. Recall that Aristotle *proves* that the syllogistic forms of the second and third figures shown in table 2.2 are valid forms. What is the form of those proofs? The proof I illustrated has the following form:

If Celarent is valid, then Cesare is valid.
Celarent is valid.
——————————————————————————————
Therefore, Cesare is valid.

This is a perfectly valid deductive argument. It has the following form:

If *P* then *Q*

P
_____

Therefore *Q*

Here *P* and *Q* stand for any complete sentences that are either true or false. *This argument is not one of Aristotle's valid syllogistic forms.* So Aristotle's own proof of the properties of his logical system uses logical principles that his system can neither represent nor account for. The argument just sketched depends on the logical properties of "If . . . then ____," where the ellipsis and the blank are filled by *sentences.* This form of argument is sometimes called a "hypothetical syllogism."

There is a third difficulty with Aristotle's theory of the syllogism. Look at the first four valid syllogisms of the third figure: Darapti, Felapton, Disamis, and Datisi. Each of them has an existential conclusion; that is, in each case the conclusion says that something exists having specified properties. So, for example, in Darapti we have the following inference:

All *B* are *A*
All *B* are *C*
_____

Some *A* are *C*

Aristotle meant "Some *A* are *C*" to be read as "There exist some things that are *A* and *C*." So understood, it is not clear that Darapti is a valid form of inference. Consider the following example:

All unicorns are animals with hoofs.
All unicorns are horses with one horn.
_____

Therefore, some animals with hoofs are horses with one horn.

This looks like an argument in which the premises are true but the conclusion is false. The problem is with the second rule of conversion:

From "All *X* are *Y*," infer "Some *Y* are *X*."

We don't think it is legitimate to infer "Some little people are leprechauns" from "All leprechauns are little people." We don't think it is legitimate to infer "Some numbers that are divisible by two are both even and odd" from "All numbers that are both even and odd are divisible by two." We reason all the time (both in fairy tales and in mathematics) about *all* things of a certain kind, even when we don't believe or mean to imply that things of that kind exist. In fact, in mathematics we often reason about such things just to prove that they don't exist! Aristotle would have agreed with our practice, but his *theory* seems not to agree.

AFTER ARISTOTLE

Aristotle's theory of deductive reasoning may have had many flaws. Yet despite minor improvements in the theory of syllogistic reasoning and some other developments in logical theory, no fundamental advances appeared for the next 2,400 years. Aristotle's successors at the Lyceum and after them the Stoic philosophers developed some of the principles of the logic of propositions. Their principles were understood by medieval logicians. For example, it was recognized that for any propositions P and Q, one could infer Q from premises consisting of the assertion of P and the assertion of "If P then Q." Medieval logicians even gave this form of inference a name, *modus ponens*:

Modus ponens   From "P" and "If P then Q," infer "Q."

Other related logical principles were also understood, for example, the principle *modus tollens*:

Modus tollens   From "Not Q" and "If P then Q," infer "Not P."

Theophrastus, who succeeded Aristotle as the head of the Lyceum, gave conditions for the truth of sentences compounded of simpler sentences. He proposed that any sentence of the form "If P then Q" is false only when P is true and Q is false. In any other circumstance, "If P then Q" is true. So in Theophrastus' view, "If P then Q" is true if P and Q are both false, if P is false and Q is true, and if both P and Q are true. In Theophrastus' conception, therefore, the truth or falsity of "If P then Q" is a function of the truth values (true or false) of P and Q. In other words, the truth value (true or false) of "If P then Q" is uniquely determined by the truth values of P and Q, just as the numerical value of the sum $X + Y$ is uniquely determined by the numerical values of X and Y. Sentences of the form "If ... then ____" are now known as *conditional sentences* or simply *conditionals*. The account of conditionals as truth functions of the simpler sentences from which they are composed was not widely accepted by logicians of the Middle Ages. They held instead that "If P then Q" is true only if the truth of P necessitates the truth of Q. With that understanding, the truth value of "If P then Q" is not a function of the truth values of P and Q. It isn't the truth or falsity of P and Q alone that determines the truth or falsity of "If P then Q," but whether the truth of P necessitates the truth of Q.

Further principles about inference with quantifiers were also recognized by Aristotle's successors. For example, they recognized the principle that from a universal claim one may infer any instance of it. From "Everything is such that if it is human, then it is mortal" one may infer "If Socrates is human, then Socrates is mortal."

Logic was extensively studied in the late Middle Ages from the twelfth through the fourteenth centuries. The theory of the syllogism was understood and extended in minor ways, and tracts were written on various sorts of quantifiers. Medieval logicians were especially interested in what we call *modal logic*, which is the study of deductive inferences that involve notions of necessity, possibility, and ability. Aristotle himself had written on the subject. Aristotle had maintained the following logical principles (which he did not clearly distinguish):

For any proposition *P*, "Necessarily *P*" is true if and only if "Not possibly not *P*" is true.

"*A* is necessarily *B*" is true if and only if "*A* is not possibly not *B*" is true.

Modal reasoning was of special concern to logicians of the Middle Ages because the motivation for their studies of logic was as much religious as it was scientific. They were concerned with features of God and with humanity's relations with God. These subjects involved complicated uses of claims about necessity and possibility. For example, Saint Anselm's proof of God's existence seems to turn on the idea that God is an entity that could not possibly not exist, an entity that necessarily exists. Notions of possibility and necessity can easily lead to paradoxes, which require a logical theory to untangle.

These and other logical investigations amounted to some limited progress in understanding valid reasoning. But at the end of the fourteenth century, Western civilization was not substantially closer to understanding deductive inference than it had been in the fourth century B.C. It was still not possible, for example, to give a systematic theory of proof that would include the proofs of geometry and exclude fallacies. Although additional logical principles had been developed after Aristotle, they had not been formed into a powerful systematic theory. The three central questions posed in chapter 1 were not much closer to being answered.

ARISTOTELIAN REASONING IN ARTIFICIAL INTELLIGENCE*

Although Aristotle's theory of demonstrative reasoning is inadequate to represent most proofs in mathematics and the sciences, a lot of simple reasoning can be represented as syllogistic.

Two puzzles

Here are two very old puzzles about the properties of God and God's relation to humans. Both involve modal reasoning. The first is concerns a claim about God that some Christians thinkers of the Middle Ages and Renaissance seem to have held:

(1) God is necessarily omnipotent; that is, necessarily God can do anything.

Consider now the question, Can God make a rock he cannot lift? Suppose God cannot make such a rock. Then (1) is false. Suppose, on the other hand, that God can make such a rock. Since God is able to make such a rock, the circumstance in which such a rock exists is possible. But in the possible circumstance in which God makes a rock he cannot lift, there is something God cannot do, namely to lift that rock. Hence there is a possible circumstance in which there is something God cannot do. So it is not the case that necessarily God can do anything. So (1) is false again. But either God can make a rock he cannot lift, or he cannot. Hence (1) is false.

The second puzzle involves two other claims that were widely believed.

(2) God is omniscient; that is, he knows beforehand everything that will happen.

(3) Humans have free will; that is, there are actions humans take such that nothing necessitates that they do that thing rather than something else.

Let A be an action freely done by some human. Then nothing necessitated A. But before A occurred, God knew that A would occur. Necessarily, God could not have known that A would occur if A did not occur. Hence God's knowledge that A would occur necessitated that A occur. Hence A was not a free action. Hence (2) and (3) are inconsistent.

Recently, Aristotelian modes of reasoning have been applied in the study of artificial intelligence. Research in artificial intelligence attempts to devise programs that will enable computers to solve problems that require intelligence in human problem solvers. Most AI work is not committed to making computers solve problems in exactly the same way in which humans solve them, but the way in which humans proceed sometimes gives the program designer useful hints about how to make a computer solve the same kind of problem. Humans *reason* in solving problems, even the most elementary kinds of problems. Computers should reason as well, or at least they should do something that looks like reasoning.

Human reasoning involves the use of an enormous amount of knowledge. If you are told that Dumbo is an elephant, you can immediately answer such questions as "Is Dumbo a mammal?" "Does Dumbo have a long nose?" "Does Dumbo have a tail?" "Is Dumbo a herbivore?" You can answer these questions because you know a great many things about elephants. If we want to design a computer program that will have the same capacities as you have, we will have to provide the computer with the same kind of knowledge. Equally important, we will have to find a way to *organize* the knowledge so that the computer can find relevant parts of it rapidly.

One of the earliest methods developed for organizing knowledge in a computer program is called an *is-a hierarchy*. An is-a hierarchy is a graph of just the kind I used to illustrate Aristotle's conception of scientific knowledge. If the subject is elephants, a simple is-a hierarchy might look like this:

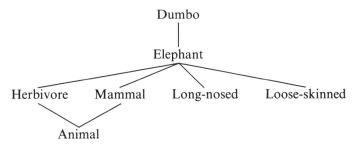

Of course, the computer does not have this *picture*. What it has is a set of instructions that link terms such as "Dumbo" and "elephant" to one another, and the links are exactly as in the graph. Each connection in the graph represents a general statement. For example,

Dumbo is an elephant.
All elephants are mammals.
All elephants are long-nosed.
All mammals are animals.

Suppose the computer is asked, Is Dumbo an animal? To answer the question, the computer searches for a path from "Dumbo" to "animal." It might, for example, go from "Dumbo" to "elephant," to "mammal," to "animal." Upon reaching "animal," it would answer that yes, Dumbo is an animal. In this sort of procedure the computer is carrying out the simplest sort of syllogistic inference.

One interesting thing about trying to simulate human reasoning using a computer is that we are forced to consider logical features that might otherwise be ignored. Suppose that instead of reasoning about elephants, the computer is to reason about birds. From the information that Tweety is a bird, the computer should be able to answer such questions as, "Does Tweety have feathers?" "Does Tweety have wings?" "Can Tweety fly?" "Is Tweety a mammal?" "Is Tweety an animal?" The relevant information about birds needed to answer these questions can be represented by a graph, just as the information about elephants is represented. The graph would encode such information as that birds have feathers, that birds have wings, that winged things can fly, and so on. The computer can then carry out simple syllogistic inferences to answer these questions. Given the information that Tweety is a bird, a person will generally answer the question, Can Tweety fly? with a yes. The computer will answer in the same way. But if you give a person a further piece of information about Tweety, you get a different answer. If a person is given the further information that Tweety is an ostrich, the person will not infer that Tweety can fly. People, in other words, make the following inference:

Tweety is a bird.
Birds can fly.
Therefore, Tweety can fly.

And they also make this inference:

Tweety is a bird.
Birds can fly.
Tweety is an ostrich.
Ostriches cannot fly.
Therefore, Tweety cannot fly.

"Tweety can fly" may look at first like the conclusion of a syllogistic inference, but actually something much more complicated is going on. Syllogistic inference, as Aristotle and his successors understood it, is *monotonic*, meaning that if a conclusion C can be validly inferred from a set of premises, then it can also be validly inferred from any set of premises that include the original premises. The Tweety example shows that the kind of reasoning humans do is sometimes (in fact quite often) *nonmonotonic*: adding information to the premises prevents us from drawing conclusions we would otherwise draw. One mark of the difference is that we are inclined to agree that birds can fly, but not that all birds can fly. In the same way, we are inclined to agree that whales give milk, but not that all whales give milk (male whales don't). Sentences such as "Birds can fly" are sometimes said to be *generalized*, whereas sentences such as "All birds can fly" are said to be *universal*. While universal and generalized sentences are sometimes synonymous, they aren't always. When they aren't, reasoning that looks syllogistic may actually be nonmonotonic. To make a computer reason as humans do in contexts where knowledge consists of generalized but not universal sentences, the computer must make inferences according to principles of nonmonotonic logic. The principles of nonmonotonic logic and their efficient implementation in computer programs are major areas of contemporary research.

Study Questions

1. Write out a graph for reasoning about birds that is like the graph shown for elephants.

2. Suppose that someone reconstructed a particular deduction as a syllogism and you wished to show that the inference principles used actually involved nonmonotonic reasoning. How could you argue for your view? Give an example.

3. Knowledge of causes is often used to reason nonmonotonically. Give an example.

4. What is the name of the syllogistic form used in the reasoning that Dumbo is an animal?

5. Explain why the theory of the syllogism cannot fully account for everyday reasoning about properties of things.

Review Questions

1. What questions should a theory of deductive argument address? How well does Aristotle's theory of deductive arguments succeed in answering these questions?

2. What are three major difficulties with Aristotle's theory of deductive argument?

3. What are the four senses of "cause" in Aristotle's philosophy?

4. Do you think that syllogistic reasoning could be used to account for proofs in arithmetic or the theory of numbers?

5. Explain Aristotle's strategy for justifying his theory of syllogisms.

6. Which of Aristotle's syllogistic forms of the second and third figures can be converted into a first-figure form without using Aristotle's second rule of conversion?

7. What role does the theory of syllogisms play in Aristotle's understanding of scientific demonstration?

Further Reading

Aristotle
Ackrill, J. L. *Aristotle's Categories and De Interpretatione.* Oxford: Oxford University Press, 1963.

Ackrill, J. L. *Aristotle, the Philosopher.* New York: Oxford University Press, 1981.

Allan, D. J. *The Philosophy of Aristotle.* New York: Oxford University Press, 1970.

Bambrough, Renford, ed. *New Essays on Plato and Aristotle.* London: Routledge and Kegan Paul, 1979.

Barnes, Jonathan. *Aristotle.* New York: Oxford University Press, 1982.

Barnes, Jonathan. *Aristotle's Posterior Analytics.* Oxford: Oxford University Press, 1975.

Barnes, Jonathan, ed. *The Complete Works of Aristotle: The Revised Oxford Translation.* Princeton: Princeton University Press, 1984.

Barnes, Jonathan, Malcolm Schofield, and Richard Sorabji, eds. *Articles on Aristotle.* Vols. 1–4. London: Duckworth, 1975–1979.

Gill, Mary Louise. *Aristotle and Substance: The Paradox of Unity.* Princeton: Princeton University Press, 1991. This book presents a very different view of Aristotle's metaphysics.

Grene, Majorie. *A Portrait of Aristotle.* Chicago: University of Chicago Press, 1963.

Hartman, Edwin. *Substance, Body, and Soul: Aristotelian Investigations.* Princeton: Princeton University Press, 1977.

Heath, T. L. *Mathematics in Aristotle.* Oxford: Oxford University Press, 1970.

Jaeger, Werner. *Aristotle: Fundamentals of the History of His Development.* New York: Oxford University Press, 1934.

Lear, Jonathan. *Aristotle and Logical Theory.* New York: Cambridge University Press, 1980.

Lloyd, G. E. R. *Aristotle: The Growth and Structure of His Thought.* New York: Cambridge University Press, 1968.

Lloyd, G. E. R., and G. E. L. Owen, eds. *Aristotle on the Mind and the Senses.* New York: Cambridge University Press, 1978.

Moravcsik, J. M. E., ed. *Aristotle: A Collection of Critical Essays.* Garden City, N.Y.: Anchor Books, 1967.

Owens, Joseph. *The Doctrine of Being in the Aristotelian Metaphysics.* Toronto: Pontifical Institute of Mediaeval Studies, 1978.

Ross, W. D. *Aristotle's Metaphysics.* Oxford: Oxford University Press, 1975.

Ross, W. D. *Aristotle's Physics.* Oxford: Oxford University Press, 1961.

Ross, W. D. *Aristotle's Prior and Posterior Analytics.* Oxford: Oxford University Press, 1965.

Solmsen, Friedrich. *Aristotle's System of the Physical World.* Ithaca, N.Y.: Cornell University Press, 1960.

Van Rijen, Jeroen. *Aspects of Aristotle's Logic of Modalities*. Dordrecht: Kluwer, 1989.

Greek science

Barnes, Jonathan, ed. *Science and Speculation: Studies in Hellenistic Theory and Practice*. New York: Cambridge University Press, 1982.

Lloyd, G. E. R. *Magic, Reason, and Experience*. New York: Cambridge University Press, 1979.

Lloyd, G. E. R. *The Revolutions of Wisdom: Studies in the Claims and Practice of Ancient Greek Science*. Berkeley: University of California Press, 1987.

Neugebauer, Otto. *The Exact Sciences in Antiquity*. Princeton: Princeton University Press, 1951.

Sambursky, Samuel. *The Physical World of the Greeks*. London: Routledge and Paul, 1956.

History of logic

Corcoran, John, ed. *Ancient Logic and Its Modern Interpretations*. Boston: D. Reidel, 1974.

Englebretsen, George. *Three Logicians*. Atlantic Highlands, N.J.: Humanities Press, 1981.

Kapp, Ernst. *Greek Foundations of Traditional Logic*. New York: Columbia University Press, 1942.

Kneale, W. C., and Martha Kneale. *The Development of Logic*. New York: Oxford University Press, 1984.

Scholz, Heinrich. *Concise History of Logic*. New York: Philosophical Library, 1961.

Syllogistic theory

Barnes, Jonathan. *Terms and Sentences: Theophrastus on Hypothetical Syllogisms*. London: Oxford University Press, 1984.

De Morgan, Augustus. *On the Syllogism and Other Logical Writings*. New Haven: Yale University Press, 1966.

Lukasiewicz, Jan. *Aristotle's Syllogistic from the Standpoint of Modern Formal Logic*. New York: Garland, 1987.

McCall, Storrs. *Aristotle's Modal Syllogisms*. Amsterdam: North-Holland Publishing Co., 1963.

Patzig, Gunther. *Aristotle's Theory of the Syllogism*. Dordrecht: D. Reidel, 1968.

Rose, Lynn E. *Aristotle's Syllogistic*. Springfield, Ill.: Thomas, 1968.

Thom, Paul. *The Syllogism*. Munich: Philosophia, 1981.

Chapter 3

IDEAS, COMBINATIONS, AND THE MATHEMATICS OF THOUGHT

INTRODUCTION

From the fifteenth through the seventeenth centuries, literature, art, and science flourished in Europe, but logic did not prosper. The careful study of the problems of deductive inference and of the relations between words and things that make reliable inference possible came to be replaced by *rhetoric*, the study of persuasive speech. Aristotle had written on rhetoric, and logic texts in the Renaissance increasingly gave their attention to that subject rather than to studies of valid argument. But in the seventeenth century there occurred such a revolution in thought, and such an explosion in knowledge, that every subject, including logic, was affected. The seventeenth century brought into vivid contrast two different ideals of reason: on the one hand, the ideal of certainty best exemplified by Euclid's geometry and Aristotelian syllogistics; on the other hand, the ideal of rational belief with uncertainty, exemplified in quantitative form by the laws of probability and the laws of nature, such as Boyle's law of gases and Newton's law of gravitation, newly discovered in the seventeenth century. One effect of this clash was to move intellectual interest away from a theory of demonstration toward theories of rational belief and rational inference. But the new mathematics of rationality also helped to unite the theory of deductive demonstration with the new quantitative theories of nature. The theory of deductive proof became the quantitative theory of *ideas* and of how they may be combined.

The seventeenth century saw the establishment of modern philosophy in the work of Galileo Galilei (1564–1642), Francis Bacon (1561–1626), René Descartes (1596–1650), Thomas Hobbes (1588–1679), Blaise Pascal (1623–1662), Gottfried Leibniz (1646–1716), Isaac Newton (1642–1727), and John Locke (1632–1704). The creation of modern philosophy went hand in hand with the creation of modern science and modern mathematics. For the most original and powerful minds of the time, science, mathematics, and philosophy were simply different aspects of a common enterprise of knowledge. Indeed, they would have found our separation of the subjects somewhat artificial. Galileo provided some of the most powerful arguments for the heliocentric conception of the solar system, and he wrote systematic attacks on the adequacy of Aristotelian physics. At the same time, his writings contain the beginnings of new conceptions of how the mind works and how knowledge is acquired. Francis Bacon not only articulated a new, empirically based conception of how knowledge is acquired; he also developed the theory of heat and conducted a number of experiments to support that theory. Descartes, except for Newton perhaps the most eminent and influential intellect of the century, invented the study of the geometrical properties of solutions to algebraic equations, the subject we now call analytic geometry, and also developed an extensive (but largely erroneous) anti-Aristotelian physical theory. Hobbes, despite many attempts, left no mathematical or scientific achievements of value, but he left something else: the idea that the study of society can be part of natural science, and the idea that moral conceptions can be explained and justified by scientific considerations of human nature and of the conditions under which humans live. Pascal invented and sold a mechanical calculator, conducted a famous experiment to demonstrate the pressure of the atmosphere, and introduced many of the fundamental ideas in the theory of probability and the theory of rational decision making. Leibniz invented the differential and integral calculus and promoted a variety of social projects in the second half of the century. He too designed and built mechanical calculators. Newton we know as the source of modern physics; his *Principia* and *Optics* revolutionized that subject. His scientific writings, especially the *Principia*, also contain a new and sophisticated philosophy of science. Locke is known for his writings on the structure of the mind, for his theory of how knowledge is acquired, and for his account of just government. His writings were heavily influenced by the new sciences emerging all around him.

Except for Leibniz, seventeenth-century philosophers did not succeed in developing a better logical theory than Aristotle's. Of Descartes, Hobbes, Pascal, Leibniz, Newton, and Locke, only Leibniz wrote extensively on logic, and most of what he wrote was not published. But the seventeenth century did establish two important ideas about deductive reasoning.

• The theory of deductive reasoning and demonstration is part of *psychology*. It should provide part of the laws of thought, just as physics provides the laws of motion.
• The laws of thought have an *algebraic structure*, just as do the laws of arithmetic or the laws of motion.

The first of these ideas turned out to be fundamentally in error—only when it was abandoned did the modern understanding of deductive inference emerge—but its very falsity creates a puzzle that we will consider at several points in this book. The second idea turned out to be correct and profound, and two centuries later, in the middle of the nineteenth century, it formed the basis for the first fundamental advance in logic since Aristotle. In the rest of this chapter we will consider how these two ideas emerged from metaphysics, mathematics, and theology in the seventeenth century.

To understand how seventeenth-century thinkers brought these views of logic and demonstration to prominence and why they were widely thought to be true, we must consider a little of the tradition of thought about mathematics and knowledge that the century inherited and drew upon.

COMBINATIONS

According to both Plato and Aristotle, the objects of knowledge have a special *formal structure*. The sort of thing a person may know is that one thing or kind or property is a *finite combination* of other things or kinds or properties. *Human* is a combination of *rational* and *animal*. *Triangle* is a combination of *closed*, *rectilinear*, *figure*, and *three-sided*. Plato and Aristotle differed about the metaphysics, of course. For Plato, the elements of these combinations are ideal objects or forms; for Aristotle, they are essential attributes of concrete objects. For both philosophers, however, all knowledge consists of knowing such combinations of forms or essential attributes of a thing or kind. For example, according to Plato, knowledge of virtue is knowledge of which simple forms are combined in the form of virtue.

This simple conjunctive view of the objects of knowledge suggests questions about combinations of properties. Ultimately, on either the Platonic or Aristotelian view, any kind or property that can be the object of scientific knowledge can be analyzed into a combination of simple properties that cannot be further analyzed. The number of distinct kinds that can be the object of knowledge then consists of the number of distinct combinations of these simple properties, whatever they are. What is the number of pairs of distinct simple properties if there are n simple properties altogether? What is the number of triples of distinct simple properties if there are n simple properties altogether? What is the number of distinct combinations of any particular number m of simple properties drawn from n simple properties? How can these distinct combinations be enumerated and surveyed? If one has the Platonic and Aristotelian conception of the form of knowledge, these are fundamental questions.

In Europe just such questions gave rise to the mathematical subject of *combinatorics*, the study of the numbers of possible combinations satisfying given conditions. The first mathematical results of this kind in Europe seem to occur in a commentary on Aristotle by Porphyry (ca. 234–ca. 305) written in the third century. Porphyry wished to comment on all of the similarities and differences among five Aristotelian categories, and so he posed the problem of enumerating all the distinct pairs of things that can be obtained from a collection of five things. He observed that one might think that this number is 20, because one can choose the first thing of a pair in any of five ways and the remaining member of the pair in four distinct ways:

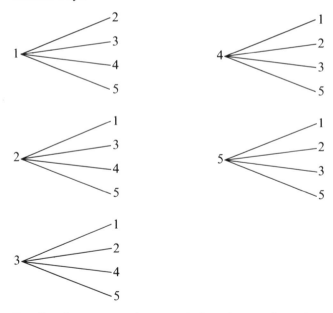

But Porphyry correctly argued that the number of pairings is not 20: "Such is not the case; for though the first of the five can be paired with the remaining four, when we come to the second, one of the pairs will already have been counted; with the third, two; with the fourth, three, and with the fifth, four; thus there are in all only ten differences: $4 + 3 + 2 + 1$."[1]

Roughly 250 years later, Boethius (d. 524) wrote commentaries on Porphyry's commentary on Aristotle, and in them he provided a more general, alternative proof. In modern terminology, his reasoning was as follows. Twenty is the number of *ordered pairs*, $\langle x, y \rangle$, in which x is distinct from y, that can be formed from five distinct objects. With ordered pairs, a change in the order counts as a distinct pair, so $\langle x, y \rangle$ is not equal to $\langle y, x \rangle$. Porphyry was interested in the number of pairs of distinct properties that could be formed from five properties, but he did not care about order. He was concerned with the number of *unordered pairs*, $\{x, y\}$. Clearly, for each ordered pair there will be another with the same objects but in the reverse order. If these two ordered pairs are thought of as together forming a single unordered pair, or if together they are counted as one object, then the number of unordered pairs will be half of the number of the ordered pairs. Ten is half of twenty, for example. The number of ways of choosing ordered pairs from n things is $n(n - 1)$, so the number of distinct unordered pairs that can be formed from n things is $n(n - 1)/2$.

In the Middle Ages, the conception of the objects of knowledge as combinations of simple attributes that make up a kind or a complex property led to a conception of the method for acquiring knowledge. The method, in so far as it deserves the name, consisted of trying to "analyze" a thing into its simple properties (*analysis*), and then trying to put it back together by combining those properties (*synthesis*). Often the analysis and synthesis were purely mental and consisted of analyzing or synthesizing a thing only in imagination, but sometimes, in Renaissance chemistry, for example, analysis meant physically decomposing a substance into "simpler" substances, and synthesis meant physically reconstituting a substance of that kind.

One would expect that Christian intellectuals would apply the methods they had adapted from Aristotle and Plato to the study of God, and, of course, they did. God too had fundamental properties, and one could consider the combinations of God's attributes. In the thirteenth century the question of how to enumerate, organize, and display God's attributes led to a fundamental insight, one that we nowadays take for granted. It concerns the odd life of the great Spanish philosopher Ramon Lull (d. 1315), a thirteenth-century Franciscan monk.

Lull grew up in a wealthy family and passed his early adulthood in the court of James II of Spain. He spent his time with games and pleasantries and is reputed to have made great efforts to seduce the wives of other courtiers. Accounts have it that after considerable effort to seduce a particular lady, she finally let him into her chambers and revealed a withered breast. Taking this as a sign from God, Lull gave up the life of a courtier and joined the Franciscan order. He determined that he would dedicate his life to converting Moslem civilization to Christianity, and in a curious way, philosophy gained from that dedication.

Lull moved to Majorca, spent several years mastering the Arabic language, and studied and wrote tracts (of which he eventually authored hundreds) against Islam and for Christianity. About 1274 Lull had a vision of the means by which Moslems could be converted to Christianity. Stimulated by the idea, he wrote another book, his *Ars Magna*. While Lull's fundamental style of thought is mystical and obscure, it contains one logical gem.

In effect, Lull's idea was that Moslems (and others) may fail to convert to Christianity because of a cognitive defect. They simply were unable to appreciate the vast array of the combinations of God's or Christ's virtues. Lull believed that infidels could be converted if they could be brought to see the *combinations* of God's attributes. Further, he thought that a *representation* of those combinations could be effectively presented by means of appropriate machines, and that was the key to his new method. Lull designed and built a series of machines meant to be used to present the combinations of God's virtues.

A typical Lullian machine consisted of two or more disks having a common spindle. Each disk could be rotated independently of the others. The rim of each disk was divided into sections or *camerae*, and each section bore a letter. According to the application for which the machine was intended, the letters each had a special significance. They might denote, for example, an attribute of God. One Lullian machine, for example, has the letters *B* through *R* around the rims of an inner disk, and around the outer disk Latin words signifying attributes of God: "bonitas" (B), "magnitudo" (C), "eternitas" (D), and so on. A Lullian machine was operated by rotating the two disks independently, much as we would a star finder or (some years ago) a circular slide rule. At any setting of the disks, *pairs* of God's attributes would be juxtaposed on the rims of the inner and outer disks. Rotating the disks would create different pairings. One would thus discover that God is good *and* great, good *and* eternal, great *and* eternal, and so forth. The heretic and the infidel were supposed to be brought to the true faith by these revelations.

Lull lectured on several occasions at the University of Paris. He traveled throughout Europe, attempting to raise money for missions to North Africa to convert Moslems to Christianity. He himself is reported to have made three such trips to Africa. Tradition has it that on his third trip, at the age of 83, he was stoned to death, but some biographers lacking in romantic sentiment dispute this account.

This may seem a bizarre and slightly amusing story of no particular philosophical significance. But buried within Lull's mysticism and his machines is the seed of a collection of powerful ideas that only began to bear fruit three hundred and fifty years later.

One of the great ideas implicit in Lull's work is that *reasoning can be done by a mechanical process.* Another equally profound idea in Lull's thought is that *reasoning does not proceed by syllogism but by combinatorics. Reasoning is the decomposition and recombination of representations.* The decomposition and recombination of attributes can be represented by the decomposition and recombination of *symbols*, and that, as Lull's devices illustrate, is a process that can be carried out by machines.

Lull's work was known even in the seventeenth century, when these ideas were taken up by Leibniz, the most eminent mind on the continent of Europe in the second half of that century. Neither in Lull nor in Leibniz, however, do these ideas form a theory that competes with Aristotle's or that offers solutions to the questions developed in the first chapter of this book. But Lull had at least taken the first step: he had an *idea* for a theory.

Study Questions

1. There are only two ways to order two distinct letters. How many ways are there to order three distinct letters?

2. One of Lull's machines had sixteen letters signifying attributes of God. How many ordered triples of three distinct letters can be formed from Lull's sixteen letters?

3. How many *unordered* triples of distinct letters can be formed from Lull's sixteen letters?

4. Let $n!$ (said "n factorial") denote the number $n \times (n - 1) \times (n - 2) \times \cdots \times 1$. The number $n!$ is clearly the number of distinct ways that n things can be put in order, because we have n choices for the first thing, $n - 1$ for the second, and so on, until there is only one thing left. The number of ways of choosing an ordered sequence of 3 distinct things from n things must be $n \times (n - 1) \times (n - 2)$. The number of ways of choosing an ordered sequence of m distinct things from n things

(where $m \leq n$) must be $n \times (n - 1) \times \cdots \times (n - (m - 1))$, or more simply, $n!/(n - m)!$ Use these facts to find a formula for the number of ways of choosing m things from n things without regard to order.

5. Suppose you have a collection of n things. How many distinct collections with 2 or more members can be formed from the collection of n things? In the sixteenth century Cardano gave the correct answer: $2^n - 1 - n$. Can you give a proof of this answer?

THE *IDEA* IDEA

The method of analysis and synthesis might be thought of as a form of *reasoning*. So conceived, it is a kind of computation or calculation in which properties are added or taken away. But in most cases those who thought of themselves as applying this method did not really add or take away any properties of things. Instead, they added or subtracted *thoughts* or *ideas* of properties. So viewed, the method of analysis and synthesis had to do with the operations of the mind.

Thomas Hobbes

Thomas Hobbes was born at the end of the sixteenth century and lived almost until the eighteenth. Educated at Oxford, he made his living by attaching himself to rich and influential families, often serving as tutor to their children. The Civil War in England raged during his adult years, and Hobbes spent most of his intellectual efforts on political theory. The general view he had of the nature of politics and the foundations of government are still influential today. Although he criticized Aristotle's system, in many respects Hobbes remained an Aristotelian thinker. Hobbes met on several occasions with one of the great intellectual revolutionaries of the first part of the seventeenth century, Francis Bacon, who along with many other figures of the period, was convinced that new empirical methods of discovery were required in science. Hobbes disagreed, and despised the experimental method that Bacon had championed and that by the middle of the seventeenth century was flourishing in England and in parts of continental Europe. Hobbes was self-taught in mathematics. He is said to have learned geometry by finding a book of Euclid's *Elements* open to some advanced proposition, which, upon reading, Hobbes did not believe. Since he did not believe the proposition, Hobbes read the proof, which depended on still other propositions, whose proofs Hobbes proceeded to read. In this way he worked back to Euclid's axioms and convinced himself of the truth of the proposition he had originally doubted.

That is just how seventeenth-century philosophers thought of it. Thomas Hobbes, for example, wrote as follows:

By ratiocination, I mean computation. Now to compute is either to collect the sum of many things that are added together, or to know what remains when one thing is taken out of another. Ratiocination, therefore, is the same with addition and subtraction; and if any man add multiplication and division, I will not be against it, seeing multiplication is nothing but addition of equals one to another, and division nothing but a subtraction of equals one from another, as often as is possible. So that all ratiocination is comprehended in these two operations of the mind, addition and subtraction.

But how by the ratiocination of our mind, we add and subtract in our silent thoughts, without the use of words, it will be necessary for me to make intelligible by an example or two. If therefore a man see something afar off and obscurely, although no appellation had yet been given to anything, he will, notwithstanding, have the same idea of that thing for which now, by imposing a name on it, we call a body. Again, when by coming nearer, he sees the same thing thus and thus, now in one place and now in another, he will have a new idea thereof, namely that for which we now call such a thing animated. Thirdly, when standing near, he perceives the figure, hears the voice, and sees other things which are signs of a rational mind, he has a third idea, though it have yet no appellation, namely that for which we now call anything rational. Lastly, when, by looking fully and distinctly upon it, he conceives all that he has seen as one thing, the idea he has now is compounded of his former ideas, which are put together in the mind in the same order in which these three single names, *body*, *animated*, *rational*, are in speech compounded into this one name, *body-animated-rational*, or *man*. In like manner, of the several conceptions of four sides, equality of sides, and right angles, is compounded the conception of a square. For the mind may conceive a figure of four sides without any conception of their equality, and of that equality without conceiving a right angle; and may join together all these single conceptions in not one conception or one idea of a square. And thus we see how the conceptions of the mind are compounded. Again, whosoever sees a man standing near him, conceives the whole idea of that man; and if, as he goes away, he follow him with his eyes only, he will lose the idea of those things that were signs of his being rational, whilst, nevertheless, the idea of a body-animated remains still before his eyes, so that the idea of rational is subtracted from the whole idea of man, that is to say, of body-animated-rational, and there remains that of body-animated and a while after, at a greater distance, the idea of animated will be lost, and that of body only will remain; so that at last, when nothing at all can be seen, the whole idea will vanish out of sight. By which examples, I think, it is manifest enough what is the internal ratiocination of the mind without words.

We must not therefore think that computation, that is ratiocination, has place only in numbers, as if man were distinguished from other living creatures (which is said to have been the opinion of Pythagoras) by nothing but the faculty of numbering; for magnitude, body, motion, time, degree of quality, action, conception, proportion, speech and names (in which all the kinds of philosophy consist) are capable of addition and subtraction.[2]

There are at least two important thoughts in this passage. One is that reasoning is a psychological process, so that a theory of logical inference should be a theory of the operations of the mind. The other is that the theory of reasoning is a theory of appropriate combinations. Just what the objects are that are combined is obscure in this passage, but other passages suggest that Hobbes thought of the mind as composed of particles, and some of these particles, or collections of them, serve as symbols (or as Hobbes would say, names) for things, and it is these physical symbols that are combined or decomposed in reasoning. As we will see later, the very same idea lies behind much of twentieth-century cognitive science.

The obvious question about the method of analysis and synthesis is why and how it should work. How are people supposed to be able to recognize which properties are simple and which are complex so that they can be decomposed into simpler combinations? Plato had an answer: recollection. The forms are "stamped on the soul," and, prompted by experience, one has only to recollect them. Aristotle had another answer: we have a faculty of intuition that tells us which properties are fundamental. Neither of these answers seems very satisfactory. They don't tell us, for example, why we should believe that intuition or recollection reliably gives us the truth. They don't explain why people who try to apply the method come to very different conclusions, or how to come to agreement about who is in error. What could the method be? How could it work? How could we be certain that it works? René Descartes had an answer, sort of.

In Descartes' view, as in Hobbes's, we do not analyze and synthesize things in themselves. We take apart our conceptions of things, our *ideas* of them. What we do in thought, then, is to try to find the simple ideas of which complex thoughts are compounded. Ideas and thoughts are mental states, not physical states. An inquiry into the basis for knowledge must therefore be an inquiry into our psychology, into the operations of the mind, and it must show why those operations, if properly conducted, are reliable. Descartes held that such an inquiry should produce a method that could be shown to be *perfectly* reliable, and he claimed that he himself had found such a method:

Science in its entirety is true and evident cognition. He is no more learned who has doubts on many matters than the man who has never thought of them; nay he appears to be less learned if he has formed wrong opinions on any particulars. Hence it were better not to study at all than to occupy one's self with objects of such difficulty, that, owing to our inability to distinguish true from false, we are forced to regard the doubtful as certain; for in those matters any hope of augmenting our knowledge is exceeded by the risk of diminishing it. Thus in accordance with the above maxim we reject all such merely probable knowledge and make it a rule to trust only what is completely known and incapable of being doubted.[3]

Moreover by a method I mean certain and simple rules, such that, if a man observe them accurately, he shall never assume what is false as true, and will never spend his mental efforts to no purpose, but will always gradually increase his knowledge and so arrive at a true understanding of all that does not surpass his powers.[4]

The fundamental operations of the mind involved in knowledge are intuition (by which we see directly that something is the case or that an immediate inference is necessary), deduction (in which we move through a sequence of intuitions to obtain a necessary conclusion), and induction (by which we infer general conclusions from particular examples). Induction does not provide certainty, but intuition and deduction do aim at certainty, which, according to Descartes, is the only proper goal of inquiry:

By intuition I understand, not the fluctuating testimony of the senses, nor the misleading judgement that proceeds from the blundering constructions of imagination, but the conception which an unclouded and attentive mind gives us so readily and distinctly that we are wholly freed from doubt about that which we understand. Or, what comes to the same thing, intuition is the undoubting conception of an unclouded and attentive mind, and springs from the light of reason alone; it is more certain than deduction itself, in that it is simpler, though deduction, as we have noted above, cannot by us be erroneously conducted. Thus each individual can mentally have intuition of the fact that he exists, and that he thinks, that the triangle is bounded by three lines only, the sphere by a single superficies, and so on.[5]

Descartes seems to think that simple deduction, as in a syllogism, requires nothing but intuition. A chain of deductions, however, also requires memory:

Many things are known with certainty, though not by themselves evident, but only deduced from true and known principles by the continuous and uninterrupted action of a mind that has a clear vision of each step in the process. It is in a similar way that we know that the last link in a long chain is connected with the first, even though we do not take in by means of one and the same act of vision all the intermediate links on which that connection depends, but only remember that we have taken them successively under review and that each single one is united to its neighbour, from the first even to the last. Hence we distinguish this mental intuition from deduction by the fact that into the conception of the latter there enters a certain movement or does not require an immediately presented evidence such as intuition possesses; its certitude is rather conferred upon it in some way by memory. The upshot of the matter is that it is possible to say that those propositions indeed which are immediately deduced from first principles are known now by intuition, now by deduction, i.e., in a way that differs according to our point of view. But the first principles themselves are given by intuition alone, while, on the contrary, the remote conclusions are furnished only by deduction.[6]

The questions for Descartes are how it is that intuition is to be used in producing knowledge, why we should believe that the deliverances of intuition are veridical, and why memory can be trusted.

Some thoughts, Descartes held, we perceive *clearly*, while others appear to us muddled or confused. Of clear ideas, some can be distinguished in imagination from all others, and some are indistinguishable from one another. The ideas of extension and of body, for example, are ideas that cannot be distinguished from one another in imagination: we cannot think of a body except by thinking of it as extended, and we cannot imagine extension without imagining some body that is extended. We have no separate idea of mind from that of substance that thinks. But we can form clear ideas of body and mind, and these ideas are distinct from one another. The idea of mind is the idea of a thinking substance, while the idea of body is the idea of an extended substance.

There is, according to Descartes, a special kind of mental state we have when we perceive a necessary truth clearly and distinctly. For example, when we see the connection between the premises of a valid syllogism and its conclusion, we see with a special clarity and distinctness that if the premises are true, then necessarily the conclusion must be true, and we do not confuse the necessary connection given by *that* syllogism with some other argument. Descartes sometimes writes of this clarity and distinctness as provided by the "natural light of reason." What he says about it is an elaboration of Aristotle's notion of the faculty of intuition.

Descartes' method rests on three principles:

• What is clearly and distinctly conceived to be true cannot be false.
• The separation of thoughts of properties is a perfect indicator of the possible separation of the properties: properties that cannot be conceived of separately are necessarily coextensive, and properties that can be conceived of separately are not necessarily coextensive.
• A genuine recollection of a sequence of clear and distinct ideas cannot be false.

These are *inner* criteria; they do not tell you what to do to check someone else's claim to know something by intuition or the natural light of reason other than to perform a thought experiment yourself. They do not even tell you very clearly what it is to clearly and distinctly conceive something or to genuinely recollect a sequence of clear and distinct thoughts. Descartes gives only a few examples, and his readers must try to learn from them what is a clear and distinct idea. Thus the idea that a triangle is a three-sided figure is, Descartes holds, a necessary truth that can be recognized by the natural light of reason. The quality, whatever it is, of the experience you have when you think of the question "Is a triangle three-sided?" is the mark of the natural light of reason and of a clear and distinct idea.

Why believe any of this? Supposing that we even understand what kinds of experiences Descartes means by the "natural light of reason" or "clear and distinct ideas" or genuine memory, why should we believe that his three principles are correct? We can ask a harder question, for Descartes claims that knowledge requires certainty: How can we be certain that the three principles are correct? Descartes' attempt to answer these questions is given in his *Meditations on the First Philosophy*, in his answers to objections to that work, and in his *Principles of Philosophy*.

First, Descartes argues that some thoughts, some clear and distinct ideas, are indubitable. While we can doubt, at least momentarily, the existence of an external world and we can doubt, at least momentarily, the truths of mathematics, we cannot doubt, even for the moment, claims that are certain. Descartes' example is the thought that I exist. I cannot doubt that I exist, for in the very attempt to doubt my existence, I show myself that I exist.

To begin with, directly we think that we rightly perceive something, we spontaneously persuade ourselves that it is true. Further, if this conviction is so strong that we have no reasons to doubt concerning that of the truth of which we have persuaded ourselves, there is nothing more to enquire about; we have here all the certainty that can reasonably be desired. What is it to us, though perchance some one feigns that that, of the truth of which we are so firmly persuaded, appears false to God or to an Angel, and hence is, absolutely speaking false? What heed do we pay to that absolute falsity, when we by no means believe that it exists or even suspect its existence? We have assumed a conviction so strong that nothing can remove it, and this persuasion is clearly the same as perfect certitude.

But it may be doubted whether there is any such certitude, whether such firm and immutable conviction exists.

It is indeed clear that no one possesses such certainty in those cases where there is the very least confusion and obscurity in our perception; for this obscurity, of whatsoever sort it be, is sufficient to make us doubt here. In matters perceived by sense alone, however clearly, certainty does not exist, because we have often noted that error can occur in sensation, as in the instance of the thirst of the dropsical man, or when one who is jaundiced sees snow as yellow; for he sees it thus with no less clearness and distinctness than we see it as white. If, then, any certitude does exist, it remains that it must be found only in the clear perceptions of the intellect.

But of these there are some so evident and at the same time so simple, that in their case we never doubt about believing them true; e.g., that I, while I think, exist; that what is once done cannot be undone, and other similar truths, about which clearly we can possess this certainty. For we cannot doubt them unless we think of them; but we cannot think of them without at the same time believing them to be true, the position taken up. Hence we can never doubt them without at the same time believing them to be true, i.e., we can never doubt them.[7]

(The argument Descartes gave was not original. In the fourth century Saint Augustine [354–430] already observed that no one can doubt his own existence.)

Second, Descartes claims that we can know with complete certainty that a benevolent God exists. He gives two arguments. The first is that one has a clear and distinct idea of God as a perfectly benevolent, necessary being. One cannot think of God without thinking that God exists. The argument is essentially Saint Anselm's, although Descartes gives him no credit for it.

That the existence of God may be rightly demonstrated from the fact that the necessity of His existence is comprehended in the conception which we have of Him.

When mind afterwards considers the diverse conceptions which it has and when it there discovers the idea of a Being who is omniscient, omnipotent and absolutely perfect, which is far the most important of all; in it it recognizes not merely a possible and contingent existence, as in all the other ideas it has of things which it clearly perceives, but one which is absolutely necessary and eternal. And just as it perceives that it is necessarily involved in the idea of the triangle that it should have three angles which are equal to two right angles, it is absolutely persuaded that the triangle has three angles equal to two right angles. In the same way from the fact that it perceives that necessary and eternal existence is comprised in the idea which it has of an absolutely perfect Being, it has clearly to conclude that this absolutely perfect Being exists.[8]

The second argument is that the cause of our idea of God must be at least as great as our idea itself. Since our idea is of a perfect and necessarily existing being, it must be caused by something at least as perfect and necessarily existing, i.e., by God. The second argument seems simply to equivocate between the perfection of an idea and the idea of something perfect. Both arguments are obscure, but Descartes is quite firm that anyone who doubts them is defective, someone wanting in "the natural light of reason."

I really do not see what can be added to make it clearer that that idea [of God] could not be present in my consciousness unless a supreme being existed, except that the reader might, by attending more diligently to what I have written, free himself of the prejudices that perchance overwhelm his natural light, and might accustom his mind to put trust in ultimate principles than which nothing can be more true or more evident, rather than in the obscure and false opinions which, however, long usage has fixed in his mind.

That *there is nothing in the effect, that has not existed in a similar or in some higher form in the cause*, is a first principle than which none clearer can be entertained. The common truth, '*from nothing, nothing comes*', is identical with it. For if we allow that there is something in the effect which did not exist in the cause, we must grant also that this something has been created by nothing; again the only reasons why nothing cannot be the cause of a thing, is that in such a cause there would not be the same thing as existed in the effect.

It is a first principle *that the whole of the reality or perfection that exists only objectively in ideas must exist in them formally or in superior manner in their causes*. It is on this alone we wholly rely, when believing that things situated outside the mind have real existence; for what should have led us to suspect their existence except the fact that the ideas of them were borne in on the mind by means of the senses?

But it will become clear to those who give sufficient attention to the matter and accompany me far in my reflections, that we possess the idea of a supreme and perfect being, and also that the objective reality of this idea exists in us neither formally nor eminently. A truth, however, which depends solely on being grasped by another's thought, cannot be forced on a listless mind.

Now, for these arguments we derive it as a most evident conclusion that God exists. But for the sake of those whose natural light is so exceeding small that they do not see this first principle, viz. *that every perfection existing objectively in an idea must exist actually in something that causes that idea*, I have demonstrated in a way more easily grasped an identical conclusion, from the fact that the mind possessing the idea cannot be self derived; and I cannot in consequence see what more is wanted.[9]

The third step in Descartes' argument should now be predictable. Since God is perfect, he cannot be a deceiver. Since we are inclined to believe whatever we clearly and distinctly perceive, whether through reflection or through experience, and since God created us, whatever we clearly and distinctly perceive must be true. For the same reason, what we genuinely recollect clearly and distinctly perceiving must be true, and so deduction can be relied upon. God is what guarantees the reliability of deductive inference. Of course, people can fail to apply the method reliably and, through acts of will, can confuse themselves. But that is not God's fault, nor is it Descartes'.

Descartes' philosophy had many critics, none more determined than Pierre Gassendi. Gassendi thought the whole thing a lot of balderdash, and he said so at length, first in objections that Descartes included in an appendix to his *Meditations* and then in a book. Gassendi revived the criticism made against Anselm: you can conceive of a perfect island, but that does not guarantee it exists. By parity of reasoning, that you can conceive of a perfect being, even one that necessarily exists, does not imply that such a being exists. Gassendi thought that many of Descartes' claims about what he clearly and distinctly perceived were simply muddled terminology, about whose meaning Descartes had no clear conception at all: "He who says that anything is infinite attributes to a thing which he does not comprehend a name which he does not understand."[10] Gassendi thought that Descartes' method was useless and in fact no method at all. We think of a method as a procedure that is more or less mechanical and will lead all users to the same conclusion. Descartes held that he had shown not only this but also that his method would lead users to the truth. Gassendi didn't believe Descartes' proof, and he thought that those who claimed to see things clearly and distinctly and to know things by the natural light of reason generally contradicted each other. Descartes replied that when they contradicted each other, it only showed that some of them had not applied the method correctly.

The content of Descartes' books on method read a little like old-fashioned versions of popular books on mental improvement. Books of the latter sort are more common nowadays than they were in Descartes' time, and they are generally held in contempt by people who do serious work on reasoning. Why were Descartes' writings taken so seriously in their own day? In part because Descartes was so vociferous and skillful at arguing; in part because his writings addressed—even if unconvincingly to a modern mind—the essential questions about the reliability of the procedures that the Renaissance still held dear: syllogistic reasoning and the method of analysis and synthesis; and in part because Descartes had to his credit a number of important mathematical discoveries. He could and did claim that his method had led him to them.

Study Questions

1. In another passage from *Rules for the Direction of the Mind*, Descartes writes, "The working of conjecture is shown, for example in this: water which is at a greater distance from the centre of the globe than earth, is likewise less dense substance, and likewise the air which is above the water, is still rarer; hence we hazard the guess that above the air nothing exists but a very pure aether, which is much rarer than air itself. Moreover, nothing that we construct in this way really deceives us, if we merely judge it to be probable and never affirm it to be true; in

fact it makes us better instructed."[11] Is this passage consistent with Descartes' remarks about "probable knowledge"?

2. How does the following remark of Descartes' accord with the Aristotelian conception of scientific method? "The upshot of the matter is that it is possible to say that those propositions indeed which are immediately deduced from first principles are known now by intuition, now by deduction, i.e., in a way that differs according to our point of view. But the first principles themselves are given by intuition alone, while, on the contrary, the remote conclusions are furnished only by deduction.

3. Rules are different from descriptions of facts. What are some of the differences?

4. Suppose you tried to follow Descartes' *Rules for the Direction of the Mind.* Could you know whether or not you had succeeded in following the rules? Could you know whether or not a conviction was an intuition guaranteed by the "natural light of reason"? If so, how, and if not, why not?

5. Suppose someone else tried to follow Descartes' *Rules.* Could you know whether or not she was doing so correctly? If so, how, and if not, again, why not?

6. How do you know when you add two numbers together and carry that you have followed the addition algorithm correctly? How do you know when someone else does the addition under your observation that they have followed the algorithm correctly?

7. Is Descartes' argument that he cannot doubt his own existence a diagonal argument? (This is for those who did the second study question from chapter 1 in the the section on infinity and cardinality.)*

THE BINOMIAL THEOREM

We have already seen that Aristotle's and Plato's conception of the structure of knowledge stimulated interest in the mathematical study of how things can be combined. By deepening the understanding of combinations, the seventeenth century took another important step toward fathoming the fundamental questions about deductive argument. One important contribution to this subject was Blaise Pascal's *Treatise on the Arithmetic Triangle.* It indirectly furthered the understanding of logic and deductive reasoning, it contained one of the first important calculations in the the theory of probability, and it helped provide the foundations of modern decision theory.

In a later chapter I will briefly consider the importance of Pascal's thought in creating the theory of probability and decision theory. For present purposes, the important aspect of his work on the arithmetic triangle is that it provided a systematic connection between the theory of combinations and ordinary algebra. Descartes had succeeded in connecting geometry with algebra by showing that geometrical figures such as the line and circle could be viewed as the collections of points that satisfy certain algebraic relations. Thus any three numbers, call them A, B, and C, determine a straight line if A and B are not both zero. The line is the set of all points (x, y) such that $Ax + By + C = 0$. Conversely, for every straight line there is some such equation. Now Pascal showed that the fundamental question of Aristotelian combinatorics, the number of ways of choosing r things from a collection of n things, concerned numbers that also have a purely algebraic significance. Pascal's result is known as the *binomial theorem*.

Consider the expression $(x + y)^n$. For different values of n we can expand this expression:

$n = 1$: $x + y$

$n = 2$: $x^2 + 2xy + y^2$

$n = 3$: $x^3 + 3x^2y + 3xy^2 + y^3$

$n = 4$: $x^4 + 4x^3y + 6x^2y^2 + 4xy^3 + y^4$

We can rewrite each expansion this way (remember that $x^0 = 1$):

$n = 1$: $x^n y^{(n-1)} + x^{(n-1)} y^n$

$n = 2$: $x^n y^{(n-2)} + 2x^{(n-1)} y^{(n-1)} + y^n$

$n = 3$: $x^n y^{(n-3)} + 3x^{(n-1)} y^{(n-2)} + 3x^{(n-2)} y^{(n-1)} + y^n$

Each term in the sum is a *binomial coefficient* multiplied by a product consisting of a power of x and a power of y. The products of the powers of x and y are always either of the form $x^r y^{(n-r)}$ or of the form $x^{(n-r)} y^r$, where r is some number between 0 and n, inclusive. So for $n = 2$, for example, the first term, x^2, has the binomial coefficient 1 and has $r = 0$, while the second term, $2xy$, has the binomial coefficient 2 and has $r = 1$. The binomial coefficients for $n = 1$ to $n = 4$ are therefore the following:

$n = 1$: 1, 1

$n = 2$: 1, 2, 1

$n = 3$: 1, 3, 3, 1

$n = 4$: 1, 4, 6, 4, 1

Binomial theorem   For a positive integral n, the binomial coefficient of $x^{(n-r)}y^r$ (or of $x^r y^{(n-r)}$) is exactly the number of ways of choosing r things from n things. In other words, the binomial coefficient is $n!/(r!(n-r)!)$

Remember that $0! = 1$.

Pascal's *Treatise* helped to make it evident that the analysis of combinations arising from the Aristotelian and Platonic traditions was an aspect of algebraic relations among numbers. Descartes' mathematical work had shown that geometry, the traditional mathematical language of the sciences, also has an algebraic side and that important geometrical properties could be characterized algebraically. By the middle and later parts of the seventeenth century, algebraic relations, usually presented as geometrical statements of ratios, had become the form in which natural science expressed the laws of nature. Kepler's third law was essentially such a relation. So were Boyle's and Mariotte's law of gases and the inverse square law of gravitation. It was only natural to suppose that the actions of the mind, thought, must also have laws that can be described by such relations, and that the combinatorics of analysis and synthesis are a hint of them. Gottfried Leibniz came to that very conclusion.

Study Questions

1. Below are the first few rows of the arithmetic triangle listing the coefficients of the monomials in the expansion of $(a + b)^n$:

$$
\begin{array}{ccccccccccc}
 & & & & & 1 & & & & & \\
 & & & & 1 & & 1 & & & & \\
 & & & 1 & & 2 & & 1 & & & \\
 & & 1 & & 3 & & 3 & & 1 & & \\
 & 1 & & 4 & & 6 & & 4 & & 1 & \\
1 & & 5 & & 10 & & 10 & & 5 & & 1
\end{array}
$$

What is the next row of the triangle?

2. The first row in the triangle gives the monomial coefficient for the expansion of $(a + b)^0$, which equals 1. The second row gives the two coefficients, (1, 1), for the expansion of $(a + b)$, which is just $a + b$. The third row gives the usual quadratic coefficients, (1, 2, 1), for the expansion of $(a + b)^2 = a^2 + 2ab + b^2$, and so on. Let (n, r) denote the coefficient of $a^r b^{n-r}$ in the expansion of a^n. What is the formula for expressing (n, r) as a function of $(n - 1, r - 1)$ and $(n - 1, r)$?

3. Verify for $n = 6$ that $(n, r) = n!/[r!(n-r)!]$.

LEIBNIZ AND THE MATHEMATICS OF REASON

Pascal's *Treatise* was published in 1665. The next year Leibniz, then 19 years of age, published his first work, a Latin treatise on logic and combinatorics, *De Arte Combinatoria*. He did not yet know of Pascal's work, but he learned of it subsequently, and in later years when he journeyed to Paris, he tried unsuccessfully to meet with Pascal, who had retreated to religious quarters at Port Royal. Pascal had shown that the same combinatorial numbers or binomial coefficients also arise in relations between the terms of certain infinite series, and reflection on the properties of series eventually helped lead Leibniz to the discovery of the differential and integral calculus.

Leibniz's first work was really a combinatorial study of logic in the Aristotelian tradition. It is the only work on logic that Leibniz ever published. Over the course of the rest of his life, Leibniz wrote a long series of unpublished and uncompleted papers on logic. They show the formation of some of the key modern ideas about deductive inference and proof, and they also show how very difficult the issues were for one of the greatest philosophers and mathematicians of the century. Leibniz's logical theory is not consistent and thorough (Leibniz had a difficult time completing anything), but it contains many ideas that were successfully elaborated in later centuries, and it also shows clearly the limitations of the Aristotelian framework.

Leibniz's viewpoint can be thought of as what you get if you do the following:

• You take the Platonic and Aristotelian view of the formal structure of what is known.
• You combine it with the method of analysis and synthesis.
• You abolish the distinction between properties that a thing has accidentally and properties that a thing has essentially and assume instead that *every* property something has, it has necessarily.

Following tradition, Leibniz assumed that every proposition consists of a predicate applied to a subject, and that in this regard the structure of language reflects the structure of the world. In the world, substances *have* attributes. But Leibniz gave this a twist. Substances don't, in his view, *have* attributes in the sense that one and the same substance could have an attribute or not have it. A substance *just is* a combination of attributes. You, for example, are nothing but the combination of all of the properties that you have. So there is no property that you in fact have that *you* could not have. An entity that didn't have some property of yours wouldn't be you. So every property you have, you have *necessarily*. The same holds of any other substance in the world. Whatever properties a substance has, it has necessarily.

In Leibniz's view, the propositions that we assert and believe and perhaps know are about *concepts*. A proposition, "Socrates is snub-nosed," for example, asserts a relation between the concept of the subject, Socrates, and the concept of the predicate, snub-nosed. It doesn't assert anything about Socrates himself. The proposition is true if and only if the concept of Socrates, which is really a combination of primitive, unanalyzable concepts, contains the concept of snub-nosed, which is also a combination of primitive concepts. Suppose, for example, that the concept of Socrates contains the concept of a nose less than 2 inches long, and the concept of snub-nosed just is the concept of a nose less than 2 inches long. Then the concept of Socrates contains the concept of snub-nosed, and so it is true that Socrates is snub-nosed. Similarly, the proposition "All perfect people are happy" is about the concept of perfect people and the concept of happiness, it is not about perfect people or about happy things. Leibniz had a reason for thinking that propositions are about concepts rather than about objects. The sentence "All perfect people are happy" may be true even though there are no perfect person. Unlike Aristotle, Leibniz did not think that a universal sentence such as "All perfect people are happy" entails that there exist perfect people. But if "All perfect people are happy" is true even though there exist no perfect person, the sentence cannot be about perfect people, for there are none. The sentence must be about something, however, and the proposal that it is about a mental entity, the concept of perfect men, seems to solve the problem.

In Leibniz's theory, every concept just is a list or combination of primitive concepts. All true propositions are true because the list of primitive concepts of the subject term is appropriately related to the list of primitive concepts of the predicate term. Leibniz says that every true proposition is true because it is an instance of the identity $A = A$. He meant that if a proposition is true, the subject and predicate lists will be such that by eliminating irrelevant parts of one or the other, the same combination of concepts of attributes is found in the subject as is found in the predicate. So every true proposition can be given a proof. The proof of a proposition consists of the following:

1. Producing the combinations of simple concepts denoted by the predicate of the proposition and the subject of the proposition.

2. Showing that the concept of the predicate is included in the concept of the subject.

Leibniz wrote extensively about these two steps. He never succeeded in making clear just how the analysis of concepts was to be obtained. Of course, neither had Aristotle nor the Scholastic tradition of analysis and synthesis. Leibniz envisioned the creation of an enormous dictionary or encyclopedia, and he attempted to get various people to actually assemble such dictionaries.

Once a universal dictionary has been assembled that expresses each concept in terms of the simplest concepts, Leibniz thought that the production of scientific knowledge would become mechanical. He thought an *algorithm* or mechanical procedure could be found to carry out the second part of the procedure for giving proofs. The way to formulate such a procedure is to treat the problem as a part of *algebra*. Each simple term and each complex term should be given a letter or other symbol (Leibniz sometimes suggested using numbers as symbols for concepts), and then one would use algebraic methods to search for algebraic identities. On other occasions he suggested representing concepts with geometrical figures, such as lines, and trying to carry out step 2 by geometrical procedures. The essential thing is that there is a *mathematics of reason* (in fact, that is the title of one of the logical papers Leibniz completed), and this mathematics can be carried out mechanically.

You can get the flavor of what Leibniz was up to from a fragment of one of many "Logical Calculi" he developed:

(1) "$A = B$" is the same as "'$A = B$' is a true proposition."
(2) "$A \neq B$" is the same as "'$A = B$' is a false proposition."
(3) $A = AA$; i.e., the multiplication of a letter by itself is here without effect.
(4) $AB = BA$, i.e., transposition makes no difference.
(5) "$A = B$" means that one can be substituted for the other, B for A or A for B, i.e., that they are equivalent.
(6) "Not" immediately repeated destroys itself.
(7) Therefore $A = $ not-not-A.
(8) Further, "$A = B$" and "A not $\neq B$" are equivalent.
(9) That in which there is "A not-A" is a "non-entity" or a "false term" e.g., if $C = A B$ not-B, C would be a non-entity.
(10) "$A \neq B$" and "$B \neq A$" are equivalent. This follows from 5.
(11) "$A = B$" and "not-$A = $ not-B" are equivalent. [Leibniz gives a proof of this claim.]
(12) If $A = B$, $AC = BC$. This is proved from 5.[12]

Leibniz goes on to state seven more claims of this kind. Clearly this looks like algebra, but it is an algebra for propositions rather than for numbers.

Leibniz was correct that the task of deciding whether all of the members of one list are members of another list can be done machanically. He was wrong in thinking that determinations of this kind are adequate for all (or even very much) of logic or of a theory of proof. He had difficulty, for example, giving an account in these terms of even the Aristotelian quantifiers. He could not give an account of reasoning that involves "or" or that involves "if ... then ____" (although in principle he could have expanded his framework to account for reasoning that depends on those connectives). Most important of all, Leibniz could not give any account of reasoning with *relations*.

We have already noted that Aristotle could not account for proofs in geometry because he could not incorporate reasoning about relations between individual objects. Leibniz had the same problem. From a logical point of view, he had no satisfactory solution. His papers contain some attempts to reduce reasoning involving relations to reasoning that involves no more than propositions of subject-predicate form. Leibniz seems instead to have adopted a *metaphysical* solution, and that may have led him to one of the strangest metaphysical positions in the history of philosophy.

The absence of a theory about how to reason with relations would be less bothersome if relations could not be the subject of knowledge. Real relations, according to the conception of the time, would have to be relations between two different substances. One way to avoid real relations, therefore, is to suppose that there is only one substance. That was Spinoza's solution. According to Spinoza, there is only one substance, God, and what can be known are his attributes. Another way to solve the problem is to suppose that there are lots and lots of substances, but none of them stand in any relations to one another, or at least not in any relations that are the subject of scientific knowledge. That was Leibniz's solution.

Leibniz claimed that the world is constituted of *monads*. Each monad is a little universe by itself. No monad has any causal relations with any other monad, so in the Aristotelian tradition the relations between monads are not subjects of scientific inquiry, since science is about causes. Some monads, such as we, have souls and so can be aware of themselves. Although each monad is separate from all others, each monad is a mirror of every other monad; some monads, those with souls, mirror one another more clearly and in more detail than do other monads. I am a monad, and so are you. We have no causal relations with one another, but God, who, being perfectly benign, has created the best of all possible worlds, has so created us that our perceptions are in perfect harmony. It *appears to each of us* that we live in a common world and have causal relations with one another. But appearance is not reality.

Leibniz's logic was never adequate, which may explain why he published so little of it, and his metaphysics was not much comfort, although he intended it to be. He did, however, accomplish several things.

• He formulated the notion of a *decision procedure* for logic: a mechanical or algorithmic procedure that will determine whether or not an inference is valid. He even attempted to give such a procedure for the theory of the syllogism.
• He made clear the notion of an *incomplete axiomatic theory*. An axiomatic theory is incomplete provided there is some sentence in its language that can be neither proved nor disproved from its axioms.
• He introduced the idea that pieces of language can be coded by abstract symbols, including numbers, and that logical relations among the propositions can be studied by considering relations among the symbols or numbers.
• He introduced and furthered the idea that logical relations among propositions have an algebraic structure.
• He developed the thought that universal subject-predicate propositions do not presuppose the existence of things satisfying their predicate or subject terms.

CONCLUSION

Although we look to the seventeenth century as the period when both modern science and modern philosophy began, it was also a time still captivated by the Aristotelian conceptions of reason and scientific knowledge. Many of the great works of seventeenth-century philosophy, especially on the continent, still assumed that the method for acquiring knowledge consists of analysis and synthesis and that real scientific knowledge requires some kind of proof analogous to the proofs of geometry. Almost all of the philosophical writers of the time assume, wrongly, that with one or another advance in these methods it will be easy to complete all of scientific knowledge. (In one of his last works Descartes chides the public for not providing him with the means to conduct a few experiments by which, he is sure, he could complete all of human knowledge.)

Even though seventeenth-century philosophers, except for Leibniz, made no fundamental advances in logic beyond the state in which Aristotle had left it, they did succeed in creating the intellectual framework for radical changes that began in the nineteenth century. Part of that framework consisted in treating logic as the theory of the operation of the faculty of reason, a faculty that acted to synthesize and analyze ideas. The mathematics of combinations became the formal basis for studying *reasoning*, which combined both logic and psychology, and it placed that study among the other new natural sciences. Geometry could be systematically connected with algebra, and the theory of combinations, which was the mathematical basis for whatever method there was to analysis and synthesis, could also be systematically connected with algebra. These connections were brought together in Leibniz's notion that deductive inference could be studied and understood through the application of algebraic methods to abstract symbols representing propositions. One hundred and fifty years later, George Boole, a professor of mathematics at the University of Cork, turned this idea into a real theory of reasoning.

Review Questions

1. Describe the method of analysis and synthesis.

2. How many ordered quadruples can be formed from seven distinct objects? How many unordered quadruples can be formed?

3. In your own words, state two significant ideas implicit in the philosophy of Ramon Lull. Explain why these ideas should be considered significant.

4. Discuss the validity of Descartes' belief that "properties which cannot be conceived separately are necessarily coextensive; and properties which can be conceived separately are not necessarily coextensive."

5. Outline Descartes' argument for the existence of God.

6. Produce the binomial coefficients for $n = 5$.

7. What is a monad? What role does it play in Leibniz's philosophy?

Further Reading

Descartes
Cottingham, John. *Descartes*. New York: B. Blackwell, 1986.

Curley, E. M. *Descartes against the Skeptics*. Oxford: B. Blackwell, 1978.

Frankfurt, Harry G. *Demons, Dreamers, and Madmen: The Defense of Reason in Descartes' Meditations*. Indianapolis: Bobbs-Merrill, 1970.

Gaukroger, Stephen. *Cartesian Logic: An Essay on Descartes' Conception of Inference*. New York: Oxford University Press, 1989.

Gaukroger, Stephen, ed. *Descartes: Philosophy, Mathematics, and Physics*. Totowa, N.J.: Barnes and Noble Books, 1980.

Grene, Marjorie. *Descartes*. Minneapolis: University of Minnesota Press, 1985.

Haldane, E., and G. Ross, eds. *The Philosophical Works of Descartes*. New York: Cambridge University Press, 1970.

Herbert, Gary B. *Thomas Hobbes: Unity of Scientific and Moral Wisdom*. Vancouver: University of British Columbia Press, 1989.

Hooker, Michael, ed. *Descartes: Critical and Interpretive Essays*. Baltimore: Johns Hopkins University Press, 1978.

Katz, Jerrold. *Cogitations: A Study of the Cogito in Relation to the Philosophy of Logic and Language and a Study of Them in Relation to the Cogito*. New York: Oxford University Press, 1986.

Kenny, Anthony John Patrick. *Descartes: A Study of His Philosophy*. New York: Random House, 1968.

Schouls, Peter A. *The Imposition of Method: A Study of Descartes and Locke*. New York: Oxford University Press, 1980.

Will, Frederick L. *Induction and Justification: An Investigation of Cartesian Procedure in the Philosophy of Knowledge*. Ithaca, N.Y.. Cornell University Press, 1974.

Williams, Bernard Arthur Owen. *Descartes: The Project of Pure Inquiry*. New York: Penguin Books, 1978.

Wilson, Margaret D. *Descartes*. Boston: Routledge and Kegan Paul, 1978.

Hobbes

Hampton, Jean. *Hobbes and the Social Contract Tradition*. New York: Cambridge University Press, 1986.

Herbert, Gary B. *Thomas Hobbes: The Unity of Scientific and Moral Wisdom*. Vancouver: University of British Columbia Press, 1989.

Hinnant, Charles H. *Thomas Hobbes*. Boston: Twayne Publishers, 1977.

Jessop, T. E. *Thomas Hobbes*. Harlow, England: Longmans, Green, 1968.

Peters, R. S. *Hobbes*. Harmondsworth: Penguin Books, 1967.

Ross, Ralph, Herbert W. Schneider, and Theodore Waldman, eds. *Thomas Hobbes in His Time*. Minneapolis: University of Minnesota Press, 1974.

Van Der Bend, J. G., ed. *Thomas Hobbes: His View of Man*. Atlantic Highlands, N.J.: Humanities Press, 1982.

Leibniz

Aiton, E. J. *Leibniz: A Biography*. Boston: A. Hilger, 1985.

Ariew, Roger, and Daniel Garber, eds. and trans. *Philosophical Essays*. Indianapolis: Hackett Publishing Co., 1989.

Hofmann, Joseph Ehrenfried. *Leibniz in Paris, 1672–1676: His Growth to Mathematical Maturity*. New York: Cambridge University Press, 1974.

Hooker, Michael, ed. *Leibniz: Critical and Interpretive Essays*. Minneapolis: University of Minnesota Press, 1982.

Ishiguro, Hide. *Leibniz's Philosophy of Logic and Language*. New York: Cambridge University Press, 1990.

Mates, Benson. *The Philosophy of Leibniz: Metaphysics and Language*. New York: Oxford University Press, 1986.

Parkinson, G., ed. and trans. *Leibniz's Logical Papers*. New York: Oxford University Press, 1966.

Rescher, Nicholas. *Leibniz: An Introduction to His Philosophy*. Totowa, N.J.: Rowman and Littlefield, 1979.

Russell, Betrand. *A Critical Exposition of the Philosophy of Leibniz*. London: Allen and Unwin, 1964.

Sleigh, Robert. *Leibniz and Arnauld: A Commentary on Their Correspondence*. New Haven: Yale University Press, 1990.

Wilson, Catherine. *Leibniz's Metaphysics: A Historical and Comparative Study*. Princeton, N.J.: Princeton University Press, 1989.

Woolhouse, R. S., ed. *Leibniz, Metaphysics, and Philosophy of Science*. New York: Oxford University Press, 1981.

Lull

Hillgarth, J. N. *Ramon Lull and Lullism in Fourteenth-Century France*. Oxford: Oxford University Press, 1971.

Yates, Frances Amelia. *Lull and Bruno: Collected Essays*. Boston: Routledge and Kegan Paul, 1982.

Pascal

Cailliet, Emile. *Pascal: The Emergence of a Genius*. New York: Greenwood Press, 1969.

Coleman, Francis X. J. *Neither Angel nor Beast: The Life and Work of Blaise Pascal*. New York: Routledge and Kegan Paul, 1986.

Edwards, A. W. F. *Pascal's Arithmetic Triangle*. New York: Oxford University Press, 1987.

Mortimer, Ernest. *Blaise Pascal: The Life and Work of a Realist.* New York: Harper, 1959.

Pascal, Blaise. *The Provincial Letters; Pensées; Scientific Treatises.* Chicago: Encyclopaedia Britannica, 1952.

Pascal, Blaise. *The Thoughts of Blaise Pascal.* Westport, Conn.: Greenwood Press, 1978.

Uspenski, V. A. *Pascal's Triangle.* Chicago: University of Chicago Press, 1974.

Seventeenth-century science and mathematics
Bell, Eric Temple. *Men of Mathematics.* New York: Simon and Schuster, 1937.

Bochner, Salomon. *The Role of Mathematics in the Rise of Science.* Princeton: Princeton University Press, 1981.

Burtt, Edwin A. *The Metaphysical Foundations of Modern Science.* London: Routledge and Kegan Paul, 1932.

Daston, Lorraine. *Classical Probability in the Enlightenment.* Princeton: Princeton University Press, 1988.

Hazard, Paul. *The European Mind, 1680–1715.* Cleveland: World, 1963.

Mahoney, Michael Sean. *The Mathematical Career of Pierre de Fermat (1601–1665).* Princeton: Princeton University Press, 1973.

Renyi, Alfred. *Letters on Probability.* Detroit: Wayne State University Press, 1972.

Rhys, Hedley Howell, ed. *Seventeenth-Century Science and Arts.* Princeton: Princeton University Press, 1961.

Shea, William R., ed. *Nature Mathematized.* Vol. 1. Boston: D. Reidel, 1983.

Struik, Dirk Jan. *A Concise History of Mathematics.* New York: Dover Publications, 1948.

Westfall, Richard. *The Construction of Modern Science: Mechanisms and Mechanics.* New York: Wiley, 1971.

Westfall, Richard. *Science and Religion in Seventeenth-Century England.* Ann Arbor: University of Michigan Press, 1973.

Watson, Richard. *The Downfall of Cartesianism, 1673–1712: A Study of Epistemological Issues in the Late Seventeenth-Century Cartesianism.* The Hague: Martinus Nijhoff, 1966.

Yolton, John W. *Philosophy, Religion, and Science in the Seventeenth and Eighteenth Centuries.* Rochester, N.Y.: University of Rochester Press, 1990.

Early history of computing
Aspray, William. *Computing before Computers.* Ames: Iowa University Press, 1990.

Aspray, William. *From Mathematical Constructivity to Computer Science: Alan Turing, John von Neumann, and the Origins of Computer Science in Mathematical Logic.* Ann Arbor: University Microfilms International, 1981.

Gardner, Martin. *Logic Machines, Diagrams, and Boolean Algebra.* New York: Dover Publications, 1968.

Williams, M. R. *A History of Computing Technology.* Englewood Cliffs, N.J.: Prentice-Hall, 1985.

Chapter 4
THE LAWS OF THOUGHT

INTRODUCTION

In the middle of the nineteenth century, George Boole, a professor of mathematics at the University of Cork in Ireland, tried to realize Leibniz's conception of an algebra of thought. Boole's work was the most important advance in logic since Aristotle, and it prepared the foundations for the emergence of modern logic some thirty years later. Boole's thought is interesting not only because of its advance in formal understanding, but also because it illuminates a fundamental difficulty in thinking of logic, the theory of perfect, deductive rationality, also as a theory of how the human mind, or some part of it, functions.

Boole's conception of logic was similar to Leibniz's:

- Logic consists of a set of laws, like the laws of physics or the laws of geometry.
- The laws have an algebraic form.
- The laws have to do with the correct operation of the mind.

One can well imagine that people think through visual images. Instead, Boole held that thinking is a way of talking to oneself in an unvoiced speech. According to Boole, rational thought is carried out in language. When we have a thought, we think a sentence. The laws of rational thought are therefore also the laws governing the use of language in reasoning. The rules of reasoning are at the same time both rules for the correct performance of various mental operations and also rules for the correct use of language. Boole's theory, like Aristotle's, therefore depends on an analysis of the structure of language. Boole's own presentation of his views about the logical structure of language was not entirely clear, and perhaps not entirely coherent. We will study a somewhat simplified version of his theory while remaining as faithful as we can to his ideas.

THE UNIVERSE OF DISCOURSE AND FIELDS OF SETS

According to Boole, every discussion, every conversation, is about some *domain*, or *universe of discourse*. The domain may be real or imaginary, the subject may be real mountains or fairy-tale mountains, but for the purposes of any specific human conversation, objects not in the domain are ignored.

In every discourse, whether of the mind conversing with its own thoughts, or of the individual in his intercourse with others, there is an assumed or expressed limit within which the subjects of its operation are confined. The most unfettered discourse is that in which the words we use are understood in the widest possible application, and for them the limits of discourse are co-extensive with those of the universe itself. But more usually we confine ourselves to a less spacious field. Sometimes, in discoursing of men we imply (without expressing the limitation) that it is of men only under certain circumstances and conditions that we speak, as of civilized men, or of men in the vigour of life, or of men under some condition or relation. Now, whatever may be the extent of the field within which all the objects of our discourse are found, that field may properly be termed the universe of discourse.[1]

Consider a particular domain of discourse. Suppose the topic is cats. The domain of discourse is the collection or set of all cats. For every conceivable property of cats, there is then a subset of the domain of discourse consisting of all of the cats that have that property. The property of being a Manx cat, for example, determines the subset of the domain of discourse that consists of Manx cats. The property of being a tailless cat determines the subset that consists of tailless cats. The property of being a black cat determines the subset that consists of black cats. I can make the idea clear with the same kinds of diagrams that I used in our study of the theory of the syllogism (Boole himself did not use such diagrams, but they were used by another nineteenth-century logician, John Venn).

If we conceive of two properties of cats, *black* and *Manx* for example, we can conceive of those properties holding of one and the same kind of thing, namely cats. We can conceive, for example, of cats that are black *and* Manx. That conception also corresponds to a subset of the domain of discourse: the set of all cats that are black and Manx, or to say the same thing, the *intersection* of the set of black cats and the set of Manx cats. I will always write the intersection of two sets M and B (for the set of Manx cats and the set of Black cats, respectively) as $M \cap B$ (figure 4.1).

Figure 4.1
The intersection of the set of black cats and the set of Manx cats

We can also conceive of cats that are black *or* Manx. The corresponding set of all cats that are either black or Manx (or both) we call the *union* of the set of black cats and the set of Manx cats. I will always write the union of any two sets M and B as $M \cup B$.

If we can conceive of any property, we can conceive of its absence (what would Saint Anselm say about *that* claim?). Since a property such as being black corresponds to a subset of the domain of discourse, namely the set of all things in the domain that have the property *black*, the absence of black will correspond to the set of all things in the domain that are not black. If U is the domain of discourse, cats in this case, and B is the subset of black things in U, the subset of nonblack things in U will be written as B'. B' is said to be the *complement of B in U*, or the complement of B relative to U. When the context makes the universe of discourse clear, I will simply say that B and B' are *complements* of one another.

Boole assumed that we can conceive of any number of compoundings of properties, and there are corresponding set operations that determine compound descriptions of sets. We can, for example, conceive of all of the cats that are *not* either black or Manx but *are* tailless. That corresponds to the subset of the domain of cats given by $(B \cup M)' \cap T'$, where B is the set of all black cats, M the set of all Manx cats, and T the set of all cats with tails.

Suppose that a piece of discourse or reasoning has to do with some definite universe of discourse U and some finite list of properties that things in that domain may or may not have. Suppose that the subsets of U corresponding to these properties are denoted by $P_1, P_2, \ldots, P_n$. The sets U and $P_1, P_2, \ldots, P_n$ implicitly determine the collection of all subsets of U that can be obtained by forming the intersections, unions, and complements of $U, P_1, P_2, \ldots, P_n$ forming the intersections, unions, and complements of *those* sets, forming the intersections, unions, and complements of *those* sets, and so on. If we consider the collection of all subsets of U that can be formed in this way, that collection is called a *field of sets over U*. A more formal formulation is the following:

Definition   A *field of sets* over a nonempty set U is any collection of subsets of U that contains U, contains the complement relative to U of any set it contains, contains the intersection of any two sets it contains, and contains the union of any two sets it contains.

It is easy to visualize simple finite fields of sets. Suppose, for example, that we are talking about cats, but (for whatever reason) we are only concerned with one property of cats, namely whether or not they have tails. Then the universe of cats divides into two kinds, those with tails and those without tails, and there are exactly four sets in the corresponding field of sets, namely the set of all cats (because U is always in a field of sets over U), the empty set (because the complement of U relative to U is the empty set), the set of cats with tails, and the set of cats without tails (figure 4.2).

It can be shown that there are no other distinct sets in *this* field of sets. For example, if we take the union of the set of all cats with tails and U, we get U again, which is a set we already have. If we take the intersection of U with the set of all cats with tails, we get the set of all cats with tails again, which is a set we already have. In the same way, any other intersection, union, or complement of these four sets generates one or another of the same four sets.

We can represent a field of sets, as in figure 4.2 on the right, by a graph with U at the top and the empty set $\varnothing$ at the bottom. A line in the graph connecting two sets means that the lower set is included in the upper set.[2] A set and its complement are never connected in such a graph, because neither set is contained in the other.

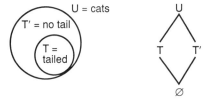

Figure 4.2
A field of sets and a graph of their containment relations

It is easy to construct other fields of sets. Simply let U be any nonempty finite set and list all of the subsets of U. The resulting collection, called the *power set* of U, is always a field of sets. If U has a single member, we get the simplest possible field of sets, consisting only of U and $\varnothing$:

The fields of sets obtained when U has three members and when U has four members are shown below:

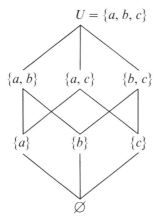

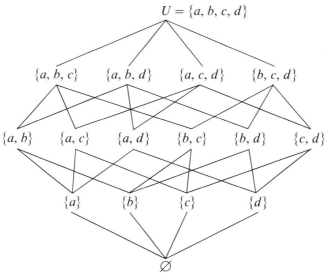

Study Questions

1. Explain why the power set of any nonempty set U is a field of sets over U. Write your explanation as a proof of that fact.

2. In the figures above, which elements of the field of sets are complements of other elements of the field?

3. Give an example of a domain of discourse and two distinct properties such that all members of the domain that have one property also have the other and vice versa.

4. Explain why there cannot exist a field of sets consisting of exactly three sets.

LANGUAGE AND THE WORLD

One of Boole's central ideas was that we can regard the world, aspects of the world, or even imaginary worlds as structured like a field of sets. Although he did not explicitly introduce the notion of a field of sets as I have defined it, he held that for any discourse, there is a domain of objects with properties and combinations of properties. Together, the set of objects in the domain and the sets of objects with any particular property or combination of properties make up a field of sets. This proposal is really a metaphysical idea, just as Aristotle's notion of objects with essential properties was a metaphysical idea. Like Aristotle, Boole proposed that language is structured to reflect metaphysics.

As a mathematical idealization of real language, Boole considered a language structured in the way in which the language of algebra is structured. Boole's mathematical language contains variables, just as ordinary algebra does. In ordinary algebra the variables range over some system of numbers; we say that the variables take numbers as *values*. The variables in Boole's language instead range over the sets that are in some field of sets. The context of the discourse or conversation determines the relevant field. Boole's variables take sets in this field as values. So, to continue the example above, the domain might consist of the set of all cats, and possible values of Boole's variables might include the set of all cats with tails, and the complement of that set would be the set of of all cats without tails.

In ordinary algebra we can write expressions that contain operation symbols and variables; we can write $x + y$, for example, and the result is a well-formed expression in the language of algebra. We understand that the plus sign signifies the operation of addition on numbers. Boole's system also allows expressions to be formed by combining his variables with symbols for operations. He allows us to write $x \cdot y$, $x + y$, and $(1 - x)$. In Boole's formulas, the symbol " $\cdot$ " signifies *set intersection*, the symbol $+$ signifies *set union*, and expression $(1 - x)$ signifies *the relative complement of x in U*. Just as we can build up arbitrarily complex expressions in ordinary algebra by combining operations and variables as often as we wish (with parentheses to make our meaning clear), so we can build complex expressions in the algebra of logic.

In ordinary algebra we can give explicit rules for how to evaluate expressions, although we don't usually state them explicitly, because they are so obvious. For example, for any algebraic formulas x and y (where x, y stand not just for variables but for well-formed expressions of any complexity), the value of $x + y$ is the sum of the value of x and the value of y, and the value of $x \cdot y$ is the product of the value of x and the value of y. Similarly, in Boole's theory we can evaluate expressions in the algebra of logic by using explicit rules. For any formulas x, y, the value of $x \cdot y$ is the intersection of the value of x and the value of y, the value of $x + y$ is the union of the value of x and the value of y, and the value of $(1 - x)$ is the relative complement of the value of x in U, the universe of discourse.

In ordinary algebra we use the identity or equals sign, $=$, to say that the value of one formula is the same as the value of another. Boole does the same thing, except that his values, as before, are not numbers but sets in a field of sets. In ordinary algebra we have names for some special numbers. In Boole's mathematical model of language we always have a name for the universe of discourse and a name for the empty set. Boole uses the numeral 1 to denote the universe of discourse and the numeral 0 to denote the empty set, $\emptyset$.

In ordinary algebra particular sentences about particular numbers can be obtained by replacing the variables in a formula with the names of numbers. For example, the true sentence $1 + 2 = 2 + 1$ can be obtained by substituting 1 for x and 2 for y in the formula $x + y = y + x$. Similarly, in Boole's system many ordinary sentences can be obtained by substituting terms for particular properties in place of variables and interpreting $\cdot$ as *and*, $+$ as *or*, and $(1 - x)$ as *not x*. For example, the sentence "Black and tailless cats are tailless and black cats" can be obtained by substituting "black" for x, and "tailed" for y in $x \cdot (1 - y) = (1 - y) \cdot x$, where the set of cats comprises the domain of discourse.

With some rearranging, many ordinary sentences can be represented by general expressions in Boole's logic. Variables are substituted for names of particular properties, and operation symbols are substituted for English (or Chinese or Martian) connectives. Consider the sentence "Manx cats are tailless." That is the same as saying, "No cats are Manx cats and cats with tails." If we understand that the set of cats is the domain of discourse, and take "no cats" to designate the empty set, this sentence can be regarded as an instance of the formula $0 = x \cdot y$, obtained by substituting "Manx cats" for x and "cats with tails" for y.

THE LAWS OF BOOLEAN ALGEBRA

In ordinary algebra we are interested in finding equalities among formulas that are *true for all possible values of the variables in the formulas.* For example, in the algebra of real numbers we know that

$x \cdot y = y \cdot x$ (commutative law of multiplication),

$x + y = y + x$ (commutative law of addition),

$x \cdot (y + z) = (x \cdot y) + (x \cdot z)$ (distributive law),

$-(-x) = x.$

What distinguishes these equations from many other equations one might write down (e.g., $x - 1 = 0$) is that these equations are true no matter what numbers the variables take as values. Equations with this property are important because they represent *fundamental laws* of the algebra of real numbers.

   Similarly, Boole was interested in finding the laws of the algebra of thought. He posed the question, *What equations in Boole's algebra will be true for all values of their variables and in every field of sets for every (nonempty) domain of discourse?* This is really the fundamental question about Boole's logic. The following equations are true in every field of sets and for all values given to the variables. They form some of the laws of Boole's system:

$x + y = y + x$ \hfill (1)

$x \cdot y = y \cdot x$ \hfill (2)

$x \cdot (y + z) = (x \cdot y) + (x \cdot z)$ \hfill (3)

$x + (y \cdot z) = (x + y) \cdot (x + z)$ \hfill (4)

$x + 0 = x$ \hfill (5)

$x \cdot 1 = x$ \hfill (6)

$$x \cdot (1 - x) = 0 \quad \text{and} \quad x + (1 - x) = 1 \tag{7}$$

$$x + (y + z) = (x + y) + z \tag{8}$$

$$x \cdot (y \cdot z) = (x \cdot y) \cdot z \tag{9}$$

$$0 \neq 1 \tag{10}$$

In modern mathematics any system of objects and operations in which all ten of these equations hold for all values of the variables is called a *Boolean algebra*. Every field of sets is a Boolean algebra.

It is easy enough to verify that these laws must hold in any field of sets. In most cases, verifying that these laws are true amounts to nothing more than saying what the operations involved mean. For example, the first of these equations says that for any set X (a value of the variable x) and any set Y (a value of the variable y), the union of X and Y is the union of Y and X. But the union of set X and set Y is the set whose members are in X or in Y, which is the same as the set whose members are in Y or in X. Again, the sixth equation says that for any set X in any field of sets over a set U, the intersection of X and U is X itself. Since by definition a set X is in a field of sets over U only if X is a subset of U, every member of X must be a member of U. The intersection of X and U, which is the set of all things that are members of X and also members of U, is therefore exactly the set of all members of X.

Study Questions

1. Show that $x \cdot x = x$ is a law in Boole's algebra. You may derive it from equations (1) through (10) above or from the definition of a field of sets.

2. Show that $x + x = x$ is a law in Boole's algebra.

3. What characteristic distinguishes a law in Boole's system from an equation that is not a law? Give an example of an equation that is not a law.

TRUTH, PROPOSITIONS, AND BOOLEAN ALGEBRA

One of Boole's principal aims was to show that language has the same structure as do algebraic formulas; he aimed to provide a metaphysical but clear account of the structures of those formulas; he aimed to find the formulas that constitute the laws of such structures; and he aimed to show that reasoning in natural language could be evaluated in the same way that we evaluate reasoning in ordinary algebra. If the last of these aims could be achieved, we would be able to use the laws of Boole's algebra to determine whether or not a particular sentence can be validly derived from other sentences, just as we can use our knowledge of the laws of ordinary algebra to determine whether or not one formula of ordinary algebra can be validly derived from a collection of other formulas.

To achieve his aims, Boole gave a second interpretation of his algebra. To understand this second interpretation, note that not every sentence that occurs in reasoning looks like an instance of one of Boole's equations. This is because of a point that should be familiar by now: not all declarative sentences are compounded out of sentences of subject-predicate form. Boole's first analysis of language works well enough for such sentences as "Tailless black cats are Manx cats" (which becomes an instance of $x \cdot y = z$), but it doesn't seem to apply at all to such a sentence as "Children love their parents, and parents love their children." The problem in this case is that "loves" is not a property but a relationship, and that in the context of the sentence, the term "parent" involves a relation between a child and the people that are the child's parents. In previous chapters we learned, you will recall, that an important defect of traditional logic was its inability to represent reasoning with relations.

Boole had no theory about how to analyze sentences that involve relations, and except in simple cases (such as "no cats"), he had no theory of quantifiers either. But he nonetheless had a clever idea for analyzing some of the logical properties of such sentences within his algebra. The idea is this: Consider the sentence "Children love their parents." That sentence is true if and only if the sentence "'Children love their parents' is true" is true. Trivial though this observation may sound, Boole made excellent use of it.

Consider again the simplest possible field of sets consisting of a nonempty set U and the empty set. Recall that Boole denotes U with 1 and the empty set with 0. Instead of thinking of 1 as a name for U and 0 as a name for the empty set, however, think of the numeral 1 as a name for the *number* 1, and think of the numeral 0 as a name for the *number* 0. Now the ordinary numbers 1, 0 will satisfy the laws of Boole's algebra if we give $+$ and $\cdot$ a new interpretation. We let Boole's symbol $\cdot$ denote the function of ordinary multiplication, but restricted to the numbers 0 and 1. In Boole's algebra, $1 \cdot 1 = 1$, and $1 \cdot 0 = 0$, and $0 \cdot 0 = 0$, just as in ordinary algebra. We let Boole's expression $(1 - x)$ denote the very same function it denotes in ordinary algebra, but with x restricted to the numbers 0 and 1. So $1 - 1 = 0$, and $1 - 0 = 1$. And we let $x + y$ denote the ordinary sum of x and y restricted to 1 and 0, with one modification. The modification is that

1 + 1 is defined to be equal to 1 (not 2, as in ordinary arithmetic). So 1 + 0 = 1, and 0 + 0 = 0, and 1 + 1 = 1.[3]

In modern mathematics the described system consisting of the ordinary numbers 0 and 1 related by the functions just defined is called the *two-element Boolean algebra*. Its structure is exactly like that of the field of sets consisting only of U and the empty set $\varnothing$. We say the two structures are *isomorphic*, by means that if we adopt the following correspondence, each structure is transformed into the other.

$U \leftrightarrow 1$

$\varnothing \leftrightarrow 0$

$$
\begin{array}{ccc}
U & & 1 \\
| & \leftrightarrow & | \\
\varnothing & & 0
\end{array}
$$

$\cup \leftrightarrow +$

$\cap \leftrightarrow \cdot$

$x' \leftrightarrow (1 - x)$

In sciences besides logic, it is perfectly routine to code properties of things by numbers. Different numerical scales are used in different sciences for different purposes. Similarly, Boole proposed to use 0 and 1 as a simple numerical scale in logic. In Boole's scale the numerical values register properties of sentences. Sentences are things that are true or false. We can think of truth and falsity as possible *properties* that sentences can have, and so we can think of the number 1 as the value a sentence has on a numerical scale when the sentence is true, and we can think of the number 0 as the value a sentence has on a numerical scale when the sentence is false. Just as we use a kilogram scale to assign particular numbers to objects according to a property, their weight, Boole proposes a scale that assigns numbers to sentences according to whether they are true or false.

Let us return now to Boole's algebraic language. Previously the variables x and y ranged over subsets of the domain of discourse, and a sentence could be obtained from an algebraic formula by replacing variables with terms for properties. Now the variables receive a different interpretation, and accordingly, sentences are obtained from algebraic formulas in a different way. The variables range over the two-element Boolean algebra. Each variable can have 1 or 0 as its value, but no other values are allowed. Ordinary sentences receive an algebraic structure in the following way. Consider the sentence

Children love their parents and parents love their children.

Replace the original sentence by the sentence that says that the original sentence is true:

"Children love their parents and parents love their children" is true.

Since 1 is the value on Boole's numerical scale for the property a sentence has when it is true, replace the phrase "is true" by "= 1":

"Children love their parents and parents love their children" = 1

Replace "and" with $\cdot$, "or" with $+$, and "not" with $(1 - \cdots)$:

"Children love their parents $\cdot$ parents love their children" = 1

Finally, replace each distinct simple sentence (that is, each sentence not compounded out of others with "and," "or," and "not") with a distinct variable. This gives us the following:

$x \cdot y = 1$

The result is the Boolean algebraic form corresponding to the original sentence.

In this way any declarative sentence can be represented in Boole's algebra. The generality is obtained at a cost, however. There is no longer any analysis of the structure of sentences except insofar as the structure involves *sentential connectives*, that is, words such as "and," "or," and "not," which can be used to build compound sentences from simpler sentences.

USE OF BOOLEAN LOGIC

Boole meant for his logical algebra to be used in settings that are quite different from the contexts in which we use ordinary algebra. He meant his algebra to apply to all deductive reasoning. To show the applicability of his algebra, he attempted to use it to reconstruct several famous philosophical arguments and to determine whether or not they are valid. Boole considered arguments from Plato, Samuel Clarke (a contemporary of Isaac Newton), and Spinoza. However, only Boole's analysis of the argument from Plato really works.

To understand Boole's account of that argument, we need to make one more concept precise. One of Boole's equations *entails* another equation if every assignment of the values 0 or 1 to the variables of the first equation that makes it true also makes the second equation true. Similarly, a set of Boolean equations, the premises, entails another Boolean equation, the conclusion, if every assignment of values 0 or 1 to the variables that makes all equations in the premise set true simultaneously also makes the conclusion true.

In *The Republic*, Plato gives the following argument (Socrates asks the questions and states the conclusions; others in the dialogue give answers to Socrates' questions):

Must not that which departs from its proper form be changed, either by itself or by another thing?

Necessarily so.

Are not things which are in the best state least changed and disturbed, as the body by meats and drinks and labours, and every species of plant by heats and winds, and such like affections? Is not the healthiest and strongest the least changed?

Assuredly.

And does not any trouble from without least disturb and change that soul which is strongest and wisest? And as to all made vessels, and furnitures, and garments, according to the same principle, are not those which are well wrought, and in a good condition, least changed by time and other accidents?

Even so.

And whatever is in a right state, either by nature or by art, or by both these, admits of the smallest change from any other thing.

So it seems.

But God and things divine are in every sense in the best state.

Assuredly.

In this way, then, God should least of all bear many forms?

Least, indeed, of all.

Again, should He transform and change Himself?

Manifestly, He must do so, if He is changed at all.

Changes He then Himself to that which is more good and fair, or to that which is worse and baser?

Necessarily to the worse, if he be changed. For never shall we say that God is indigent of beauty or of virtue.

You speak most rightly, said I, and the matter being so, seems it to you, O Adimantus, that God or man *willingly* makes himself in any sense worse?

Impossible.

Impossible, then, it is, that a god should wish to change himself; but ever being fairest and best, each of them ever remains absolutely in the same form.[4]

Boole took Plato's argument to be the following:

Premise 1: If the Deity suffers change, then the Deity is changed either by the Deity or by another.

Premise 2: If the Deity is in the best state, then the Deity is not changed by another.

Premise 3: The Deity is in the best state.

Premise 4: If the Deity is changed by the Deity, then the Deity is changed to a worse state.

Premise 5: If the Deity acts willingly, then the Deity is not changed to a worse state.

Premise 6: The Deity acts willingly.

Conclusion: The Deity does not suffer change.

Using his algebra, Boole aimed to show that the conclusion is a necessary consequence of the premises, that is, if the premises are true, then the conclusion is true. To show that, he demonstrated that the algebraic form of the premises is such that whenever they are true, the conclusion is true. First he assigned variables to the simple sentences of which the premises are composed:

x: The Deity suffers change.
y: The Deity is changed by the Deity.
z: The Deity is changed by another.
s: The Deity is in the best state.
t: The Deity is changed to a worse state.
w: The Deity acts willingly.

Boole represented sentences of the form "If A then B" as "not(A and not B)," or in other words, by equations of the form "$A \cdot (1 - B) = 0$."

Boole's formulas for the six premises and conclusion of Plato's argument are as follows:

$x \cdot (1 - y) \cdot (1 - z) = 0$

$s \cdot z = 0$

$s = 1$

$y \cdot (1 - t) = 0$

$w \cdot t = 0$

$w = 1$

$x = 0$

Now it is easy to show algebraically that the conclusion must follow from the premises. (Recall laws (4.1) to (4.10) of Boole's algebra.)

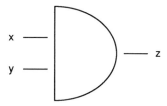

Figure 4.3
An electrical device that is a physical realization of the Boolean formula
$z = x \cdot y$

Since $w = 1$ and $w \cdot t = 0$, t must equal 0.
Since $s = 1$ and $s \cdot z = 0$, z must equal 0.
Since $t = 0$, $0 = y \cdot (1 - t) = y \cdot (1 - 0) = y$. So $y = 0$
Since $y = 0$ and $z = 0$, $0 = x \cdot (1 - y) \cdot (1 - z) = x \cdot (1 - 0) \cdot (1 - 0) = x$.
Hence, $x = 0$.

In the twentieth century Boole's algebra has found applications that he could not have imagined. His theory is used every day by electrical engineers who design microchips. Every computer you have ever used was designed using principles of Boole's algebra. Electrical current (on or off) can be used to code the Boolean values of propositions, 1 and 0. The presence of a current stands for the value 1, and the absence of a current stands for the value 0. In Boole's formulas, if you put in values 0 or 1, you get a value of 0 or 1 for the entire formula. Bits of circuitry behave exactly as do Boolean formulas. For example, suppose an electrical device, a little bit of a microchip, has two input leads and one output lead, as in figure 4.3. If the device behaves so that the current arrives at z when and only when the device receives current from x and y at the same time, then the device is a physical realization of the Boolean formula $z = x \cdot y$. Systems of such devices function together to do binary arithmetic in a pocket calculator or a computer. The central processing unit of such devices can thus be described a system of Boolean formulas, and knowledge of the properties of such formulas is important in designing the devices and in diagnosing their flaws.

SOME LIMITATIONS OF BOOLE'S LOGICAL THEORY

In the first chapter of this book I argued that a theory of deduction should answer at least three questions:

- How can we determine whether or not a piece of reasoning from premises to a conclusion is a valid deductive argument?
- How can we determine whether or not a conclusion is necessitated by a set of premises? If a conclusion is necessitated by a set of premises, how can we find a valid deductive argument that demonstrates that necessary connection?
- What features of the structure of the world, the structure of language, and the relation between words and thoughts and things make deductive reasoning possible?

Boole did not give us a theory that says whether a piece of reasoning is or is not a genuine proof. Instead, he relied on our understanding of an algebraic proof. He had no real answer to the first question, but his theory does tell us when a proof is possible and how to find one if it exists. He in effect offers an answer to the second question. There are algorithms that will determine, for any finite set of Boolean formulas (the premises) and any other Boolean formula (the conclusion), whether or not the premise set entails the conclusion. So once we have represented a set of premises and a conclusion as Boolean equations, there is a completely mechanical process to determine entailment. If the results of such a procedure say that the premises do entail the conclusion, then the application of the algorithm itself will constitute a proof of that fact.

Boole also gave an answer to the third question, but the answer does not seem satisfactory. Boole's problem was that he had represented logic as a kind of physics of the mind. Logic, he assumed, describes the laws by which the mind moves, just as physics describes the laws by which bodies move. But we know that everyone makes errors in reasoning. So Boole's theory cannot possibly *describe* how we reason, because in fact we don't always reason that way. Instead, Boole's theory seems to prescribe how we *ought* to reason. Theories that prescribe standards are *normative*. The laws of physics are not normative: they don't say how bodies ought to move; they say how bodies *do* move in various circumstances.

Here is what Boole himself says on this and related issues:

The truth that the ultimate laws of thought are mathematical in their form, viewed in connexion with the fact of the possibility of error, establishes a ground for some remarkable conclusions. If we directed our attention to the scientific truth alone, we might be led to infer an almost exact parallelism between the intellectual operations and the movements of external nature. Suppose any one conversant with physical science, but unaccustomed to reflect upon the nature of his own faculties, to have been informed, that it had been proved, that the laws of those faculties were mathematical; it is probable that after the first feelings of incredulity had subsided, the impression would arise, that the order of thought must, *therefore*, be as necessary as that of the material universe. We know that in the realm of natural science, the absolute connexion between the initial and final elements of a problem, exhibited in the mathematical form, fitly symbolizes that physical necessity which binds together effect and cause. The necessary sequence of states and conditions in the inorganic world, and the necessary connexion of premises and conclusion in the processes of exact demonstration thereto applied, seem to be coordinate....

Were, then, the laws of valid reasoning uniformly obeyed, a very close parallelism would exist between the operations of the intellect and those of external Nature. Subjection to laws mathematical in their form and expression, even the subjection of an absolute obedience, would stamp upon the two series one common character. The reign of necessity over the intellectual and the physical world would be alike complete and universal.

But while the observation of external Nature testifies with ever-strengthening evidence to the fact, that uniformity of operation and unvarying obedience to appointed laws prevail throughout her entire domain, the slightest attention to the processes of the intellectual world reveals to us another state of things. The mathematical laws of reasoning are, properly speaking, the laws of *right* reasoning only, and their actual transgression is a perpetually recurring phenomenon. Error, which has no place in the material system, occupies a large one here. We must accept this as one of those ultimate facts, the origin of which it lies beyond the province of science to determine. We must admit that there exist laws which even the rigour of their mathematical forms does not preserve from violation. We must ascribe to them an authority the essence of which does not consist in power, a supremacy which the analogy of the inviolable order of the natural world in no way assists us to comprehend.[5]

In this passage Boole has reluctantly and halfheartedly come to the conclusion that the conception of logic as a kind of physics of thought, a conception inherited from the seventeenth century, is in error. Logic is a normative theory and a metaphysical theory. It is metaphysical in telling us which propositions are necessary consequences of others. It is normative in telling us that *if* we believe certain things (the premises), then we *ought* to believe other things (the necessary consequences of things we believe). But it doesn't describe how our minds work.

There is another kind of difficulty with Boole's theory. The first aim of a logical theory is to distinguish the arguments that are valid deductions from the arguments that are not valid deductions. Can Boole's theory really do that? Clearly, his theory includes many arguments that we would regard as valid, but it does not include all of them.

As we have seen, Boole really had two theories. The first theory supposes that a sentence is of subject-predicate form or is compounded out of simple sentences of subject-predicate form with "and," "or," and "not." With this theory Boole can account for the validity of many syllogistic inferences. For example, we can represent the premises and the conclusion of the syllogistic form Camestres as Boolean equations, and the result is a valid argument in Boole's system:

No A are B	$A \cdot B = 0$
All C are B	$C \cdot (1 - B) = 0$
No A are C	$A \cdot C = 0$

It is easy to see that the Boolean argument is valid: Since it is assumed as a premise that $A \cdot B = 0$, (i) either $A = 0$ or $B = 0$ or both. Since it is assumed that $C \cdot (1 - B) = 0$, (ii) either $C = 0$ or $B = 1$ or both. Necessarily, either $B = 1$ or $B = 0$. If $B = 1$, then by (i), $A = 0$, so $A \cdot C = 0$. If $B = 0$, then by (ii), $C = 0$, so $A \cdot C = 0$. Hence, in either case $A \cdot C = 0$.

Boole's second theory does not assume that sentences have a subject-predicate form, but it only accounts for logical properties that depend on *sentential connectives*, such as "and," "or," and "not." Neither of Boole's theories can account for logical inferences that depend on quantifiers and relations. For example, Boole's theories do not explain why the following simple inference is valid:

Someone loves everyone.
Therefore, everyone is loved by someone.

Boole's theories are not sufficient to reconstruct the arguments in Euclid's *Elements* or in any other mathematically sophisticated work. Nonetheless, in several respects Boole's work provided a real improvement on all preceding logical theories. Boole showed that logic really could be studied by modern mathematical methods, and he helped to distinguish logic from psychology. But he was not yet very close to an adequate theory of deductive reasoning. That achievement was begun thirty-five years later by Gottlob Frege.

Study Questions

1. We could introduce the notion of *inequality* into Boole's algebra, and then "Some A are C" could be represented as $A \cdot C \neq 0$. However, "Some A are C" means that something is A and C, or in Boole's terms, the class of things that are both A and C is not empty. If B is the empty set (remember that in his first theory Boole used 0 to denote the empty set), both Boolean premises are true, and the intersection of A and B can be empty. Aristotle assumed that if "All B are A" is

true, then there exist some B. Boole did not. Modern logicians follow Boole. How can you represent "Not all A are B" in Boole's theory?

2. The form Darapti does not correspond to a valid Boolean argument, because no Boolean equation represents "Some A are C." For each of the Aristotelian syllogistic forms in the third figure, determine whether or not the corresponding arguments are valid in Boolean logic.

All B are A	$B \cdot (1 - A) = 0$
All B are C	$B \cdot (1 - C) = 0$
Some A are C	?

3. For each of the valid Aristotelian forms in the first and second figures, construct a parallel argument using Boolean equations (or inequalities), and show that the Boolean argument is valid.

Review Questions

1. In what ways might Boole's logical theory be considered a continuation of Leibniz's ideas?

2. Explain the differences between Boole's two theories. Is it a good objection to Boole's work that he does not provide a single, unified theory?

3. What is a simple sentence in Boole's logic? What is a compound sentence?

4. How did Boole think that the truth or falsity of simple sentences determines the truth or falsity of compound sentences?

5. What are the limitations in the answers Boole's theory provides for the three principal questions at issue in a theory of proof?

Further Reading

Boole
Boole, George. *An Investigation of the Laws of Thought on Which Are Founded the Mathematical Theories of Logic and Probabilities*. New York: Dover Publications, 1951.

Boole, George. *The Mathematical Analysis of Logic, Being an Essay Towards Deductive Reasoning*. Oxford: B. Blackwell, 1948.

Boole, George. *Studies in Logic and Probability*. London: Watts, 1952.

Hailperin, Theodore. *Boole's Logic and Probability: A Critical Exposition from the Standpoint of Contemporary Algebra, Logic, and Probability Theory*. New York: Elsevier Publishing Company, 1986.

Smith, G. C., ed. *The Boole–De Morgan Correspondence, 1842–1864*. New York: Oxford University Press, 1982.

Logic, Boolean algebra, and its applications
Adelfio, Salvatore A., and Christine F. Nolan. *Principles and Applications of Boolean Algebra*. New York: Hayden Book Company, 1964.

Adler, Irving. *Thinking Machines: A Layman's Introduction to Logic, Boolean Algebra, and Computers.* New York: John Day Company, 1961.

Arnold, Bradford Henry. *Logic and Boolean Algebra.* Englewood Cliffs, N.J.: Prentice-Hall, 1962.

Brzozowski, J. A., and Michael Yoeli. *Digital Networks.* Englewood Cliffs, N.J.: Prentice-Hall, 1976.

Halmos, Paul Richard. *Lectures on Boolean Algebras.* New York: Springer-Verlag, 1974.

Monk, J. Donald, and Robert Bonnet, eds. *Handbook of Boolean Algebras.* New York: Elsevier Science Publishing Co. 1989.

Sikorski, Roman. *Boolean Algebras.* Berlin: Springer, 1960.

Stiazhkin, N. I. *History of Mathematical Logic from Leibniz to Peano.* Cambridge: MIT Press, 1969.

Stoll, Robert Roth. *Sets, Logic, and Axiomatic Theories.* San Francisco: W. H. Freedman, 1974.

Chapter 5

FREGE'S NEW LOGICAL WORLD

INTRODUCTION

Aristotle and Descartes each gave similar answers to the questions, How do we *know* what is true? How do we know the truths of geometry and arithmetic and physics, for example? Each of them held that we know the truths of these subjects because certain fundamental principles are known through intuition and other truths are validly deduced from these fundamental principles. By the eighteenth century this understanding of the structure of knowledge had almost dissolved. At the end of the nineteenth century, new developments gave birth to modern logic, to modern conceptions of proof and logical necessity, and to radical changes in metaphysics. In this chapter I will describe some of the developments that led to this new understanding.

The seventeenth century succeeded in throwing off most of Aristotle's conception of knowledge and inquiry by establishing new and impressive sciences through other methods. The most striking example was Newton's *Principia*, which established a science of motion that seemed at least as profound and powerful as Euclid's geometry. But Newton did not argue for his new science from intuition or from the natural light of reason. He argued for it from observations that anyone (with appropriate instruments) could make, and he made his methods of argument a central point of the *Principia*. Francis Bacon did not succeed in constructing a science as impressive as Newton's, but his *Novum Organum* did call for a new experimental method of discovery, and he illustrated that method by constructing an (essentially correct) theory of heat. William Harvey used simple observations and experiments to argue for the circulation of the blood, and William Gilbert described experiments to determine the properties of the lodestone, or magnet. In England, France, Germany, Italy, and Holland, those interested in physics, biology, and chemistry began to think that the way to knowledge was via the path of experimentation. Newtonian and Baconian science competed with Cartesian science in the late seventeenth and early eighteenth centuries, and Newtonian and Baconian science won.

The new science and its methods brought new philosophical problems. One problem, which will concern us in later chapters, is this: Why are the experimental and observational methods of modern science reliable? How can we know, or why are we justified in believing, that these methods lead to truth? Another problem, which will concern us in this chapter, is this: If science depends on inferences made from observation and experiment, what is the basis for our knowledge of mathematics and for the special certainty that propositions in geometry and arithmetic seem to have? What is it that guarantees that arithmetic applies to everything and that geometry applies everywhere?

Reflection on such questions began to create new divisions among the sciences. In the eighteenth century, the new sciences of physics and chemistry seemed different from geometry and arithmetic. Unlike the new sciences, geometry and arithmetic *did* seem to depend on self-evident principles. How could anyone who understood the matter doubt Euclid's axioms or that addition is commutative? For most thinkers, geometry and arithmetic did not seem (in the eighteenth and nineteenth centuries anyway) altered by or elaborated through experimentation in the way theories in physics, chemistry, and biology are changed as the evidence from observation changes. There seemed to be two different kinds of sciences, one founded on experience and observation, the other founded on reason alone. A few philosophers disagreed with this division. For example, John Stuart Mill, perhaps the most influential English philosopher in the nineteenth century, held that geometry and arithmetic really are sciences exactly like physics, biology, or chemistry. Arithmetic, according to Mill, is an experimental subject; the fundamental principles of arithmetic seem certain to us only because they have so often been tested and confirmed by our experience. The same is true with geometry.

Prior to Mill's work, another attempt to distinguish between various sciences emerged from the psychological perspective of the seventeenth century. Descartes and Leibniz, following Aristotelian tradition, had thought of physical objects as bundles of properties attached to a substance. Descartes thought of mental objects in the same way: bundles of properties attached to a mental substance. *Ideas* are collection of properties attached to a mental substance. So an idea may be simple or complex; it may consist of a single irreducible property or of a bundle of properties together. Descartes' way of thinking about ideas was shared by English philosophers who opposed him in other respects. John Locke, George Berkeley, and David Hume rejected Cartesian substances and Cartesian method, but they thought of *ideas* in roughly the way Descartes had. Hume, an eighteenth-century Scottish philosopher and historian, used the *idea* idea to give a rather traditional answer to questions about our knowledge of arithmetic and geometry.

Some propositions, Hume proposed, are about *matters of fact*. That the sky is blue, that the earth has but one moon, that Italy has a sea coast—these are matters of fact. Matters of fact can be discovered only from experience (if at all). The empirical sciences concern themselves with discovering matters of fact. Other propositions are about (or are true because of) *relations among ideas*. Since an idea is just a bundle of (mental) properties, some ideas may contain other ideas. Descartes insisted, for example, that the idea of *body* includes the idea of *extended thing*. Hume proposed that the propositions that we judge to be certain and to be known without observation or experimental testing are propositions about the relations of ideas. We can know them without performing experimental tests, it seemed to Hume, because our mental life, our ideas, are immediately apparent to us and we can just see with the mind's eye that some ideas contain other ideas.

Hume's proposal really comes to this: True propositions that are about the relations among ideas can be known a priori, that is, in a way not founded on any experience, essentially by a combination of what Descartes would have called "natural light" and the method of analysis and synthesis. Propositions that are not about relations among our ideas but instead are about the external world cannot be known in this way.

Unfortunately, Hume's proposal has an obvious flaw. Insofar as we understand what is meant by "idea," it does not seem that mathematical truths can be obtained as relations among ideas. Consider simple arithmetic. It is a truth of arithmetic that $2 + 2 = 4$, and this seems as certain as anything can be. But does the idea of the number 4 contain the idea of the sum of 2 with itself? If so and if this is why it is true that $2 + 2 = 4$, then it would seem that the number 4 must contain an infinity of other ideas as well, for it is also true that $3 + 1 = 4$ and that $5 - 1 = 4$ and that $8 - 4 = 4$ and so on. No one (save possibly Leibniz) thought of ideas as entities that contain infinities of other ideas. Immanuel Kant, the greatest philosopher of the second half of the eighteenth century and one of the thinkers who most influenced science and philosophy in the nineteenth century, recognized this flaw in Hume's proposal and built a system to try to account, nonetheless, for the a priori character of arithmetical and geometrical truths.

Kant distinguished between propositions (or *judgments* as he would have said) that are *analytic* and those that are *synthetic*. Kant thought that judgements always have a subject-predicate form, and he wrote of *concepts* rather than ideas. He put the distinction between analytic and synthetic judgements thus: in analytic judgements, but not in synthetic judgements, the concept of the predicate contains the concept of the subject. Kant's distinction between analytic and synthetic judgements is essentially the same as Hume's distinction between relations of ideas and matters of fact, and Kant took the distinction (with profuse acknowledgments) from Hume. Kant also distinguished between a priori and a posteriori judgments. *A priori* judgements can be known by reason alone; *a posteriori* judgements cannot be known by reason alone but require the evidence provided by experience.

Kant took the foremost question of epistemology and metaphysics to be this: How are synthetic a priori judgements possible? That was Kant's technical way of asking how, for example, the truths of mathematics can be known with certainty by reason alone. The truths of mathematics are not, in his view, analytic, so their truth cannot be established merely by unpacking the relevant concepts; the method of analysis cannot succeed in establishing their truth. Nonetheless, it is true that $2 + 2 = 4$, and we can know that truth without doing experiments, and our conclusion is not subject to any possible refutation by experience. Kant's question was how this can be so.

We will consider Kant's answer and its implications in some detail in a later chapter, but we first need to consider it very briefly here. Kant's answer is this. The world we experience and come to know is partly a world of our own creation. Our sensory and our cognitive apparatuses act on whatever they receive to construct a world of colors, objects, spatial and temporal relations, and so on. The way in which we create the world and the world that we create are not subject to our will, but they are nonetheless partly our creation. We cannot make up a world of experience simply by imagining whatever we please. The world of experience is determined by our cognitive apparatuses, which is not subject to our will, and by how the world is in itself, which we will never know. The world in itself

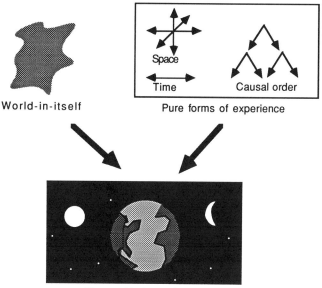

Figure 5.1
Kant's picture of metaphysics

does not, or at least need not, have red things or extended things or even things. The world we experience depends on two factors: the world in itself and our cognitive apparatuses. We could say, as Kant sometimes suggests, that the world in itself provides the matter or raw input for experience, and we ourselves provide the *form of experience*. A picture may help (see figure 5.1).

Kant argued that judgements of arithmetic and geometry can be synthetic and yet known a priori because they constitute the form of experience. That is, our cognitive apparatus is so constructed that arithmetic will apply to every sequence of objects in experience and is so constructed that Euclidean geometry will apply to every system of objects in experience. We can imagine creatures who do not have cognitive apparatuses like ours and who might therefore have very different a priori sciences. For such creatures, arithmetic or Euclidean geometry might not even be true. But for us, the propositions of these mathematical theories are certain to be true of anything we experience. With Kant, the content and epistemology of mathematics became an essential part of psychology.

Study Question

Suppose that Kant was correct that the human cognitive apparatus imposes Euclidean geometric forms on experience. Could Kant *know* that to be true? If so, could he have a priori knowledge of it or only a posteriori knowledge?

FREGE, LOGICISM, AND LOGIC

In the late nineteenth century there seemed to be few alternative accounts of mathematical knowledge besides those of Mill and Kant. Gottlob Frege invented an entirely new approach. Frege was Professor of Mathematics at the University of Jena in Germany in the closing years of the nineteenth century and the early years of the twentieth century. He was as much a philosopher as a mathematician, and the two subjects were intimately combined in his work. Despite the obscurity of his writings during his lifetime, Frege's efforts opened the way to much of modern mathematics, modern logic, modern approaches to topics in economics, and the modern theory of computation. Many people (including me) think that most work of value in twentieth-century philosophy is in some way indebted to Frege's ideas. His work had enormous practical consequences as well: every time you use a computer you take advantage of a device that emerged in the twentieth century as a result of Frege's work. Frege stands to logic roughly as Newton stands to physics.

Frege's alternative to Kant and Mill was this: arithmetic and geometry are certain and can be known by reason alone because arithmetic and geometry are *nothing but logic*, and logic is certain and can be known by reason alone. According to the this idea, now called *logicism*, the notions of number, numerical order, sum, and product can all be defined in purely logical terms, and with those definitions, the basic laws of arithmetic should turn out to be purely logical propositions that are necessarily true. Similarly for geometry, the notions of congruence and betweenness might be reduced to purely logical terms, and the laws of geometry shown to reduce to logical truths.

In the late nineteenth century this proposal seemed to face insuperable obstacles. The best logical theory available was Boole's, and as we have seen, Boole's theory could not account for the simplest geometric proofs, and it was equally inadequate for proofs in arithmetic. Frege did not know of Boole's work when he first began publishing on these questions, and the logical theories available to him were even less adequate. How could one reduce mathematics to logic when the available logical theories did not even permit one to derive the consequences of mathematical axioms? Frege offered an astonishing and ambitious solution: *invent a better a logic*. That is exactly what he did.

The logicist program begun by Frege was continued in the twentieth century by Bertrand Russell and Alfred North Whitehead, but it eventually failed. The program helped logic to flourish, but it did not succeed in convincing most scholars that mathematics is nothing but logic. For one thing, mathematical theories such as ordinary arithmetic require that there exist an infinity of objects—the infinite series of numbers—and no matter how ingenious the attempts at reducing mathematics to logic, the existence of an infinite collection of objects does not seem to be a matter of logic alone. For another thing, by the earlier years of the twentieth century, developments in mathematics and science made it appear that Mill was correct in claiming that geometry is an experimental science. In the nineteenth century several new geometrical theories were developed. They came to be known as *non-Euclidean geometries*. Karl Gauss, one of the discoverers of the first non-Euclidean geometry, viewed the theory exactly as Mill would have: as an alternative empirical theory about space. Gauss tried unsuccessfully to perform a test that would determine whether space is Euclidean or non-Euclidean. Furthermore, by 1915 Albert Einstein and David Hilbert had developed a new physical theory of gravitation, the general theory of relativity, which postulated that the geometry of space is a physical quantity that changes with the density of matter and radiation.

Frege first presented his new theory of logic in a work entitled (in English translation) *Conceptual Notation: A Formula Language of Pure Thought Modeled on the Formula Language of Arithmetic*. The book contained not only new logical ideas but a notation in which formulas were spread out in two dimensions on the page. Like logicism, Frege's notation did not succeed, and it is never used today. So I will present Frege's theory in conventional notation.

Let A, B, C, stand for any sentences. Then the formulas $\neg A$, $\neg B$, $\neg C$ stand for the sentences "A is not the case," "B is not the case," "C is not the case." The formula $A \rightarrow B$ stands for the sentence "If A then B."

All of the operations in Boole's logic can be expressed with such formulas. For example, in Frege's system the sentence "If A then B" is equivalent to "It is not the case that A and not B." "If A then B" is also equivalent to "Either it is not the case that A, or it is the case that B, or both." So Frege obtained the following equivalences. The sentence "A and

B" is equivalent to the sentence "It is not the case that if *A* then not *B*," and so the sentence "*A* and *B*" can be represented by the formula $\neg(A \to \neg B)$. The sentence "Either *A* or *B* or both" is equivalent to the sentence "If *A* is not the case, then *B*," and so the sentence "Either *A* or *B* or both" can be represented by the formula $\neg A \to B$. "Equivalent" means that *necessarily* a sentence of one form is true if and only if the sentence of the equivalent form is true.

Notice that parentheses are used to make clear the intended *scope* of an operator. In the formula $\neg A \to B$, the symbol $\neg$ has only *A* in its scope. In the formula $\neg(A \to B)$ the symbol $\neg$ has the entire formula $A \to B$ in its scope.

Since formulas representing "or" and "and" can be given for any sentences, we can make things more convenient by using *A* & *B* to abbreviate $\neg(A \to \neg B)$ and *A* ∨ *B* to abbreviate $\neg A \to B$.

Recall that Boole really had two logical theories. His second theory gave an account of how to reason with "and," "or," and "not" for sentences whose structure was not further analyzed. His first theory gave an account of reasoning that used the subject-predicate structure Boole assumed for sentences. Frege integrated the two theories into one, but he did not assume that sentences have a subject-predicate structure. Instead, Frege introduces names, variables, function symbols, and predicates, and he uses these logical categories to represent the structure of sentences.

For Frege a *name* is any term that denotes a particular object: "the Moon," "Bertrand Russell," "Plato," "the number 3" are all names for different objects.

A *variable* is a letter, *x*, *y*, *z* used in place of a name. It does not name an object but ranges over objects, the way a numerical variable in algebra ranges over numbers.

A *function symbol* is a term that denotes some object when applied to a name or sequence of names. "Father of," "sum of," "product of" are function terms. Applied to an appropriate name or sequence of names, each function term denotes an object: "father of Gottlob Frege" denotes Karl Alexander Frege, "sum of 2, 2" denotes 4, "product of 2, 3" denotes 6, and so on. Functions can be classified according to how many arguments they need in order to denote an object. "Father of" requires that one name be specified. We say that it is a *unary* function. "Sum of" requires that two arguments be specified (names of the two numbers to be added together). Two descriptions must be specified even if they describe the same number, as in the sum of 2, 2. We say that sum is a *binary* function. Similarly, we can consider function terms that require three arguments, four arguments, and so on. In logical notation, lower case letters such as f, g, h, are often used for function symbols.

A *predicate symbol* denotes a property of individual things or a relation among things. When applied to a name or a sequence of names, a predicate forms a sentence that asserts that the named objects in the sequence stand in the relation that the predicate denotes. "Loves," for example, is a predicate, and so are "is red" and "is between." "Sam loves Mary" is a sentence, and so are "Mars is red" and "Point b is between point a and point c." In logical notation, predicate symbols are often given by capital letters, such as P, Q, R, and the names to which they attach are given in sequence after them. So if B is the predicate that denotes the property of betweenness, and a, b, and c are names for points, the formula $Babc$ says that point b is between point a and point c. Frege introduced a special predicate for identity: for any names a and b, $a = b$ always means that the object named by a is the very same object named by b.

Finally, a *quantifier* is a phrase such as "every," "all," "some," "there exists," "there is," "there are." In Frege's theory the phrases "every" and "all" are represented by the symbol $\forall$, called the *universal quantifier*. The universal quantifier is always immediately followed by a variable, x, y, z, etc. The universal quantifier followed by a variable can be attached to the beginning of any formula to form another formula. So, for example, to the formula $Baxc$ we can attach $\forall x$ to make the formula $\forall x\ Baxc$, which says that every point is between points a and c, or equivalently, for any point, call it x, x is between a and c. Quantifier phrases that assert existence (phrases such as "some," "there exists," and so forth) can be represented by using $\neg$ and the universal quantifier together. So the sentence "There exists a point between points a and c" says the same thing as the sentence "It is not the case that every point is not between a and c." With the universal quantifier, the latter sentence can be represented by $\neg \forall x\ \neg Baxc$. We use $\exists x$ to abbreviate $\neg \forall x\ \neg$. Every quantifier also has a *scope*, often indicated by parentheses. In the formula just written, the scope of the quantifier is the formula $\neg Baxc$, but in the formula $\forall x(\neg Baxc \lor Bxxx)$ the scope of the quantifier is the entire formula $\neg Baxc \lor Bxxx$. In the formula $\forall x(\neg Baxc) \lor Bxxx$ the scope of the quantifier is again just the formula $\neg Baxc$.

Frege's logic allows us to put formulas together using any of these logical structures. If we form a formula with $\rightarrow$ and $\neg$, we can put a universal quantifier in front of it. We can put a whole sequence of quantifiers together in front of a formula. With these logical categories we can easily represent important differences in sentences that Aristotle and Boole could not distinguish. For example, we can say say that someone loves everyone: $\exists x \forall y(Lxy)$. We can say that everyone loves someone: $\forall x \exists y(Lxy)$. We can say that everyone is loved by someone: $\forall x \exists y(Lyx)$. We can say that someone loves himself: $\exists x(Lxx)$. Frege's notation represents the differences among these English sentences clearly.

Frege introduced a series of formulas that he took to be *logical truths*. Every sentence having the form of one of these formulas is necessarily true, that is, true in every logically possible world. Frege's list of logical truths is not intended to be complete. There are an infinity of other formulas that are also logically truth and that can be derived from those that Frege gave. Here are some of Frege's forms of logical truths:

$A \rightarrow (B \rightarrow A)$

$(C \rightarrow (B \rightarrow A)) \rightarrow ((C \rightarrow B) \rightarrow (C \rightarrow A))$

$(D \rightarrow (B \rightarrow A)) \rightarrow (B \rightarrow (D \rightarrow A))$

$(B \rightarrow A) \rightarrow (\neg A \rightarrow \neg B)$

$\neg \neg A \rightarrow A$

$A \rightarrow \neg \neg A$

$(c = d \rightarrow K) \rightarrow Kc/d$ (where Kc/d is the result of substituting d for c wherever c occurs in formula K)

$c = c$

Besides his logical formalism, Frege introduced a series of *rules of inference*. The rules of inference permit one to infer one formula from others. Frege's idea was that a proof consists of a sequence of sentences that can be represented as a sequence of logical formulas in which each formula is either an assumption of the proof (a premise) or else is derived from preceding formulas by means of one of the rules of inference.

I will not give all of Frege's rules of inference, but here are a few rules that hold for his system of logic.

Substitution   From any set of premises at all, infer the result of substituting any formulas for A, B, C, and D, and of substituting any names for c and d in any of the forms of logical truths given above.

Modus ponens   From $A \rightarrow B$ and A, infer B, where A and B are any formulas.

Quantifier deletion   From $\forall x(Fx)$, infer Fx for any formula F.

Conjunction introduction   From any formulas A, B, infer A & B.

Notice that these rules of inference are given entirely in terms of the structure of the formulas themselves. They do not depend on the *meanings* of the formulas.

A *proof* in Frege's system is just a finite sequence of formulas such that every formula in the sequence either follows from preceding formulas by one of the rules of inference or else is an assumption of the proof.

Using nothing more than these rules of inference, Frege was able to account for deductive arguments that would have baffled Aristotle and Boole. The details of a system of proof derived from Frege's are given in the next chapter.

The virtue of Frege's system is *not* that the formal proofs it gives are short or simple. The virtues of Frege's system are quite different:

• The rules of proof are sufficient to reconstruct valid deductive arguments in mathematics and science.
• The rules of formal proof are entirely explicit.
• They are so explicit, in fact, that it is a completely mechanical matter to determine whether or not a sequence of formulas is a proof. All that is required to test whether a purported proof is indeed a proof is to check whether the rules of inference have been properly applied.

Study Questions

1. Explain what constitutes a *proof* in Frege's logic. If we prove something *about* Frege's logic are we giving a proof *in* his logic?

2. Explain informally why the first six of Frege's logical truths should be regarded as necessarily true. In other words, why should one think that sentences of these forms cannot possibly be false on the intended meanings of the symbols $\neg$ and $\rightarrow$.

3. Use the list of Frege's logical truths and the rules of substitution and modus ponens to give proofs of the following formulas:

$A \rightarrow (A \rightarrow A)$

$(A \rightarrow A) \rightarrow (A \rightarrow A)$

$A \rightarrow (\neg A \rightarrow A)$

$A \rightarrow A$

THE THEORY OF MEANING: LANGUAGE AND THE WORLD

Frege's logical theory was founded on an analysis of the logical structure of language, and his theory of proof uses nothing but grammatical features of formulas in a logical language. But what are formulas in such a language *about*? The "logical truths" Frege assumed are supposed to be forms of sentences that are necessarily true. But what is *truth*, and why are these sentences necessarily true? Do the proofs that can be constructed in Frege's system necessarily preserve truth? Does a proof exist for every valid deductive inference? Answering these questions about Frege's theory requires a theory of *meaning*. Frege himself thought a great deal about the question of meaning, and after the turn of the century, philosophers and logicians developed a mathematical theory of meaning to correspond to Frege's logic.

Frege distinguished the *reference* of a phrase or a sentence from its *sense*. The phrases "morning star" and "evening star" refer to the same object, the planet Venus, but they have different senses. Frege held that each declarative sentence refers to its truth value. So true sentences refer to truth, and false sentences refer to falsehood. But, of course, not every true sentence means the same thing, so sense and reference must be distinguished. Reference does not determine sense, nor does sense determine reference, but according to Frege, two expressions that have the same sense must have the same reference. Frege's picture suggests a linguistic transformation of metaphysics. Instead of searching for the essences of things, we should search for the senses, the meanings, of expressions. We will consider in later chapters some of the consequences of this way of thinking.

The mathematical theory of meaning that developed for Frege's logic is really an elaboration of ideas implicit in George Boole's work. Boole had emphasized that every conversation tacitly presupposes a universe of discourse. Suppose there is a set, called the *domain*, that contains all of the objects we wish to talk or reason about in a particular context. If we are reasoning about whole numbers, the domain will consist of the natural numbers. If we are doing anthropology, the domain will consist of people and the objects people possess or know about. In other contexts, other domains will be assumed.

In Boole's conception, the objects in a domain have properties. For example, if the domain is the natural numbers, some of the numbers are even, some are odd, some are prime, some are perfect squares, and so forth. As with Boole's first theory, consider for each property of interest the set of all objects in the domain having that property. The property of being even determines in the natural numbers the set of all even numbers, the property of being odd determines the set of all odd numbers, and so on for any property that we want to talk about. Like Boole, I will assume that a discourse is about a domain and a specific collection of properties of members of that domain, and that each property determines the set of all objects of the domain having that property.

Suppose E and O are one-place predicates in a formal language that we wish to use to represent arithmetic reasoning. We might *specify* that E denotes the set of all even numbers and O denotes the set of all odd numbers in a domain that consists of all the whole numbers. If the language has numerals as names, we might further specify that "0" denotes the number 0, "1" the number 1, "2" the number 2, and so on. Then the formula $E2$ will say something true about numbers. What makes $E2$ true? The fact that "2" denotes an object (the number 2) that really is in the set denoted by E (the set of even numbers). A formula is true or false only in relation to a structure (a domain and subsets of that domain) and some rule that connects particular predicates with particular subsets of the domain and particular names with particular objects in the domain.

A formula such as Ex is neither true nor false, since x is a variable. However, if we let the variable x have a particular value, say the value 2, then the formula Ex will be *true of* that value. Ex is neither true nor false by itself, but in the domain we are considering, Ex is true of the number 2, false of the number 1, and so on. The formula $\neg Ex$ will be true of a value of x whenever that value of x is *not* in the set denoted by E. The formula $\neg Ex$ is true of the number 3, for example. Now the formula $\forall x(Ex)$ says that Ex is true of everything in the domain. So $\forall x(Ex)$ is true if and only if Ex is true of every value of x. The formula $\exists x(Ex)$ says that some number is even. It is true if and only if the formula Ex is true of some number or other, in other words, if and only if Ex is true of some value of x.

When is a formula such as $Ex \lor Ox$ *true* of a value of x? When the value of x is in the set denoted by E *or* is in the set denoted by O. That is the same as saying that $Ex \lor Ox$ is true of a value of x if and only if that value of x is a member of the union of the set denoted by E and the set denoted by O. For example, in the interpretation of E and O we are considering, E denotes the set of even numbers, and O denotes the set of odd numbers, and since every number is even or odd, the union of E and O is the set of all numbers. So $Ex \lor Ox$ is true of every number in the domain. It follows from what was said in the preceding paragraph that $\forall x(Ex \lor Ox)$ is true. In parallel fashion, the formula $Ex \,\&\, Ox$ will be true of any object that is a member of both the set denoted by E *and* the set denoted by O. In other words, it will be true of any member of the intersection of those sets. Since no number is both even and odd, $Ex \,\&\, Ox$ is true of no number. Hence $\exists x(Ex \,\&\, Ox)$ is false.

If the terms of a formal language are given their meanings according to the procedures just described, some formulas will come out true no matter what domain we choose, as long as it is not empty, and no matter what subsets of the domain individual predicates denote. For example, the formula $\forall x(Ex \lor \neg Ex)$ is true no matter what domain we consider and no matter what subset of that domain E denotes. $\forall x(Ex \lor \neg Ex)$ *is a logically true formula.* It is easy to see why: $\forall x(Ex \lor \neg Ex)$ is true in a domain under any particular specification of what E denotes if and only if $Ex \lor \neg Ex$ is true of every element of the domain. $Ex \lor \neg Ex$ is true of a member of the domain if that individual is a member of the set denoted by E or a member of the complement (in the domain) of the set denoted by E. But every member of every nonempty domain is a member of E or of the complement of E, no matter what set E is. So $Ex \lor \neg Ex$ is true of every value of x. So, finally, $\forall x(Ex \lor \neg Ex)$ is always true.

Study Questions

The mathematical theory of meaning for Frege's logic can be extended to relations as follows. A two-place relation between members of a domain determines the set of *pairs* of objects in that domain that stand in the relation. In the natural numbers, the relation *less than* determines the set of all pairs of numbers where the first member of the pair is less than the second. So the pair $\langle 1, 2 \rangle$ is determined by this relation, but not the pair $\langle 2, 1 \rangle$ and not the pair $\langle 1, 1 \rangle$. A *two-place predicate* in a formal language forms a sentence when followed by two names, but the names may also be replaced by variables. Such a predicate may be taken to denote the set of all pairs in a domain that stand in some relation. For example, let the domain be the natural numbers 0, 1, 2, 3, ..., and let L be a two-place predicate that denotes the relation "less than." Then $L(1, 2)$ is true, but $L(2, 1)$ and $L(1, 1)$ are false. The formula Lxy is true of the pair $\langle 1, 2 \rangle$ but false of the pair $\langle 2, 1 \rangle$ and false of the the the pair $\langle 1, 1 \rangle$. The same thing may be done with three-place relations and three-place predicates, four-place relations and four-place predicates, and so on.

1. Given the definitions in the paragraph above, what pairs of natural numbers is the formula Lxx true of?

2. Is the formula $\exists x \forall y\, Lxy$ true in the domain of natural numbers? Is the formula $\exists x \forall y\, Lyx$ true? Explain what each of these formulas says.

3. Explain what the following formula says, and determine whether or not it is true:

$\forall x \forall y \exists z((Lxy) \to (Lxz \,\&\, Lzy))$

4. Write a formula that says that for every two distinct points, there is a point between them. Use whatever symbols you need.

IMPLICATIONS OF FREGE'S THEORY

The proof of the logical truth of $\forall x(Ex \lor \neg Ex)$ given in the preceding section is the basis for an explanation of why logical truths are necessarily true. *Logical truths are true because of how we use our language.* If we use "and," "or," "not," "for every," "some," and other logical phrases in the way Frege describes, then the truth or falsity of complex sentences will depend on the truth or falsity of simpler sentences from which they are compounded, and the truth or falsity of sentences with quantifiers will depend on what the formulas without quantifiers are *true of.* These dependencies of complex sentences on simpler sentences will make some formulas come out true no matter whether their simpler sentences are true or false and no matter what the predicates they contain denote. The sentences or formulas that come out true in every possible world are the sentences or formulas that are true as a matter of logical necessity, true in every conceivable world. In Frege's theory, there is no longer a great mystery as to how some sentences can have this kind of necessity.

The mathematical theory of meaning for the part of Frege's logic I have described (sometimes called *first-order logic*) provides a formal notion of *entailment.* Recall that one sentence entails another if the truth of the first sentence logically necessitates the truth of the second sentence, in other words, if it is not logically possible for the first sentence to be true and at the same time for the second sentence to be false. Similarly, we say that a set of sentences entails another sentence if it is not logically possible for all of the sentences in the set to be simultaneously true and the entailed sentence to be false. We can analyze entailment as follows:

Definition   Let Γ be a collection of sentences, and let S be a sentence. Γ *entails* S if and only if for every nonempty domain D and every rule assigning subsets of D to predicates occurring in Γ or S, if all sentences in Γ are true, then S is also true.

With the theory of meaning and this definition of entailment, various fundamental questions about the adequacy of Frege's logical theory become mathematical questions that can be answered by (often difficult) mathematical investigations. One such question is whether proofs in Frege's logic necessarily preserve truth. This question becomes the more precise question, In every proof in Frege's logic, do the assumptions of the proof entail the conclusions? Logicians succeeded in proving that the answer to this question is affirmative, and that is why proofs show that premises entail conclusions. Another question is whether for every entailment there is a corresponding proof. More precisely, if Γ entails S, is there a proof of S from assumptions in Γ? In 1931 Kurt Gödel, then a young Viennese logician, proved that the answer to this question is also affirmative.

I began our study of the idea of a deductive argument with three principal questions.

1. How can we determine whether or not a piece of reasoning from premises to a conclusion is a valid deductive argument?
2. How can we determine whether or not a conclusion is necessitated by a set of premises? If a conclusion is necessitated by a set of premises, how can we find a valid deductive argument that demonstrates that necessary connection?
3. What features of the structure of the world, the structure of language, and the relations among words, thoughts, and things make deductive reasoning possible?

Frege's theory provides an answer to the first question. Given a deductive argument, we can now determine whether or not it is a *good* deductive argument. We put the premises, the conclusion, and the intermediate steps of the argument into formal notation and then determine whether or not each step of the formal argument follows from preceding steps or from the premises by Frege's rules of proof or by rules that can be derived from Frege's rules. Moreover, this constitutes an *adequate* answer to the question. Using Frege's theory, we can represent proofs in number theory, algebra, geometry, set theory, and those empirical sciences that use mathematical reasoning. In previous chapters I illustrated the limitations of theories of proof with the problem of reconstructing the very first proof in Euclid's *Elements*. I emphasized that Aristotle's theory of the syllogism could not account for Euclid's proof and later noted that George Boole's logical theory could not do much better. Frege's theory can do better.

Frege himself claimed that his system could be used to reconstruct proofs in geometry as well as other types of deductive arguments, such as Saint Anselm's ontological proof of the existence of God. (Frege even wrote a paper on Anselm's argument.) But it turns out to be a considerable task actually to develop a formal system in which Euclid's geometrical assumptions can be stated and all of Euclid's propositions can be proved. David Hilbert presented the first such system after the turn of the century, using some stronger logical principles than those I have discussed.

Frege's theory also provides a kind of answer to the third question. The answer is given through the theory of meaning, which connects formulas in Frege's logical notation with domains and their subsets, and specifies what it means for a formula to be true (or to be false) when its variables range over a domain and its predicates are assigned to subsets of that domain. The idea is that the names and predicates of a language *denote* objects, properties, and relations, and in the actual world some objects may happen to exemplify any particular property or relation, and some may not. The denotations and the facts of the world determine the truth values of sentences. What constitutes the relation of denotation between words on the one hand and things, properties, and relations on the other remains mysterious. This sketchy theory of meaning, together with the logicians' mathematical demonstration that proofs in Frege's system show that the premises of the proof entail the conclusion and Gödel's proof that if a set of sentences entails a conclusion, then there exists some proof in Frege's system that derives the conclusion from the premises, provide a partial answer to the third question.

Only the second question remains untouched, but it is a very important. Recall that Leibniz hoped that by formulating all of science in a formal language, an "alphabet of thought," we would obtain an algorithm, a mechanical means, to derive all of the consequences of any proposition. If Leibniz's vision were fulfilled, all of the tedious work of investigating the consequences of any set of assumptions could be done by machine. We would never need to be in ignorance of the implications of any theory: a computer could calculate them for us. On Frege's logical theory, the second part of the second question amounts to the following: Is there an algorithm that, if run forever, will list every proof in Frege's logic? The answer is that there is such an algorithm. If a finite set of sentences entails a conclusion, this algorithm will find a proof of that conclusion from premises in the set. But when we formulate the question in this way, we realize that the answer is a little disappointing, for what if we don't know whether or not a set of premises entails a conclusion and want to find out? An algorithm that runs forever looking for a proof and doesn't find one will never tell us at any finite time that there is no proof to be found. It seems that to fulfill Leibniz's vision what we really want is a positive answer to the following question: Is there an algorithm, a mechanical, computable procedure, that will determine for every formula whether or not that formula is a logical truth in Frege's system? If there were such an algorithm or computational procedure, we could use it to determine whether or not any particular set of premises logically necessitates any particular conclusion. For suppose that the premises are A, B, C, ..., D, and suppose that the conclusion is E. Then if the premises logically necessitate the conclusion, whenever the premises are true, the conclusion is also true; in other words, in no possible circumstance are the premises true and the conclusion false. Thus if the premises necessitate the conclusion, then the sentence $(A \ \& \ B \ \& \ C \ \& \ ... \ \& \ D) \to E$ must be true in every possible world, that is, it must be a logical truth. Conversely, if the formula $(A \ \& \ B \ \& \ C \ \& \ ... \ \& \ D) \to E$ is logically true, then in every world in which the formula $A \ \& \ B \ \& \ C \ \& \ ... \ \& \ D$ is true, E is also true. So the premises necessitate the conclusion. Therefore, to determine whether or not the premises $A \ \& \ B \ \& \ C \ \& \ ... \ \& \ D$ necessitate the conclusion E, we have only to determine whether the formula $(A \ \& \ B \ \& \ C \ \& \ ... \ \& \ D) \to E$ is logically true. So an algorithm that would determine whether or not a formula in Frege's system is logically true would realize Leibniz's dream. But is there such an algorithm?

There is not. *No algorithm exists that will determine for every formula whether or not that formula is logically true. Hence no algorithm exists that will determine for every set of premises and every possible conclusion whether or not the premises entail the conclusion.* Leibniz dreamed an impossible dream.

To obtain this answer, logicians in the 1930s had to formulate a precise theory of what is and what is not computable, and they had to formulate precise mathematical descriptions of idealized machines for carrying out computations. These logical studies created the mathematical subject now known as the theory of computation. That theory was developed by a number of people in the 1930s and 1940s, including Gödel, whom I have already mentioned; Alonzo Church, then a professor of mathematics at Princeton; and his students, including Alan Turing, then a young Englishman whom Church brought to Princeton. Their work led to the modern understanding of computation and provided the ground work for theoretical computer science. At the close of World War II, the new theory of computation and the emerging understanding of programming systems guided the construction of the first programmable electronic computers.

MYSTERIES

Frege's theory leaves a number of problems unsolved. For example, Frege thought that his formula $\forall x(Ax \rightarrow Bx)$ captured the logical properties of scientific laws about causality. But "Smoking causes cancer" cannot be represented very well by a logical formula of the form $\forall x(Sx \rightarrow Cx)$. The sentence "Smoking causes cancer" does not imply that everyone who smokes gets cancer. Logicians have sought formal systems that better represent causal reasoning. Again, Frege's logic does not succeed very well in capturing the logical properties of conditional senses whose antecedents are known to be false. For example, "If George Bush were not president, then Dan Quayle would be president" is true (at least in 1991), but "If George Bush were not President and he had emigrated to Chile in 1987, then Dan Quayle would be president" is false. But in Frege's logic, if any sentence of the form $A \rightarrow B$ is true, then so is $(A \,\&\, C) \rightarrow B$. Elegant formal systems have been developed to account for counterfactual reasoning. There are many other problems of this sort, but in each case modern solutions continue to use both Frege's fundamental ideas and the basic principles of the theory of meaning that later logicians developed for Frege's theory.

Frege's theory also leaves or creates a number of other philosophical problems that we do not yet fully understand. Frege's theory supposes that names denote objects, and predicates denote properties (or the sets that are the extensions of properties). One of the fundamental concerns of twentieth-century philosophy has surrounded the following questions: What is the relation of denoting? What makes it the case that a particular word or phrase on a particular occasion of utterance denotes a particular object or property? What are meanings or senses?

One answer to these questions is that people have a mysterious and irreducible capacity to make words mean things. On this view, the relation of denoting cannot be explained in any natural way. Most philosophers today regard such a view as unfounded, but finding a scientifically acceptable alternative is not easy. A plausible proposal is that denoting is some sort of *causal* relation between objects or properties on the one hand and utterances of words or phrases on the other. The idea is, for example, that when we say or write "Cicero," we denote the Roman orator because our use of the word "Cicero" is connected by a millennium long causal chain of uses to the event in which Cicero was named "Cicero." A use of the word "red" denotes the property red because somewhere in the prehistory of language, ancestral users picked a word for the property red, and that word evolved through history into the English word "red." On this view, utterances of "red" and the presences of red things may be correlated, but the relation of denotation does not consist in that correlation. The correlation is what makes it useful to have a term for the property red and what makes it possible for us to learn what "red" denotes. Children are able to learn what "red" denotes because their teachers arrange circumstances in which the property denoted, red, is strongly correlated with utterances of "red."

But what makes a particular action an act of *naming*? We need a natural account of naming quite as much as we need an account of denoting. The obvious explanation of naming appeals to what the namer *intends* for a word to denote. But to intend something seems to require having thoughts that have a linguistic structure and whose component simple thoughts stand in denoting relations to things and properties. Is the causal account therefore inevitably circular, and circular in a way that makes it unenlightening and unscientific? These questions have been the subject of considerable debate in philosophy in the last twenty years.

A third approach to the question of denoting denies that there is any such relation. In effect, it claims that the theory of meaning developed for Frege's logic is a mistake. This approach is generally attributed to the American pragmatists Charles Sanders Peirce, William James, and John Dewey, who wrote during the first decades of this century, and also to various continental philosophers writing in the same period. It continues to be held today by some philosophers. The pragmatists denied that there are relations between language and a world (independent of language) in virtue of which sentences are true or false. Peirce, for example, claimed that *truth is what will be believed in the long run*. The radical reading of this slogan is that whatever people come to believe in the long run *constitutes* the truth. This idea is puzzling for several reasons, including the following: For an utterance or a writing to express a *belief*, and not be just ink marks or noise, requires that parts of the utterance or writing have a meaning, which seems to require that they denote properties or things (or at least possible properties and possible things). So the idea that beliefs could completely determine the world seems curiously incoherent, since the idea of something being a *belief* seems to require a world and meaning relations. Perhaps for reasons such as these, some contemporary pragmatists explicitly do not follow Peirce's program. Instead, they emphasize that the fundamental property of sentences is not their truth or their falsity but their *assertability*. In some contexts it is appropriate to assert a sentence, and in other contexts it is not appropriate. The proper study of language and logic on this view is not the study of entailment but the study of assertability. A convincing development of this view of language faces formidable tasks, including explaining how linguistic competence is acquired, explaining how we can use assertions to reliably manipulate the world ("Jump! There's a truck coming"), and explaining the basis for our intuitions about entailment and logical implication. I will return to some of these topics in a later chapter.

Meaning is not the only profound problem that has followed Frege's logic. Another difficulty has to do with twentieth-century physics. We can give perfectly adequate formal-logical reconstructions of many branches of physics. In essence, this has been done for classical particle mechanics, for the special theory of relativity, and for several other physical theories. There is one branch of twentieth-century physics, however, for which it seems that it cannot be done, and unfortunately, that part of physics, *quantum theory*, is the most fundamental. Quantum theory emerged in the first decades of this century from ideas due to Max Planck, Albert Einstein, and Niels Bohr. In the middle of the 1920s the theory was changed dramatically by Erwin Schrödinger, Werner Heisenberg, and others. The "new quantum theory" that emerged has a *mathematical framework* that can be perfectly well represented in a formal logical system. However, when we try to say what the entities of the theory are and what their properties are, things begin to come apart.

The fundamental problem can be thought of this way. Consider a box that has two sides, and suppose that there is an electron in the box. According to quantum theory, it can be *true* that an electron is in the left side of a box *or* in the right side of the box, while at the same time it is *false* that the electron is in the left side of the box and it is *false* that the electron is in the right side of the box. This phenomenon is known as *superposition*. Let Le mean the electron is in the left-hand side of the box, and let Re mean the electron is in the right-hand side of the box. Then it is true that

Le ∨ *Re* and false that *Le* and false that *Re*. So we have that (*Le* ∨ *Re*) & ¬*Le* & ¬*Re*, which is a contradiction according to Frege's logical theory (and according to Boole's as well).

What do we do when a fundamental physical theory involves a contradiction? Well, ordinarily we might reject the physical theory and look for a better theory that does not involve a contradiction. Many physicists have attempted to do just that, but they have found no theory without superposition that is able to account for the statistical relations found among properties of subatomic particles. The same phenomenon is present even in more recent fundamental theories, such as the quantum theory of fields. Another response is to conclude that the physical theory is an excellent calculating device for predicting the outcomes of experiment but that the theory really *says nothing* about the constitution of matter. This view, often known as *instrumentalism*, avoids the problem of inconsistency by treating sentences that seem to be about individual particles as not about such things at all. Instrumentalism saves us from paradox, but only at the cost of enormous disappointment. After all, we thought that modern physics would tell us about the structure of the universe. On the instrumentalist view, modern physics does no such thing; it only tells us how to predict the outcomes of experiments.

There is another way to resolve the problem. If our fundamental physical theories seem to involve a contradiction, perhaps we should change our ideas about what is and what is not a contradiction. Perhaps the difficulty is not with physics but with Frege's logic, and perhaps we should look for a logical theory in which the formula (*Le* ∨ *Re*) & ¬*Le* & ¬*Re* is consistent. Philosophers, physicists, and logicians have developed several logical systems of this kind, called *quantum logics*. Quantum logics avoid the logical paradox in modern physics, and some of them are still strong enough to permit the reconstruction of classical mathematical reasoning, but they have not yet been provided with a theory of meaning as clear as the system of domains and subsets that provides the theory of meaning for Frege's logic. Perhaps the theory of meaning for quantum logic never will be so clear. Niels Bohr argued that quantum phenomena are essentially *complementary*, by which he meant that there is a coherent picture not of all properties of a quantum system taken together but only of one or another aspect of quantum systems considered independently. If he is right, then we should not expect to find an unequivocal theory of meaning that includes the foundations of modern physics.

CONCLUSION

Frege's logical theory solves the problems I posed for a theory of deductive argument. It characterizes a notion of proof adequate to encompass mathematical proofs in a wide range of subjects. When elaborated with a theory of meaning, the theory of proof turns out to be complete in the sense that for every entailment, there exists a corresponding proof. Moreover, the theory of meaning explains why proofs reveal entailment, since the theory of meaning can be used to show that whenever there is a proof of a conclusion from a set of premises, the premises necessitate the conclusion. It is disappointing but certainly enlightening to learn that no possible algorithm can tell us, for every finite set of premises and every possible conclusion, whether there exists a proof of the conclusion from the premises. The work that led to understanding this limitation also created the modern theory of computation.

With all of its benefits and insights, Frege's logical theory and the theory of meaning that was built upon it also left us with many puzzles. Some of the puzzles require extending the logical theory or introducing modifications while keeping the same general picture of how language relates to the world. Other puzzles, including explaining what constitutes meaning relations and reconciling Frege's logic with modern physics, seem more fundamentally difficult.

Review Questions

1. What is logicism, and to what views of Mill and Kant is it opposed?

2. Explain Frege's logical categories and his conception of a formal proof.

3. What does Frege's theory say about the three fundamental questions concerning deductive argument?

4. Explain the basic idea of the mathematical theory of meaning developed for Frege's logic.

5. Many previous theories were limited because they could not account for reasoning about relations. Explain how Frege's theory can account for such reasoning.

6. Describe some contemporary difficulties for Frege's theory and some proposed solutions to them.

7. Suppose that we could present Frege's theory to Aristotle and to Leibniz. How do you suppose each of them would evaluate Frege's theory? If they accepted Frege's logical theory, what implications would that have for their own metaphysical theories?

8. What roles did each of the following people have in the story of this chapter: Alfred North Whitehead (1861–1947), Immanuel Kant (1724–1804), John Stuart Mill (1806–1873), David Hume (1711–1776), Bertrand Russell (1872–1970), Alan Turing (1912–1954), David Hilbert (1862–1943), Albert Einstein (1979–1955), Alonzo Church (1903–present), Niels Bohr (1995–1962), Charles Sanders Peirce (1839–1914).

9. Briefly explain the views of Hume, Mill, and Kant about the nature of mathematical knowledge.

Further Reading

Frege
Dummett, Michael A. E. *The Interpretation of Frege's Philosophy*. Cambridge: Harvard University Press, 1981.

Frege, Gottlob. *Collected Works on Mathematics, Logic, and Philosophy*. Ed. Brian McGuinness. New York: B. Blackwell, 1984.

Frege, Gottlob. *Philosophical and Mathematical Correspondence*. Ed. Gabriel Gorrfried. Chicago: University of Chicago Press, 1980.

Haaparanta, Leila, and Jaakko Hintikka, eds. *Frege Synthesized: Essays on the Philosophical and Foundational Work of Gottlob Frege*. Boston: D. Reidel, 1986.

Resnick, Michael D. *Frege and the Philosophy of Mathematics*. Ithaca, N.Y.: Cornell University Press, 1980.

Sluga, Hans D. *Gottlob Frege*. Boston: Routledge and Kegan Paul, 1980.

Weiner, Joan. *Frege in Perspective*. Ithaca, N.Y.: Cornell University Press, 1990.

Wright, Crispin, ed. *Frege: Tradition and Influence*. New York: B. Blackwell, 1984.

Counterfactuals and conditionals
Jackson, Frank. *Conditionals*. Cambridge, England: B. Blackwell, 1987.

Lewis, David K. *Counterfactuals*. Cambridge: Harvard University Press, 1973.

Pollock, John L. *Subjunctive Reasoning*. Boston: D. Reidel Publishing Co., 1976.

Peirce
Peirce, Charles S. *The Philosophy of Peirce: Selected Writings*. Ed. Justus Buchler. New York: Harcourt, Brace, 1940.

Philosophy of language
Blackburn, Simon. *Spreading the Word: Groundings in the Philosophy of Language*. New York: Oxford University Press, 1984.

Chomsky, Noam. *Language and Problems of Knowledge: The Managua Lectures*. Cambridge: MIT Press, 1988.

French, Peter A., Theodore Edward Uehling, and Howard K. Wettstein, eds. *Contemporary Perspectives in the Philosophy of Language*. Vol. 2. Notre Dame, Ind.: University of Notre Dame Press, 1989.

Schwartz, Stephen P., ed. *Naming, Necessity, and Natural Kinds*. Ithaca, N.Y.: Cornell University Press, 1977.

Quantum logic

Hooker, Clifford Alan, ed. *The Logico-algebraic Approach to Quantum Mechanics*. Boston: D. Reidel, 1979.

Pitowsky, Itamar. *Quantum Probability, Quantum Logic*. New York: Springer-Verlag, 1989.

Chapter 6

MODERN LOGIC*

In this chapter we will take a more careful look at logic as it has developed since Frege. We will consider many of the same ideas discussed in the previous chapter, but we will proceed more rigorously, and I give more details.

RELATIONAL STRUCTURES

One might be asked to find the *roots* of the polynomial $x^2 - 1$. That is really just to ask for the values of x that satisfy the following formula:

(1) $x^2 - 1 = 0$

The answer, of course, is $\{1, -1\}$. The formula states a condition satisfied only by special values of the variable x. We could say that the equation is *true of* the number 1 and *true of* the number -1. But it would not make sense to say that the equation is, all by itself, true, nor would it make any sense to say that the equation is false. The formula is true of some numbers, those that satisfy it, and false of other numbers, those that do not satisfy it. Compare these sentences:

(2) For all x, $x^2 - 1 = 0$.

(3) For all x, if $x^2 = 1$ then $x^2 - 1 = 0$.

(4) These exists an x such that $x^2 - 1 = 0$.

Sentence (2) is simply false if the domain over which the variables range is the real numbers. It is not *true of* some numbers and false of others. It is simply false. Sentence (3) is true; it is not true of some numbers but not others. Sentence (2) is false because it says that $x^2 - 1$ is satisfied by *every* number, and that is false. Sentence (3) is true because it says that every number satisfying $x^2 = 1$ satisfies $x^2 - 1 = 0$, and that is true. Sentence (4) is true, not true of some numbers and false of others, but simply true. There are, however, particular numbers that *make* (4) true, specifically the numbers 1 and -1. They make (4) true because they satisfy (1), and what (4) says is that some numbers satisfy (1).

The difference between (1), which is true of some numbers but not others, and (2) through (4) is that (1) has a *free variable*, x, whereas in (2) through (4), the variable x is *bound*. In (2) and (3), every occurrence of the variable x is governed by the phrase "for all," and we say that when a variable occurs in such a context, it is bound. Similarly, in (4) every occurrence of the variable x is governed by the phrase "there exists," and we also say a variable occurring in such a context is bound. We say that formulas with free variables are *open* formulas and that formulas without free variables are *closed* formulas. Closed formulas will also be called *sentences*.

Other phrases can be used to bind variables. "Every" means the same as "for all." "There exists" and "for some" are synonymous with one another, but they bind variables in a different way than does "for all."

Why is the formula $x^2 - 1 = 0$ satisfied by $\{1, -1\}$? Well, because if we take the number 1 and square it, we get the number 1 back, and if we take that number and subtract from it the number 1, we get 0. We get the same result if we take the value of x to be -1, but not if we take x to have any other value besides 1 or -1. So we are really thinking of the numbers in the real line as the possible values of x, and we are thinking of these numbers as things for which such functions as addition, subtraction, and multiplication are defined. Further, we think of the real numbers as each standing in a special relation to itself and to no other number, the relation of identity or equality.

So the picture we have when we do algebra is of a domain—perhaps the real line, perhaps the real plane, perhaps sometimes some other system of objects. When we write algebraic expressions using variables, the variables range over the objects of the domain. When we say "for all," we mean for all members of the domain, and when we say "there exists," we mean that there exists a member of the domain. The objects of the domain are related to each other by some definite collection of functions and by some definite collection of properties or relations.

Let us call a *relational structure* any *nonempty* set D, which we will call the *domain of* the structure, together with any finite collection of functions defined on all members of D, all ordered pairs of D, or all ordered triples of D, and so on, according to whether the functions require one argument or two arguments or whatever. The functions also have their values in D. We further allow that a relational structure may have any finite number of relations or properties. A property is just a subset of D, a two-place relation is just a subset of all of the ordered pairs of D, and so on. We write *the set of all ordered pairs of D* as $D \times D$, sometimes called the *Cartesian product of D with itself*, or *the second Cartesian power of D* (after Descartes, of course).

The *natural numbers* form one relational structure. The domain consists of an infinite collection of objects. There are three functions—successor, addition, and multiplication—defined on the domain. The successor function, s, maps each number to its immediate successor, that is $s(x) = x + 1$. There is one constant or distinguished individual, namely the number 0. There are two relations in the structure: one is the relation of identity that each number has to itself; the other is the relation of order $(a < b)$, which holds of numbers $\langle a, b \rangle$ if and only if a is less than b. We write this structure as $[N, 0, s, +, \times, =, <]$ and denote it by $\mathcal{N}$.

We can consider the structure that has the same domain as the natural numbers but has no functions, no constant, and two relations: identity and the less-than relation. The structure is $[N, <, =]$. The structure just defined is sometimes described as *discrete order with a first element* because there is an object in the domain, namely the number zero, that is less than every number.

The integers, denoted by $\mathcal{Z}$, form a relational structure, $[Z, 0, s, +, \times, =, <]$, that can be thought of as an extension of $\mathcal{N}$. The integers include the positive numbers, zero, and the negative numbers. Successor, addition, and multiplication are all part of this relational structure, just as with the natural numbers. Whereas in the natural numbers there is a number, zero, that is not the successor of any number, in the integers every number is the successor of a number. In the integers we can define an operation, subtraction, that we cannot define on the natural numbers. (By our conventions a function can only be introduced if it is defined on all members of the domain of the structure, or on all ordered pairs if it is a two-place function. Subtraction does not have a value in the natural numbers for all pairs of natural numbers.)

If we ignore the functions in $\mathcal{Z}$ and consider just the identity and the ordering relations, we obtain a structure sometimes called *discrete order without first or last elements*, $[Z, =, <]$.

Another familiar number domain is the collection of *rational numbers*. The rational numbers can be described in various ways. They are, for example, the real numbers that have repeating decimal expansions. Another way to think of the rationals is as those numbers that can be represented by a ratio of integers. Of course, one and the same rational number can often be represented by more than one ratio of integers. Thus $1/2$ is the same number as $2/4$, as $3/6$, as $4/8$, and so on. Two ratios of integers a/b and c/d, represent the same number provided that $ad = cb$. So, starting with the integers, $\mathscr{Z}$, we can consider the set $\mathscr{Z} \times \mathscr{Z}$ of all ordered pairs of integers, except for those ordered pairs whose second element is 0 (because we cannot divide by 0). We can then define an *equivalence relation*, call it E, between such ordered pairs by the condition that $E(\langle a, b \rangle, \langle c, d \rangle)$ if and only if $ad = cb$. For each ordered pair of integers $\langle a, b \rangle$ in $\mathscr{Z} \times \mathscr{Z}$ (except ordered pairs whose second element is 0), we can consider the set of all ordered pairs $\langle x, y \rangle$ such that $E(\langle a, b \rangle, \langle x, y \rangle)$. We can call this set the *equivalence class of* $\langle a, b \rangle$ and denote it by $[\langle a, b \rangle]$. So if $E(\langle a, b \rangle, \langle c, d \rangle)$ holds, that is, if $\langle a, b \rangle$ and $\langle c, d \rangle$ are equivalent ratios of integers, then they determine one and the same equivalence class, that is to say, $[\langle a, b \rangle] = [\langle c, d \rangle]$.

Now take the domain of the rational numbers to be the set of all equivalence classes just constructed. In other words, treat the equivalence classes as themselves the fundamental objects. We can define operations $+$ and $\cdot$ on these equivalence classes in terms of the operations of addition and multiplication on the integers. To understand the point of the definitions, recall that a fraction, say $1/2$, is simply one way of representing the ordered pair $\langle 1, 2 \rangle$, and recall that in adding fractions, say $1/2 + 2/4$, we multiply the numerator of each fraction by the denominator of the other, add the results, and divide by the product of the denominators. The definitions are as follows:

Definition of sum $[\langle a, b \rangle] + [\langle c, d \rangle] = [\langle ad + bc, bd \rangle]$

Definition of product $[\langle a, b \rangle] \cdot [\langle c, d \rangle] = [\langle ac, bd \rangle]$

The first of these equations says that the operation $+$ operating on the two equivalence classes $[\langle a, b \rangle]$ and $[\langle c, d \rangle]$ is defined to be the equivalence class of the ordered pair of numbers $\langle ad + cd, bd \rangle$, where the $+$ between ad and cd means ordinary addition of integers. The second equation is to be read in an analogous way.

We can also define an ordering relation, denoted by $<$, on the rational numbers from properties of the integers. Thus we have the following definition of order:

Definition of order $[\langle a, b\rangle] < [\langle c, d\rangle]$ if and only if there exists a rational $[\langle u, v\rangle]$ such that $u > 0$ and $v > 0$ and $[\langle a, b\rangle] + [\langle u, v\rangle] = [\langle c, d\rangle]$.

Using the integers, we have constructed the rational numbers. Actually, we had to use a good bit more than just the integers; we also had to use principles of *set theory*.

The rational numbers form a relational structure that has an infinite domain with the operations of addition and multiplication (but *not* the successor operation). Informally, we think of the rational numbers as *including* the integers, so that each integer x is identified with a particular rational number, $[\langle x, s(0)\rangle]$. Just as with the natural numbers and the integers, we can use addition to define the relation of less than on the rational numbers, and we can think of the structure obtained from $\mathscr{Q}$ by deleting all relations and functions except for identity and less than. This ordering differs from the ordering on the integers in the following way: between any two rational numbers, there is another rational number. So the sentence "For every object x and for every object y, if x is less than y, then there is an object z such that x is less than z and z is less than y" is true in the rationals but false in the integers. An ordering for which this sentence is true is said to be *dense*.

Number systems are not the only relational structures. Euclidean geometry is concerned with such structures. Consider a structure whose domain consists of all ordered pairs of real numbers. Intuitively, each object in the domain is a point of two-dimensional Euclidean space. The points can be taken to stand in two relations (besides identity): betweenness and congruence. Betweenness is a three-place relation. Informally, a point z is between two points x and y just in case there is a Euclidean (straight) line segment from x to y containing z. Congruence is a four-place relation. Again informally, a pair of points x, y is congruent to a pair of points u, w just in case the line segment with endpoints x and y has the same length as the line segment with endpoints u and w.

In fact, any set of objects, together with functions and relations defined on the objects, can form a relational structure. The domain can be the set of streets in Pittsburgh. Properties might be the set of paved streets, and the set of cobblestoned streets. One relation might be the set of pairs of streets such that the first intersects the second.

Study Questions

1. For each of the following formulas, describe the set of natural numbers (i.e., nonnegative whole numbers) satisfying it:

$$x - 2 = 0$$
$$x^2 < 5$$
$$x + (x - 3) = 4$$
$$x - x = 0$$

2. Which of the following are true in the structure of a discrete order with a first element? (a) There is an object such that every object is less than it. (b) For any two distinct objects, there is a third such that the third object is less than one of the first two and the other object of the first two is less than the third object. (c) No object is less than itself. (d) If one object is less than a second and the second object is less than a third, then the third object is less than the first. (e) If one object is less than another, then the latter is also less than the former.

3. Specify the set of numbers in the domain of the structure just described that satisfy the following (note that what follow are *not sentences*; they are *formulas*): (a) x is less than all other numbers; (b) x is less than all numbers; (c) x is less than 3, and 1 is less than x; (d) x is less than 3, and 2 is less than x; (e) x is less than 3, or 2 is less than x.

4. Can you give a *formula* that cannot be satisfied in the domain of the integers but can be satisfied in the domain of natural numbers?

5. Let E be the relation defined in the construction of the rational numbers from the integers. Prove that for all ordered pairs $u = \langle x, y \rangle$, $w = \langle k, z \rangle$, $v = \langle m, n \rangle$, the following hold: $E(u, u)$; if $E(u, w)$, then $E(w, u)$; and if $E(u, w)$ and $E(w, v)$, then $E(u, v)$. Any two-place relation that has these three properties (called, respectively, reflexivity, symmetry, and transitivity) is an *equivalence relation*.

6. Show that the following open formula (open because x and y are free variables) can be satisfied by some pairs of numbers in the integers: if x is less than y, there is an object z such that x is less than z and z is less than y.

7. Prove that the ordering of the rational numbers is dense.

FORMAL LANGUAGES

Consider the sentence "For any two objects, there is a third such that the third object is less than one of the first two and the other object of the first two is less than the third object." What makes this sentence clumsy is the need for *coreference*. Different parts of the sentence must refer to one and the same unnamed object and not to other objects. In this case we can introduce the device of *variables* in such sentences in lieu of names. So we might say, "For any two distinct objects x, y, there is a third object z such that z is less than x or z is less than y, and if z is less than x then y is less than z, and if z is less than y then x is less than z." This restatement ought to be clearer, even though it is still complicated. One reason logicians work with formalized languages is to remove such ambiguities. Another reason is that logicians want to prove things about properties of languages, and doing so requires that a *language* be a definite mathematical object.

In a formalized language there is a basic vocabulary consisting of expressions that serve as names for particular objects in the domain (analogous to the names "zero" and "0," which we use for the number zero), expressions that serve as variables, expressions that denote properties and relations, expressions that denote functions, expressions that serve as quantifiers (analogous to "for all" and "there exists"), expressions that serve as sentential connectives (analogous to the & and $\vee$ and $\neg$ of chapter 5), and items, such as parentheses, that serve a role analogous to that of punctuation marks in English.

For example, we can take the vocabulary for the basic language of arithmetic to consist of the following:

Names: 0
Variables: x_i for any i in N
Two-place predicate symbols: L, $=$
One-place function symbol: s
Two-place function symbols: $+$, $\times$
Quantifiers: $\forall$, $\exists$
Sentential connectives: &, $\vee$, $\neg$, $\rightarrow$
Parentheses: (,)

This basic vocabulary is infinite, but only because we allow an infinity of distinct variables.

Clearly there are an infinite number of finite strings of elements from this vocabulary, for example, the following are all strings from this vocabulary:

$(\forall L - =)($

$(\forall x)Lx_3 0$

$((((((((((((((((((())))))))))))))$

In a natural language such as English, not every string from the vocabulary makes sense. "English, up goes the, to tree. not; ;;? who" is a string of English words and punctuation marks, but it is not a sentence; it has no meaning in the English language. We say it is not *well formed*.

In the same way, we want only special strings from our formal vocabulary to count as being well formed, but we want it to be perfectly definite which strings are, and which are not, well formed. In English and in other natural languages there is no bound on the length or number of well-formed strings, or sentences, and so the collection of sentences in English is infinite. We want the same to be true of the well-formed strings in formalized languages. After all, the number of truths is infinite, and we hope to be able in principle to state any of them.

How can we characterize this infinite class *exactly*? We do so by giving an *inductive definition*. The inductive definition will begin by saying that a certain perspicuous collection of strings is well formed. Then it will specify rules or operations from which a new well-formed string can be made from previous well-formed strings. Finally, it will say that the set of all well-formed strings is exactly the set of all strings that can be generated by applying these rules to the initial finite set of well-formed strings any finite number of times. In this way the set of well-formed strings will be "built up."

For the vocabulary I have just given, the characterization of the set of well-formed strings is as follows:

Definition of a term   (1) The symbol 0 is a term. (2) Every variable is a term. (3) If t_1, ..., t_n are terms and f is an n-place function symbol, $f(t_1, \ldots, t_n)$ is a term. (4) Nothing else is a term.

Definition of an atomic formula   An *atomic formula* is a string of the form $Lt_i t_k$ or of the form $t_i = t_k$, where t_i and t_k are any terms.

Definition of a well-formed formula   (1) Every atomic formula is well formed. (2) If M is well formed, so is (M). (3) If M is well formed, so is $\neg M$. (4) If M and N are well formed, so are $(M \& N)$ and $(M \vee N)$ and $(M \to N)$. (5) If M is well formed, so are $\forall x_i M$ and $\exists x_i M$, where x_i is any variable. (6) Nothing else is well formed.

The inductive definition of a well-formed string implicitly provides a procedure for determining whether or not an arbitrary string is well formed. If there is a means of determining whether a symbol is a variable, the procedure can be made completely mechanical.

When we first considered examples from algebra, I noted the difference between variables that occur free and variables that are governed by a quantifier expression such as "there exists" or "for all." We can make the notion of a free occurrence of a variable precise for any formalized language of the kind we are considering. Recall first of all that one and the same variable can occur in several places in one and the same well-formed formula, so that what must be defined is the notion of a free occurrence of a variable in a well-formed formula:

Definition of a free occurrence of a variable in a well-formed formula   (1) Every occurrence of a variable in an atomic formula is a free occurrence. (2) An occurrence of a variable in $\neg S$ is free if and only if that occurrence is free in S. (3) An occurrence of a variable is free in $(M \lor N)$ if and only if that occurrence is free in M, if it occurs in M, or free in N, if it occurs in N. (4) An occurrence of a variable is free in $(M \ \& \ N)$ if and only if that occurrence is free in M, if it occurs in M, or free in N, if it occurs in N. (5) An occurrence of a variable is free in $(M \to N)$ if and only if that occurrence is free in M, if it occurs in M, or free in N, if it occurs in N. (6) An occurrence of a variable x_i is free in $\forall x_k S$ or in $\exists x_k S$ if and only if that occurrence is free in S and i does not equal k.

An occurrence of a variable that is not free is said to be *bound*.

We say that a well-formed formula is *closed* or is a *sentence* if it contains no free occurrences of variables. Otherwise, the formula is said to be *open*.

One great advantage of formal languages is that the language itself becomes a perfectly definite mathematical object, so that one may proceed to prove things about it, just as one proves things about numerical or geometrical objects. The importance of formal languages is not so much in their actual use but rather in showing that everything can in principle be made precise. In practice, completely formal languages are much too clumsy to use, and I will abbreviate formulas in obvious ways, for example, by ignoring extraneous parentheses required by the formation rules but unnecessary for seeing what is meant.

The formulation and study of formalized languages was concurrent with the development of logic early in this century. In the 1950s this aspect of logic served as a model and stimulus for the science of linguistics. Since then a principle aim of many linguists, following the work of Noam Chomsky, has been to characterize natural languages as systems with explicit rules of formation, or *parsing rules*. Like the rules of our simple formalized language, these linguists search for a formulation of grammatical principles that will make it possible to determine mechanically whether or not a string of symbols from a language is grammatical.

Study Question

Which of the following are terms if f is a two-place function symbol and g is a one-place function symbol and x and y are variables:

$f(x, f(x))$
$f(g(x), y)$
$g(f(x, g(y))$
$g(g(g(g(x))))$

TRUTH AND SATISFACTION

We know the basic idea for connecting formulas in a formal language to relational structures. The aim is to connect symbols with objects, properties, and relations in such a way that formulas in the language will be true or false of objects or sequences of objects in the domain and sentences in the language will be true or false. The basic idea is that each predicate of each type (that is, one-place, two-place, etc.) is mapped to a subset of members of the domain (or subset of ordered sequences of members of the domain) satisfying a property or relation. One-place predicates are mapped to subsets of the domain, two-place predicates are mapped to sets of ordered pairs of members of the domain, and so on. In the same way, unary-function symbols in a formal language are mapped to unary functions in the relational structure, binary-function symbols to binary functions, etc. I will call an *interpretation* any mapping that connects the names, predicates, and function symbols of a language with the relations and functions of a relational structure.

We also know from chapter 5 what it is that makes an atomic formula with a free variable *true of* an object in the domain of a relational structure on an interpretation connecting the language of the formula with the relational structure. A formula such as Mx is true of an object d in the domain of a relational structure under an interpretation, call it $\mathscr{I}$, provided that d is in the subset of the domain that $\mathscr{I}$ connects with the predicate M. Logicians tend to say that d *satisfies* Mx, keeping the terminology familiar from algebraic formulas. More formally, if we let $\mathscr{I}(M)$ be the subset of the domain D to which $\mathscr{I}$ maps M, then d satisfies Mx with respect to $\mathscr{I}$ if and only if $d \in \mathscr{I}(M)$. If the predicate is two-place, then a formula such as Bxy is true of, or satisfied by, an ordered pair of objects from the domain, say $\langle c, d \rangle$, provided that $\langle c, d \rangle$ is in the set of ordered pairs connected to B by $\mathscr{I}$. That is, $\langle c, d \rangle$ satisfies Bxy with respect to $\mathscr{I}$ if and only if $\langle c, d \rangle \in Bxy$. We also know that a formula of the form $\exists x\, Mx$ will be true with respect to an interpretation if and only if some object in the domain is in the set to which $\mathscr{I}$ maps M, in other words, if and only if *some* object in the domain satisfies Mx. $\forall x\, Mx$ will be true with respect to interpretation $\mathcal{I}$ if and only if every object in the domain is in the set to which $\mathcal{I}$ maps M, other words, if and only if *every* object in the domain satisfies Mx. A general definition of truth of sentences and satisfaction of formulas can be given inductively.

Study Question

Think of an assignment function $\mathcal{K}$ as a rule that specifies, for each variable in a formal language, an object in a domain D. Then we say that $\mathcal{K}$ *satisfies* $M(x)$ if $\mathcal{K}(x)$ is in $\mathcal{I}(M)$, where the interpretation $\mathcal{I}$ is assumed. Try to give an inductive definition of "Mapping $\mathcal{K}$ of variables in language L to domain D of relational structure R *satisfies* formula S." Assume a fixed interpretation $\mathcal{I}$ of the predicate and function symbols and the names in the language. Start with clauses for atomic formulas in the language. For each sentential connective (&, $\vee$, $\neg$), add a clause saying when $\mathcal{K}$ satisfies a compound formula with the connective (for example, $P \& Q$) in terms of when $\mathcal{K}$ satisfies the components (P and Q in the example). For existential quantifiers, take $\mathcal{K}$ to satisfy $\exists x\, S(x, y, z)$, for example, if *some* assignment function $\mathcal{J}$ that has the same value as $\mathcal{K}$ for all variables except possibly for the variable x satisfies $S(x, y, z)$. For universal quantifiers, take $\mathcal{K}$ to satisfy "$\forall x\, S(x, y, z)$ if *every* assignment function $\mathcal{L}$ that has the same values as $\mathcal{K}$ for all variables except possibly for variable x satisfies $S(x, y, z)$.

PROOFS

There are many different ways to formulate a theory of proof for the kinds of formal languages I have discussed. Different formulations may start from different sets of logical truths and use different rules of inference. All of the many formulations turn out to be equivalent in the sense that if a formula is provable from a set of assumptions in one formulation, it is also provable from the same set of assumptions in other formulations. I will give a system of proof that is based loosely on Frege's treatment.[1]

To obtain a consistent and adequate system of proof, we must be careful about the substitution of variables. The problem is that we cannot permit the substitution of an arbitrary term in an arbitrary universally quantified formula. Where t is an arbitrary term, we cannot without restriction infer a formula of the form $\forall x\, St$ or the formula St from a formula of the form $\forall x\, Sx$. For example, suppose that the formula we are considering is $\forall x \exists y\, \neg(x = y)$. This sentence says there are at least two things in the domain. If we substitute the term y for the variable x in this sentence, we would get the sentence $\forall x \exists y\, \neg(y = y)$, which, by quantifier deletion, entails $\exists y\, \neg(y = y)$. This sentence is a contradiction asserting there exists something that is not identical with itself.

Definition of substitutable   (1) For atomic S, any term is substitutable for x in S. (2) Term t is substitutable for x in $\neg S$ if and only if t is substitutable for x in S. (3) Term t is substitutable for x in $M \to N$ if and only if t is substitutable for x in both M and N. (4) Term t is substitutable for x in $\forall x\, S$ if and only if either x does not occur free in S or x does not occur in t and t is substitutable for x in S.

Our formal characterization of proof is given by a system of axioms and inference rules. There are an infinity of different axioms, but they may all be obtained from a finite number of *axiom schemata* either by substituting any well-formed formulas in an axiom scheme or by substituting and then placing universal quantifiers in front of the formula.

Definition   Formula S is a *generalization* of formula S' if and only if S is obtained from S' by prefixing S' with any finite number of universal quantifiers in any variables.

Every generalization of any formula obtained by substituting any well-formed formulas for A, B, and C and any names or variables for x, c, and d and any term for t in the following axiom schemata is an *axiom*.

$A \to (B \to A)$

$(C \to (B \to A)) \to ((C \to B) \to (C \to A))$

$(D \to (B \to A)) \to (B \to (D \to A))$

$(B \to A) \to (\neg A \to \neg B)$

$\neg\,\neg A \to A$

$A \to \neg\,\neg A$

$c = d \to K \to (Kc/d)$ (where K is an atomic formula and Kc/d is the result of substituting d for c in zero or more occurrences of c in formula K)

$c = c$

$\forall x\, Sx \to St$ (where St is substitutable for x in Sx)

$\forall x (M \to N) \to (\forall x\, M \to \forall x\, N)$

$S \to \forall x\, S$ (where x does not occur free in S)

There is a single rule of inference:

From $S \to T$ and S, infer T.

Finally, I define a *proof of formula S from a set of assumptions* Γ to be a finite sequence of formulas such that the last formula in the sequence is S and each formula in the sequence is in Γ, is an axiom, or follows from two preceding formulas in the sequence by the rule of inference.

Actual proofs in this system may be quite lengthy and very difficult to construct. The important thing, once more, is not that this characterization of proof provides a convenient system in which actually to construct proofs. It does not. Rather, the important thing is that the notion of a proof in a formal language becomes perfectly definite, so that we can informally prove things about formal proofs, just as we give informal proofs about other definite mathematical objects, such as numbers or sets.

SOUNDNESS AND COMPLETENESS

I have developed the logic of quantifiers from several points of view. First I described relational structures, which I took to be the abstract structure of the possible worlds or circumstances that are of concern in mathematics and the sciences. Then I described *formalized languages*, which differ from natural languages in their simplicity and in having explicit rules that make it possible to determine in a mechanical way whether or not a string of symbols is well formed. Third, I developed a *semantics* for formalized languages. The semantics specifies precisely the conditions under which a set of values for variables in the language *satisfies* a formula in the language. Using these notions, one can say precisely what is meant by the claim that a collection of formulas in the language *entails* another formula. Recall that a set of sentences Γ *entails* a sentence S if and only if S is true in every relational structure for which all sentence in Γ are true. Fourth, I sketched a theory of *proof*. Although the intent of the theory of proof is that proofs will preserve truth, the theory of proof given made no use of any of the semantic notions; it did not use the notion of a relational structure or the notion of a set of values satisfying a formula. Nonetheless, it is possible (informally) to prove that the theory of proof and the semantic account of entailment coincide perfectly: a collection of formulas entails a formula if and only if the latter is provable from a finite subset of the former. More exactly, we have the following theorems for formalized languages of the kind considered in this chapter.

Soundness theorem   If Δ is any finite set of formulas and there is a proof of a formula S from Δ, then Δ entails S.

A much more difficult result is the converse, first proved by Kurt Gödel in his doctoral dissertation in 1930:

Completeness theorem   If Δ is any collection of formulas and Δ entails S, then there is a proof of S from formulas in Δ.

Since a proof must be a finite sequence of formulas and therefore only a finite number of assumptions can occur in any proof, an immediate corollary is the following:

Compactness theorem   If S is entailed by Δ, then S is entailed by some finite subset of Δ.

These results, which will not be proved here, tend to show that the semantics and the proof theory are in accord. It remains to be shown, however, that the logical theory I have described is really adequate to reconstruct deductive reasoning in the mathematical sciences.

THEORIES AND MODELS

The logical theory I have developed in this chapter is usually referred to as *first-order logic* because it permits quantifiers to bind variables that range over individuals but it does not contain variables that range over properties nor does it have quantifiers that bind such variables. One of the best ways to consider the richness of first-order logic is to consider some collections of sentences and formulas in formalized languages, and the collections of relational structures in which those sentences or formulas are true. First we need some convenient terminology.

Relational structures are often called *models*. In particular, a relational structure in which sentence S is true is called a model of S. Any collection Δ of formulas in a formalized language has a set of logical consequences, denoted $Cn(\Delta)$. $Cn(\Delta)$ is the set of all well-formed formulas that can be deduced from Δ or, in other words, that are entailed by Δ. For any set Δ, $Cn(\Delta)$ is *deductively closed*; that is to say, every logical consequence of $Cn(\Delta)$ is already in $Cn(\Delta)$. A deductively closed collection of formulas is called a *theory*. A theory is *consistent* if and only if it has a model. Two sentences in a language are said to be consistent if and only if their conjunction has a model.

Given a theory T, if there exists a collection Δ of formulas for which (1) there is an algorithm that determines for any formula in the language whether or not it is in Δ, and (2) $Cn(\Delta) = T$, then T is said to be *axiomati-*

zable. If there exists a *finite* set of formulas Δ such that $Cn(\Delta) = T$, then T is said to be *finitely axiomatizable*.

A theory is said to be *complete* if for every sentence S in the language of the theory, either S is in the theory or $\neg S$ is in the theory. If a relational structure is for a formal language, then every sentence in that language is either true or false in that relational structure. Hence for any relational structure, the set of all sentences true in that structure is a complete theory.

The Theory of Identity

Consider the following sequence of sentences:

$\exists x_1 \exists x_2 (\neg x_1 = x_2)$

$\exists x_1 \exists x_2 \exists x_3 (\neg x_1 = x_2 \,\&\, \neg x_1 = x_3 \,\&\, \neg x_2 = x_3)$

$\vdots$

The first sentence says that there are at least two things. The second sentence says that there are at least three things. The next sentence in the sequence will say that there are at least four things, and so on.

All models of the first sentence have two or more elements in their respective domains. Every relational structure $[D, =]$ in which D has at least two members is a model for the first sentence. Every model of the second sentence has three or more elements in its domain, and every structure with identity that has a domain of three of more members is a model of the second sentence.

Notice that every model of the second sentence above is also a model of the first sentence. Every model having a domain with at least three members is a model with a domain having at least two members. So the second sentence *entails* the first sentence. Since the second sentence has a model, the two sentences are *consistent*. We can form the set of sentences consisting of both of these sentences. Call that set Δ_3 to indicate that it is a set of sentences that says there are at least three things. By including more and more sentences in the sequence of sentences indicated above, we can form a sequence of sets of sentences, $\Delta_4, \Delta_5, \ldots, \Delta_n, \ldots$. The set Δ_n is a collection of sentences that are true in all and only structures having at least n members in their respective domains.

Now suppose we form the set that is the union of all sets Δ_n for all $n > 1$, and call the set of sentences that results Δ_ω. We use the symbol $\bigcup_n(\ldots)$ to denote the operation of taking the union of an arbitrary collection of sets indexed by n. Accordingly, $\Delta_\omega = \bigcup_n(\Delta_n)$.

The set Δ_ω contains each sentence that occurs in any of the Δ_n. $\mathrm{Cn}(\Delta_\omega)$ is a theory. In what structures is the theory true? For every $n > 1$, there is a sentence in Δ_ω that says there are at least n things. That sentence is false in any domain having fewer than n members. So for every number $n > 0$, Δ_ω is not satisfied in any domain having exactly n elements and no more. So the only structures in which all sentences in Δ_ω are true are structures having infinite domains. In fact, one can prove that all structures for the language having infinite domains are models of Δ_ω.

There is an obvious algorithm for determining, for any given sentence, whether or not that sentence is in Δ_ω. So $\mathrm{Cn}(\Delta_\omega)$ is an axiomatizable theory. It is easy to prove that it is not a finitely axiomatizable theory. One can also prove that the theory is complete.

How Can It Be Proved That $\mathrm{Cn}(\Delta_\omega)$ Is Not Finitely Axiomatizable?

First I prove a lemma needed for the proof of the theorem:

Lemma   If Δ is any set of sentences and $\mathrm{Cn}(\Delta)$ is finitely axiomatizable, then there is a finite subset of Δ that axiomatizes $\mathrm{Cn}(\Delta)$.

Proof   Suppose that A is a finite set of sentences such that $\mathrm{Cn}(A) = \mathrm{Cn}(\Delta)$. Then certainly Δ entails A. Hence by the completeness and compactness theorems, there is a finite subset of Δ, call it Φ, such that Φ entails A. So Φ is a finite subset of Δ that axiomatizes $\mathrm{Cn}(\Delta)$. Q.E.D.

Theorem $\mathrm{Cn}(\Delta_\omega)$ is not finitely axiomatizable.

Proof   Now suppose, contrary to what is to be proved, that Δ_ω is finitely axiomatizable. Then by the lemma just proved, there is a finite subset of Δ_ω that axiomatizes Δ_ω. Any such finite subset must be the same as Δ_n for some n. So Δ_n entails Δ_ω. But all the sentences in Δ_n are true in any domain that has at least n members. So they are all true in a domain that has exactly n members and is therefore finite. But Δ_ω has no finite models. So there are models of Δ_n that are not models of Δ_ω. So Δ_n does not entail Δ_ω, which is a contradiction. Since the supposition that Δ_ω is finitely axiomatizable implies a contradiction, Δ_ω is not finitely axiomatizable. Q.E.D.

Study Questions

1. Write a sentence that says there are at least four things.

2. Write a sentence that says there are exactly four things.

3. Give an argument to show that $Cn(\Delta_n)$ is not a complete theory for any n. (Hint: Show how, for any given n, to find a sentence true in one model of $Cn(\Delta_n)$ and false in another model.)

The Theory of Successor

Consider the structure $[N, 0, s, =]$, obtained from the natural numbers by ignoring the functions of addition and multiplication. Since this structure has an infinite domain, Δ_ω is true in it. So, of course, are other sentences and formulas. Consider the following:

$\forall x \neg(s(x) = 0)$ (Zero is not the successor of any number.)

$\forall y \exists x\, s(y) = x$ (Every number has a successor.)

$\forall x \forall y (s(x) = s(y) \rightarrow x = y)$ (No two distinct numbers have the same successor.)

$\forall x \neg s(x) = x$ (No number succeeds itself.)

These four sentences are true in $[N, 0, s, =]$ but do not entail all that is true in that structure. In fact, the complete theory of $[N, 0, s, =]$ can be axiomatized but it cannot be finitely axiomatized. But the four sentences just given *do* entail all of the sentences in Δ_ω. So while the theory $Cn(\Delta_\omega)$ is not finitely axiomatizable, we can extend that theory with extra vocabulary (in this case, the constant symbol 0 and the symbol for the successor function) to a finitely axiomatizable theory. Moreover, the extension is *conservative*: the extended theory entails $Cn(\Delta_\omega)$ but no other sentences that can be stated with identity alone.

Study Questions

1. Finish the proof of the following theorem:

Theorem   If theory T is any extension of $Cn(\Delta_\omega)$ that is *not* conservative, then T is inconsistent.

Proof   Since a sentence and its denial cannot both be true in a relational structure, it suffices to show that if T is a nonconservative extension of $Cn(\Delta_\omega)$, then $Cn(T)$ includes some sentence and its denial, and hence T has no model. T is an extension of $Cn(\Delta_\omega)$ means that $Cn(T) \supseteq Cn(\Delta_\omega)$; that is, every consequence of Δ_ω is a consequence of T. That T is not a conservative extension of $Cn(\Delta_\omega)$ means that there exists a sentence in the language of Δ_ω (the language with only identity as a predicate) that is a consequence of T but is not a consequence of Δ_ω. Let S be such a sentence. Since Δ_ω is complete, either S is in $Cn(\Delta_\omega)$ or $\neg S$ is. But since S is by assumption a sentence that is not a consequence of Δ_ω, $\neg S$ is in $Cn(\Delta_\omega)$. Etc.

2. Explain why the set consisting of the four sentences for the theory of successor given above has no finite model.

The Theory of Successor and Discrete Order

If we add the order relation on the natural numbers to the identity and successor relations, we are considering the structure $[N, 0, s, <, =]$. The theory of this structure is rather different from the theory of identity or of successor for the natural numbers. The complete theory of $[N, 0, s, <, =]$ is finitely axiomatizable. Here is a set of axioms:

$\forall y(\neg(y = 0) \rightarrow \exists x(y = s(x)))$

$\forall x \forall y(Lxs(y) \rightarrow (Lxy \vee x = y))$

$\forall x \forall y((Lxy \vee x = y) \rightarrow Lxs(y))$

$\forall x \neg Lx0$

$\forall x \forall y(Lxy \vee (x = y \vee Lyx))$

$\forall x \forall y(Lxy \rightarrow \neg Lyx)$

$\forall x \forall y \forall z(Lxy \rightarrow (Lyz \rightarrow Lxz)$

By adding structure to a structure that can only be described with an infinite set of axioms, we get a structure that can be completely described by a *finite* set of axioms.

The Theory of Dense Order

The ordering on the rational numbers gives the structure $[Q, <, =]$. The complete theory of this structure is also finitely axiomatizable, and it too has no finite models. The theory can be axiomatized by the following axioms:

$\forall x \forall y(Lxy \rightarrow \exists x(Lxz \,\&\, Lzy))$

$\forall y \exists x\, Lxy$

$\forall y \exists x\, Lyx$

$\forall x \neg Lxx$

$\forall x \forall y \forall z(Lxy \rightarrow (Lyz \rightarrow Lxz))$

$\forall x \forall y(Lxy \vee (x = y \vee Lyx))$

Study Questions

1. Give English paraphrases for each of the axioms in the two axiom systems just given.

2. Suppose that you are allowed to look only at a finite number of elements and their order relations. Imagine that either all of the objects are selected from a domain that is either densely ordered or discretely ordered, but you are not told which. Could you determine from the finite sample whether the objects came from a discretely ordered domain or from a densely ordered one?

TWO PARADOXES

Many familiar theories can be formalized in first-order logic. The postulates of arithmetic developed by Guiseppe Peano (1858–1932) in the nineteenth century can be formalized. In fact, I have formalized parts of that theory in the examples of previous sections. The theory of sets has been given a first-order formalization, and Euclidean geometry, hyperbolic geometry, and the geometry of spherical surfaces have also been given nice formalizations. Algebraic theories, such as the theory of real algebra, have been formalized and extensively studied. Moreover, theories that are not purely mathematical have also been given first-order formalizations. These include the classical mechanics of particles, classical rigid-body mechanics, parts of genetics, the special theory of relativity, parts of cosmology, and many other theories. There are, however, some fundamental notions that escape representation in first-order theories. Various conceptions of cardinality cannot be represented, even though they seem to be fundamentally important ideas. The notion of truth cannot be adequately represented, even though the notion is essential to the semantics of first-order logic.

The Finite and the Infinite

I have already described a formal theory, Δ_ω, that expresses the concept of infinity. Every model of the theory has an infinite domain, and every infinite domain serves as a model of the theory. But consider the concept of *finiteness*. Every domain that is not infinite is finite. So it might seem reasonable to expect that if the idea of infinity can be represented in a first-order theory, so can the idea of finiteness. Such a representation would consist in a theory that has every finite domain as a model and has no models with infinite domains. We cannot form such a theory by asserting the denial of Δ_ω, because Δ_ω is not a sentence but rather an infinite set of sentences. Sets do not have denials; sentences do. Intuitively, to express the idea of finiteness, we would need to find a way to assert within the language of Δ_ω that *some sentence* in that set is false. It turns out that there is no way to do that. In fact, the following can be proved:

Theorem   In any first-order language, every theory that has models of every finite cardinality has an infinite model.

Traditional metaphysics held that the notion of infinity is obscure, but the notion of finiteness is not troublesome. In modern logic things seem to get reversed. Infinity is easy, finitude is obscure.

But infinity is not that easy. Recall that in chapter 1 we considered theorems of Cantor's that show that for any set Ω, the set of all subsets of Ω (the power set of Ω) has a larger cardinality than Ω. So the set of all subsets of the set of natural numbers is larger than the set of natural numbers, and the set of all subsets of the set of all subsets of the natural numbers is larger still, and so on. There are infinities, bigger infinities, still bigger infinities, and so on forever. But the differences among infinite sets with different cardinalities cannot be represented by any first-order theory. One of the remarkable results proved early in this century is the following:

Löwenheim-Skolem theorem   In any first-order language, every theory that has an infinite model has an infinite model of every cardinality.

The Löwenheim-Skolem theorem is sometimes described as a paradox. It states a fact about first-order theories, but since that fact presupposes that we can distinguish between infinite sets with different cardinalities, the fact itself cannot be faithfully represented as a claim within any first-order theory.

The moral seems to be that not everything that it makes sense to say can be said in a first-order language. Many philosophers and logicians have drawn that conclusion. More powerful logical systems (systems that in fact originated in Frege's work) permit one to distinguish between different infinities. The essential thing is that while sentences in first-order languages have only variables that range over individuals in a domain, more powerful logical systems have variables that also range over arbitrary subsets of a domain. In first-order logic we can say that all individuals in the domain have some property or that there exists an individual with some property, but in more powerful logical systems we can also say that there exist properties and relations with some *second-order* property.

Some philosophers and logicians resist the conclusion that first-order logic is inadequate and hold that everything can be said in a first-order language. They may do so, for example, because they doubt that such abstract objects as sets, properties, and relations really exist, and they do not want to use a formal language that logically commits them to the existence of such entities. Those with such a view seem to be stuck with the position that there are no *absolute* notions of finitude or of infinite cardinalities. Or more radically and skeptically, they may recall Gassendi's riposte to Descartes: he who says that anything is infinite attributes to a thing that he does not comprehend a name that he does not understand. Perhaps the same is true for he who says that anything is finite.

The Liar

In the the Old Testament, the Cretan says that all Cretans are liars. Suppose he had said that all Cretans lie whenever they speak. Then what he said could not have been true, since if it were true, everything said by a Cretan is false, and since what he said was said by a Cretan, if it were true it would be false.

The biblical paradox leads to a modern logical paradox. This time the paradox is not peculiar to first-order logic but intrinsic to the very idea of giving a theory of truth for a language. Let us make one assumption about truth and falsity:

Assumption   No sentence in a language is both true in that language and false in that language.

It is easy to show that if a language is strong enough to say certain things about the truth or falsity of sentences in that language, then the assumption must be contradicted. Consider the following sentence:

(1) Sentence (1) is false.

There are only three possibilities: (1) is true in English, (1) is false in English, or (1) is neither true nor false in English. Suppose that (1) is true. Then since (1) says that (1) is false, what it says is false. So if (1) is true, it is also false, which contradicts the assumption. Suppose that (1) is false. Then since (1) says that (1) is false, what it says is true. Hence (1) is true. So if (1) is false, then it is true, which contradicts the assumption. Finally, suppose that (1) is neither true nor false. Then since (1) says that it is false and it is neither true nor false, what it says of itself is false. Hence if (1) is neither true nor false, it is false, which is a logical contradiction.

There are several responses to this argument. One response is to try to find some logical flaw in the proof. One might think that there is something unclear about the idea of English as a definite object about which one can produce proofs. One of the great logicians of this century, Alfred Tarski, showed that essentially the same result can be obtained for certain formalized first-order languages. So the paradox does not result from the vagueness of the English language. Some think that the argument contains some subtle equivocation in the notion of truth, but there is little agreement about what the equivocation might be. Another response is to accept the conclusion. If one accepts the conclusion, then any of several lines of thought suggest themselves. One is to try to introduce a new technical notion that is like the notion of truth but does not have the unwelcome property that for some sentences it both applies and does not apply. Another is to attempt to isolate all discourses that, like sentence (1), produce paradox, and to avoid applying semantic notions to them. There is no single widely accepted solution.

In a way, the liar paradox is refreshing. We started with a pre-Christian problem, to characterize valid deductive arguments, and that quest led 2,500 years later to a modern, mathematical theory of proof, meaning, and deductive argument. It is amusing and ironic to find the resulting theory perplexed by a simple remark recorded more than 2,000 years ago.

Study Questions

1. Sentence (1) refers to itself, but not all forms of the liar paradox require self-reference. What can be inferred about the truth or falsity (or lack thereof) of sentences (2) and (3) below?

(2) Sentence (3) is true.

(3) Sentence (2) is false.

2. What can be inferred about the truth or falsity (or lack thereof) of sentences (4) and (5) below?

(4) Sentence (5) is neither true nor false.

(5) Sentence (4) is neither true nor false.

Review Questions

1. In this chapter I have given a theory of proof and proofs of theorems about the theory of proof. What is the relation between the two?

2. What is meant by an *inductive definition*?

3. Give examples of each of the following: (a) two complete, finitely axiomatizable theories that each has no finite model but that are inconsistent with one another, (b) a theory that is not finitely axiomatizable, (c) a theory that is finitely axiomatizable and has no finite models but is not complete.

4. Explain the difference between discrete order and dense order.

5. Explain why the compactness theorem follows from the completeness theorem.

6. Suppose that you are given a finite sample of objects and the facts about their relations with one another, either all drawn from a relational structure that has discrete order with first endpoint or all drawn from a relational structure that has discrete order without endpoints. Could you tell from the sample which structure it came from? Why or why not?

7. Explain how to construct the rational numbers from the integers.

8. Suppose that someone devised a theory of proof for which no completeness theorem is true. What would you conclude about the adequacy of the theory of proof, and why? Suppose that someone devised a theory of proof for which no soundness theorem is true. What would you conclude about the adequacy of the theory of proof, and why?

Further Reading

Studies in mathematical logic

Bell, J. L., and M. Machover. *A Course in Mathematical Logic*. Amsterdam: North-Holland, 1977.

Copi, Irving. *Introduction to Logic*. New York: Macmillan, 1972.

Etchemendy, John. *The Concept of Logical Consequence*. Cambridge: Harvard University Press, 1990.

Gabbay, Dov M., and Franz Guenthner, eds. *Alternatives to Classical Logic*. Boston: D. Reidel, 1986.

Gödel, Kurt. *Collected Works*. Vol. 1. Ed. Solomon Feferman. Oxford: Oxford University Press, 1986.

Henkin, Leon, ed. *The Axiomatic Method*. Amsterdam: North-Holland Publishing Co., 1959.

Hintikka, Jaakko, ed. *The Philosophy of Mathematics*. London: Oxford University Press, 1969.

Mates, Benson. *Elementary Logic*. New York: Oxford University Press, 1965.

Quine, W. V. O. *Philosophy of Logic*. Englewood Cliffs, N.J.: Prentice-Hall, 1970.

Salmon, Nathan U., and Scott Soames, ed. *Propositions and Attitudes*. New York: Oxford University Press, 1988.

Tarski, Alfred. *Logic, Semantics, Metamathematics.* Oxford: Oxford University Press, 1956.

Van Heijenoort, Jean. *From Frege to Gödel: A Source Book in Mathematical Logic, 1879–1931.* Cambridge: Harvard University Press, 1967.

Liar paradox
Barwise, Jon, and John Etchemendy. *The Liar: An Essay on Truth and Circularity.* New York: Oxford University Press, 1987.

Martin, Robert L., ed. *The Paradox of the Liar.* New Haven: Yale University Press, 1970.

Part II

EXPERIENCE, KNOWLEDGE, AND BELIEF

Chapter 7
SKEPTICISM

INTRODUCTION

Euclid's geometry was the paradigm of science shared by Aristotle, Descartes, and many people in between. At roughly the same time that Descartes was reaffirming this conception of knowledge and attempting to give arguments for a "method" adapted to it, revolutionary developments in science were replacing the Cartesian view of how knowledge is acquired with a quite different conception. Andreas Vesalius had examined human cadavers to produce new revelations about human anatomy; Galileo had discovered sunspots, found the satellites of Jupiter, and observed their rotation about that planet; William Gilbert had investigated the properties of the magnet; and William Harvey had done experiments to argue for the circulation of the blood.

These and other discoveries did not seem to have the form expected by either Aristotelian or Cartesian science. There were no intuitions of general principles about lodestones or human physiology from which everything else in these subjects was deduced. Instead, examples of particular phenomena were observed, found to be repeatedly and regularly produced, and thus taken to hold generally. Inferences from particular instances to general conclusions were called *inductive*, and they were contrasted both with the direct intuition of general principles and with deductive inferences.

Induction might lead to general conclusions from observed regularities, but the goal of the new science was to go beyond simple generalizations of observed regularities to find their causes and the laws governing those causes. Scientists of the time searched for the hidden powers, causes, and structures that produce appearances, and they searched for the laws that govern such powers, causes, and structures. In the sky the sun and the stars appear to move, but according to Copernicus, that is only appearance, and in fact, it is the earth that moves. Harvey observed that living humans invariably have a pulse, but he explained the pulse by postulating a hidden mechanism not available to the eye: the heart acts as a pump and sends the blood through tubes in the body. Copernicus and Harvey and Galileo seemed to be penetrating the "hidden springs" of nature, but how could they do so? What could the method be? Different answers to these questions were offered by two great English scientists and philosophers: Francis Bacon and Isaac Newton.

BACON'S INDUCTIVE METHOD

Francis Bacon's *Novum Organum*, published in 1620, was an influential statement of the goals and methods of the new science. Bacon saw clearly that the aims of science are not just to generalize observed regularities but more fundamentally to find the causes of those regularities. In keeping with the scholastic terminology of the day, Bacon usually wrote not of causes but instead of "forms"; even so, by that term he meant those properties of things that together are responsible for phenomena of scientific interest. Rather like Aristotle, he thought of the content of scientific

---

Francis Bacon

Francis Bacon was born in 1561 to a politically prominent English family. He studied at Cambridge University, where he learned and came to dislike Aristotelian philosophy. After a period on the Continent, he returned to England and studied law, thereafter making his living through law, the patronage of various nobles, and a small inheritance. When James I succeeded Elizabeth I to the throne of England, Bacon prospered and eventually became Chancellor. In 1621 he was accused of taking bribes; he was found guilty of the accusations by a Parliamentary court and sentenced to an enormous fine, imprisonment, and disbarment. Most of the sentence was not carried out, but Bacon never again held public office, and he died five years later. He wrote systematically on scientific method between 1605 and the end of his life, but he missed many of the scientific developments of his day. He did not know William Gilbert, although Gilbert was a contemporary and was the physician of both Elizabeth I and James I. William Harvey was Bacon's own physician, but Bacon seems not to have known of Harvey's work on the circulation of the blood. But others knew of Bacon. Harvey said that he "writes philosophy like a lord chancellor."

laws as conjunctions of conditions necessary and sufficient for observed effects.

Bacon thought that scientific laws are to be discovered by applying the appropriate kind of reasoning to observations of particular cases. If one is studying the cause of heat, for example, then instances of hot things and cold things must be observed, and from those instances Reason must draw a conclusion as to the general cause of heat. The important questions for scientific method concern what observations to make and how to reason from the observations to conclusions about causes.

Bacon's answer was clear but not fully precise. To discover the cause of a phenomenon such as heat or light or gravity, one should collect three different kinds of instances. Bacon thought of the instances of each kind as formed into "tables" or lists. One should first collect a list of *positive instances* of the phenomenon in question. A list of positive instances of heat should include many instances of distinct kinds, incorporating as much variety as possible. Second, one should collect a list of *negative instances*. The negative instances should be chosen to be as similar to the positive instances as is possible while still failing to exhibit the phenomenon to be explained. Third, one should form a list of *degrees*. The list of degrees is like the list of positive instances but the instances in it are ordered by the intensity of the effect. A list of degrees of heat contains positive instances of heat, ordered from instances in which heat is least apparent and least intense to those in which heat is most apparent and most intense.

Bacon's primary example was the investigation of the cause of heat. He provided lengthy lists, of which the following are only a selection of the instances:

Positive instances of heat
• The rays of the sun, especially in summer and at noon
• The rays of the sun reflected and condensed, as between mountains or on walls, and most of all in burning glasses and mirrors.
• Fiery meteors
• Burning thunderbolts
• Eruptions of flame from the cavities of mountains
• All flames
• Ignited solids
• Natural warm baths
• Liquids boiling or heated

Negative instances of heat
· Rays of the moon, stars, and comets
· The rays of the sun on the tops of mountains where the air is thin
· The rays of the sun in the polar regions
· The rays that emerge from a reverse burning glass
· Rotten wood that shines by night but is not hot
· The scales of fish and the body of the glowworm, which give light but
are not warm

Degrees of heat
· Everyday inanimate substances, such as rocks and metals
· Substances formerly hot, such as horse dung, lime, and ashes from fires
· The heat of animals
· Animal heat is increased by motion and exercise, wine, feasting, sex,
fevers, and pains
· The heat of the sun in warm climates
· The heat of a flame, which depends on the body ignited

Bacon supposed not only that the investigator has such lists of positive
and negative instances as well as instances of various degrees but also
that the investigator knows the properties of each instance. Sometimes
his own lists include commentaries that indicate properties he takes to
be relevant. Thus he tells us that on mountaintops the air is thin and
that the body of the glowworm gives light.

From the lists, Bacon proposed that the cause or "form" be found by
seeking a conjunction of properties such that

· each property in the conjunction occurs in every positive instance,
· in every negative instance, some property in the conjunction is absent,
· the combination of properties increases in intensity as the phenomenon
increases in intensity.

Bacon did not explain how the intensity of a combination of distinct
properties is to be measured, nor did he explain how a combination
of the kind required is to be found. But he did give an example, the
cause of heat, which he concluded is the chaotic motion of the very
small parts of a thing, but the procedure by which he found this explanation is not fully clear.

Bacon's method became a standard for the new science in the late
seventeenth century and after, and it has been subsequently redescribed in
many different ways, sometimes in more detail than Bacon himself pro-

vided. In the nineteenth century John Stuart Mill wrote an influential logic text, *A System of Logic*, that treats induction almost exactly as Bacon did (but without giving Bacon any credit). Mill proposed three "methods" for inferring causes: the method of agreement, the method of difference, and the method of concomitant variation. The method of agreement is simply the rule, Infer that the properties common to all instances of an effect are its causes. The method of difference is the rule, Infer that the properties common to all instances of an effect and absent from all noninstances of the effect are the causes. The method of concomitant variation is the rule, Infer that the combination of properties that increases in intensity as the effect increases in intensity, and decreases in intensity as the effect decreases in intensity is the cause of the effect to be explained. Mill's methods are simply a decomposition of Bacon's procedure. In the 1950s a number of psychologists became interested in how children learn new concepts from old concepts. One of the very first proposals is that they do so by a procedure that is essentially Bacon's. Today elaborations of Bacon's procedures find little application in studies of human psychology, but they are widely used in artificial intelligence procedures that simulate learning.

THE NEWTONIAN REVOLUTION

In 1686 Isaac Newton published the first Latin edition of his *Philosophiae Naturalis Principia Mathematica* (Mathematical Principles of Natural Philosophy). If ever a work of ideas shook civilization, Newton's *Principia* did. Not only did it establish the content and methods of much of physics as we still understand that subject, it also provided *the* example for the next century of how scientific knowledge is to be acquired.

Newton's masterpiece is divided into four parts. The first part is a statement of the purpose of the work, together with a system of definitions and axioms. The second part, book 1, is a series of theorems on the motions of bodies subject to forces of various mathematical forms. Together with the definitions and axioms of the first part, book 1 forms an axiomatic system much like Euclid's *Elements* (and in fact Newton assumes without comment all of Euclidean geometry), but the subject is motion rather than the relations of figures. Book 2 concerns hydrostatics (the motions of bodies in fluids, such as air and water) and wave motion. It too proceeds axiomatically, investigating the laws of motion that follow from the axioms under various assumptions about forces of resistance. Newton's theorems are illustrated by applications to various hydraulic experiments. In book 3, Newton uses the theorems deduced in book 1, together with observed laws of planetary motion, to argue for the law of universal gravitation and then to deduce consequences of that law and the laws of motion.

Newton was not concerned with providing a theory that merely generalizes observed regularities. His goals were deeper. In Newton's conception, what we see and observe are apparent motions—the motions of bodies relative to one another and relative to the position we inhabit. The effects we see in nature—the motions of the planets, the tides, falling bodies—are effects compounded of several different causes or forces. But in Newton's conception, besides apparent motions there are *real motions*, that is, motions with respect to absolute space. And there are real causes as well, those fundamental forces that apparent causes are composed of.

Newton thought simple experiments could demonstrate that there is real motion with respect to absolute space and that real motion is different from the relative motion of one body with respect to another. If a bucket of water is rotated, at first the bucket moves relative to the water within it, and initially the surface of the water is flat. But shortly the rotation of the bucket is communicated to the water and the water begins to rotate as well, until eventually the water is rotating as fast as the bucket, and the two, water and bucket, are no longer rotating relative to one another. But as the water in the bucket begins to rotate, the surface of the water ceases to be flat and becomes more and more concave, so that when the water is rotating with the rotating bucket and the two are no longer rotating with respect to one another, the water has crept up the sides of the bucket (figure 7.1). Thus there are two states in which the bucket and the water are at rest with respect to one another. In one of them, the initial state

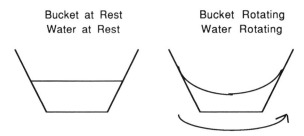

Figure 7.1
The rotating-bucket experiment

before rotation, the surface of the water is flat. In the other state, when both water and bucket are rotating, the surface of the water is concave. The difference must be caused by something, and it cannot be caused by the relative motion of the water and the bucket, since there is none in either case. Newton concluded that the difference is caused by different states of motion with respect to absolute space: rotation with respect to absolute space causes the water to recede from the axis of motion and makes the surface of the water concave.

The point of the *Principia* is to show how to infer true motions and causes from apparent motions and causes.

It is indeed a matter of great difficulty to discover, and effectually to distinguish, the true motions of particular bodies from the apparent; because the parts of that immovable space, in which those motions are performed, do by no means come under the observation of our senses. Yet the thing is not altogether desperate; for we have some arguments to guide us, partly from the apparent motions, which are the differences of the true motions partly from the forces which are the causes and effects of the true motions. . . . But how we are to obtain the true motions from their causes, effects, and apparent differences, and the converse, shall be explained more at large in the following treatise. For to this end it was that I composed it.[1]

Aside from the assumptions of Euclidean geometry, Newton's axioms consist of his three laws of motion:

• Every body continues in its state of rest or of uniform motion in a straight line unless it is compelled to change that state by forces impressed upon it.
• The change of motion is proportional to the motive force impressed and is made in the direction of the straight line in which that force is impressed.
• To every action there is always opposed an equal reaction; that is, the mutual actions of two bodies upon each other are always equal and directed to contrary parts.

Newton's evidence for these three laws consisted of a variety of simple experiments with pendulums conducted by Newton's contemporaries—Christopher Wren, John Wallis, and Christian Huygens ("the greatest geometers of our times")—and by Newton himself. Other evidence included Galileo's law (that bodies falling freely toward earth cover a distance proportional to the square of the time of fall), the motions of projectiles, the motions of magnets floating on water, and simple mechanical experiments. Experiments of these kinds exhibit either the composition of forces required by the first two laws or the conservation of momentum required by the third law.

In these experimental arguments for the laws of motion, Newton assumed that something about the *forces* is known. For example, he assumes that in Galileo's experiments with falling bodies, it is known that the force of gravity acting on each body is constant and the "quantity of matter" or mass of the falling body does not change. "When a body is falling, the uniform force of its gravity acting equally, impresses, in equal intervals of time, equal forces upon that body, and therefore generates equal velocities; and in the whole time impresses a whole force, and generates a whole velocity proportional to the time. And the spaces described in proportional times are as the product of the velocities and the times; that is, as the squares of the times."[2] In other words, given that the force of gravity is constant in a falling body, the second law requires that the acceleration of each body be constant, and hence that the distance a body falls is proportional to the square of the time elapsed.

Galileo's law also provides the basis for a more detailed argument for the second law of motion, an argument that does not *assume* that the force of gravity is constant. For finding that for one class of bodies the distance traveled in free fall is proportional to the square of the elapsed time, you might *use* Newton's second law to infer that for this class of bodies the force of gravity is constant for each body. Then by induction you might conclude that for any body in free fall near the surface of the earth, the force of gravity is constant. And finally, by applying this conclusion to a new class of bodies in free fall and measuring the time elapsed to cover a fixed distance of fall, you might conclude that the second law of motion is satisfied. This argument pulls the second law of motion up by its own bootstraps by assuming that the law is true of one system of bodies in order to obtain a generalization about the force of gravity, which it then applies to another system of bodies in order to test the second law. Later, in book 3 of the *Principia*, Newton gives a much more complex argument with a similar structure.

While book 1 of the *Principia* is a work of great mathematical power, it is book 3 that shows Newton's new method in its most dramatic application. Here Newton gave an argument for the law of universal gravitation. The argument has an intricate structure, but the general idea is quite simple. Newton started with observed regularities about the motions of the sun, moon, and planets and the properties of pendula here on earth. Using these regularities and logical consequences of his three laws as *premises*, he then deduced that there exists a force attracting the planets to the sun, a force attracting the satellites of Jupiter to the planet Jupiter, and a force attracting the moon to the earth. He further proved from these premises that the force in question varies inversely as the square of the distance between the bodies and that the force is proportional to the products of the masses of the bodies. Accordingly, from generalizations induced from observed regularities and from his three laws of motion, Newton deduced that there exist bodies in which one body attracts the other with a force given by the equation $F = GMM'/r^2$, where G is a constant, M is the mass of one of the bodies, M' is the mass of the other body, and r is the distance between them.

Newton then inferred *inductively* that for *every* pair of particles in the universe, there is such a force between them. Using the law of gravitational force, he was able to compute the relative masses of many of the planets and the sun and hence to estimate the center of mass of the solar system, which he hypothesized to be at rest with respect to absolute space.

Newton placed his argument, which he called a "general induction from the phenomena," within a general method for the conduct of science. He prefaced the argument with a system of "Rules of Reasoning in Philosophy" and then applied the rules to justify particular steps in his general induction of the law of gravitation. The rules of reasoning have to do with the circumstances in which one may legitimately induce general conclusions about causes:

Rule I   We are to admit no more causes of natural things than such as are both true and sufficient to explain their appearances.

Rule II   Therefore to the same natural effects we must, as far as possible, assign the same causes.

Rule III   The qualities of bodies, which admit neither intensification nor remission of degrees, and which are found to belong to all bodies within the reach of our experiments, are to be esteemed the universal qualities of all bodies whatsoever.

Rule IV   In experimental philosophy we are to look upon propositions inferred by general induction from phenomena as accurately or very nearly true, notwithstanding any contrary hypotheses that may be imagined, till such time as other phenomena occur, by which they may either be made more accurate, or liable to exceptions.[3]

Rule I sounds circular: How are we to know which are the "true" causes? But Newton used the rule in a way that was not circular. When he argued for the existence of a force in nature, such as the force of gravitation, and found that force sufficient to explain some phenomenon, such as the tides, he took rule I to justify the conclusion that no other explanation need be sought. Rules I and II together amount to a complex (and rather vague) claim that in science we should proceed as though the world is causally simple. Rule III is the basic inductive rule, applied to properties things either have or don't have, but not to values of variable quantities. Rule IV was meant to exclude alternative explanations of phenomena. In Newton's argument for the law of universal gravitation, *instances* of the law were obtained by applying independently confirmed laws of motion to phenomena. The law of gravitation and the laws of motion in turn explain the motions of the planets and pendula used to derive instances of the law of gravitation. Alternative explanations of the motions of the planets and the motions of pendula might be concocted, but if these alternative explanations postulate regularities for which instances cannot be obtained from the phenomena (by independently confirmed laws, such as the laws of motion), then rule IV says that these alternative explanations are to be rejected.

Newton's argument for universal gravitation and the general achievement of the *Principia* formed the framework for much of science in the eighteenth and even the nineteenth centuries. Later physicists sought to establish the existence of other forces and their laws through arguments that paralleled Newton's, while philosophers of science believed that they saw in Newton's arguments the most penetrating insights into the structure of nature.

ANCIENT INDUCTIVE SKEPTICISM

Whether in Newton's "general induction" or in Bacon's simpler framework, inductive inference is subject to an important objection. The objection was apparent to the ancient Greeks, and it is one of the reasons why Plato, for one, sought other grounds for claims to knowledge.

In one passage in *The Meno*, Plato pointed out the difficulty with inference from particular facts to general conclusions. In the dialogue, Socrates and his acquaintance, Meno, are applying the Socratic method to attempt to answer the question, What is virtue? The method is to consider various hypotheses about what constitutes virtue and to confront each hypothesis with various cases to see whether the cases accord with the hypothesis or provide a counterexample to it. (Socrates and Meno agree as to whether or not something is virtuous.) When a counterexample is found to the current hypothesis, a new hypothesis is tried. Eventually Meno tires of the enterprise and asks Socrates a pointed question about how, by this method, one could ever know the correct characterization of virtue:

Meno: How will you look for it, Socrates, when you do not know at all what it is? How will you aim to search for something you do not know at all? If you should meet with it, how will you know that this is the thing that you did not know?[4]

Many commentators, including Aristotle in his *Posterior Analytics*, understand this passage to pose a problem about recognizing an object of which only a description is known, or about referring to an object that is unknown in one or another respect. But Plato has hit on a point that is at once simpler, deeper, and more precise. Consider any universal hypothesis, such as "All ravens are black" or "All virtuous people are just" or "All pure water boils at 100 degrees centigrade at 1 atmosphere of pressure." Suppose that we collect particular cases of things that are ravens and things that are not or, as the case may be, of people that are virtuous and people that are not or of the boiling points of samples of pure water. Suppose that after looking at a sufficiently large sample, we conclude that all ravens are indeed black, that virtuous people are just, or that all pure water boils at 100 degrees centigrade at 1 atmosphere pressure. And suppose that when we draw these conclusions, we are right, the conclusions are in fact true. Plato has Meno ask how we will *know* the conclusions are true. For even if we are in fact right about the boiling point of water, it is still *logically possible* that some as yet unexamined sample of pure water will boil at a different temperature at 1 atmosphere of pressure. Even if we are really in a world in which no such sample exists and we believe we are in such a world, how, after examining only a finite sample, can we know that we are in such a world?

The answer depends on what is meant by *knowledge*. For Plato, someone can know a proposition only if the proposition is true, the person believes it, and the person also knows *why* the proposition is true. Plato had a detailed theory of what is required to know why a proposition is true, but for our purposes, the important point is that Plato held that knowledge of a proposition requires that one believe it through a process that *guarantees* or *necessitates* the truth of the belief. Thus, according to Plato, for someone to know that all ravens are black after having examined a finite sample of ravens, the person must have formed a belief in such a way that the occurrence of the belief guarantees the truth of "All ravens are black." The belief must be brought about by a mark or, as the ancients would have said, a *criterion* of its truth. A belief occasioned by a criterion of truth will be certainly true, and no further evidence need be examined. Meno's objection is that from a logical point of view the evidence of a finite sample contains no such criterion for a universal claim.

Plato's solution to Meno's problem is to claim that there is an internal criterion within the inquirer. By some method, one considers hypothesis after hypothesis, confronting each with the evidence, according to the Socratic procedure. When eventually one hits upon the true hypothesis, some inner recognition guarantees its truth. The criterion is not in the evidence that the inquirer has used to reject other hypotheses before arriving at the true one; the criterion is in the inquirer. All that the evidence does is to prompt the inquirer to recognize a conclusion that the inquirer already implicitly knew. Discovery is recollection. The latter part of the dialogue attempts to illustrate this claim by having Socrates prompt a slave boy, supposed ignorant of all geometry, to produce the Pythagorean theorem by considering a sequence of examples and counterexamples.

The skepticism of Meno's question was endorsed by a number of Hellenistic writers. Several schools of thought developed in the fourth century B.C., and many of them continued to be developed into the second century A.D. One of these schools of thought, Pyrrhonism, took its name from Pyrrho of Elis (circa 360–275 B.C.). The main source of the views of this school of thought is the writings of Sextus Empiricus (circa A.D. 200). He argues for a great variety of skeptical doubts. One of his doubts is that there is any such thing as a criterion, whether internal or in the evidence itself, and hence Sextus doubts that induction can provide knowledge:

It is also easy, I consider, to set aside the method of induction. For, when they propose to establish the universal from the particulars by means of induction, they will effect this by a review either of all or of some of the particular instances. But if they review some, the induction will be insecure, since some of the particulars omitted in the induction may contravene the universal; while if they are to review all, they will be toiling at the impossible, since the particulars are infinite and indefinite. Thus on both grounds, as I think, the consequence is that induction is invalidated.[5]

The arguments given by Plato and Sextus depend on a purely mathematical point: no procedure is mathematically possible that, in every logically possible world or circumstance, will correctly decide the truth or falsity of a universal hypothesis from a finite sample of singular facts. It is not simply that we haven't chanced to think of such a procedure. None is possible, any more than it is possible that $2 + 2 = 5$. Although Plato and Sextus don't give rigorous proofs, they make it plain that they see the idea for a proof: Suppose there were a procedure that reliably decides the truth or falsity of a universal hypothesis H in every logically possible world. Then in any logically possible world W in which H is true, there must exist finite evidence E true in W such that when the procedure is given E, it decides that H is true. But for *any* finite evidence E consistent with a universal hypothesis H, there is, besides the logically possible world W in which E is true and H is true, another logically possible world V in which E is true and H is *false*. So the procedure will give the wrong output on evidence E in world V. Hence, no reliable procedure of the kind desired is logically possible.

Study Questions

1. Imagine a procedure that is given a series of particular facts about a domain and after each new fact outputs one of the following: *, T, F. The asterisk indicates that the procedure makes no conjecture, "T" indicates that the procedure claims some hypothesis H is true, and "F" indicates that the procedure claims H is false. Once T or F are output, the procedure continues to output the same value ever after. Assume that every singular fact in the domain will eventually be presented to the procedure, but the facts may be presented in any order, and any fact may be repeated any number of times. Say that H can be *verified* if there exists a procedure that will output T in every possible domain in which H is true; say that H can be *falsified* if there exists a procedure that will output F in every possible domain in which H is false; say that H can be *decided* if there exists a procedure that will output T in every possible domain in which H is true and will output F in every possible domain in which H is false. Which of the following kinds of hypotheses can be verified, falsified, or decided: (a) a singular claim about a particular fact, e.g., "Sam is a black raven," (b) a universal hypothesis, e.g., "All ravens are black," (c) an existential hypothesis, e.g., "There exists a black raven."

2. Give an example of a sentence that cannot be verified or falsified by any collection of singular sentences or facts.

3. Prove that if hypothesis H can be verified and also falsified, then H can be decided.

4. Suppose that we change the requirements of the procedure. Once the procedure outputs T or F, it is no longer required to keep outputting the same conjecture. The procedure is allowed to change its conjecture: if T or F is output on some evidence E, the reverse (F or T, respectively) may be output on some larger finite set of evidence E' including E. Say that H can be *verified in the limit* if there exists a procedure that outputs only T in all and only possible domains in which H is true, after some finite number of conjectures. Say that H can be *falsified in the limit* if there exists a procedure that outputs only F in all and only possible domains in which H is false, after some finite number of conjectures. Say that H can be *decided in the limit* if there exists a procedure that output only T in every possible domain

in which H is true, after some finite number of conjectures and that outputs only F in every possible domain in which H is true, after some finite number of conjectures. Which of the following kinds of hypotheses can be verified, falsified, or decided in the limit: (a) a singular claim about a particular fact, e.g., "Sam is a black raven," (b) a universal hypothesis, e.g., "All ravens are black," (c) an existential hypothesis, e.g., "There exists a black raven."

5. Can the example you gave in answer to question 2 be verified or falsified in the limit? Can you think of a sentence that cannot be verified or falsified in the limit?

HUME'S INDUCTIVE SKEPTICISM

The difficulty with inductive inference is that it can be *unreliable*. If every observed object has a certain feature, it is logically possible that some (or even all) objects that have not yet been observed will not have that property, or that objects that have the property at all observed times will not have it at subsequent times. Many of the ancient Greeks thought the heavens were perfect and unalterable, for they exhibited perfectly regular motions that seemed never to change. But then in the sixteenth century there appeared a new star (now thought to be a supernova): the heavens did change. Until the eighteenth century, no means had ever been found to synthesize a biological chemical from inorganic chemicals, but then Friedrich Wöhler found a way to synthesize urea. Whenever we draw conclusions about the unobserved based on samples in our experience, we risk the possibility that our conclusions will be false. If our conclusions may be false, we cannot be justified in being certain of them. If we cannot be justified in being certain of our conclusions, then, according to the conception of knowledge that endured from Plato to Descartes, we cannot have knowledge.

The new science of the seventeenth century prospered by ignoring the traditional objections to induction, but those objections were not altogether forgotten. The writings of the ancient skeptics were known in the sixteenth and seventeenth centuries, and the problem was obvious enough in any case. Thomas Hobbes complained that inductive inference was no more than guessing, and Cartesian scientists resisted the empirical arguments of Newton and Boyle and others. But in the writings of David Hume, an eighteenth-century philosopher and historian, the old skeptical concerns about induction were revived and elaborated most forcefully in a new philosophical idiom.

Hume's skeptical arguments were formulated within a psychological theory that he adopted from other English philosophers, notably John

Locke and George Berkeley. Among the contents of mental life, Hume distinguished between ideas and impressions. *Impressions* are the contents of sensation, of experience, whether of the external world or of our own feelings and thoughts. In Hume's way of talking, *ideas* are either memories of impressions or thoughts formed by combining such memories. Hume writes of ideas and impressions as though they are so many pieces that can be combined together or taken apart. An impression is not the entire gestalt of experience at any moment; instead, it is some aspect of experience. If you see a red ball at rest on the green grass in a yard on a day when the sky is blue, you have separate impressions of red, green, and blue, as well as an impression of a round thing and so on. Any of these separate impressions may be copied in memory to form ideas and may be combined with other ideas to form new complex ideas. There is nothing novel in this part of his psychological theory: we see much the same view in the writing of Descartes and Hobbes. But Hume goes further.

Ideas combine and separate in thought according to natural law. The principles that determine whether or not ideas are associated with one another have to do with the contents of those ideas, with what they are ideas about. One idea tends to lead to another if the two ideas have a similarity in their content (*resemblance*, Hume called it), if they are ideas of events that are close to one another in time or space (*contiguity*, Hume called it), or if one of the ideas is of a cause and the other idea is of the effect of that cause.

Ideas can be obtained as copies in memory of impressions or by combining copies of impressions stored in memory, but with minor exceptions, ideas can be obtained in no other way. There are no innate ideas: "When we think of a golden mountain, we only join two consistent ideas, *gold* and *mountain*, with which we were formerly acquainted. A virtuous horse we can conceive; because, from our own feeling, we can conceive virtue; and this we may unite to the figure and shape of a horse, which is an animal familiar to us. In short, all the materials of thinking are derived either from our outward or inward sentiment. The mixture and composition of these belongs alone to the mind and will."[6]

Finally, in Hume's psychology the mind has traditional faculties or capacities. The capacities of the mind are composed of the faculties of will, imagination, understanding, and so on. Reason is the operation of the understanding, and Hume thought of reasoning as deduction, analysis, and synthesis. Hume sometimes gave a peculiar psychological formulation to the question of the reliability of inductive inference as a means to produce knowledge. The issue, as he formulated it, is whether it is the understanding that acts in inductive inference, or something else.

If, as Bacon and Newton seem to suggest, inductive inference is the inference to causes from effects (and effects from causes) and to general principles about causes and effects, then the question, as Hume saw it, is how such relations may be discovered and what it would be to discover them. By "discover" Hume meant *come to know*, and he regarded knowledge as something more than an inner state of complete conviction. To know something must not only you have come to believe it, but it must also be true, and you must have come to believe it by a *reliable* means. How, then, can we acquire knowledge of causes and effects? Not by reason alone, for any attempt to predict causes from effects without experience would be arbitrary and unreliable. From the point of view of reason, the actual effect of any given cause is an arbitrary selection from a myriad of possibilities:

I shall venture to affirm, as a general proposition, which admits of no exception, that the knowledge of this relation is not, in any instance, attained by reasonings *a priori*, but arises entirely from experience, when we find, that any particular objects are constantly conjoined with each other. Let an object be presented to a man of ever so strong natural reason and abilities; if that object be entirely new to him, he will not be able, by the most accurate examination of its sensible qualities, to discovery any of its cause or effects. Adam, though his rational faculties be supposed at the very first, entirely perfect, could not have inferred from the fluidity, and transparency of water, that it would suffocate him, or from the light and warmth of fire, that it would consume him. No object ever discovers, by the qualities which appear to the senses, either the causes which produced it, or the effects which will arise from it; nor can our reason, unassisted by experience, ever draw any inference concerning real existence and matter of fact.[7]

In a word, then, every effect is a distinct event from its cause. It could not, therefore, be discovered in the cause, and the first invention or conception of it, *a priori*, must be entirely arbitrary. And even after it is suggested, the conjunction of it with the cause must appear equally arbitrary; since there are always many other effects which, to reason, must seem fully as consistent and natural. In vain, therefore, should we pretend to determine any single event, or infer any cause or effect, without the assistance of observation and experience.[8]

Hume's point could be put this way: from premises that consist of a description of how an object or collection of objects appear to us, there is no reliable course of reasoning that leads to conclusions about how the object or objects will behave.

Even *after* we have experience with an object or kind of object or circumstance, any conclusions we may draw cannot be founded on reason "or any process of the understanding."

These two propositions are far from being the same, I have found that such an object has always been attended with such an effect, and I foresee, that other objects, which are, in appearance, similar, will be attended with similar effects. I shall allow, if you please, that the one proposition may justly be inferred from the other; I know in fact, that it always is inferred. But if you insist, that the inference is made by a chain of reasoning, I desire you to produce that reasoning. The connexion between these propositions is not intuitive. There is required a medium, which may enable the mind to draw such an inference, if indeed it be drawn by reasoning and argument. What that medium is, I must confess, passes my comprehension; and it is incumbent on those to produce it, who assert, that it really exists, and is the origin of all our conclusions concerning matter of fact.[9]

Hume did not leave the matter as a challenge; he went on to give an argument that there can be no reasoning that leads from experience to general conclusions about causes and effects. The argument is that all reasoning is either deductive (or "demonstrative," as Hume called it) or else inductive (or "moral reasoning," as Hume called the latter). In the cases at issue, nothing in the premises about the experience of causes, or the experience of the succession of causes and effects, permits one to deduce a general proposition that says that a certain cause will always and everywhere have a certain effect. If we analyze the concept of causality, we find no impression corresponding to the notion of a necessary connection between cause and effect; we cannot see a connection that would warrant us in always inferring the effect from the cause. But, Hume claimed, reasoning from experience to universal claims about causes and effects cannot be a kind of inductive or moral reasoning either, on pain of circularity. His argument is a little compressed:

If we be, therefore, engaged by arguments to put trust in past experience, and make it the standard of our future judgement, these arguments must be probable only, or such as regard matter of fact and real existence, according to the division above mentioned. But that there is no argument of this kind, must appear, if our explications of that species of reasoning be admitted as solid and satisfactory. We have said, that all arguments concerning existence are founded on the relation of cause and effect, that our knowledge of that relation is derived entirely from experience, and that all our experimental conclusions proceed upon the supposition, that the future will be conformable to the past. To endeavour, therefore, the proof of this last supposition by probable arguments, or arguments regarding existence, must be evidently going in a circle, and taking that for granted which is the very point in question.[10]

The thought behind this passage seems to be something like this: The question is why the inference is reliable from the premise "I have found that such an object has always been attended with such an effect" to the conclusion "Other objects in all appearance similar will be attended with similar effects." In other words, what guarantees that whenever the premise is true, the conclusion is true, or even that in most cases in which the premise is true the conclusion is true? The answer cannot be that the inference is reliable because in most cases (or always) in our experience it has been reliable, and therefore it will be reliable in every (or almost every) instance, for that reasoning is a particular case of the inference whose reliability is in question.

Hume's conclusion is that inductive inference is not founded on reason. We have no rational grounds for believing such inferences to be reliable, and so when we do empirical science, we are not engaged in a rational activity. Inductive inferences, Hume concluded, are founded on *custom* and *habit* rather than reason. We are so constructed psychologically that from observed instances of regularities we come naturally to expect the same regularity in future instances. We cannot in many circumstances help but form such expectations. But the fact that we are driven by nature to hold certain convictions does not mean that we have any reason for holding them; it does not mean that we can give a sound argument for such convictions.

Hume's skepticism was based on the fact that there are many alternative logically possible continuations of the world we have so far experienced, as diagramed in figure 7.2. Bread has always nourished humans, but it is logically possible that after tomorrow it no longer will. Hydrogen has always had less mass than oxygen, but it is logically possible that after tomorrow it no longer will. Any conclusion we draw now about the future is potentially false. Whether or not a conclusion is true depends on which of the many logically possible alternative futures turns out to be the actual future. In some possible futures the claim that bread will nourish will be false, and in others it will be true. Whichever is actually the case, Hume's view is that *now* we don't have knowledge that bread will always nourish, because even if we happen to be correct, our conclusion was not obtained by a procedure we can know to be reliable. Lucky guesses are not knowledge.

METAPHYSICAL SKEPTICISM

Suppose somehow that we had before us all possible facts of a certain kind; suppose that by magic we could survey an infinity of possible experiences. Then Hume's or Sextus' skepticism would not apply. But one can

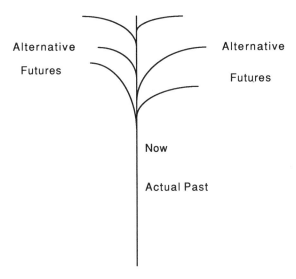

Figure 7.2

imagine that skeptical doubt would remain even then. In his *Meditations*, Descartes offers the following consideration:

> I will suppose not a supremely good God, the source of truth, but rather an evil genius, as clever and deceitful as he is powerful, who has directed his entire effort to misleading me. I will regard the heavens, the air, the earth, colors, shapes, sounds and all external things as nothing but the deceptive games of my dreams, with which he lays snares for my credulity. I will regard myself as having no hands, no eyes, no flesh, no blood, no senses, but as nevertheless falsely believing that I possess all these things.[11]

A modern version of Descartes' thought is this: Imagine that you are a brain in a vat, with your sensory nerves stimulated according to a schedule controlled by a powerful computer so as to create in you the illusion of a coherent life. In the illusion created by the stimulations of your nerves, you move about through the world, talk to other people, and so on, none of which you really do. Having imagined such a circumstance, now ask yourself how you know that it isn't true. It seems that nothing in experience, not even in an infinity of experiences, will distinguish between the case in which you are a brain in a vat and the case in which you are not.

Descartes' demon is the basis for a whole class of skeptical problems distinct from the problems of inductive inference. Consider the following claims, which every reader of this book believes:

(1) Ordinary objects and persons continue to exist when I do not perceive them.

(2) Other persons have minds.

(3) Some past events really took place.

(4) The world I perceive really exists.

The skeptical arguments that we don't *know* any of these things almost always follow the same strategy. They try to show that there is a logically possible world in which my experience will be *exactly the same* as in the real world, but in the logically possible alternative world, one or another of these three claims will be false. For me to know that (1) is true, for example, I should be able to form my conviction that (1) is true by a procedure that can reliably discriminate between worlds in which (1) is true and worlds in which (1) is false. But if there is a logically possible world in which (1) is false and in which I have the very same experiences as I actually do, then no evidence provided by experience can tell me whether or not I am in that world rather than in a world in which (1) is true. And since I cannot know that (1) is true by reason alone, I cannot know that (1) is true. The idea is that if God were to place me a number of times into worlds in some of which (1) is true and in some of which (1) is false but in all of which my experience is like what I have in *this* world, then I would never be able to tell into which kind of world I had been placed. Because I cannot discriminate, I cannot know that (1) is true, even though I believe that (1) is true and even if, as it turns out, I am correct in my belief.

We can certainly imagine a world in which objects vanish from existence when they are not perceived. George Berkeley, an English philosopher of a generation before Hume, claimed that such is actually the case. Things exist, Berkeley held, when and only when they are perceived. Berkeley maintained, however, that things do not vanish from existence when you or I are not perceiving them because God is always perceiving them. But if God should blink while we are sleeping, the world would disappear and reappear like some flashing neon sign.

The relation between mind and body is mysterious. Nothing about the physical appearance of an object shows directly that it feels or thinks. Your experience would be the same if, contrary to Newton's rules of reasoning, you and you alone had feelings and thoughts, while all other animals and persons do no more than act as if they sometimes have feelings and thoughts. That seems to be a logically possible world, and one that you cannot reliably discriminate from the world in which the second claim is true.

In the nineteenth century the growing evidence of evolution provided by geology and fossils discomforted many members of the clergy (as it does even now). Calculations based on the Old Testament led to the conclusion that according to Holy Writ the world was created less than 5,000 years ago. Rocks and fossils suggested that creatures lived and became extinct thousands and even millions of years before that. The Reverend Phillip Gosse found a way of reconciling scripture and science. Gosse proposed that when God created the world some 5,000 years ago, he created it complete with geological strata and fossils. The geological strata and the fossils within them are thus not the traces of a real past but only evidences created to make things look as if there were a real past. Gosse's strategy can be carried out more generally, as Descartes realized. There is nothing inconsistent in your assuming that all of your memories are illusory and that in fact the world was created yesterday along with your memories and the physical circumstances that corroborate your memories. For all you could experience, the two worlds, one in which memories are true or veridical, the other in which they are illusory, would be indistinguishable.

Each of these skeptical arguments uses the same strategy; in each case the object is to show that some simple and fundamental belief is underdetermined by any possible experience. It cannot even be said that the beliefs in question are inconsequential or that it would make no difference whether we believed them or not. There are any number of things in my life that I regret and wish I had done otherwise. The same is true of most people. But if I believed that the past is a fiction, I would have no regrets. Each of us judges others by their character and their history, and we probably put more weight on individual history than is useful in predicting future behavior. But if we believed the past to be an illusion, we would let go our grudges against others and take account of their fictive past only insofar as it proves useful in predicting their future behavior. If I believed that others besides myself had neither feelings nor thoughts, my moral inhibitions would vanish. Prudence tells me to avoid actions for which I might be punished, but given the chance to make use of another person without retribution, there would be no reasons to inhibit me. Metaphysics matters.

CONCLUSION

Both inductive skepticism and metaphysical skepticism challenge the thought that there is a reliable method for getting from evidence or experience to the conclusions of everyday life and science. Knowledge requires that belief be formulated in a reliable way, and therefore, skepticism argues, we have and can have no knowledge of the claims of everyday life and science. There seem to be only two ways of avoiding the skeptical conclusion:

• We can deny the skeptical description of our situation. We can maintain, for example, that we do have available all facts at once, or we can maintain that we directly experience other minds, bodies, the past, and so on, so that no inference is required to know them.
• We can deny that knowledge or rational belief requires a process of belief formation that is reliable in all logically possible worlds.

Plato took the first solution, and so have a number of English philosophers, including G. E. Moore early in this century and others even to the present. Bertrand Russell thought Moore's view had a single advantage, "the advantage of theft over honest toil," and presumably he would have thought the same of contemporary philosophers who claim we just *know* that others have minds, that there is a past, and that the world in which we live and move is no illusion.

In one way or another, attempts to develop the second response to skepticism have generated a large part of the theory of knowledge and metaphysics from the eighteenth century up to the present. These efforts have had enormous consequences outside of philosophy. They are at least in part responsible for the foundations of much of contemporary economic theory, statistics, cognitive science, and computer science. We will see some of these implications in later chapters of this book. In the next three chapters I will consider two major versions of the second response. Each variant forms a rich tradition of work that has occupied philosophers and many others besides.

Review Questions

1. Describe Bacon's method for inductively reasoning.

2. How did Newton use the rotating bucket as an argument for motion with respect to absolute space? Reproduce his reasoning in sufficient detail.

3. State Newton's rules of reasoning in your own words.

4. What constitutes knowledge for Plato? For Hume?

5. What is meant by the term "criterion of truth"?

6. Discuss the distinction between ideas and impressions for Hume.

7. Explain why there can be no innate ideas in Hume's philosophy.

8. Characterize Hume's skepticism concerning inductive inference.

9. How does the relationship between the external world and your perception of this world lead to metaphysical skepticism? How is metaphysical skepticism different from inductive skepticism?

Further Reading

Francis Bacon

Bacon, Francis. *Advancement of Learning; Novum Organum; New Atlantis.* Chicago: Encyclopaedia Britannica, 1952.

Bowen, Catherine. *Francis Bacon: The Temper of a Man.* Boston: Little, Brown, 1963.

Stephens, James. *Francis Bacon and the Style of Science.* Chicago: University of Chicago Press, 1975.

David Hume

Braham, Earnest G. *The Life of David Hume (the Terrible David).* Altrincham: J. M. Stafford, 1987.

Baier, Annette. *A Process of Sentiment: Reflections on Hume's Treatise.* Cambridge: Harvard University Press, 1991.

Fogelin, Robert J. *Hume's Scepticism in the Treatise of Human Nature.* Boston: Routledge and Kegan Paul, 1985.

Hume, David. *Enquiries Concerning the Human Understanding and Concerning the Principles of Morals.* Westport, Conn.: Greenwood Press, 1980.

Hume, David. *The Natural History of Religion.* Oxford: Oxford Universsity Press, 1976.

Hume, David. *A Treatise of Human Nature.* Oxford: Oxford University Press, 1965.

Stove, David Charles. *Probability and Hume's Inductive Scepticism.* Oxford: Oxford University Press, 1973.

Strawson, Galen. *The Secret Connection: Causation, Realism, and David Hume.* New York: Oxford University Press, 1989.

Isaac Newton

Glymour, C. *Theory and Evidence.* Princeton: Princeton University Press, 1980.

Hall, A. Rupert. *Philosophers at War: The Quarrel between Newton and Leibniz.* New York: Cambridge University Press, 1980.

Manuel, Frank Edward. *A Portrait of Isaac Newton.* New York: Da Capo Press, 1968.

Newton, Isaac. *Newton's Philosophy of Nature: Selections from His Writings.* New York: Hafner Publishing Co., 1953.

Newton, Isaac. *Sir Isaac Newton's Mathematical Principles of Natural Philosophy and His System of the World.* Berkeley: University of California Press, 1962.

Westfall, Richard S. *Never at Rest: A Biography of Isaac Newton.* New York: Cambridge University Press, 1980.

Skepticism

Barnes, Jonathan. *The Toils of Skepticism.* New York: Cambridge University Press, 1990.

Burnyeat, Miles, ed. *The Skeptical Tradition.* Berkeley: University of California Press, 1983.

Dancy, Jonathan, ed. *Perceptual Knowledge.* New York: Oxford University Press, 1988.

Stroud, Barry. *The Significance of Philosophical Scepticism.* Oxford: Oxford University Press, 1984.

Unger, Peter. *Ignorance: A Case for Scepticism.* Oxford: Oxford University Press, 1975.

Chapter 8

BAYESIAN SOLUTIONS*

NATURAL RELIGION

Sophisticated Enlightenment intellectuals may have been annoyed by the difficulties about the rationality of science presented in David Hume's arguments, but others were at least as troubled by the difficulties that Hume presented for religion. At the time an influential conception of Christianity in the British Isles (and nowhere more so than in Hume's own Scotland) held that religion is an extension of science. The same rational sense that produced arguments that revealed a universe obeying Newton's laws could also produce, it was firmly believed, arguments to show the existence of God and the truth of Christianity. Hume set out the principal arguments in his *Dialogues Concerning Natural Religion*, and then refuted them.

The *argument from design* was a favorite of advocates of natural religion. Hume stated the argument through the voice of his conversationalist Cleanthes:

Look round the world: Contemplate the whole and every part of it: You will find it to be nothing but one great machine, subdivided into an infinite number of lesser machines, which again admit of subdivisions to a degree beyond what human senses and faculties can trace and explain. All these various machines, and even their most minute parts, are adjusted to each other with an accuracy which ravishes into admiration all men who have ever contemplated them. The curious adapting of means to ends, throughout all nature, resembles exactly, though it much exceeds, the productions of human contrivance—of human design, thought, wisdom, and intelligence. Since therefore the effects resemble each other, we are led to infer, by all the rules of analogy, that the causes also resemble, and that the Author of Nature is somewhat similar to the mind of man, though possessed of much larger faculties, proportioned to the grandeur of the work which he has executed. By this argument *a posteriori*, and by this argument alone, do we prove at once the existence of a Deity and his similarity to human mind and intelligence.[1]

Hume's skeptic, Philo, objects that in science inferences from effect to cause are founded on many examples, and when applied to a new case require that the case be as similar as possible to those already known. But the inference from little parts of the universe and their design by humans to the universe as a whole and its creation according to a design of God's is an extraordinary change of context, circumstances, and scale quite unlike the careful, detailed similarities that natural science requires.

Hume had even more disconcerting objections to the argument from design. The argument supposes that like effects have like causes, and that since the universe shows pattern and structure as do human artifacts, the universe must have been designed, just as watches and ships are designed. But the designs of watches and ships are caused by the ideas of such designs in men's minds, and these ideas are themselves the effects of various complicated causes operating to produce them. So by the same principle that like effects are due to like causes, we must conclude that the idea of the design of the universe in the mind of the designer, God, has causes. So God's thoughts, like ours, are caused by something else.

There are worse problems, Hume argued:

• The argument from design cannot establish the infinity of any of God's attributes, for the part of the universe that falls within the compass of our observations is, however large, necessarily finite, and "the cause ought always to be proportioned to the effect."

• God cannot be perfect, because nature is not, or at least seems not to be on the basis of the evidence available to us. We live in a world in which children die horrible deaths from disease and in which evil sometimes triumphs over good. If the cause must be like the effect and the world is imperfect, then so must be the creator or creators of the world. To judge from the design that nature shows to us, either God is not all powerful, or else God is malicious. In either case, God is imperfect.

• Even the perfections of the world do not, according to the analogy, give evidence that God is correspondingly perfect. A workman may produce an excellent piece of work only after many failed and bungled attempts. For all we know, God has tried to make many worlds and bungled most attempts.

• The analogy provides no grounds for believing that there is a single God. To the contrary, when large complex projects are executed by humans, many designers and builders are required. The argument from design therefore seems to require us to conclude that there are many creators acting in consort, not one.

Hume's philosophy raised two kinds of difficulties for natural religion: First, the kinds of arguments applied in the sciences did not lead to Christian doctrine when applied more broadly, as in the argument from design. Second, according to Hume's general skeptical arguments, natural science itself is a matter of habit rather than reason. The second difficulty was the most fundamental, and in the eighteenth century the theory of probability offered a solution.

THE THEORY OF PROBABILITY

The modern mathematical theory of probability emerged from the Renaissance through the work of many people, including some, such as Pascal and Leibniz, whom I have already discussed. Games of chance and astronomical observations were two main sources of problems that led to the development of the theory, but theoretical arguments also provided a motive for developing the theory of probability as an account of the weight and bearing of evidence. By the eighteenth century probability theory was sufficiently developed that people attempted to apply it in more general settings, and an important use of the theory was to reply to skepticism and atheism. Before we turn to some of the applications of the theory of probability, let us consider some basic features of the theory itself.

One standard model of circumstances in which probabilities arise consists of drawing balls from an urn (figure 8.1). Suppose that all the balls are the same shape, but some are black and some are white. The probability of drawing a black ball is taken to be equal to the proportion of black balls in the urn. Suppose a number b of the balls are black, and a number w are white. Then the probability p of drawing a black ball is $p = b/(b + w)$, and the probability of drawing a white ball is $(1 - p) = w/(b + w)$.

Drawing a black ball from the urn is an *event*. Drawing a white ball from the urn is a different event. These two events are incompatible (as outcomes of one and the same drawing): if one of them occurs, the other does not. They are also complementary: if one of them does not occur, the

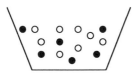

Figure 8.1
Black and white balls in an urn

other one must, on the assumption that some ball or other is drawn. We can describe other relevant events, for example, the event that either a white ball *or* a black ball is drawn. If a ball is drawn, this event is certain to occur. We can consider the event that neither a black ball nor a white ball is drawn. If a ball is drawn and the urn contains only black balls and white balls, this event is impossible.

The events described can be viewed as forming a field of sets or a Boolean algebra. Consider the set $D = \{B, W\}$ that has two members: B, representing the drawing of a black ball, and W, representing the drawing of a white ball. Consider the subsets of D: $\{B, W\}$, $\{B\}$, $\{W\}$, $\varnothing$. They form a field of sets over D and represent the events of drawing either a black ball or a white ball, drawing a black ball, drawing a white ball, and drawing neither a black ball nor a white ball.

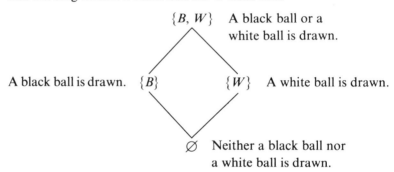

$\{B, W\}$ A black ball or a
              white ball is drawn.

A black ball is drawn. $\{B\}$ $\{W\}$ A white ball is drawn.

                        $\varnothing$ Neither a black ball nor
                                          a white ball is drawn.

I have already noted that event of drawing a black ball has probability $b/(b + w)$. Drawing a white ball from the urn is a different event, with probability $w/(b + w)$. *Whatever numerical values b and w have, so long as they are not both zero, these ratios must have values between 0 and 1.*

The sum of the probability of drawing a white ball and the probability of drawing a black ball is $b/(b + w) + w/(b + w) = 1$. In other words, if a ball is drawn from the urn, it is certainly either black or white. Drawing a white ball *or* a black ball is also an event, but one that is certain to happen if any ball is drawn at all. Thus if we assume that a ball is drawn, it is certain that the ball drawn is black or white. *Events that are certain have a probability of 1.*

The event of drawing a white ball on a specific draw is incompatible with the event of drawing a black ball on that turn. These two events are therefore systematically related: if one happens, necessarily the other does *not* happen. The probability of $\{B, W\}$, the event of drawing a black ball *or* a white ball, is the probability of a disjunction (or union) of two incompatible events. It is thus the sum of $b/(b + w)$ and $w/(b + w)$, or 1. *The probability of two incompatible events is the sum of their probabilities.*

These features characterize the mathematical properties of probabilities whenever the collection of alternative events is finite. From a formal point of view, probabilities do not have to be associated with drawings from urns. They can be associated with any system of events that form a Boolean algebra or field of sets. All that are required for a mathematical function to be a probability measure or probability distribution in the formal sense are that it be defined on a collection of events that form a field of sets and that the numerical assignments given to the events satisfy the principles in italics in the previous paragraphs. In other words, the following:

Definition   A (finitely additive) probability measure on a field F of sets over a nonempty set D is any function p defined on all sets in F and assigning each set a real number between 0 and 1 such that (1) $p(D) = 1$ and (2) for any two sets R and S in F that have an *empty* intersection, $p(R \cup S) = p(R) + p(S)$.

Study Questions

1. Show that for any probability measure over any field of sets, the probability of the empty set is 0.

2. Show that for any probability measure p over any field of sets F, if R and S are sets in F and if R is a subset of S, then $p(R) \leq p(S)$.

BERNOULLI TRIALS

Late in the seventeenth century Jacob Bernoulli studied the properties of sequences of draws from an urn with balls of two kinds, say black and white. Whatever ball is drawn, it is returned to the urn (and the urn mixed up again) before the next draw. (Bernoulli sometimes wrote of drawing "tiles" and rather than drawing black or white balls. He assumed each tile either had or lacked some property that made it "fertile," i.e., desired or useful. Of course, for philosophical and mathematical purposes, it makes no difference whether the examples we consider are about black and white balls or fertile tiles.)

Bernoulli was motivated by considerations of the following sort. Suppose that you don't know the proportion of black balls in an urn but you can draw a ball at random, see whether or not it is black, and return it to the urn. You can repeat this procedure as many times as you like, mixing the balls in the urn thoroughly after each trial. After you have carried out

Newton's problem

Late in the seventeenth century Isaac Newton, who was then rightly regarded as the greatest living natural philosopher and mathematician, was asked a simple problem about repeated trials. Newton's problem was the following: A man who is condemned to death is given a chance to save his live and regain his liberty. He has a choice of three different options: (1) throw 6 dice and be freed if and only if exactly 1 die comes up 6, (2) throw 12 dice and be liberated if and only if exactly 2 dice show a 6, (3) throw 18 dice and be liberated if and only if exactly 3 dice show a 6. Which should he choose? Newton's (correct) answer was that the prisoner should choose the first alternative. Why?

a number of trials, there will be a proportion of the trials in which a black ball was drawn and a remaining proportion in which a white ball was obtained. The proportion of trials in which a black ball is obtained ought to be a rough estimate of the proportion of black balls in the urn. We would expect that the larger the number of trials made, the better this estimate would be. Bernoulli aimed to do two things: first, to *prove* that as the number of trials increases, the proportion of trials in which a black ball is drawn will converge to the proportion of black balls in the urn, and second, to determine how the accuracy of this estimate depends on the number of trials made. Apparently because Bernoulli did not think he had satisfactorily answered the second problem, he did not publish his work. Fortunately, in 1713, eight years after Jacob Bernoulli's death, his nephew published the work as the book *Ars Conjectandi*.

The events associated with repeated trials of draws from an urn can also be viewed as a field of sets or a Boolean algebra, and probabilities can be assigned to those events subject to the rules I have just given. The algebras become very large very fast. So let us consider only the algebra of events associated with two trials in which a ball is drawn from an urn of black and white balls, with the understanding that after the first trial, the ball drawn is returned to the urn and the contents are mixed up.

If we let B_1 denote drawing a black ball on the first trial and W_2 denote drawing a white ball on the second trial, then the list of possible outcomes of the two trials is this:

$$\{B_1 B_2\}, \{B_1 W_2\}, \{W_1 B_2\}, \{W_1 W_2\}$$

Each outcome of two trials in this list is an event. In one sense, these events are the most fundamental in the problem. All other events having to do with the outcomes of the trials are unions of these simple events. For example, the event of drawing a black ball on the first trial is $\{B_1 B_2, B_1 W_2\} = \{B_1 B_2\} \cup \{B_1 W_2\}$. If the Boolean algebra or field of sets for this problem is drawn, the events in the list each are immediately above the impossible event, $\emptyset$. In another sense, however, the events in this list are not fundamental, since each is a composite of an outcome on the first trial, which is an event in the simpler Boolean algebra we drew earlier, and an outcome on the second trial, which is an event in an isomorphic simpler Boolean algebra. The algebra for the two trial problem can be thought of as a product of two simpler algebras: one for the first trial and one for the second trial.

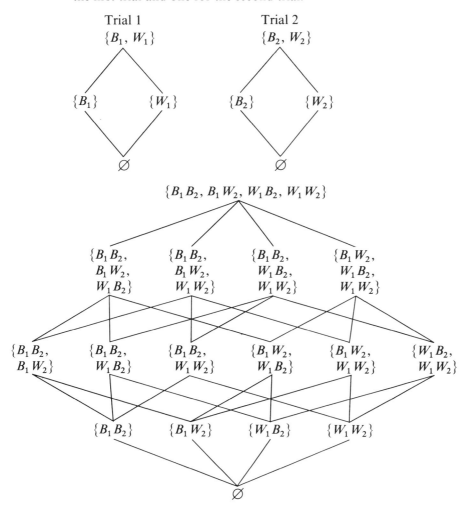

The fundamental events (called *atoms* of the algebra) just above $\varnothing$ in the large algebra are composites of the fundamental events (also called atoms) just above $\varnothing$ in the simpler algebras. The larger *product algebra* is then constructed simply by taking unions of the composite atomic events.

A probability measure for the two trials will assign a number between 0 and 1 to each event in the product algebra. What relation should there be between the probabilities assigned to events in the product algebra and the probabilities of events in the separate trials? Bernoulli's claim is this:

Bernoulli's rule   If the trials are conducted independently of one another, so that the outcome of one trial has no effect on the outcome of the other trial, then the probability of a composite event should be the ordinary product of the probability of the separate events that compose it.

Suppose 1/3 of the balls in an urn are black. Then on any trial the probability of drawing a black ball is 1/3, and the probability of drawing a white ball is 2/3. According to Bernoulli, the probability of drawing a black ball on the first trial and a black ball on the second trial, $p(\{B_1 B_2\})$, is therefore $1/3 \times 1/3 = 1/9$. The probability of drawing a white ball on the first trial and a black ball on the second trial, $p(\{W_1 B_2\})$, is $2/3 \times 1/3 = 2/9$. In the same way Bernoulli's rule for assigning probabilities to atomic events determines values for $p(\{B_1 W_2\})$ and $p(\{W_1 W_2\})$.

The probabilities of the atoms in an algebra determine unique probability values for all other events in the algebra. For example, consider $p(\{B_1 W_2, B_1 B_2\})$. The set $\{B_1 W_2, B_1 B_2\}$ is the union of the sets $\{B_1 W_1\}$ and $\{B_1 B_2\}$. These sets have $\varnothing$ as their intersection. Hence by the rules for probability measures, $p(\{B_1 W_2, B_1 B_2\}) = p(\{B_1 W_2\}) + p(\{B_1 B_2\}) = (1/3 \times 2/3) + (1/3 \times 1/3) = 2/9 + 1/9 = 1/3$.

The example is perfectly general. The probabilities of atomic events in the product algebra for a number of independent trials are the products of the probabilities of atomic events in the algebras for the individual trials. Any two atoms are disjoint sets having an empty intersection. In the product algebra, every event is a union of atoms. So the probability of any event in the product algebra is obtained simply by adding up the probabilities of the atoms contained in that event. For the simple example of two independent trials, if $p(B) = 1/3$, we get the following values:

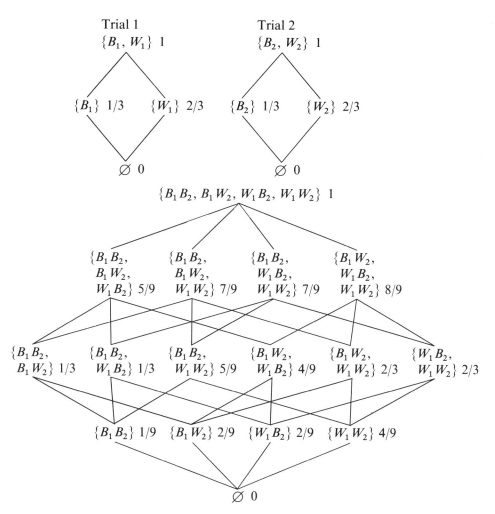

What is the probability of getting no black balls in two independent draws from an urn? There are two ways to compute this probability, each, of course, yielding the same value. One way is to apply Bernoulli's principle about composite events directly. The event of getting no black balls in two draws is composed of the events of getting a white ball on the first draw ($p = 2/3$) and a white ball on the second draw ($p = 2/3$). Since the events have no effect on one another, the probability of the composite event is obtained by multiplying and is $4/9$. The other way is simply to look at the event in the product algebra that represents getting no black balls, $\{W_1 W_2\}$, and see that its probability is $4/9$.

What is the probability of getting exactly one black ball in two trials? This event is the union of two disjoint events, namely the event $\{B_1 W_2\}$ and the event $\{W_1 B_2\}$. By Bernoulli's rule, the probability of $\{B_1 W_2\}$ is 2/9, and the probability of $\{W_1 B_2\}$ is also 2/9. Since these events have an empty union, the probability of their union is the sum of their probabilities, or 4/9, which is the answer.

What is the probability of getting exactly two black balls in two trials? This event is a composite event consisting of drawing a black ball on the first trial ($p = 1/3$) and drawing a black ball on the second trial ($p = 1/3$). So by Bernoulli's rule, the probability is 1/9.

Study Question

Suppose that the probability of drawing a black ball is 1/6. Calculate the probabilities of all events in the algebra representing two trials with this probability.

THE BINOMIAL DISTRIBUTION

Bernoulli, like Newton and other students of probability in the seventeenth century, was interested in the general formula for obtaining any number, say k, of successes (or "fertile" cases) in n independent trials when the probability of success in each trial is p (and so the probability of an outcome other than a success is $1 - p$). For example, we could call drawing a black ball a success and ask such questions as, What is the probability of drawing a black ball 5 times in 10 trials when the probability of drawing a black ball on any one trial is 1/3?

One way to obtain the answer to such questions is as follows. Suppose a sequence of $n = 10$ trials yields 5 draws of black balls. Suppose, in particular, that the first 5 draws yield black balls and the next 5 draws yield white balls. Each draw of a black ball is an event with probability $p = 1/3$, and each draw of a white ball is an event with probability $q = 1 - p = 2/3$. The trials are all independent, so the probability of a composite atomic event consisting of 5 draws of black balls on the first 5 trials and 5 draws of white balls on the next 5 trials will be the product of the probabilities of the outcomes of the individual trials that compose it. In other words, the probability of the composite event consisting of 5 draws of black balls followed by 5 draws of white balls will be $1/3 \times 1/3 \times 1/3 \times 1/3 \times 1/3 \times 2/3 \times 2/3 \times 2/3 \times 2/3 \times 2/3 = (1/3)^5 \times (2/3)^5 = (1/3)^5 \times (2/3)^{n-5} = p^5 q^{n-5}$. Now drawing black balls on the first 5 draws and drawing white balls on the next 5 draws is only *one* member of the event of drawing exactly 5 black balls in 10 trials. For we could draw the 5 black balls on any 5 of the 10 trials; it is not necessary that we draw the 5 black balls on the first 5 trials. For example, the event of drawing exactly 5 black balls in 10 trials also includes the case in which we draw a white ball on the first trial, then draw 5 black balls, then draw 4 white balls; it also include the case in which we draw a white ball, then a black ball, then a white ball, then a black ball, and so on. Each different way of drawing 5 black balls in 10 trials will have the same probability, namely $p^5 q^{n-5}$. No two distinct ways of drawing 5 black balls can both occur; considered as events, their intersection is empty. So, to answer the question with which we began— What is the probability of drawing a black ball 5 times in 10 trials when the probability of drawing a black ball on any one trial is 1/3?—we must calculate how many different ways there are of selecting, from 10 trials, 5 trials that result in black balls and we multiply that number by $p^5 q^{n-5}$.

The number of different members of the event of drawing exactly 5 black balls in 10 trials is given by the number of different ways in which we can select 5 things (the 5 trials on which a black ball occurs) from 10 things. From chapter 3 we know that number is $C(5, 10) = 10!/(5!(10 - 5)!)$ So finally we obtain the conclusion that the probability of drawing 5 black balls in $n = 10$ independent trials, on each of which the probability of drawing a black ball is $p = 1/3$ and the probability of drawing a white ball is $q = (1 - p) = 2/3$, is given by

$$\frac{10!}{5!(10 - 5)!} \left(\frac{1}{3}\right)^5 \left(\frac{2}{3}\right)^5.$$

The reasoning used is perfectly general:

Theorem   The probability of k successes in n independent trials each having a probability p of success and a probability $q = (1 - p)$ of failure is $C(k, n)p^k q^{(n-k)}$.

You may recall that Pascal proved that $C(k, n)$, the number of ways of choosing k things from n things, is also the value of the kth binomial coefficient in the expansion of an nth power binomial such as $(x + y)^n$. In fact, the formula for the probability of k successes in n independent trials each with probability p of success is the very same as the formula for the kth monomial in the expansion of the binomial $(p + q)^n$. For this reason the probability measure that assigns the probability $C(k, n)p^k q^{n-k}$ to the event of k successes in n trials is called the *binomial distribution*. For $n = 8$ and $p = q = 1/2$, the binomial distribution is as shown in figure 8.2.

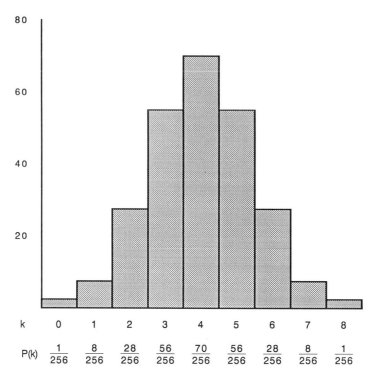

Figure 8.2
The binomial distribution for $n = 8$ and $p = q = 1/2$

Recall that Bernoulli wanted to determine how good an estimate of the proportion of black balls in an urn is provided by the proportion of black balls actually drawn in a sequence of trials. The first question, however, is whether it can be shown that as the number of trials gets larger, the proportion of black balls drawn comes closer and closer to the proportion of black balls in the urn. In the probability distribution shown in figure 8.2, where 8 draws are made from an urn that is half filled with black balls, the probability is a little over .27 that half the balls drawn will be black, and the probability that either 3, 4, or 5 of the balls drawn will be black is roughly .71. In other words, the probability is .71 that the proportion of black balls drawn will be within 1/8 of the proportion of black balls actually in the urn. Let us consider the binomial distribution for 16 trials rather than just 8, again with $p = 1/2$. Then we would find that the probability of getting black balls on exactly half of the draws is just under .20, and the probability is about .79 that the proportion

of black balls drawn is within 1/8 of the proportion of the black balls in
the urn (1/2).

*As the number of trials increases, the probability goes down that the
proportion of successes will be exactly equal to the probability of a success
on a single trial, but as the number of trials increases, the probability of
obtaining a proportion of successes within a fixed interval of the probability
of success on a single trial increases.* Bernoulli himself made the point this
way:

I suppose that without your knowledge there are concealed in an urn 3000 white
pebbles and 2000 black pebbles, and in trying to determine the numbers of these
pebbles you take out one pebble after another (each time replacing the pebble you
have drawn before choosing the next, in order not to decrease the number of
pebbles in the urn), and that you observe how often a white and how often a black
pebble is withdrawn. The question is, can you do this so often that it becomes ten
times, one hundred times, one thousand times, etc., more probable (that is, it be
morally certain) that the numbers of whites and blacks chosen are in the same 3:2
ratio as the pebbles in the urn, rather than in any other different ratio?

To avoid misunderstanding, we must note that the ratio between the number of
cases, which we are trying to determine by experiment, should not be taken as
precise and indivisible (for then just the contrary would happen, and it would
become less probable that the true ratio would be found the more numerous were
the observations). Rather, it is a ratio taken with some latitude, that is, included
within two limits which can be made as narrow as one might wish. For instance,
if in the example of the pebbles alluded to above we take two ratios 301/200 and
299/200 or 3001/2000 and 2999/2000, etc., of which one is immediately greater
and the other immediately less than the ratio 3:2, it will be shown that it can be
made more probable, that the ratio found by often repeated experiments will fall
within these limits of the 3:2 ratio rather than outside them.[2]

In fact, Bernoulli succeeded in proving essentially the following theorem, which is now sometimes known as the weak law of large numbers.

Bernoulli's theorem   For any small positive number ε and any large positive number c and any value of p ($0 \le p, \le 1$), there is an n such that for the
binomial distribution with n trials, each with probability p of success, if x
is the number of successes in n trials, then

$\mathrm{Prob}(|x/n - p| > \varepsilon) < 1/(c + 1).$

Bernoulli and his successors, such as Abraham De Moivre, took this
result to form the basis for a rebuttal to skepticism, or at least to Hume's
kind of skepticism. If some quantity (analogous to the true proportion of
black balls) is constrained by nature to have a particular value and we can
make repeated experiments to measure the quantity (which is analogous

to making repeated trials and using the frequency of black balls in the trials to estimate the proportion of black balls in the urn), then the probability that our estimate is within a given small interval of the truth gets larger and larger. We are justified, as the number of experiments or trials we make increases, in having more and more confidence that our estimate of the quantity is within any given interval of the true value. The argument depends, however, on our granting the analogy between urn problems and scientific problems, and the appropriateness of urn problems as a general model for empirical inquiry might be doubted.

In the middle of the eighteenth century, the Reverend Thomas Bayes provided the basis for a more powerful argument against Hume.

Study Questions

1. How does the binomial distribution (for any $n > 0$) look when $p = 1$?

2. Compute the values and graph the results for the binomial distribution with $n = 8$ and $p = 3/4$ (as in figure 8.2).

WHAT IS PROBABILITY?

During the seventeenth and eighteenth centuries philosophers and mathematicians were uncertain about the *metaphysics* of probability. Much of that uncertainty remains today. On the one hand, probability was thought of as a measure of a feature of events, their *chance*. *Games of chance*, such as dice games, are so called because they determine specific chances for various outcomes. It is the physical properties of dice that determines the chance that they will show one side or another when thrown. So chance is a kind of complex physical property. On the other hand, probability was thought of as a *measure of opinion*, a measure of degree of belief or credence.

The view of probability as a measure of opinion or degree of belief was strengthened by the effects of Newtonian philosophy. In problems in dynamics, an initial description of the state of a physical system is given, positions and momenta at one time, for example, and Newtonian laws then entail unique values for the state of the system at subsequent times. The Newtonian laws provide a *function* between possible states of a system at one time and possible states of the system at certain subsequent times. Each initial state *determines* unique subsequent states. Pierre Simon de Laplace, the greatest mathematical physicist and probabilist of the eighteenth century, drew a bold conclusion from this feature of Newtonian dynamics:

Laplacian determinism   From a complete description of the mechanical state of the universe at one moment of time, the Newtonian laws of dynamics determine a unique state of the universe at any subsequent moment of time. The latter state can in principle be computed from the initial description and the laws.

We now know that, even if we assume Newtonian laws, Laplace's view is false and requires considerable qualification, but from the eighteenth century until the twentieth century Laplacian determinism was accepted not only by physicists but by many other scientists as well. Laplace provided a picture of the universe in which there is no such thing as a real physical property of chance except for the extreme cases (chances of 0 or of 1), and the appearance of chance variation in events is simply the result of our ignorance.

This was, in fact, the view that Hume endorsed in his section on probability in the *Enquiry*: "Though there be no such thing as Chance in the world; our ignorance of the real cause of any event has the same influence on the understanding, and begets a like species of belief or opinion."[3] If one took Hume's view quite literally, then the study of probability would become the study of belief, its degrees, and its variations. But that was something no one in the eighteenth century knew how to attempt. Probabilists knew how to count and observe frequencies, and they knew how to compute some of the mathematical consequences of mathematical probabilities, but they did not know (or really care) about variations of belief in actual people. Perhaps one result of this tension was that astute writers were carefully equivocal about the meaning of probability.

Thomas Bayes, who wrote one of the most important studies of probability in the eighteenth century, defined the notion this way: "The *probability* of any event is the ratio between the value at which an expectation depending on the happening of the event ought to be computed, and the value of the thing expected upon its happening. By *chance* I mean the same as probability."[4]

The idea behind Bayes' definition can be seen by thinking what a promise would be worth to you if you knew that it would be kept. A lottery ticket is a kind of promise, and lottery tickets can generally be sold or exchanged. Suppose you are offered a lottery ticket that will pay $2 if a 6 comes up on a roll of a die. To compute what the ticket is worth to you ("the value at which an expectation depending on the happening of the event ought to be computed") multiply $2 ("the value of the thing expected upon its happening") by the probability of the event:

Value of an expectation depending on the happening of the event

= (probability of the event)

× (value of the thing received if the event happens)

So the value at which an expectation depending on the happening of the event ought to be computed, divided by the value of the thing expected upon its happening, is just the probability of the event:

Probability of the event

$$= \frac{\text{(probability of the event)} \times \text{(value received if the event occurs)}}{\text{value received if the event occurs}}$$

The ambiguity in Bayes' definition arises because of his use of the phrase "ought to be." What probability *ought to be* given to a possible outcome of a lottery? One that is the measure of some physical property? One that is somehow logically correct? Bayes does not say. If Bayes had instead used the phrase "is," then his account would amount simply to a reformulation of Hume's, in which the degree of belief in an outcome is measured indirectly through assessments of the value of bets or lotteries on the outcome of the event.

BAYES, PRICE, AND HUME

Bayes was a Scottish minister and a contemporary of David Hume. He was known for his mathematical skills, but published almost nothing during his lifetime. After his death a remarkable manuscript was found among his papers, a manuscript that eventually came to revolutionize the theory of probability. Bayes' "Essay towards Solving a Problem in the Doctrine of Chances" was read, with an introduction and postscript by Richard Price, to the Royal Society of London in 1763, and it was subsequently published in the Proceedings of the Society. While the essay itself was entirely mathematical, Price presented it as a response to Hume's skepticism.

Consider one of Hume's examples: How can reason together with experience justify our belief that the sun will rise tomorrow? Hume, of course, argued that they could not, and that our belief is founded on experience and habit rather than on experience and reason. Price thought of the issue in terms of Bernoulli trials and the binomial distribution. The days and nights we experience can be thought of as so many draws from Nature's urn: periods of night followed by periods of day are successes; a period of night that lasts a long while and is not followed (in central latitudes) by a day (after roughly twelve hours) would count as a failure. In Hume's terminology, Nature's "hidden springs" determine the probability that a day will follow a night. So as Price conceived the issue, our experience of nights and days constitute so many trials from a binomial distribution, in which the probability of observing k successes in n trials is $C(k, n)p^k q^{n-k}$, where q is by definition equal to $1 - p$. If we knew the value of p, the chance that the sun will rise tomorrow would be represented by the value of the parameter p. If $p = 1$, the sun will certainly rise tomorrow (and the day after that, and the day after that, forever). If $p = 0$, then the sun will certainly not rise tomorrow, or ever. If we are uncertain of the value of p, we are uncertain whether the sun will rise tomorrow.

In Bayes' theory, the value of p itself has a probability. In formal terms, for example, that p is between $1/2$ and $2/3$ is an event to be assigned a probability. The idea may be a little confusing, since p itself is a number that determines a probability. In draws from urns, for example, p is a proportion that determines the probability of k successes in n draws from the urn. But quite aside from that, Bayes supposed that the event that p lies within an interval of values is measured by a probability. In general, to follow Bayes' reasoning you must keep in mind that several different probability measures will be talked about at once.

The probability distribution on p determines, for any n and k, a probability that there will be k successes on n trials. To obtain that probability, for each value of p, compute the probability of k successes in n trials, then multiply that probability by the probability of the value of p used, and then sum over all of the values of p. Since the values of p form a continuum, we must actually *integrate* rather than sum. If we let Prob(x) signify the function representing the initial probability that parameter p has the value x and let Prob(k, n) signify the probability of obtaining k successes in n trials, then the formula for Prob(k, n) becomes

$$\text{Prob}(k, n) = \int_0^1 C(k, n) x^k (1 - x)^{(n-k)} \frac{d\,\text{Prob}(x)}{dx}\,dx.$$

Changing the function Prob(x), which measures the probability of values of p, will generally result in changes in Prob(k, n), the probability of k successes in n trials.

In Price's view, the central question about induction, therefore, is to determine how much probability should be assigned to any interval of values of p in light of evidence about a number of successes and failures in Bernoulli trials. Once that is known, it will be understood how we can rationally learn from experience: "the number of times in which an unknown event has happened and failed being given, to find the chance that the probability of its happening [in a single trial] should lie somewhere between any two named degrees of probability."[5]

Bayes supposed that before any trials are made, the probability that p lies in the interval between a and b is $b - a$ ($0 \le b < a \le 1$). We now call the initial probability distribution for p that Bayes assumed a *uniform distribution*. Accordingly, the mathematical and conceptual problem that Bayes addressed concerns how the initial uniform probability distribution for p should be changed as Bernoulli trials are conducted and their outcomes noted.

For a uniform distribution, $1 = d\,\mathrm{Prob}(x)/dx$, and therefore, the expression for $\mathrm{Prob}(k, n)$ simplifies to

$$\mathrm{Prob}(k, n) = \int_0^1 C(k, n)x^k(1 - x)^{(n-k)}\,dx.$$

If we regard n as fixed, this is Bayes' expression for the probability that k successes will be obtained.

What is the probability that k successes will be obtained *and* that the value of p lies between two numbers a and b? Bayes argued that it is just the sum (or integral) of the probability of k successes taken over each value of p from a to b. In other words,

$$\mathrm{Prob}(k \text{ successes in } n \text{ trials } \& \ a \le p \le b) = \int_a^b C(k, n)x^k(1 - x)^{(n-k)}\,dx.$$

Finally, Bayes argued that the probability of event A given event B is the probability of A and B jointly occurring, divided by the probability that B occurs. (We now call the notion that event A occurs given that B occurs *the probability of A conditional on B*, and write it $\mathrm{Prob}(A|B)$). Applying this principle to his problem, Bayes concluded that the probability that p is between a and b, given that k successes have been observed in n trials, is

$$\mathrm{Prob}(a \le p \le b|k \text{ successes in } n \text{ trials}) = \frac{\int_a^b C(k, n)x^k(1 - x)^{(n-k)}\,dx}{\int_0^1 C(k, n)x^k(1 - x)^{(n-k)}\,dx}.$$

The most difficult problem for Bayes was to evaluate these integrals. He showed that the denominator is always equal to $1/(n + 1)$, no matter what value of k is considered, but the numerator is more difficult, and Bayes was not able to give a general solution. He was able to give an analysis for the numerator only when either k or $(n - k)$ is small.

It is easy to see what happens to the probability of values for p as one gathers trials in which only successes occur. Starting with a uniform probability distribution over p, suppose that there are k successes in k trials, i.e., that $n = k$. $C(k, k) = 1$, and $(n - k) = 0$, so we have that

$$\text{Prob}(a \leq p \leq b | k \text{ successes in } k \text{ trials}) = \frac{\int_a^b x^k \, dx}{1/(k + 1)} = b^{k+1} - a^{k+1}.$$

As the number of trials k becomes large, this quantity approaches 0 for any interval that does not include the value $p = 1$, and it approaches 1 for any interval that does include the value $p = 1$. In other words, if we start from an initial uniform distribution over values of p, as the number of trials without failure increases, the probability distribution becomes concentrated around $p = 1$. Moreover, we do not have to wait for a large number of trials before the probability of values of p in intervals of interest that do not include 1 becomes very small. After 10 successes in 10 trials, for example, the probability that p lies between 0 and $1/2$ is less than .001, and the probability that the value of p lies between $3/4$ and 1 is greater than .94.

Price thought such results as these to be a decisive reply to Hume:

Let us imagine to ourselves the case of a person just brought forth into this world and left to collect from his observation of the order and course of events what powers and causes take place in it. The Sun would, probably, be the first object that would engage his attention; but after losing it the first night he would be entirely ignorant whether he should ever see it again. He would therefore be in the condition of a person making a first experiment about an event entirely unknown to him. But let him see a second appearance or one *return* of the Sun, and an expectation would be raised in him of a second return, and he might know that there was an odds of 3 to 1 for *some* probability of this. This odds would increase, as before represented, with the number of returns to which he was witness. But no finite number of returns would be sufficient to produce absolute or physical certainty. For let it be supposed that he has seen it return at regular and stated intervals a million of times. The conclusions it would warrant would be such as follow—There would be the odds of the millionth power of 2 to one, that it was likely that it would return again at the end of the usual interval. . . .

It should be carefully remembered that these deductions suppose a previous total ignorance of nature. After having observed for some time the course of events it would be found that the operations of nature are in general regular, and that the powers and laws which prevail in it are stable and permanent. The consideration of this will cause one or a few experiments often to produce a much stronger expectation of success in further experiments than would otherwise have been reasonable; just as the frequent observation that things of a sort are disposed to gather in any place would lead us to conclude, upon discovering there any object of a particular sort, that there are laid up with it many others of the same sort. It is obvious that this, so far from contradicting the foregoing deductions, is only one particular case to which they are to be applied.[6]

Study Question

1. For the binomial distribution with $n = 8$ and $p = 1/2$, calculate the conditional probability that exactly 5 successes are obtained, *given* that more than 4 successes are obtained.

THE MODERN REVIVAL

Bayes' ideas did not have much influence in the eighteenth or even the nineteenth centuries. Laplace used similar but less explicitly developed methods. There was a small school of Bayesians at the University of Cambridge in the nineteenth century, but they seem to have published very little. In the twentieth century, in the hands of the philosopher Frank Ramsey and the statistician Bruno De Finnetti, Bayes ideas were rekindled and developed into a major branch of modern statistics, as well as an influential approach to philosophical issues about knowledge.

Three distinct problems beset the Bayes and Price response to Hume's inductive skepticism:

1. What is probability? Bayes, De Moivre, Leibniz, and others suggested that it is the degree of belief or confidence that *ought to be* given to an event or state of affairs, but they gave no clear account of what this means.
2. Bayes showed how to compute simple cases of a conditional probability for a parameter of a binomial distribution, and we have seen that the conditional-probability distribution may quickly come to be localized around a particular value for the parameter. But does the process of changing probabilities by forming conditional probabilities as new evidence arises always converge to the truth?
3. Price's response to Hume assumes that our inquiries into nature are accurately represented as attempts to infer a parameter in a binomial distribution from a sequence of Bernoulli trials. But he gave no argument for the accuracy of this representation, and it is not obviously correct in

general. Perhaps in nature the value of p varies from trial to trial; perhaps our sample is not randomly selected from any binomial distribution.

Ramsey's solution to the first question was to argue that *probability is a measure of rational degree of belief*. In Ramsey's conception, different rational agents may assign different degrees of belief, and hence different probability measures, to the *same* system of events. Thus you may judge that a coin is fair and have confidence equal to 1/2 that it will land heads if flipped, while I may judge that the coin is biased and have confidence equal to 1/3 that it will land heads if flipped. Moreover, Ramsey allowed that different rational agents may assign different degrees of belief to the same system of events even though the rational agents have available to them exactly the same body of evidence. You and I may each have observed the same fifty flips of the coin in question and have no other specific information about it, but we may still differ in the probability we assign to heads on a given flip. According to Ramsey, the rationality of a system of degrees of belief requires only two things:

• The measure of degrees of belief must satisfy the axioms for probability measures.
• As new evidence is acquired, the measure of degrees of belief in a system of events must change to their conditional probabilities (under that same measure) on the evidence.

If probability is a measure of degree of belief, how can degree of belief be measured? Ramsey proposed a method that assumes one further principle about rational agents. To explain it requires that we be clear about the notion of *expected value*, which Bayes himself used.

Definition   For an action with a finite set of possible outcomes, each outcome having a definite value, the *expected value* of the action is the sum over all possible outcomes of the measure of degree of belief that the outcome will occur multiplied by the value of the outcome.

Ramsey assumed the following principle:

Ramsey's assumption   Given a set of alternative actions one of which must be chosen, a rational agent will choose the action with the largest expected value.

Ramsey was then able to show that under quite general conditions the degrees of belief of an agent that satisfies this assumption can be inferred from the agent's choices among gambles. In appropriate circumstances,

---

An illustration

The problem is to find dollar values A, B, and C such that the rational agent is indifferent between the following prospects:

1. Getting $\$A$ for sure
2. Getting $\$B$ if proposition q is true and getting $\$C$ if q is not true

Suppose further that we have determined that the agent's degree of belief in $\neg q$, $\mathrm{DOB}(\neg q)$, is one minus the agent's degree of belief in q, $1 - \mathrm{DOB}(q)$. Since the agent is indifferent between choice 1 and choice 2, they must have the same expected value. Hence, $A = B \times \mathrm{DOB}(q) + C(1 - \mathrm{DOB}(q))$. Therefore, by simple algebra, $\mathrm{DOB}(q) = (A - C)/(B - C)$.

---

degrees of belief are measurable features of ideally rational agents (see boxed illustration).

The second question concerning Price's response to Hume has to do with whether or not one will converge to truth if one follows the strategy of adopting an initial (or prior) probability distribution and then changing it by forming conditional probabilities as new evidence is acquired. In the context of Ramsey's account of probability as rational degree of belief, the question about convergence is quite general. There is no reason, on Ramsey's account, why we should start with a uniform distribution.

Modern studies of probability have shown that in very general circumstances, changing probability by conditionalizing does result in convergence to the truth. There are, however, some important restrictions on this claim.

1. If the initial distribution gives 0 prior probability to a set of values that contains the true value of a parameter, that set will continue to receive 0 probability no matter how much evidence is obtained.

2. If the evidence has the same probability on alternative hypotheses, then the ratios of the probabilities of those hypotheses will be unchanged by conditionalizing on the evidence.

The first of these limitations means that a dogmatic Bayesian agent who happens to be wrong cannot recover from that error. The second means that if two (or more) hypotheses give the same likelihood to every possible body of evidence, then conditioning on evidence will never change the initial ratio of their probabilities. And this means, of course, that if exactly one of them is true, then we will not converge toward giving probability 1 to the true hypothesis by conditioning on ever larger bodies of evidence.

The third problem for Price's argument against Hume has to do with the appropriateness of the binomial model as a representation of inquiry into nature. Instead of relying on the binomial representation, using modern logic, we can state the essential points of Price's argument much more generally. Imagine a Fregean formal language that has an infinite number of predicate and function symbols. That is, suppose that the language is large enough that every hypothesis can be expressed in it (up to the limits of expressibility of formalized languages). Say that two sentences in the language are *equivalent* if they are logically equivalent, if each of them can be deduced from the other. Then numbers representing degrees of belief can be assigned to sentences in such a way that equivalent sentences receive the same degrees of belief. The degrees of belief can then satisfy the axioms of probability, and it can be shown under general conditions (provided restrictions numbered 1 and 2 above are not violated) that a Bayesian agent who changes degrees of belief by conditionalizing on the evidence will converge to the truth.

The Bayesian picture does not refute metaphysical skepticism. Rather, it tries to render it harmless. Metaphysical skepticism imagines alternative hypotheses that generate exactly the same experiences, so the ratio of the initial probabilities of the alternatives will always be the same as their ratio after conditioning on any evidence. This means that we cannot learn, even in the long run, that the skeptic's hypothesis that we are brains in vats is false. But so what? How will our ignorance harm us in either deliberation or action?

The modern Bayesian picture of rational action and deliberation derives as much from Pascal and Ramsey as from Bayes, and this very picture forms the foundation of much of contemporary economic theory and of an influential branch of contemporary statistics. The individual is considered to be someone who must decide what to do. Alternative courses of action are available, and each alternative course of action may produce outcomes of interest to the individual, depending on how the world really is. The individual has preferences regarding the possible outcomes: some may be valuable, some may be disastrous, and so on. The value of the alternatives is assumed to be measurable on some scale, and these measured values of outcomes are traditionally called *utilities*. The individual also has views about the likelihood or probability of the various alternative states of the world; in the modern subjective Bayesian tradition, following Ramsey, these probabilities are nothing more than the individual's degrees of belief in the various alternative states of the world. If the individual can frame her preferences, measure the utility to her of the various possible outcomes, formulate the probabilities of the alternative states of the world, and determine which outcomes will result from which actions in which states of the world, then she can calculate her *expected utility* for each alternative action. The expected utility of action A is just the sum, over each possible state W of the world, of the utility of the outcome of action A in world state W multiplied by the subjective probability of state W of the world.

On the modern Bayesian view, to act rationally, the individual must choose an action that has as large an expected utility as possible. Nothing more is required for rationality than degrees of belief that satisfy the axioms of probability, preferences that are coherent, and actions taken to maximize expected utility. It is perfectly rational, therefore, for an individual to recognize the logical possibility that she is a brain in a vat, or that other minds don't exist, and to give such claims 0 probability or infinitesimal probability so that they make no difference to expected utility calculations. It is also possible to give such hypotheses some substantial probability but to judge that they will make no difference whatsoever to outcomes of value. The modern Bayesian may even be a metaphysical skeptic, but that skepticism makes no difference to rational deliberation or rational action.

Study Question

Pascal provided a famous argument for the rationality of causing oneself to believe in God. He realized that one cannot simply choose to believe in God, but by going to church, avoiding temptation, and pious behavior, one can so act that one comes to believe in God. Pascal's argument that this is the rational course of action contains the central ideas of the probabilistic study of rational decision making, or *decision theory*, as the subject is now called. It also uses an interpretation of probability according to which all alternative circumstances are equally probable. Pascal assumes that it is rational to act so that your expected utility is maximized.

One of Pascal's arguments is this: If God exists and you act so as not to believe in him, you will be condemned to hell for eternity and suffer an infinite loss in utility; if God exists and you do believe in him, you will spend eternity in Heaven and have an infinite gain in utility; if God does not exists and you do believe in him, you will suffer a small finite loss in utility in having given up sinful pleasures; if God does not exist and you do not believe in him, you will gain a small, finite utility from sinful pleasures. Either God exists, or he does not. So the probability is $1/2$ for either case. Thus the expected utility of acting so as to believe in God is $1/2 \times \infty = \infty$, and the expected utility of not acting so as to believe in

God is $1/2 \times -\infty = -\infty$. A rational person will therefore choose to act so as to believe in God.

What is wrong with Pascal's argument?

BOUNDED RATIONALITY AND BAYESIAN PROBLEMS

Altogether, the results obtained by modern Bayesians provide a powerful response to Hume's inductive skepticism and an interesting response to metaphysical skepticism. But as so far developed, it is a response for an *ideally* rational agent, that is, an agent who

1. never makes logical mistakes,
2. never needs to consider novel hypotheses not previously thought of,
3. can compute anything,
4. never accepts anything false as data.

And that's not us. Some of the reasons we do not satisfy these four conditions have to do with human perception. Let's consider point 4. The Bayesian account of belief and learning as presented assumes that the data the rational agent uses in forming conditional probabilities is free of error. But there is no reason to believe this to be the case with us humans. We often describe data, or aspects of data, in ways that subsequently come to be thought of as erroneous. Richard Jeffrey, a distinguished Bayesian philosopher, offers the example of observing the colors of objects by candlelight. What you see may alter your degree of belief that an object is blue (or green or red, as the case may be), but it is unlikely to make you *certain* that the object is blue.

Various responses to this problem have been proposed by those who are sympathetic with Bayesian approaches to the theory of knowledge. One is to claim that the uncertain descriptions of our data are themselves inferences made from simpler descriptions that are certain. It might be argued, for example, that there are "sense data" events, from which any ordinary report of things seen are tacitly inferred. From a mathematical point of view, the algebra of events in which we describe possible outcomes of experiments can always be enlarged to include such hypothetical events, and measures of our degree of belief can be extended to such events to give some of them the value 1. A second response is to suggest that we should *not* change our degrees of belief by forming conditional probabilities on the data, because that process results in giving the data a degree of belief of 1. Instead, we could suppose that, as with observation by candlelight, experience causes us to change our degrees of belief in some propositions (e.g., that the object is blue) but does not cause us to change them to 1. We then must readjust our degrees of belief in the propositions so that the total system of degrees of belief will again satisfy the axioms of probability. Jeffrey proposed a rule for doing so. One difficulty with this approach is that we lose the general guarantee of convergence to the truth.

Another reason we don't satisfy the four conditions has to do with the limitations of human logical powers. It is obvious that we humans are not able, at any moment in our history, to consider all possible hypotheses about the world. The history of science is filled with episodes in which novel theories were introduced, theories that had never before been articulated. If at a given moment we have a set of alternative hypotheses about which we have degrees of belief, and a novel hypothesis not previously thought of is introduced, we must decide what degree of belief to give to this novel hypothesis. We cannot do this by conditioning on empirical data, since no new empirical data have been obtained (other than the existence of the novel hypothesis). What happens when a new hypothesis is introduced is that the relevant algebra of events is changed. But unfortunately, nothing in the Bayesian story tells us how to alter our degrees of belief when this happens.

Perhaps the most profound difficulty for the Bayesian conception arises from a combination of philosophy, of mind, psychology, and the theory of computation. One of the most powerful ideas of the twentieth century—and an idea that we will consider in detail in subsequent chapters—is that the human brain is a biological computer and the cognitive activities of humans are produced by computational procedures within this biological computer. If we assume for the moment that this is so, then we humans cannot determine the answers to mathematical problems that are in principle beyond the capacity of any possible computer to decide.

A perfectly nondogmatic Bayesian must be able to determine a degree of belief for each of an infinity of sentences. For any declarative sentence, the perfect, ideally rational nondogmatic Bayesian agent has a degree of belief in that sentence. Moreover, initially the only sentences given a degree of belief of 0 are logical contradictions, for what it means to be perfectly nondogmatic is that no sentence whose truth is logically possible is given a 0 degree of belief. That, recall, is one condition required to show that an ideal Bayesian agent can converge to the truth, whatever it is. For brevity, let me call such a probability measure *nondogmatic*. One of the results of modern logic and the modern theory of computation that developed from it in this century is that *no possible computer can compute a nondogmatic probability function defined on all sentences in a formalized first-order language that contains even one two-place predicate*. If no possible computer can do it, and if no human can do it unless some possible computer can do it, then no human can do it.

In fact, it turns out that only very dogmatic probability functions are feasible to compute. But if such probability measures are used, then of course reliability must be sacrificed, and the claim to have a general answer to Hume's skepticism is lost.

CONCLUSION

Although in many ways religious belief was one of the great motivations for the study of probability, probability has not, on the whole, been kind to religious belief. How much comfort, if any, Bayes' ideas provide to natural religion is not clear. When asked what place God has in his system of the universe, Laplace is said to have replied, "I have no need of that hypothesis," and insofar as he was correct about what he needed to explain the motions of the planets, his remark illustrates that Bayesian doctrine does not provide much support for natural religion. Insofar as natural phenomena can be explained by theories that do not invoke God (or at any rate, do not invoke a *nice* God), Bayesian approaches provide no special case for religious belief. On the other hand, Bayesian doctrine is extremely tolerant, and nothing in it argues that religious belief is in any way irrational.

Historically, another "natural" argument for religious belief is founded on miracles: a God who can intervene in the course of nature is said to be the best explanation for miracles. Hume ridiculed such arguments on the grounds that natural laws are confirmed by billions of instances known to mankind, and in the case of any miracle it is more probable that the testimony of witnesses is false than that the laws of nature have failed. In the late nineteenth century, Francis Galton, one of the chief inventors of modern social statistics, gave a probabilistic argument against the efficacy of prayer. He compared the longevity of clerics and kings, whose health was presumably prayed for a great deal, with that of more ordinary folk, who presumably got less prayer on their behalf. He found that on the average there were no differences in the lifespans of the two groups.

Nonetheless, religion aside, the study of probability is one of the great successes of skepticism. Although serious skeptics would not welcome the gratitude, contemporary economic and statistical theorists owe an intellectual debt to the skeptical tradition.

Review Questions

1. State the argument from design, and explain Hume's objections to it.

2. What response could be given to Hume's objection to arguments for the existence of God founded on miracles?

3. Give the definition of a probability measure.

4. What is a field of sets?

5. What is meant by a "Bernoulli trial"?

6. State Bernoulli's theorem.

7. Describe the binomial distribution, and explain in detail why it is called the *binomial* distribution.

8. What is Laplacian determinism?

9. Explain Hume's conception of probability.

10. What is a uniform probability distribution?

11. Using any appropriate mathematical examples, explain how Bayes proposed that probabilities should be changed as evidence is acquired.

12. Explain how Price used Bayes' results as a response to Hume's skepticism. How might Hume reply?

13. Describe Frank Ramsey's contributions to Bayesian conceptions of probability and inference.

14. Discuss some difficulties with the Bayesian conception of rationality.

Further Reading

Daston, Lorraine. *Classical Probability in the Enlightenment*. Princeton, N.J.: Princeton University Press, 1988.

Earman, John. *Bayes or Bust*. Cambridge: MIT Press, 1992.

Fisher, R. A. *Statistical Methods and Scientific Inference*. Edinburgh: Oliver and Boyd, 1956.

Hacking, Ian. *The Emergence of Probability*. New York: Cambridge University Press, 1975.

Harper, W., and B. Skyrms, eds. *Causation, Chance, and Credence*, Vol. 1. Dordrecht: Kluwer Academic Publishers, 1988.

Howson, Colin, and Peter Urbach. *Scientific Reasoning: The Bayesian Approach*. La Salle, Ill.: Open Court, 1989.

Jeffrey, Richard. *The Logic of Decision*. Chicago: University of Chicago Press, 1983.

Jeffreys, H. *Scientific Inference*. 3rd ed. New York: Cambridge University Press, 1973.

Pearson, K. *The History of Statistics in the Seventeenth and Eighteenth Centuries against the Changing Background of Intellectual, Scientific, and Religious Thought*. London: Charles Griffin, 1978.

Rescher, Nicholas. *Pascal's Wager: A Study of Practical Reasoning in Philosophical Theology*. Notre Dame, Ind.: University of Notre Dame Press, 1985.

Rosenkrantz, R. D. *Foundations and Applications of Inductive Probability*. Atascadero, Calif.: Ridgeview, 1981.

Savage, L. J. *Foundations of Statistics*. New York: J. Wiley, 1954.

Skyrms, Brian. *Choice and Chance: An Introduction to Inductive Logic*. 3rd ed. Belmont, Calif.: Wadsworth Publishing Co., 1986.

Stigler, S. M. *The History of Statistics*. Cambridge: Harvard University Press, 1986.

Chapter 9
KANTIAN SOLUTIONS

INTRODUCTION

At the beginning of this century the great American physicist Josiah Willard Gibbs introduced his revolutionary book on statistical mechanics and thermodynamics with the remark that its aim was to reduce the study of heat to an a priori science. Gibbs's purpose shows the extraordinary influence of an eighteenth-century philosopher, Immanuel Kant. Kant claimed to have demonstrated that the fundamental principles of physics, ranging from the conservation of matter to Newton's three laws of motion, are founded on reason alone, are not induced from experience, and could not be falsified by any possible experience. More than a century later, Gibbs, along with many others, still believed him.

Kant spent all of his life in or near Königsburg, in the eastern part of Prussia. He is the first philosopher we have considered who was so by profession: in 1770, after fifteen years as a lecturer, he became professor of logic and metaphysics at the University of Königsburg. Until 1770 Kant wrote on scientific topics, particularly questions of geophysics. From 1781 he produced in rapid succession a sequence of books on epistemology, ethics, and aesthetics. One of his principal philosophical works, *The Prolegomena*, is explicitly directed to an audience of teachers of philosophy, something quite uncommon before the eighteenth century.

Kant's theory of knowledge was developed in response to Hume's skeptical arguments. In *The Critique of Pure Reason*, *Prolegomena to Any Future Metaphysics*, and *Metaphysical Foundations of Natural Science*, Kant claimed to explain why arithmetic and geometry can be known a priori with certainty and to provide a demonstration of the a priori certainty of the most fundamental laws of physics, a demonstration that every event must have a cause, a demonstration that every sequence of causes and effects must follow some rule, and a refutation of Hume's skepticism about induction.

All of these works are written in a very obscure and forbidding style. Kant introduced an enormous variety of technical terms, which he seldom defined clearly and did not use in an obviously consistent way. He was fond of classifications and subclassifications, and so each part of his work received a separate special name or title, always in technical terms that sometimes mystify even those who are immersed in his system. Kant's combination of obscurity and influence have naturally produced a great many commentaries intended to clarify and evaluate his views and arguments, and several excellent secondary works have been published in the last twenty years.

Kant's three works on epistemology are filled with arguments. Unfortunately, the major arguments appear either invalid or too obscure to assess with confidence. While some modern writers report Kant's arguments without comment, few are willing to defend the soundness of the crucial inferences. Unlike Descartes and Hume, Kant's importance does not rest with his arguments themselves. Instead, the value of Kant's work for the theory of knowledge rests in the *kind* of argument he thought he could give for his theory, and in the general picture of knowledge presented in that theory, regardless of the arguments for it.

THE KANTIAN PICTURE

The world we experience is a world of enduring things arranged in space and of events involving those things. Some events occur simultaneously with one another, and others occur in succession. If we look out upon a scene, we do not see separate patches of color and luminosity on a two-dimensional surface. Instead, we see things, objects. We see trees and houses and clouds and fences and other objects arranged in three-dimensional space. And yet it would seem that it is just such patches and their boundaries that are presented to each of our eyes. Somehow our mind puts together the inputs to each eye, transforming them into something quite different. If we follow a scene, we do not see a succession of patches of color and luminosity, but again it seems that just such a succession is presented to each of our eyes. We see causal processes involving changes in things and in their relations with one another. A bird flies through the sky, the clouds move with the wind, a leaf falls from a tree and drops to the ground. Somehow our mind transforms the inputs into intelligible causal changes in objects. If we move about in the world, or close our eyes and reopen them, we do not just see two or more different systems of patches of color and luminosity, although that is what is presented to our eyes. Instead, we may see the *same* objects once more. We recognize that we are home again, back in places we have been before, looking at the faces of our neighbors or friends. Our mind somehow *reidentifies* objects of experience.

These examples indicate the radical difference between what is presented to the eye and what we *see*. Patches of light and color are not presented to the retina with such tags as "house"; sequences of patches are not presented to us with such tags as "causal process"; two arrangements of patches are not presented to us linked with such identifiers as "patches of the same thing you saw this morning." We see things identified, objectified, and causally ordered, but that is *our* doing. Kant saw in reflections such as these a fundamental point: *the world we experience is a world constructed by our minds*. Kant called this process *synthesis*. We have seen the Kantian picture before, but it is worth seeing again (figure 9.1).

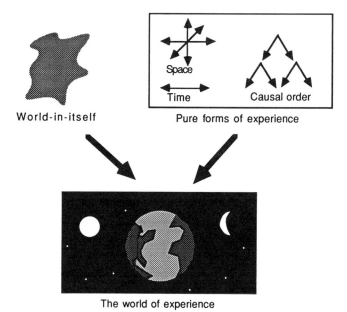

Figure 9.1
Kant's picture of metaphysics

For the most part, the construction of the empirical world from sensory inputs is automatic; it is done by our minds but not by our wills. We do not have to deliberately and consciously assemble things out of patches of color and illumination. But sometimes higher-order versions of these processes are deliberate, as when scientists introduce atoms and other unseen particles to explain experimental results or when Newton introduced the universal gravitational force. These inferred objects and processes also belong to the world of experience in a broad sense. Atoms and gravitational forces are not patches of color and illumination; they are objects, properties, and processes in three-dimensional space and in time. Such theoretical objects and processes are postulated to explain other objects and processes more apparent in experience. Kant's interests included the deliberate, scientific construction of the unseen features of the world, but his primary concern was with the construction of the pre-scientific world of experience by our minds.

In view of these conclusions, we might expect to learn about general features of our experience by investigating *how* our minds construct the world from sensory inputs. That is exactly what cognitive scientists attempt to do in our own time, but in the eighteenth century no one had suggested such an inquiry, nor, exactly, did Kant. For one thing, neither Kant nor anyone else in the eighteenth century had any idea of how such an experimental inquiry into the operations of the mind could be conducted. But in any case, Kant would not have thought that such experimental inquiries could be important in responding to Hume's skeptical arguments. For any conclusions obtained from experiments about how the mind works, and thus about general features of any possible experience, would be subject to Hume's doubts about induction. If from experiments we learned that mental operations always produce experiences with a certain feature, that information would not provide any response to Hume's skepticism about induction. Indeed, conclusions about the operations of the mind founded on experiment would themselves be subject to the general doubts that Hume advanced about the conclusions of inductive inference.

Kant never suggested an experimental inquiry into the operations of the mind. Instead, he claimed to *deduce conditions necessary for any possible experience*. The premises of such an argument are to be nothing more than that the mind produces experience of reidentifiable objects undergoing regular changes in time and in three-dimensional space. The conclusions of such arguments are that Euclidean geometry is true of the space we experience, that every event has a cause, that every sequence of causes and effects follows a general rule, and that the most general fundamental laws of natural science necessarily hold in the world we experience. Kant called such arguments *transcendental*. Kant took Hume's skepticism to be refuted by the principles that every event has a cause and that a sequence of causes and effects must satisfy general laws. Moreover, the demonstration of these claims is supposed to be immune to Hume's doubts about inductive inference, because the argument that leads to the reliability of induction is not an inductive inference or a deductive argument but a transcendental argument premised only on the possibility of experience. Kant thought he had shown, in other words, that inductive inference can be reliable for any possible course of experience.

Kant emphasized repeatedly that he retained a certain form of skepticism. What Kant doubted was that we could have any knowledge of how the world is in itself, as distinct from our knowledge of things in the world of experience constructed by our minds. Of course, through experimental investigations we can acquire knowledge about how external circumstances produce radiation on our retinas and about the correlation between our perceptions and those external things. But all knowledge of that kind is knowledge of things within the world of experience, not knowledge of things in themselves. In distinguishing *external causes* of our *internal perceptions*, we already presuppose that there are things, that they are located in three-dimensional space, and that they are subject to a causal order. All of these suppositions are products of the application of our minds to the data of sensation. They are true of the world of experience—indeed, necessarily true, according to Kant—but we have no reason whatsoever to believe that they are true of the world in itself.

Unfortunately, none of Kant's transcendental arguments are sound. Kant in fact gives no direct argument that Euclidean geometry is true or is imposed by the mind on the data of sensation. Instead, he assumed that Euclidean geometry is true of the space of experience, and he further assumed that it is necessarily true (no possible experience could contradict it), and that we can know a priori that it is true. His *argument* is that his theory *explains* how this could be so: if Euclidean geometrical relations are an artifact of how we synthesize the manifold of experience, then all possible experience must satisfy Euclidean geometry, and we can be certain (Kant says "apodeictically certain") of its truth, so we do not have to resort to inductive inference. Despite Kant's claim, this is not even an adequate explanation. The hypothesis that in creating experience from the data of sensation the operations of the mind guarantee that spatial representations satisfy Euclidean geometry would explain why space is Euclidean (if that were true, which it is not), but it would not of itself explain the *certainty* that Euclidean geometry is true. In fact, it seems that if the mind constructs experience so that Euclidean geometry is true, we still have no means other than induction from experience to *learn* that Euclidean geometry is true. There are at least two senses of a priori, and it seems that Kant sometimes does not clearly distinguish them. In one sense, a feature of the world is a priori if it is due to our minds; in another sense, a feature is a priori if without induction we can come to know the proposition that says that the feature obtains. Even in Kant's own story, Euclidean geometry is a priori in the first sense but not in the second sense.

Kant's arguments for an a priori physics are given in the *Metaphysical Foundations of Natural Science*. One example will show the flavor of his demonstrations:

Proposition 3: second law of mechanics   Every change of matter has an external cause. (Every body remains in its state of rest or motion in the same direction and with the same velocity unless it is compelled by an external cause to forsake this state.)

Proof   (In universal metaphysics there is laid down the proposition that every change has a cause; here [in mechanics] there is only to be proved of matter that its change must always have an external cause.) Matter as mere object of the external senses has no other determinations than those of external relations in space and hence undergoes no changes except by motion. With regard to such change, insofar as it is an exchange of one motion with another, or of motion with rest, and vice-versa, a cause of such change must be found (according to the principle of metaphysics). But this cause cannot be internal, for matter has no absolutely internal determinations and grounds of determination. Hence all change of a matter is based upon an external cause.[1]

Aside from the vagueness of the notions used in this argument ("determinations," for example), nothing in the "proof" explains why changes in *velocity* require external causes but changes in *position* or *acceleration* do not. In fact, the proposition is not even clear: Kant does not explain in what frame of reference this principle is to apply. A motion that has a constant velocity with respect to one frame of reference does not have a constant velocity with respect to other frames of reference accelerated with respect to the first. Kant provides no basis for distinguishing absolutely accelerated frames of reference from other frames of reference.

The physical argument just considered is at least succinct. In contrast, Kant's argument for the reliability of inductive inference is very elaborate

Table 9.1
Logical table of judgements

Quantity	Quality	Relation	Modality
Universal	Affirmative	Categorical	Problematic
Particular	Negative	Hypothetical	Assertoric
Singular	Infinite	Disjunctive	Apodeictic

and very obscure. The general picture is quite simple, but how it works is neither clear nor simple. The general picture is roughly as follows: In synthesizing the manifold of experience, the understanding makes *judgements*. Judgments all have a logical structure. There are only a few possible logical structures for judgements, and they can be completely described (according to Kant) in a simple table (table 9.1). There are 81 distinct logical forms. Each logical form is determined by a value for quantity, quality, relation, and modality, and each of these four has three possible values.

Kant, I think, would have classified the judgement that necessarily, all Manx cats are tailless, as universal ("all"), infinite (it neither affirms nor denies a property of a particular thing), categorical (it is not a conditional or disjunctive claim), and apodeictic ("necessarily"). The classification is a version of the logical theories current late in the eighteenth century, of which Kant had his own. The important thing is that Kant claimed that with each value of quantity, quality, relation, and modality there is a corresponding *concept of the understanding*. For example, the concept of the understanding that corresponds to hypothetical judgements (expressed by conditional sentences) is *cause*.

When we form the manifold of experience from the matter of experience, we apply the concepts of the understanding to make judgements, and some of these judgements are hypothetical. Hypothetical judgements incorporate the concept of causality, and so we form the world of experience so that sequences of events (in the world of experience) make appropriate sentences of the form "If A then B" always true. Thus we have an a priori concept of causality and of necessary connection, which we do not need to form *from* experience but rather *use to form* experience. And the construction of the world of experience guarantees that the causal relations that experience presents to us in particular sequences of events can be generalized and will always be true.

What we have is a sequence of claims that together form a general picture of how the world of experience is constituted, why geometry and parts of physics are irrefutable by any possible experience, and why induction is reliable.

There are really two different themes in Kant's philosophy. One is *idealism*: the world of experience is constructed by the mind, and aspects of the world of experience may therefore be artifacts of that construction. The other theme is *transcendental argument*: necessary conditions of any possible experience can be established by deductive arguments from general features of experience. Variations on Kant's form of idealism captivated a great many philosophers and philosophically inclined scientists in the nineteenth and twentieth centuries. Despite the failure of Kant's own attempts at transcendental arguments, many others have since been given. Indeed, the idea of a transcendental argument has been broadened to include, for example, arguments for necessary conditions of any possible belief from general features of belief. In one way or another, Kant's picture posed the issues for much of modern philosophical thought about knowledge. In the remainder of this chapter I will consider some of those developments.

CONSTRUCTIONAL SYSTEMS

Kant held that the objects of experience are constructed or "synthesized," but he was not at all clear about what they are constructed from, or how the details of such a construction could work. After Frege's work, a few philosophers began to have novel ideas about what a "construction" or "synthesis" might be. The three most important philosophers first influenced by Frege were Bertrand Russell, Ludwig Wittgenstein, and Rudolf Carnap. Russell had an important correspondence with Frege, and Carnap went to Jena to study with him.

Russell and Carnap each proposed (at about the same time) that extensions of Frege's logical theory, or Frege's logic in combination with set theory, could be used to describe the construction of physical objects from the data of sensation. Russell and Whitehead developed techniques to carry on Frege's logicist program to reduce mathematics to logic; Russell and Carnap independently thought that the same techniques could be used to give an account of our knowledge of the external world.

Russell's idea was that with variables ranging over basic entities (the sense data) and with predicates denoting properties of sense data (such as *red*) one could *define* terms that would denote *sets* of sense data. Physical objects would literally be sets of sense data, or sets of sets of sense data, or sets of sets of sets of sense data, and so on. Similarly, higher-order properties of physical objects (such as the property of being a tree) would also be appropriate sets of sense data (or sets of sets of sense data, etc.). Russell sketched these ideas in a popular book, *Our Knowledge of the External World*, but he made no attempt to describe any logical details. Meanwhile, Carnap actually produced an outline of such a system.

Carnap's book, *The Logical Construction of the World*, was published in 1929. Carnap assumed that the fundamental entities over which the variables of his system range are what he called *elementary experiences*. An elementary experience is all that appears to someone at a particular moment. In addition, he assumed one relation between elementary experiences is given in experience, namely the relation that obtains when one recollects that two experiences are similar in some respect or other. (For example, they might both be experiences that contain a red patch somewhere.) The construction of the world begins with a finite list of pairs of elementary experiences; for each pair in the list, the person whose experiences they are recollects that the first element in the pair is in some respect similar to the second element in the pair. Qualities such as color and tone are then defined as certain sets (or sets of sets, etc.) formed from this list. Objects are to be constructed in the same way.

One of the most remarkable things about Carnap's logical construction of the world is that it is presented not only as a collection of logical formulas to be applied to terms denoting elementary experiences and the relation of recollection. Carnap also described the construction as a *computational procedure*. That is, along with each logical construction he gave what he called a "fictitious procedure" that shows how to calculate a representation of the object constructed from any list of pairs of elementary experiences. The procedures are perfectly explicit, and they could be represented in any modern computer language, such as Pascal or LISP. *Carnap was the first philosopher (indeed, the first person) to present a theory of the mind as a computational program.* The use of logical representations immediately suggested (to Carnap, anyway) that computation can be done not just on numbers but on symbols that represent nonnumerical objects. This was really Ramon Lull's idea, and Hobbes's idea after that, but in Carnap's work it begins to look much more serious.

Contemporary work in artificial intelligence (AI) aims to produce computer programs that describe procedures that, when implemented on a computer, will produce intelligent behavior. Many AI workers build programs that are in the general spirit of Carnap's procedures. There is even a popular AI programming language, PROLOG, that represents procedures as logical formulas. Such programs operate on inputs to create data structures that play the role of beliefs, desires, or interests and that describe objects and properties, which the programs infer from the data given to them. Of course, when Carnap wrote his book, there were no electronic digital computers, no computer programs, and no programming languages. Those did not begin to appear until fifteen years later. Even so, a great deal of contemporary work in artificial intelligence has descended from Carnap's ideas.

CONVENTIONALISM AND ANALYTIC TRUTH

Kant's goals were to put geometry and the laws of motion on an a priori foundation and in addition to solve the problem of inductive skepticism that Hume had posed. His strategy was to see the world as a system of objects, properties, and relations constructed by the mind in such a way that Euclidean geometry and Newton's laws of motion are always satisfied and inductive inference is reliable. The problem was that Kant could not really demonstrate these claims. Carnap's *Logical Construction of the World* gave a more detailed and clearer description of procedures by which features of the world *could be* constructed by the mind from simpler data. But Carnap's work did not show (nor did Carnap claim) that our minds *actually* construct the world of experience in the way Carnap described. That would be an empirical claim for which Carnap had no evidence. In addition, Carnap's construction did not guarantee that induction will be reliable or that the laws of motion are satisfied. So Carnap's construction formed a kind of logical bridge between Kant's project and modern cognitive science, but Carnap's work did not help to fulfill Kant's epistemological goals. For that, we must consider another modern line of thought, *conventionalism*.

Henri Poincaré (1854–1912) was one of the great mathematicians, mathematical physicists, and philosophers of the late nineteenth century. Poincaré held that Euclidean geometry is true a priori, and that, as Kant maintained, it is *we* who make Euclidean geometry true. But Poincaré's account of *how* we make Euclidean geometry true is quite different from Kant's.

Poincaré thought that nothing in experience could contradict geometry by itself, because pure geometry makes no predictions about the world. Only geometry in combination with physics makes predictions that can be tested by experience. Suppose, for example, that you wish to test the Pythagorean theorem. You might measure the two sides and the hypotenuse of a right triangle and see if the sum of the squares of the lengths of the sides equals the square of the length of the hypotenuse. But how would you measure the lengths? Perhaps you would use a measuring stick of some kind, laying it off against the sides and against the hypotenuse of the triangle. Suppose now that you do the measurements and that to your surprise you discover that the sum of the squares of the lengths of the sides *does not* equal the square of the length of the hypotenuse of the triangle. Must you conclude that the Pythagorean theorem is false? Poincaré thought not.

Rather than reject the Pythagorean theorem, you are free to conclude that as the measuring stick was moved from one position to another when measuring the sides and hypotenuse of the triangle, it was subject to forces that changed its length; you are also free to conclude instead that the triangle was not really a *right* triangle. If you get the imagined results, you are free to change physics rather than geometry. Poincaré thought that if we made observations inconsistent with the combination of geometry and physics, we would always prefer to change physics and keep Euclidean geometry unaltered. The truth of Euclidean geometry is therefore, in Poincaré's view, a matter of *decision*, of human convention. We always have a choice about how to interpret observations, and we always choose to interpret them so that geometry is true. The reason, according to Poincaré, is that maintaining Euclidean geometry and altering physics as needed will keep our total system of beliefs *simpler* than would adopting a non-Euclidean geometry. We happen to prefer simpler systems of belief.

Poincaré's account of geometrical truth reminds one of the account of logical truth developed from Frege's theory. In that view, logical truths are true in virtue of our use of such simple parts of language as quantifier phrases ("every," "no," "all") and sentential connectives ("and," "or," "not"). It is our linguistic practice that makes certain sentences logical truths, just as, according to Poincaré, it is our linguistic and inductive practice that makes geometrical claims immune to refutation. Poincaré's explanation of geometrical truth could readily be extended to other kinds of mathematical truths. Philosophers influenced by his views offered a parallel explanation for truth in arithmetic. On this view, arithmetic is true because we do not allow anything in experience to contradict it. When we use a scientific theory and arithmetic to make a prediction that turns out false, we blame the scientific theory, not arithmetic.

Poincaré's conventionalism provided an alternative to Kant's account of mathematical truth, and it saved an important Kantian theme. For both Kant and Poincaré, mathematics is not founded on inductive inference and is not subject to refutation by any possible experience.

Conventionalist explanations might be extended to parts of physics as well. Might it not be that, like geometry, certain parts of physics cannot be tested separately but only in conjunction with other parts of physics? And might the parts of physics that cannot be tested in isolation be made true by convention, that is, by our decision not to let any unexpected observations count against them but rather to always put the blame for failed predictions elsewhere? Influenced by Poincaré, Albert Einstein argued that some determinations of simultaneity relations between physical events are conventional.

Imagine that you are trying to determine whether two events A and B that occur in regions of space some distance from one another are simultaneous (figure 9.2). Light travels with a finite velocity. Imagine that the two events occur close enough together in time so that no light pulse could be sent from the place where A occurs, when A occurs, to arrive at the

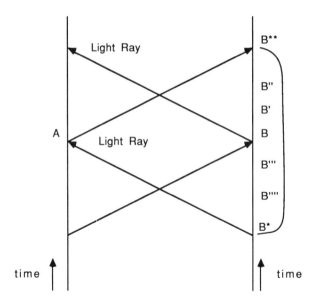

Figure 9.2
The problem of simultaneity

place where B occurs before or at the moment B occurs, and symmetrically, that no light pulse could be sent from the place where B occurs, when B occurs, to arrive at the place where A occurs before or at the moment A occurs.

One of the fundamental principles of Einstein's special theory of relativity is that no causal process can move faster than light. If a light ray cannot be sent from A to B or to an event in the same place prior to B, then no signal of any kind can be sent from event A to event B. The same is true for signals from B to A. Einstein maintained that whether or not events A and B are simultaneous is a matter of convention. One could just as well decide to take any of the events between B^* and B^{**} as simultaneous with A. But certain choices about which distant events are simultaneous lead to a simpler system of physics than do other choices, and that is why, Einstein claimed, we should adopt appropriate conventions about simultaneity.

Hans Reichenbach (1981–1953), Einstein's student, developed the conventionalist idea still further. According to Reichenbach, the fundamental laws of motion, whether Newton's or Einstein's, are true by convention if they are true at all. The first law of Newtonian mechanics says that a body subject to no force will move through space in a straight Euclidean line with a constant speed (when viewed from an unaccelerated frame of reference). The first law picks out certain motions through space and time and says that they are the motions possible for a body subject to no force. But no experiment could contradict such a law of motion, Reichenbach argued. For suppose we found that when we eliminate all known forces, bodies do not move in straight Euclidean lines. Then instead of abandoning Newton's first law of motion, we could postulate a new "universal" force that acts on all bodies all the time, keeping them from moving in straight Euclidean lines with constant speed. In fact, Reichenbach claimed, gravity is such a "universal force." It affects everything and keeps bodies that are otherwise isolated from more specific forces from moving in straight Euclidean lines at constant speed. When Newton and Newtonians treated gravity as a force that disturbs bodies from their natural, unforced motion, they were exercising a convention, not drawing an experimentally founded generalization. Whether we use Newton's laws of motion, Einstein's laws of motion, or some other system, according to Reichenbach it is our decision or convention that makes the laws of motion we choose true and irrefutable.

For Kant, as for Leibniz, Hobbes, and others, *analytic truths* are judgements that are true because one concept is contained in another concept.

Philosophers in the twentieth century influenced by the conventionalist approach gave the term "analytic truth" quite a different interpretation. It came to mean any sentence that is true because of the conventions implicit in our use of language or because of our general inductive practice about which parts of our theories we blame when the unexpected occurs. Logical truths thus count as analytic truths, according to conventionalists, and so do geometry, arithmetic, parts of physics, and even such everyday truths as "All bachelors are unmarried men."

DOUBTS

Several of the accounts of knowledge that emerged in the first half of this century share a similar structure. They postulate some kind of fundamental level of appearances—whether Russell's "sense data," Carnap's "elementary experiences," or whatever—that can be described and reported. The claims of other minds, of an external world, of physical objects, of the objects and laws of science are connected with claims about fundamental appearances by means of conventions (or stipulations or analytic truths). The connections aren't deductive, they are part of the very *meanings* of our terms for describing the world and its contents. Versions of this picture were developed by Russell, by Carnap, and by such American philosophers as Roy Wood Sellars and Clarence Irving Lewis. Elements of this picture are still advocated by a number of philosophers, but its central tenets were critically attacked in the middle of this century.

One challenge was to the very idea of a category of statements that provide a "foundation" for knowledge. The idea of a foundational class of statements is that statements not in this class are justified by their logical or conceptual connections to claims in the foundational class and, of course, by the truth of the appropriate claims in the foundational class. For example, Russell's sort of foundationalism seemed to say that our claims about physical objects are ultimately justified by claims about sense data. The claims that we assert from the foundational class need no justification whatsoever: no justification is or can be given for my claim about how something appears to me. A number of philosophers denied that any such foundational class of statements exists. They acknowledged that for the purposes of some inquiry or for resolving some question, we might very well distinguish the hypothesis at issue from a class of possible sentences that could be evidence for or against the hypothesis. But, they argued, other considerations could always induce us to broaden or narrow the evidence class, or to reject some purported piece of evidence. For reports of appearances to be beyond the requirement of justification, there must be no way of calling such judgements into doubt, and the critics argued that every judgement in public language can be called into doubt. If you say "The cat looks black to me," one can ask how you know you are using "black" correctly, how you know there is a cat before you, how you know that it's you who are the subject of this experience.

Willard Van Orman Quine was one of the most influential critics of the conventionalist solutions. Quine argued that there is no mark that distinguishes claims that philosophers such as Reichenbach and Carnap called conventional from any other claims of science. There is nothing special about geometry or simultaneity or the laws of motion.

Quine's argument really has two sides. First, it cannot be said that geometry or theories about simultaneity or the laws of motion are immune from revision. These claims have changed a great deal in the course of the history of science. In the general theory of relativity, Euclidean geometry has been replaced by dynamic non-Euclidean geometries. The laws of motion of the theory of relativity and of quantum theory are not the laws of motion that Newton postulated. Simultaneity relations according to the theory of relativity are different from such relations according to Newtonian theory. Just like the rest of science, the parts that neo-Kantians called "conventional" have been altered over time.

Second, Quine argued that there is no *logical* distinction between claims that are called conventional and other parts of science. The change that takes place when we alter the laws of motion is not a change of a different logical kind from the change that takes place when we alter the laws of electrodynamics. It is not true, according to Quine, that some parts of science are subject to refutation from experience and other parts of science are immune from any such refutation. If we are determined enough and ingenious enough, Quine argued, no matter what unexpected observations we make, we can revise science so as to keep unchanged any particular claim we wish. We simply have to be willing to make enough alterations in other parts of our scientific theories. As Quine put it, *anything can be held true, come what may*. It is true that our science is in some measure conventional, if that means our scientific theories are a human creation that serve a purpose, which alternative creations might serve as well. But it is not true, according to Quine, that the conventionality is located in particular parts of our system of beliefs. On the contrary, a bit of arbitrariness is diffused over the whole system.

Quantum logic?

Does the diffused conventionalism extend even to logic? Could we, to save our physical theories, literally change our principles of inference in the face of unexpected experiences? Quine himself was equivocal on the question, but subsequent philosophers were not. Many philosophers proposed that the phenomena of quantum mechanics call for a change in logical principles. Recall that there are physical phenomena of the following kind: An electron is in a box divided into two sides, the left side (L) and the right side (R). According to common interpretations of the quantum theory, it can happen that $\neg Le$ is true and $\neg Re$ is also true, but at the same time it *is* true that $Le \vee Re$. These circumstances are impossible according to classical, or Fregean, logic. One might think, therefore, that the remedy is to change the physical theory, but for many reasons, physicists are not willing to do that. A number of philosophers, physicists, and mathematicians have proposed that what has happened in quantum theory is a change in logic itself. One philosopher, Hilary Putnam, has compared the change in logic implicit in quantum theory with the change in geometry implicit in the adoption of the general theory of relativity. But a change of logic is in a sense more radical than any change in a particular theory. A change in logic is not simply a change in beliefs but a change in the consequences that one draws from any proposition whatsoever.

Quine realized that we can start with conventions or analytic truths. We can introduce a new term as an abbreviation for a combination of old terms. But as soon as we begin to form generalizations and to conjecture laws that involve the new term, we create an option for ourselves. If a counterexample to the new conjectures is produced that involves the connection between the original term and the new term, then rather than giving up the conjectures, we have the option of abandoning the definition while keeping the new term and the new conjectures. We can make conventions for the moment, but if they are useful in empirical science, they soon cease to be any different from other scientific claims.

Arguments such as these undermined the conventionalist road to Kant's goals, and in particular to the special status of geometry and the laws of motion.

IDEALISM, SKEPTICISM, AND RELATIVISM

One of the unexpected effects of Kant's philosophy was to produce a concern with the historical development of belief and culture. The initial source of the connection between idealism and history was Hegel, who thought of all of human history as a kind of Kantian synthesis in the mind of God, or (as Hegel called the deity) the Absolute. The synthesis Hegel imagined was not carried out by the categories of the understanding but by what Hegel called *dialectic*; history produces a condition and an opposing condition that works against the first, a *thesis* and an *antithesis* as Hegel called them, and the two opposing forces produce a synthesis, which then faces another antithesis, and so on. Hegel's views have been one important source for the development of historicist conceptions of knowledge and truth.

In its boldest form, *historicism* is the view that the world changes as human culture and belief about the world change, or equivalently, that the contradictory beliefs of human cultures at different epochs are all equally true. For example, in Aristotle's time there were final causes because Aristotle and the Greeks believed in them, but now there are no final causes. There were witches in Salem in the days of Cotton Mather, but now there are none. There are few contemporary thinkers who explicitly endorse such bold historicist claims, but many writers implicitly use the historicist perspective.

In any period there are bound to be groups with conflicting beliefs. A view closely related to but distinct from historicism is *cultural relativism*, which asserts that the beliefs of all human communities are equally well founded and that none are more or less true than others. While cultural relativism is liberal and tolerant, it also offends almost every moral sensibility. It entails, for example, that we should not censure those who organize their families differently than we, who have different religious views, or who have different medical practices. But it also entails that if a physician in rural Oklahoma believes that women of a local religious community are dying because of infection produced by incompetent midwives but the male elders of the religious community believe that the women are dying only because it is God's will, there is no truth to the matter, and no one, neither physician nor religious authority, can have the better reasons. It also means that if Hitler caused many to believe that Jews form an inferior race, he and his followers were not less right or less warranted in their beliefs than were those who opposed such opinions.

Historicism was associated with idealism through Hegel's influence, and the association of these themes continues today even among those who have never read a word of Hegel. Cultural relativism has many of the same sources, but it was also supported by twentieth-century movements in cultural anthropology. Cultural relativism seems little different from radical skepticism of the kind that Descartes imagined but never seriously entertained and that Hume thought philosophically warranted but absurd and impossible in practice. Recently, however, neo-Kantian replies to skeptical arguments have come to be widely replaced by views that are quite close to cultural relativism. Many of the arguments for these views have to do with psychology and the history of science.

The History of Knowledge

One of the striking facts about the history of science is that, judged from our present perspective, almost every scientific theory ever proposed has been false in some respect. Moreover, there are sometimes radical breaks in scientific tradition. When these breaks or *scientific revolutions* occur, new theories emerge that may postulate a different fundamental structure for the world or for some aspect of the world. New scientific theories do not simply propose novel laws for the same quantities that occur in the theories that proceed them. Instead, when a scientific revolution occurs, old quantities and old entities may be disregarded altogether —even their existence may be denied—while new laws are proposed that govern novel properties and entities.

Newton's dynamics was about motion with respect to *absolute space*. In the theory that succeeded Newtonian dynamics, the theory of relativity, there is no such thing as absolute space. In relativity, a property of bodies, *relativistic mass*, varies with the velocity of the moving body. There is no such quantity in Newtonian dynamics. In the theory of heat that dominated the nineteenth century, heat was regarded as a fluid called *caloric*, and the study of heat was the study of the properties and motions of that fluid. There is no such fluid according to modern theories of heat. In eighteenth-century chemistry, combustion involved the loss of a chemical species, *phlogiston*. Much of eighteenth-century chemistry concerned the properties of various gases from which some measure of phlogiston had been removed. Phlogiston chemists called samples of light, colorless gas *dephlogisticated air*. In the chemistry of the nineteenth century and afterwards, there is no such thing as phlogiston, and so there is no such process as removing the phlogiston from a gas. There is hydrogen gas, and oxygen gas, but there is no such thing as dephlogisticated air.

Thomas Kuhn, a contemporary historian and philosopher whose influential book *The Structure of Scientific Revolutions* emphasized these aspects of scientific development, argued that changes in scientific theory constitute changes in how the world is *seen*. Kuhn's thought was that scientists before and after a scientific revolution may literally perceive different entities in circumstances that might otherwise seem similar. Faced with the same light, colorless gas, an eighteenth-century chemist would see dephlogisticated air, while a nineteenth-century chemist would see hydrogen. Examining the water in a spinning bucket, a Newtonian scientist sees rotation with respect to absolute space, whereas an Einsteinian scientist sees only absolute acceleration but no motion with respect to absolute space.

Furthermore, Kuhn argued, revolutionary changes in scientific theory change the very meanings of words. There are no fixed senses to claims made in different scientific paradigms. When the Newtonian talks of "mass," something different is meant than when the relativist talks of "mass." Because there are no fixed meanings, scientists in different paradigms cannot describe their observations in neutral terms, which means that there is no possible empirical procedure by which advocates of different paradigms can resolve their differences. Phlogiston chemists and oxygen chemists could not even agree on how to describe experimental results, nor could classical ether theorists and relativity theorists. Kuhn says that the language in one scientific paradigm is *incommensurable* with language in a competing paradigm.

Finally, scientific revolutions change scientific method. In practice, scientific method in any subject consists of elaborate and often tacit criteria for good observational studies, criteria for experimental designs, particular statistical methods for analyzing data, and restrictions on the form and content of scientific explanations. Alternative paradigms differ in some or all of these aspects of scientific method. So even if advocates of different paradigms could agree on empirical premises, they would make very different inferences.

The radical conclusion that some philosophers have drawn from Kuhn's picture of the history of science is that the world of experience depends upon variable features of human beings or communities of human beings. Different worlds of experience arise because of different *conceptual schemes*, and any empirical knowledge must be relative to such a scheme. An even stronger conclusion is that there are absolutely no normative principles that can or should regulate the transition from one conceptual scheme to another. Nothing can be said about whether one conceptual scheme was better than another or whether evidence warranted any historical transition from one paradigm to another over the course of human intellectual history.

In one respect, conceptual relativism can be viewed as a philosophical position that frees a parameter fixed in Kant's framework. According to Kant, the world of experience is a function of the world in itself, which is unknown and unknowable, and what we might call the human conceptual scheme. The two together determine the world of experience of each person and guarantee their correlation. Our notions of possibility involve counterfactual worlds of experience, presumably those that might occur if things in themselves were different. The relativist framework retains the Kantian view that the world of experience is determined by the individual's conceptual scheme and the world in itself, but allows the conceptual scheme to vary from person to person and for each person from time to time. Within each conceptual scheme, the counterfactual worlds of experience are those that might occur if things in themselves were different. Viewed in this formal way, conceptual relativism looks like a natural extension of the Kantian framework, but in substance, it represents a collapse of the Kantian solution into skepticism, in which there is and can be no rational basis for agreement between people committed to different paradigms or conceptual schemes. We will see in the next chapter, however, that even this apparently radical view of the human condition leaves room for normative principles about how best to conduct inquiry.

Study Questions

1. Does conceptual relativism entail that whatever one believes is true?

2. What do you think that Quine would say about the doctrine of incommensurability across paradigms?

3. Do you think that there is a level of description of the outcomes of experiments at which phlogiston and oxygen chemists would agree as to what happened? If so, what becomes of Kuhn's thesis?

AFTER KANT

Language Games

If the Kantian and neo-Kantian replies to skepticism fail, what reply can be given to metaphysical and inductive skepticism? What answer can we give to questions about how it can be known that we are not brains in vats, or how any one of us can know that others have minds, or why the results of scientific inquiry should be trusted? More fundamentally, if the project of giving a priori foundations for knowledge is impossible, what is there for philosophical inquiry about knowledge to do?

One line of thought in the twentieth century tries to answer these questions by outlawing them. They can be outlawed in either of two ways. One way is to argue that the questions themselves are incoherent, self-contradictory, or meaningless. This response to the collapse of Kantian theory was taken by the logical positivists of the 1920s, who proposed the *verification principle*, which held that the meaning of a claim is exhausted by whatever would verify it. The principle still has advocates, principally among philosophers associated with Oxford University. More elaborate attempts to dismiss metaphysical and inductive skepticism are based on claims that the questions violate standard linguistic practice. In the middle of this century John Austin argued that skeptical doubts and claims about the evidence of the senses involve linguistic improprieties. Peter Strawson argued that reliance on inductive inference is just part of the meaning of "rational," so that no one can coherently ask why it is rational to believe in the results of inductive inference. More recently, Donald Davidson has argued that the very idea that most of our beliefs could be wrong is incoherent. Other arguments claim that we don't infer the existence of an external world or of others minds; we simply recognize them immediately and without inference.

None of these responses provide very satisfactory responses to skepticism, although the detailed analyses of the informal logical properties of parts of language given by Austin are fascinating in their own right. Even if our inductive practices are part of what we mean by "rational," it still makes sense to ask why we should think that these practices are reliable, and it still makes sense to ask why, if we are interested in coming to believe the truth, we should be "rational." It certainly *seems* to make sense to ask how I know I'm not a brain in a vat. Whether or not I go through a process of inference when recognizing objects or other persons seems irrelevant to the skeptical challenge, which is to show that my practice or habit or capacity for recognizing persons and things would reliably discriminate the real thing from particular conceivable illusions.

Descartes' question as to how he can know that he is not dreaming, or parallel questions about how anyone can know she is not a brain in a vat, or how anyone with a mind can know other people have minds, and so on, are fundamentally questions about how to reliably distinguish whether our beliefs are correct or illusory. Remarks about language and practice are attempts to show a priori in each case that one of the alternatives is impossible. They are near relatives to Kant's transcendental arguments, and about as convincing.

Primitivism

A second contemporary approach to skepticism and the problems of knowledge, an approach that can best be called *primitivism*, rejects the concern for rational, true belief that such problems presuppose. The primitivist response claims that intellectuals ought not to bother with such questions or with trying to answer them, sometimes hinting darkly that the questions are not really profound or that they have hidden confusions that need not be detailed (e.g., there is no such thing as *true* belief) or even that the skeptical questions and responses to them indicate a kind of cultural decay. Primitivism rejects the scientific description of the world as a place of things, events, and processes that are in themselves indifferent to human concerns, and in which the emergence of human consciousness and intentionality constitute phenomena to be explained. Primitivism instead insists on the sort of anthropomorphic conception of the world that we use in our everyday lives, a conception in which we think of things in terms of their utility to us and others and their significance as symbols. In the writing of the most influential primitivist of the twentieth century, Martin Heidegger, primitivism tends to be associated both with a holism that denies that any particular sort of object can be characterized and defined, or its essence given, in any way that separates that kind from the whole system of Being. Heidegger's primitivism emphasizes the authority of the community over the individual. Indeed, Wilhelm Dilthey, a German philosopher who is the source of much of contemporary primitivism and who influenced both Heidegger and such American pragmatists as John Dewey, suggested that individuals do not really exist; all that really exists is the social role an individual plays. After World War II, versions of these views were taken up by a number of French philosophers, notably Jean-Paul Sartre, Maurice Merleau-Ponty, and (less clearly) Albert Camus, whose doctrines came to be popularly known as *existentialism*. In recent years primitivism has been championed by a number of American philosophers, and in one version or another it has become the standard philosophical opinion of many scholars in the humanities other than professional philosophers.

Primitivism doesn't have much to offer those interested in the possibilities and limits of knowledge, in how we must be constituted and how the world must be constituted for us to know the world, in the nature of reason, demonstration, or meaning, in how the phenomena of mind can arise in a mindless world. Indeed, primitivists do not *want* to offer any results about these topics, nor, often enough, do they want others to.[2]

Naturalized Epistemology

A third response to the collapse of attempts to give an a priori foundation for human belief is quite different. That response is to start with whatever we think we know about the world and ourselves and to work backward and sideways, asking what we mean by *knowledge*; what the limits of knowledge are and are not for creatures such as ourselves; how to make a coherent metaphysical picture of the world, ourselves, and our interactions with the world that fits with our scientific understanding; and how creatures such as ourselves living in worlds such as ours can best achieve the goals of knowing and understanding. These projects are often called *naturalized epistemology*. Naturalized epistemology is not psychology, although it may very well use psychological results. Naturalized epistemology is not an empirical inquiry into how people learn. Instead, naturalized epistemology is partly a matter of analyzing the very goals and presuppositions of inquiry, partly a matter of trying to put together what we believe about the physical and the psychological realms into a coherent story of the human condition, and partly a matter of discovering how creatures such as ourselves can best conduct inquiry to achieve our goals. Some aspects of naturalized epistemology aren't even particularly about people but instead are about norms for any possible agents that share certain features of the human condition, agents that might be androids or computers, for example.

The questions of naturalized epistemology are a mixture of vivid contemporary issues and traditional philosophical concerns: How does mind relate to body? Could people be computers? How do the phenomena of meaning work? How can and should a computationally bounded agent reason? How can and should such an agent conduct inquiry? What can it learn, and what can it not learn? Given what we think we know about the world and ourselves, what questions can and cannot be answered in principle? Some of these questions have a vaguely Kantian ring, even though no attempt is made in naturalized epistemology to give a priori foundations for knowledge. A hypothesis about the substantive assumptions concerning causal structure, space, and time that a human must make to get around in the physical world is not any sort of a priori proof that those assumptions are correct, but it has an aspect of the transcendental about it. A mathematical proof characterizing the class of questions that a computationally bounded agent can and cannot reliably discover sounds a bit like a Kantian transcendental deduction. One difference is that the proofs of naturalized epistemology, unlike Kant's, are valid. Another difference is that the natural epistemologist doesn't claim to have shown a priori that the world we experience must be such that procedures of inquiry succeed.

Bertrand Russell's intellectual career illustrates the transition from neo-Kantianism to naturalized epistemology. Russell began his philosophical career as a neo-Kantian; his doctoral work was, in fact, a defence of the a priori claims of geometry in response to the development, in the nineteenth century, of consistent non-Euclidean geometries. Early in the twentieth century he focused on the problem of how, a logically powerful individual could "construct" the external world from sense data, that is, how he could define set-theoretic structures, based on possible sense data, that would play the roles of things in space and time and their properties and relations. Russell derided the idea of doing philosophy while simply assuming that there is an external world; that procedure, he wrote, has the advantage of theft over honest toil. By the time he wrote his last major philosophical work, *Human Knowledge: Its Scope and Limits*, Russell had decided that this kind of honest toil was work for Sisyphus. In this book Russell tried to characterize the assumptions about causal structure that humans must somehow have wired into them if they are to succeed in learning about the world as we believe it to be.

Naturalized epistemology does not provide a reply to skepticism, any more than does primitivist philosophy. But unlike primitivism, naturalized epistemology abandons neither reason nor clarity and offers a rich structure of problems, solutions, and results. In the remaining chapters of this book we will consider some of each.

Review Questions

1. Discuss in your own words the claim that the world we experience is a world constructed by our minds.

2. For Kant, why must Euclidean geometry and the fundamental laws of natural science necessarily hold for all human experiences of the world?

3. What is a transcendental argument?

4. Kant rejected Hume's skepticism but retained another form of skepticism. Explain the distinction between these two, and discuss why Hume's skepticism is denied by Kant.

5. Outline Kant's logical structure for judgements of the understanding.

6. Discuss the role of the concept of causality in the formation of the manifold of experience from the matter of experience.

7. What is meant by the term "idealism" as used in Kant's philosophy?

8. Outline Carnap's idea of a constructional system based on elementary experiences.

9. Discuss Poincaré's argument for the necessary truth of Euclidean geometry (now called *conventionalism*).

10. How did Quine argue against conventionalism?

11. Define "historicism." Define "cultural relativism." How are they different?

12. Describe what you think Kuhn means by a scientific *paradigm*.

13. What does Kuhn mean when he says that languages of distinct paradigms are *incommensurable*?

Further Reading

For contemporary replies to skepticism from Lockean and Kantian points of view, see respectively the following:

Goldman, Alan. *Empirical Knowledge*. Berkeley: University of California Press, 1988.

Grayling, A. C. *The Refutation of Scepticism*. La Salle, Ill.: Open Court, 1985.

Kant

Bennett, Jonathan Francis. *Kant's Analytic*. New York: Cambridge University Press, 1966.

Bennett, Jonathan Francis. *Kant's Dialectic*. New York: Cambridge University Press, 1974.

Brittan, Gordon G. *Kant's Theory of Science*. Princeton: Princeton University Press, 1978.

Kant, Immanuel. *Critique of Pure Reason*. New York: St. Martin's Press, 1968.

Kant, Immanuel. *Metaphysical Foundations of Natural Science*. Indianapolis: Bobbs-Merrill, 1970.

Kitcher, Patricia. *Kant's Transcendental Psychology*. New York: Oxford University Press, 1990.

Martin, Gotfried, and Judy Wubnig. *Arithmetic and Combinatorics: Kant and His Contemporaries.* Carbondale: Southern Illinois University Press, 1985.

Nagel, Gordon. *The Structure of Experience: Kant's System of Principles.* Chicago: University of Chicago Press, 1983.

Scruton, Roger. *Kant.* New York: Oxford University Press, 1982.

Strawson, P. F. *The Bounds of Sense: An Essay on Kant's "Critique of Pure Reason."* London: Methuen, 1966.

Walker, Ralph. *Kant on Pure Reason.* New York: Oxford University Press, 1982.

Constructional systems
Carnap, Rudolf. *The Logical Structure of the World: Pseudoproblems in Philosophy.* Berkeley: University of California Press, 1967.

Carnap, Rudolf. *The Logical Syntax of Language.* London: Routledge and Kegan Paul, 1937.

Goodman, Nelson. *The Structure of Appearance.* 3rd ed. Boston: D. Reidel, 1977.

Goodman, Nelson. *Ways of Worldmaking.* Indianapolis: Hackett Publishing Co., 1978.

Lewis, Clarence Irving. *Mind and the World-Order: Outline of a Theory of Knowledge.* New York: Dover Publications, 1956.

Russell, Bertrand. *Our Knowledge of the External World.* New York: Norton, 1929.

Conventionalism and its critics
Austin, John. *How to Do Things with Words.* 2nd ed. Cambridge: Harvard University Press, 1975.

Earman, John. *World Enough and Space-Time: Absolute versus Relational Theories of Space and Time.* Cambridge: MIT Press, 1989.

Poincaré, Henri. *The Foundations of Science; Science and Hypothesis; The Value of Science; Science and Method.* Trans. Bruce Halsted. New York: Science Press, 1929.

Quine, W. V. O. *From a Logical Point of View.* New York: Harper and Row, 1963.

Quine, W. V. O. *Philosophy of Logic.* Englewood Cliffs, N.J.: Prentice-Hall, 1970.

Quine, W. V. O. *Word and Object.* Cambridge: MIT Press, 1960.

Reichenbach, Hans. *The Philosophy of Space and Time.* New York: Dover, 1958.

Idealism, skepticism, and relativism
Benedict, Ruth. *Patterns of Culture.* Boston: Houghton Mifflin Co., 1934.

Douglas, Mary. *Implicit Meanings: Essays in Anthropology*. Boston: Routledge and Kegan Paul, 1978.

Hooker, Clifford Alan, ed. *The Logico-algebraic Approach to Quantum Mechanics*. Boston: D. Reidel, 1979.

Krausz, Michael. *Relativism*. Notre Dame, Ind.: University of Notre Dame Press, 1989.

Kuhn, Thomas. *The Essential Tension*. Chicago: University of Chicago Press, 1977.

Kuhn, Thomas. *The Structure of Scientific Revolutions*. 2nd ed. Chicago: University of Chicago Press, 1970.

Mead, Margaret. *From the South Seas: Studies of Adolescence and Sex in Primitive Societies*. New York: W. Morrow and Co., 1939.

Whorf, B. L. *Language, Thought, and Reality*. Cambridge: MIT Press, 1956.

Language games
Ayer, Alfred. *Logical Positivism*. Glencoe, Ill.: Free Press, 1959.

Dummett, Michael. *Truth and Other Enigmas*. Cambridge: Harvard University Press, 1978.

Warnock, Geoffrey. *J. L. Austin*. London: Routledge, 1989.

Primitivism
Dreyfus, Bert. *Being-in-the-World*. Cambridge: MIT Press, 1990.

Farias, Victor. *Heidegger and Naziism*. Philadelphia: Temple University Press, 1988.

Heidegger, Martin. *Being and Time*. New York: Harper, 1962.

Rorty, Richard. *Philosophy and the Mirror of Nature*. Princeton: Princeton University Press, 1979.

Sartre, Jean Paul. *Being and Nothingness*. New York: Philosophical Library, 1972.

Naturalized epistemology
Goldman, Alvin. *Epistemology and Cognition*. Cambridge: Harvard University Press, 1986.

Quine, W. V. O. *Ontological Relativity and Other Essays*. New York: Columbia University Press, 1969.

Russell, Bertrand. *Human Knowledge: Its Scope and Limits*. New York: Simon and Schuster, 1948.

Chapter 10
KNOWLEDGE AND RELIABILITY

INTRODUCTION

The challenges of metaphysical and inductive skepticism can be met in at least two different ways. One way is to change the conception of reliability used by Plato and Sextus. The Platonic conception of reliability requires that, whatever the truth may be, after a finite amount of evidence is obtained, we will believe the truth and know that we believe the truth. Another way is to loosen the connection between reliability and knowledge. The arguments of Meno, Sextus, Descartes, and even Hume demand that for knowledge in the actual world, we be able to reliably determine the truth in arbitrary imaginable worlds. But perhaps knowledge requires only reliability in some possible worlds, not in all imaginable circumstances. These are two of the most serious contemporary responses to skepticism.

We have already considered the Bayesian response to skepticism. Modern Bayesians abandon the notion of knowledge altogether, focusing instead on the notion of rational degrees of belief and rational changes of degrees of belief. Rather than obtaining the truth after a finite amount of evidence has appeared and knowing when one has obtained the truth, Bayesians conceive reliability as at most convergence to the truth in the limit, so that as evidence increases without bound, one's probability distribution becomes concentrated more and more tightly around the true hypothesis. Rather than requiring that inquiry lead to the truth in all logically possible worlds, Bayesians allow many logically possible worlds to have a zero initial probability; if the truth lies in such a world, it will not be found. And finally, Bayesians maintains that for deliberation, decision, and action, only expected utilities matter, and these may be defined and computable even in the presence of skeptical hypotheses.

In this chapter we will consider two additional contemporary responses to skepticism. One involves analyzing the notion of knowledge in a novel way; the other involves analyzing the notion of reliability in a novel way. The novel analyses of knowledge have been developed almost entirely by philosophers; the novel analyses of reliability were first introduced by the contemporary philosopher Hilary Putnam, but they have been further investigated by linguists, psychologists, computer scientists, and economists. How we respond to skepticism turns out to have many implications for disciplines besides philosophy.

KNOWLEDGE

The skeptic claims that we don't know things we ordinarily think we know very well. One response to the skeptic is to define "knowledge" so that it follows from the definition that the skeptic's claims are false. This is a dicey strategy, because we will not be very satisfied if the definition also has the consequence that lots of things we think aren't really knowledge turn out to be knowledge according to the definition. Nothing much is gained if we refute know-nothingism by embracing know-everythingism.

Here is a nice account of knowledge, proposed by the great American philosopher Clarence Irving Lewis:

Lewis's account of knowledge   Someone, *s*, *knows* proposition *p* if and only if (1) *s* believes that *p*, (2) *p* is true, (3) *s* is justified in believing that *p*.

The key terms used in the analysis—"believes," "true," and "justified"— are all vague in one way or another, but the notion of justification is especially vague. If we understand justification in a sufficiently broad way, this kind of analysis of knowledge offers a reply to skepticism. We might say, for example, that we are justified in a belief if we have formed it in the ordinary ways through seeing, touching, hearing, or other senses. To the skeptical claim that we do not know that there is an external world, we can reply that we do indeed. For we believe there is an external world, there truly is an external world, and we are justified in our belief because we formed it in the ordinary ways in which people form beliefs.

There is something unsatisfactory about this answer. If we came to recognize for some reason that many of our ordinary ways of justifying beliefs were in fact wildly unreliable, so that false beliefs were as likely to be justified as true beliefs, we might think that someone whose true belief was justified only by such unreliable methods really did not have knowledge. Traditional skeptical arguments depend on the fact that our standard methods of acquiring beliefs, such as perception, are not infallible. Indeed, sometimes our standard methods of forming beliefs are not even close to infallible. Psychological investigations in the last fifty years have shown that in many contexts people's ordinary ways of forming beliefs and making judgements are in fact quite unreliable. People are unreliable, for example, in forming probability judgements when they are given information sufficient to determine the right judgement according to the probability calculus. In many cases, even people with a good deal of experience in using statistics make predictable errors in judging probabilities. People are also known to be unreliable in judging certain forms of risk. Few people are afraid of driving in cars, while many people are afraid of flying, but driving in a car is much more risky. Moreover, human unreliability isn't limited to probability judgements. There is a great deal of evidence that most medical experts are unreliable at many forms of diagnosis, that psychiatric experts are unreliable at predicting future behavior, and that textbook methods standardly used in the social sciences to determine causal facts are unreliable. In any of these cases a person using an unreliable method could claim to be justified in belief, but if the method used was unreliable we might question whether she really had knowledge, even if by chance her belief was true and even if the method was widely accepted and used.

In a short paper famous among philosophers, Edmund Gettier gave a refutation of the account of knowledge as justified, true belief.[1] Some of his examples go like this: Suppose you believe that Barishnikov is in town because you have seen an advertisement for a dance performance; seeing the advertisement justifies your belief. But suppose Barishnikov's performance was canceled because, unknown to you, the orchestra went on strike. Nonetheless, Barishnikov is in your town because he has a chronic health problem and your town is where the specialist he sees maintains a practice. According to Gettier, your belief that Barishnikov is in town is true, and you are justified in having the belief, but in fact you have no knowledge that Barishnikov is in town.

It is easy to produce further examples in which someone has a true belief and has acquired that belief by a means that we ordinarily think justifies the belief, and yet the reason why the person holds the belief is not the reason why the belief is true. Many people think that in such a state, belief is not knowledge; something is missing. Gettier's examples produced a number of attempts to say what that something is. Here are a few possibilities:

Defeasibility. Say that a true belief *p* that someone holds is *defeasible* for that person if there is some other true proposition such that if the person believed that proposition, she would not believe *p*. The proposal is that true beliefs that are knowledge must not be defeasible.

Truth of reasons. For knowledge, the reasons one would give to justify a belief must themselves all be true.

Causal relations. For knowledge, the circumstances justifying the belief that *p* must stand in appropriate causal relations to the truth that *p* and to the belief that *p*.

Reliability. The belief that *p* must have been acquired by a process that reliably yields the truth.

There are objections to all of these remedies. The appeal to reliability, for example, seems to offer little aid in avoiding Gettier's objection, since in the sorts of examples Gettier gives, a true belief is acquired by a method that generally is reliable and yet knowledge does not seem to result.

One of the most appealing answers to Gettier's problem was developed in recent years by Robert Nozick. It also forms a response to the skeptical claim that nothing is known. Nozick's idea is that one knows a proposition *p* if the proposition is true and if one's belief in it was acquired by a method such that if the proposition *p* were not true, the method would lead one to believe $\neg p$, and if *p* were true, one would believe *p*.

The force of the idea is that in saying that method *m* would lead one to believe $\neg p$ if *p* were false, Nozick is not claiming that the method must be reliable in every imaginable or logically possible circumstance. When we consider the conditions for the truth of sentences using subjunctives, such as "if the dancer were not in town," we do not consider arbitrary logically possible worlds. Instead, we consider only those possible circumstances that we would expect if things were very much as they are except that the indicated circumstance of the subjunctive phrase (the dancer is in town) were true. Consider Gettier's sort of example again. A person truly believes that Barishnikov is in town from reading an advertisement. Barishnikov is indeed in town, not because of the concert, which has been canceled, but for reasons of heath. If Barishnikov *were not* in town, it would be because he did not have an appointment with the physician. From reading the advertisement, the person in question would nonetheless believe that Barishnikov is in town. So the person does not have knowledge, and Gettier's objection is nicely sidestepped.

Many objections have been offered against Nozick's analysis of knowledge. I will consider just a few of them. One objection is this. On Nozick's analysis, one can know that p, and also know that p logically entails q, but fail to know that q. Nozick himself welcomed this feature of his account. I can, for example, know very well that I am typing, since if I were not typing, I would not believe that I am. But that I am typing entails that I am not a brain in a vat, and I know that the entailment holds. Nonetheless, on Nozick's analysis of knowledge, I do not know that I am not a brain in a vat, since if I were a brain in a vat, I would not then believe that I am a brain in a vat. Many commentators find it absurd that we should not be credited with knowing the known logical consequences of what we know. One way of fixing the analysis to meet this objection is suggested in the next set of study questions.

Another problem with Nozick's analysis concerns reliability. Sometimes a very reliable method will give the truth whenever some condition is met but will give no output or a random output in cases where the condition is not met. There are familiar examples from logic and mathematics. There is a method, for example, that, when given any logical formula, will return "yes" if the formula is a logical truth but is not guaranteed to return anything if the formula is not a logical truth. The same sort of one-sidedness can happen with methods or strategies for forming empirical beliefs. Nozick's analysis, however, requires something much stronger, something apparently too strong. It requires that the method m for resolving the question of whether p be a sort of decision procedure for p: it must return p if p is true and return the denial of p if p is not true. But if p is in fact true and we believe p and the method by which we formed the belief that p is reliable for positive assertions but not for denials, it would seem that we still know p.[2]

Study Questions

1. The problem of logical closure in Nozick's analysis might be removed by modifying the analysis to say that subject s knows that p if there exists a proposition q such that s knows that p entails q and if s acquired the belief that q by a method m that would have led s to believe the denial of q if q were not true. Is it a good objection to this revised analysis that the notion of knowledge of logical consequence is used to analyze the notion of knowledge?

2. The proposed analyses of knowledge in the text are more or less Socratic: knowing that p is analyzed in terms of a conjunction of other conditions not

involving the notion of knowledge. Could knowing that p instead be usefully analyzed in terms of knowledge that ____, where the blank is filled in by something other than p? Could knowing that p at time t be usefully analyzed in terms of knowledge of other propositions at times prior to t?

3. In mathematical logic, definitions are often *recursive*. The addition of natural numbers, $+$, for example, is often defined recursively in terms of 0 and the successor function s on the natural numbers. (By definition, $s(x)$ equals the number immediately following x.) The definition of addition is that $x + 0 = x$ and $x + s(y) = s(x + y)$. A recursive definition determines the value of a predicate or function for each object in a series in terms of some base case (the addition of 0 in the example just given) and in terms of the values of the predicate or function for succeeding members of the series. Can you use a time ordering to give a recursive analysis of knowledge?

4. Nozick proposes his account as an analysis of empirical knowledge, not of mathematical knowledge. What difficulties would his analysis meet if it were applied to mathematical knowledge?

RELIABILITY AND JUSTIFICATION

It may be a waste of time to spend a great deal of effort on attempting an analysis of knowledge. Perhaps, as Bayesians maintain, *knowledge* isn't really the central concept of human inquiry. For what ends should one want knowledge rather than merely true belief? For purposes of prediction or deciding action, it seems sufficient to believe truly and unnecessary to meet the further conditions, whatever they are, for knowing. Plato put this issue plainly in *The Meno* and answered it with the suggestion that knowledge has the further virtue of *stability*: we are less likely to forget or to change beliefs we know; we are more likely to change opinions concerning what we truly believe but do not know.

Socrates: If someone knows the way to Larissa, or anywhere else you like, then when he goes there and takes others with him he will be a good and capable guide, you would agree?

Meno: Of course.

Socrates: But if a man judges correctly which is the road though he has never been there and doesn't know it, will he not also guide others aright?

Meno: Yes he will.

Socrates: And as long as he has a correct opinion on the points about which the other has a knowledge, he will be just as good a guide, believing the truth but not knowing it.

Meno: Just as good.

Socrates: Therefore true opinion is as good a guide as knowledge for the purpose of acting rightly. That is what we left out just now in our discussion of the nature of virtue, when we said that knowledge is the only guide to right action. There was also, it seems, true opinion.

Meno: It seems so.

Socrates: So right opinion is something no less useful than knowledge.

Meno: Except that the man with knowledge will always be successful, and the man with right opinion only sometimes.

Socrates: What? Will he not always be successful so long as he has the right opinion?

Meno: That must be so, I suppose. In that case, I wonder why knowledge should be so much more prized than right opinion, and indeed how there is any difference between them.

Socrates: Shall I tell you the reason for your surprise, or do you know it?

Meno: No, tell me.

Socrates: It is because you have not observed the statues of Daedalus. Perhaps you don't have them in your country.

Meno: What makes you say that?

Socrates: They too, if no one ties them down, run away and escape. If tied, they stay where they are put.

Meno: What of it?

Socrates: If you have one of his works untethered, it is not worth much: it gives you the slip like a runaway slave. But a tethered specimen is very valuable, for they are magnificent creations. And that, I may say, has a bearing on the matter of true opinions. True opinions are a fine thing and do all sorts of good so long as they stay in their place, but they will not stay long. They run away from a man's mind; so they are not worth much until you tether them by working out the reason. That process, my dear Meno, is recollection, as we agreed earlier. Once they are tied down, they become knowledge and are stable. That is why knowledge is something more valuable than right opinion. What distinguishes one from the other is the tether.[3]

Modern views of the tether are different from Plato's. The contemporary answer is that knowledge is necessarily associated with having a *justification* for belief, and with justification comes stability. A justification is a kind of argument. Besides promoting stability of true beliefs, arguments can also be used to excuse one's beliefs to others and to persuade others of their truth.

These reasons for wanting something more than true belief are met by having arguments sufficient to persuade oneself if one should fall into doubt, sufficient to excuse one from complaints about actions based on what one believes, and sufficient to persuade others of what one believes.

Arguments that serve such purposes may be of many sorts, depending on the beliefs and dispositions of whomever they are arguments for. For some people and some communities citing a holy book may always suffice to remind, excuse, or persuade. What more than truth should members of such a community want of beliefs that they know can be thus justified? Holy writ suffices for the devout because the devout believe it to be reliable. The same sort of argument is available to the rest of us: Anyone can remind himself of a belief temporarily called into doubt by recalling that it was acquired by a procedure he believes to be reliable. If recollection of one's own history is in doubt, one may sometimes be able to reacquire the belief by applying such a method again. Similarly, one may excuse a belief to others by showing that it was acquired by a method believed to be reliable. One may try to persuade others of the truth of something one believes by showing them that a reliable method produces the same conclusion.

Such arguments have a common structure. They appeal to a background of beliefs that limit the possible alternative circumstances or hypotheses that need to be considered as possible truths; they appeal to a method believed to reliably yield the truth in any of those possible circumstances; they appeal to beliefs about evidence; and they show or claim that the method yields a particular result. For example, those who appeal to a holy book to decide some question imagine at least two alternatives: either a proposition at issue is true or its denial is true. They believe that a reliable method to determine the truth, whatever it may be, is to consult the holy book, and they cite evidence as to what the book says. If there is something wrong in their procedure, it is that the testimony of the book may not be reliable. But not every justification involves a direct appeal to reliability.

Lots of justifications don't seem to involve claims of reliability directly but do rest on them indirectly. A woman can justify a claim that there are giraffes in Pittsburgh by saying that she saw a giraffe in Pittsburgh. But on reflection it seems that justifying beliefs by appeals to perception has a great deal to do with showing that the belief was acquired by a reliable method. One need not be a grand skeptic here, or worry about the existence of an external world: if tests reveal the woman can't distinguish a giraffe from a plum tree and there are lots of plum trees in Pittsburgh, we may conclude that her appeal to perception fails to establish her knowledge that there are giraffes in Pittsburgh, and, depending on subtleties of context, we may even deny that her claim to have seen giraffes, or the corresponding perceptual events, justify her belief that there are giraffes in Pittsburgh.

Many justifications have no immediate connection to truth or reliability. For example, your belief in a proposition p can be justified by showing that you learned it from someone else who *ought to know*, someone who is an accepted authority. If you formed your belief on good authority, whether or not the authority really did know that p is irrelevant to whether you are justified in your belief. Again, in court testimony and elsewhere, when professional engineers or professional statisticians serve as expert witnesses, they often justify their opinions by claiming that the opinions were obtained in accordance with accepted professional standards. Of course, in some cases accepted professional standards might prove to be quite unreliable guides to the truth, but for the purpose of the legal context, the expert witness need offer no guarantee of reliability to claim to be justified in her opinion. However, even in these cases there is a second level of justification that has to do with reliability. *You* may be justified in a belief obtained from an accepted authority, in the sense that you are excused from any charge that your belief was wanton, formed carelessly, or without foundation. But if we are interested in believing the truth, the question of the reliability of your authority, or of accepted professional standards, still remains and should not be avoided.

Philosophers of science have proposed any number of *confirmation relations* between evidence and theory, and they claim that belief in, or acceptance of, a hypothesis is justified if the hypothesis is confirmed by known evidence. But few of these confirmation relations have any connection with truth or reliability. The confirmation theories either evade a straightforward question or deny its presupposition: If we are interested in believing the truth, predicting the future, or predicting the effects of alternative actions, why should be give credence to hypotheses that are "confirmed" by the evidence? One idea is to try avoid this question by reanalyzing the notion of truth so that the questions just posed become meaningless. One analysis of truth, for example, sometimes called the *redundancy* or *prosentential* theory of truth, holds that to claim something to be true is merely an indirect method of referring to and endorsing some definite proposition or system of propositions. On this view, "It is true that snow is white" is an emphatic way of saying snow is white. "Whatever John thinks is true" is merely an indirect way of endorsing whatever propositions John thinks (even if the person making the endorsement does not know exactly what John thinks). Various standard usages of the notion of truth might be thought to be unintelligible on this account of truth, especially the very usages that have to do with inquiry. If truth is simply a device for referring to and endorsing sentences otherwise described and not any property of sentences, then it might seem that we can make no sense of such sentences as "Find out the truth about the greenhouse effect," "Find out the truth about torture and murder around the world." These injunctions seem to make no sense on the redundancy account of truth because they do not refer to any definite propositions that are independently characterized by some other description; on the redundancy theory of truth, no propositions can be characterized simply as the truth about some issue or domain. Likewise, it seems to make no sense to say, "We are interested in believing the truth." So it might seem that no challenge about reliability can be posed about confirmation relations.

Using a simple logical device, however, we can easily formulate questions about inquiry and reliability consistent with the redundancy or prosentential theory of truth. We need to use variables that range over propositions. Then we can say, "Find the propositions p about the greenhouse effect such that p." "Find out the propositions p about torture and murder around the world such that p." "We are interested in believing those propositions p such that p." Using propositional variables and subjunctives ("if it were the case that p"), we can ask whatever we wish to about the reliability of a proposal for forming or changing beliefs, and to do so, we do not need to explicitly use the notion of truth.

THE MATHEMATICS OF RELIABILITY

These considerations suggest that emphasis on the analysis of knowledge and of justification may be unprofitable. Perhaps instead we should directly consider the notion of *reliable methods of forming opinion*. What can we discover about reliable inference? I begin with the twentieth-century philosopher Hans Reichenbach. Reichenbach claimed that the goal of science is to determine the probabilities with which events of various kinds will occur, or the probabilities with which certain events will occur, given that others have occurred.

Suppose that you flip a coin four times and it comes up heads three of the four times. Then the *relative frequency* of heads in the sequence of four flips is the number of times the coin landed heads, divided by the total number of flips. In this case the relative frequency is 3/4. Suppose that you flip a coin 12 times and it comes up heads 7 of those times. In that case the relative frequency of heads in the sequence is 7/12. Suppose that we flip a fair, evenly balanced coin a number of times, and suppose that the flipping has no effect on the balance of the coin. The relative frequency of heads will change as we flip the coin more and more often. But as the number of flips grows ever larger, the *change* in the relative frequency of heads will tend to become smaller and smaller. If we flip the coin 1,000 times, we cannot expect that it will land heads exactly 500 times, but the relative frequency of heads should be very close to 1/2, and it should remain close to 1/2 if we flip the coin 10,000 times.

Imagine flipping the coin forever, so that there is an infinite sequence of flips. Then there is a corresponding sequence of relative frequencies of heads.

H	T	T	H	H	H	T	H	T	T	H	...
1	1/2	1/3	1/2	3/5	2/3	4/7	5/8	5/9	1/2	6/11	...

Assuming that the coin is fair and perfectly balanced and remains that way through all flips, the infinite sequence of relative frequencies of heads should *converge* to 1/2. Or in other terms, 1/2 should be the *limit* of the infinite sequence of numbers giving the relative frequencies. According to Reichenbach, *probabilities are limits of relative frequencies.* So, according to Reichenbach, the aim of science is to determine limits of relative frequencies.

Now some infinite sequences of numbers have limits and some do not. The sequence 1/2, 2/3, 3/4, 4/5, 5/6, 6/7, 7/8, 8/9, ..., if continued forever, converges to 1. But the sequence 1/2, 1, 1/2, 1, 1/2, 1, 1/2, 1, ... does not converge at all. It oscillates forever between 1/2 and 1. So, in Reichenbach's view, probabilities do not always exist, and therefore sometimes the goal of scientific knowledge cannot be achieved. But when probabilities do exist and there are limits of relative frequencies for events of kinds that interest us, then there is a method of conjecturing hypotheses that will *always* lead to the truth. Reichenbach called this method the *straight rule.*

Straight rule of induction   Always conjecture that the limit of the relative frequency of events of kind *a* in a sequence of events of kind *b* is the relative frequency so far observed of events of kind *a* among events of kind *b*.

Reichenbach's argument that the straight rule of induction is reliable is very simple. Consider (1) an infinite sequence of flips of a coin, (2) the corresponding infinite sequence of relative frequencies of heads, and (3) the corresponding infinite sequence of conjectures about the limit of the relative frequency of heads by the straight rule:

H	T	T	H	H	H	T	H	T	T	H	...
1	1/2	1/3	1/2	3/5	2/3	4/7	5/8	5/9	1/2	6/11	...
1	1/2	1/3	1/2	3/5	2/3	4/7	5/8	5/9	1/2	6/11	...

The sequence (3) of conjectures according to the straight rule is the same as the sequence (2) of relative frequencies. If the sequence of relative frequencies converges to a limiting value, then so does the sequence of conjectures about that limiting value, made in accordance with the straight rule. Any method of conjecturing the limit of relative frequencies can converge to the truth only if the sequence has a limit. If an infinite sequence of relative frequencies has a limit, the straight rule will converge to it. Thus if any method will succeed in converging to the probability of an event in a sequence, the straight rule will.

Reichenbach called his argument a *pragmatic vindication of induction*. He meant something like the following: We can imagine that some procedures for making inductive inferences will work, will converge to the truth, in certain circumstances, and other procedures will work in other circumstances. One problem about induction is how to know which procedures are reliable in which circumstances, since different rules for conjecturing might lead to different conjectures on the same evidence. Since the straight rule is maximally reliable, in practice the only sensible thing to do is to form conjectures according to the method of the straight rule.

Many objections to Reichenbach's vindication of induction concern his understanding of the goals of science. No real coin will ever be flipped an infinity of times, let alone an infinity of times without having its center of gravity altered. Why should scientists be concerned with the limit of an *imaginary* infinite sequence?

There are other objections as well. Suppose that we flip a coin a number of times and after each new flip apply the straight rule to estimate the probability of heads on a flip. Then we obtain, as before, a sequence of outcomes (1), a sequence of relative frequencies (2), and a sequences of conjectures about the limit of the relative frequency of heads in flips of the coin (3). If we form conjectures according to the straight rule, we are guaranteed to converge to the true limit of the sequence if there is such a limit. But the same is true if we form our conjectures according to any of an infinity of different rules.

For example, consider the following rule:

Alternative rule   If the observed relative frequency of events of kind a in a sequence of n events of kind b is r, conjecture that the limit of the relative frequency of events of kind a in the sequence of events of kind b is $(1/n) + (n-2)r/n$.

As n becomes large, the first term in this sum approaches 0, and the second term in the sum (equal to $r - 2r/n$) approaches r. So in the limit, the conjectures produced according to this rule converge to r, the relative frequency. If the straight rule converges to a limiting value when applied to a given sequence, the alternative rule also converges to the same value. The conjectures of the straight rule and the alternative rule will differ, but they will converge to the same value. Let us call any alternative rule that converges to the same limit as the straight rule a *convergent* rule.

For any sequence of events of kind b and any relative frequency of events of kind a in the first n members of this sequence, and for any number l between 0 and 1, there is a convergent rule that conjectures l from the first n members of the sequence. In other words, a pragmatic justification can be given for any conjecture one pleases on any evidence. This is a rather mathematical way of pointing out that Reichenbach's pragmatic vindication of induction helps only in the long run but does not help at all in the short run. But, as the great economist John Maynard Keynes objected, in the long run, we're all dead.

PUTNAM'S FRAMEWORK

About 1960 Hilary Putnam transformed Reichenbach's frequency analysis of reliability to create a general framework for analyzing the reliability of methods for deciding the truth or falsity of any sort of hypothesis. We have already seen the basic idea in a study question from an earlier chapter. Imagine, for example, that we want to determine the truth or falsity of "All ravens are black." To make things simple, let's suppose that there are no difficulties in determining the color of any individual object we meet, and no difficulties in determining whether or not any object we come across is a raven. Further, let's suppose that we can continue searching for ravens forever; I assume that every raven that ever exists will eventually be seen, even though the same raven may be seen repeatedly and even though there may be no time at which all ravens have been seen. After each new piece of evidence is collected, the scientist conducting this inquiry for us can make a conjecture about the truth or falsity of the

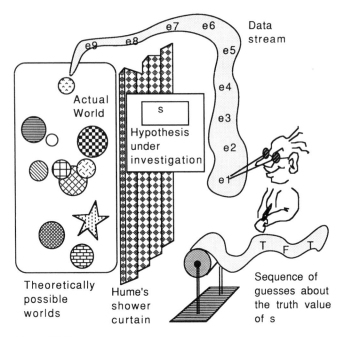

Figure 10.1
A scientist conjectures about the hypothesis that all ravens are black, using rule *R*.

hypothesis that all ravens are black. Finally let's suppose that the scientist uses some rule *R* for forming conjectures. We can picture the setup as in figure 10.1.

Mathematically, rule *R* is simply a function from finite sequences of evidence to the two-member set {True, False}. What does it mean for such a rule to be *reliable*? Putnam's criterion for the reliability of any such rule *R* is this:

Putnam's criterion   In every logically possible world *W* in which the conditions above are met and for every possible order of presentation to the investigator of the individual facts in *W*, there exists some finite number of facts after which *R* outputs only T if the hypothesis is true and outputs only F if the hypothesis is false.

In other words, the investigator eventually gets it right and sticks with the right answer. The difference between Putnam's conception of reliability and Plato's conception is that Plato requires that a reliable method never output T unless the hypothesis is true or output F unless the hypothesis is false. Putnam's reliable learner is allowed to vacillate and change the conjecture an arbitrary but finite number of times. In general, we cannot say how large or how small *finite* will be. A method that is reliable in Putnam's sense is guaranteed to arrive at the correct hypothesis at some time, but usually no guarantee can be given as to when that time will be.

It is easy to apply Putnam's criterion to methods for investigating whether or not all ravens are black. Carl Hempel, a twentieth-century philosopher of science, proposed that a body of evidence E that consists of singular sentences describing the color and ravenhood of a finite number of objects confirms "All ravens are black" if and only if E, together with the assumption that nothing exists that is not named in the evidence, logically entails "All ravens are black." Hempel's analysis of confirmation can be transformed into a rule for forming conjectures: conjecture T if the evidence confirms the hypothesis, and F otherwise. It is easy to see that, in Putnam's sense, this rule is not a reliable method for determining the truth value of any universal hypothesis such as "All ravens are black." Let the hypothesis be true in a world with an infinity of black ravens, but let the evidence be ordered so that the investigator always discovers a new raven at a stage prior to discovering its color. The body of evidence consisting of sentences asserting for n things that they are ravens and black and for one other thing that it is a raven doesn't entail (even with the assumption that nothing else exists) that all ravens are black. The status of the $(n + 1)$th raven is not settled by the evidence at that stage. So a scientist using Hempel's rule could be made to change her mind infinitely often about the hypothesis. In contrast, Karl Popper, another influential twentieth-century philosopher of science, proposed that inquiry should proceed by conjecturing the most easily refutable hypothesis and sticking with it until efforts to refute it succeed. By Popper's method, we would conjecture the truth of "All ravens are black" until (and if) the evidence contains a description of a raven that is not black. It is also easy to see that Popper's method is reliable in Putnam's sense for the question of whether ravens are black: If we follow the rule and are in a world in which all ravens are black, we will always be right in our conjecture. If we follow the rule and are in a world in which there is a raven that is not black, then eventually that raven will be put in evidence, and we will change our conjecture to F and be right ever after. Either way, we will always get to the correct conjecture and stick with it after a finite body of evidence is collected.

Popper's rule is more reliable than the one derived from Hempel's confirmation theory, but Popper's rule is defective in other respects. It can be shown that Popper's rule is not the most reliable procedure that can be constructed. There is, in fact, a *maximally* reliable rule of inference, and there are problems for which Popper's rule fails but the maximally reliable rule succeeds.

Other common methodological recommendations also turn out to reduce reliability. For example, some philosophers of science recommend that scientific change be *conservative*: a theory or hypothesis should not be given up until it is contradicted by the evidence. Popper's rule is conservative, but so are many others. It can be shown that any conservative rule is less than maximally reliable. Another common recommendation is that theories should be simple, but it can be shown that various precise versions of a preference for simple hypotheses sacrifice simplicity.

Putnam's framework was discovered independently by a computer scientist, E. Mark Gold, and it has since been developed by computer scientists, linguists, psychologists, and philosophers. It forms one standard used to evaluate procedures to make computers learn, and it is the basis for a technique for studying language learning in children.

My presentation may make it seem that Putnam's framework is rather artificial: the imaginary investigator gets to receive data, but he never gets to conduct experiments, the way real investigators do; the data the imaginary investigator receives are never erroneous, but real data sometimes are; every fact about the world eventually occurs among the evidence the imaginary investigator receives, but that may very well not be true of us; the imaginary investigator inquires about hypotheses in a formal first-order language, but real investigators usually have other formulations of their hypotheses; the imaginary investigator is given the hypothesis to investigate, but real human investigators often have to generate their hypotheses themselves; our imaginary investigator knows little or nothing about the world, but real investigators know a great deal. But in the last thirty years Putnam's framework has been generalized so that each of these aspects of real inquiry are represented, and mathematical results about reliable procedures are still obtained. The framework does not have to be limited to hypotheses that can be expressed in a formal first-order language; it has been adapted so that it applies to a great variety of ways of representing hypotheses. Reliability can be studied over any arbitrary set of possible infinite sequences of data (the exclusion of some sequences amounts to background knowledge brought to the inquiry). The data need not be free of error, nor need the investigator be merely a passive recipient of the data. The hypothesis does not have to be specified in advance; instead, we can study the reliability of procedures that try to *discover* true hypotheses about a domain. Reliability can be studied when various restrictions are put on the learning rule. One of the most interesting restrictions is that the rule be computable. When that restriction is imposed, many of the theoretical results obtained are reinterpretations of mathematical results in the theory of recursion, a subject we will briefly consider in a later chapter.

What is the relation between the analysis of knowledge and Putnam's sense of reliability? If we settle for Putnam's sense of reliability rather than Plato's stronger requirement, the force of inductive skepticism is weakened a little. From data consisting of particular facts, no universal claim can reliably be established in Plato's sense, as Sextus pointed out. We know that universal claims can be reliably established in Putnam's sense. From a logical point of view, a formal sentence can be reliably verified (that is, we will converge after finite evidence to saying the hypothesis is true if and only if it is true) provided the sentence is logically equivalent to a sentence with a string of existential quantifiers, followed by a string of universal quantifiers, followed by a formula without quantifiers. So, for example, "There exists a smallest particle" is verifiable in this sense. A sentence can reliably be falsified provided it is logically equivalent to a sentence with a string of universal quantifiers, followed by a string of existential quantifiers, followed by a formula without quantifiers. So a sentence is reliably verifiable and falsifiable if it is logically equivalent to both sorts of quantified sentences. What this means is that it is easy to think up claims—even perhaps claims we believe—that cannot be reliably verified or falsified in Putnam's sense unless some possible worlds and data sequences are ruled out by prior knowledge. An example is "For every compound there exists a temperature at which the compound is a liquid for all pressures greater than 1 atmosphere." But although the truth or falsity of such a sentence cannot be reliably decided, it may be a logical consequence of some sentence that can be reliably decided, or it may simply be that we are committed to prior beliefs relative to which the sentence is decidable.

Study Questions

1. Suppose that for a particular set of infinite sequences of possible data and a particular proposition that is true in the worlds described by some possible se-

quences of evidence but not in the worlds described by other possible sequences of evidence, there is an inference rule that is reliable in Putnam's sense and that, when the inference procedure has finally settled on a value, it will not change. That is, suppose that the inference rule can announce that it has settled down. Show that there is then an inference rule that is reliable in Plato's sense.

2. Consider an arbitrary set S of infinite sequences of possible data and a set of mutually exclusive and exhaustive hypotheses. Suppose that there is a prior probability distribution on the evidence and data that in every infinite data sequence in S converges by Bayesian conditionalization to probability 1 for the true hypothesis. Show that there is a conjecturing rule (a function from finite data sequences to hypotheses) that is reliable in Putnam's sense.

3. Does Keynes's objection to the Reichenbach's "vindication of induction" also apply to results about the existence of inference methods that are reliable in Putnam's sense?

4. If the truth or falsity of p can be reliably determined in Putnam's sense and p logically entails q, does it follow that q can be reliably determined in Putnam's sense?

RELIABILITY WHEN TRUTH IS RELATIVE

There are many familiar ways in which what we say or believe changes the very truth value of what we are talking about. The predictions of Wall Street "gurus" may help to make their own predictions come true. If everyone in a community believes everyone else is going to act selfishly, they may all reason that it is in their interest to act selfishly as well, and so the beliefs come true. Some philosophers have suggested much more radical ways in which truth may depend on belief, so radical that people with different beliefs or different *conceptual schemes* may literally live in different worlds of experience. In that case, if two such people meet and dispute, there is no fact of the matter as to who is correct.

Philosophers who think that truth is in this way relative to something about the speaker—her conceptual scheme, her social role, or whatever —sometimes hold a modified Kantian picture of the human condition. According to Kant, there is an unknown world in itself that, together with the conceptual scheme fixed in all of us, determines our common world. According to the relativist, there are many possible conceptual schemes, and the world of any individual's experience is a function of the world in itself and her conceptual scheme. If, through a scientific revolution, a leap of faith, or immigration, the person were to change her conceptual scheme, then, according to the relativist, what is true of her world of

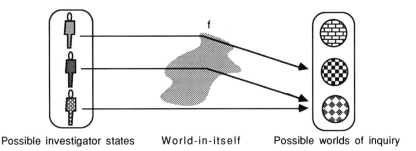

Possible investigator states   World-in-itself   Possible worlds of inquiry

Figure 10.2
One's world of experience is determined by the world in itself and one's conceptual scheme.

experience would also change. The picture is something like figure 10.2. A picture like figure 10.2 does not imply that whatever the investigator thinks is true therefore *is* true. Just because the truth varies with her conceptual scheme or beliefs doesn't mean that the truth varies in such a way as always to *agree* with her beliefs.

The picture of inquiry when truth is not relative allows us to try to satisfy two requirements at once: to reach agreement with one another and to reach the truth. If truth is relative in this way, however, we cannot ensure reaching agreement, but we can still ask when it is that someone can reliably get to the truth, although what the truth is will depend on features of the person herself. Most philosophers who have thought about relative truth have thought that the very idea is inconsistent with any normative standards of inquiry, but in fact that is not so. Indeed, the issue of reliable methods of inquiry becomes more interesting when truth depends on the conceptual scheme of the inquirer. It turns out that if you want to get to the truth of the matter about some question when the truth of the matter depends on you, and even depends on what you *think* is the truth of the matter, there are still more reliable and less reliable ways to proceed.

Let us suppose that an investigator can alter his conceptual scheme as he chooses and that the data he gets will depend on how the world is in itself and on the conceptual scheme he adopts. To make things more interesting still, let us suppose that there are alternative possible worlds in themselves about which nothing substantive can be known but that may combine differently with conceptual schemes to produce a world of inquiry from which data is obtained. If the investigator changes from conceptual scheme 1, say, to other conceptual schemes and then returns to

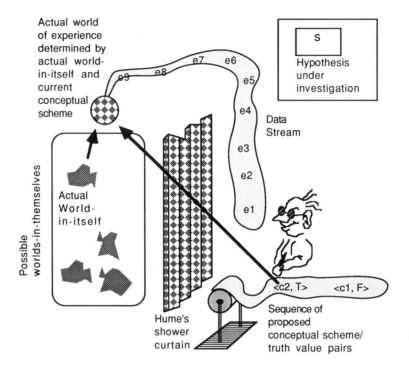

Figure 10.3
One's conceptual scheme and the world in itself determine the data stream and
hence the truth values of sentences under that conceptual scheme.

conceptual scheme 1, he receives data that continue where he left off. If,
therefore, he adopts a given conceptual scheme infinitely often, he will
receive a complete set of data for that conceptual scheme. The picture
of inquiry now looks something like figure 10.3.

Changing conceptual schemes may change proposition *s* from true to
false or from false to true, or even make the proposition meaningless.
Suppose that the investigator wants to have his conjectures about *s* converge to a truth value, true or false, that is correct. Already the relativist
picture shows itself to be more complicated and more interesting that the
realist picture, because there are at least three different senses that might
be given to this convergence (see figures 10.4 to 10.6).

We can think of a relativistic inquiry problem as given by a set of
possible worlds in themselves, a set of conceptual schemes, and a function
that determines a world of inquiry for each pair consisting of a world in
itself and a conceptual scheme. The worlds of inquiry are just like ordinary

Figure 10.4
The conceptual scheme is stable. Converge to a conceptual scheme, stabilize the truth value of *s* (that is, converge to a world of inquiry), and then converge to the truth value of *s* for that conceptual scheme.

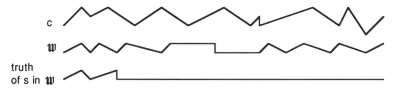

Figure 10.5
The truth value is stable. Stabilize the truth value of *s*, and then converge to its truth value.

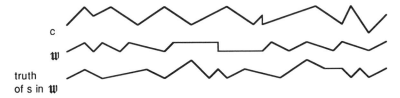

Figure 10.6
Unrestricted. Permit the truth value of *s* to fluctuate forever, so long as you are eventually always right about it.

worlds from which ordinary data are presented (until the investigator changes the conceptual scheme). In some of them the matter under investigation, *s*, is true, and in some of them it is false (and in some of them *s* is neither true nor false). In addition, to make a relativistic discovery problem definite, we need to specify a sense of convergence. Once all of these components are specified, it is a mathematical fact whether or not there exists a method that will reliably converge to the right truth value for *s*. It turns out that the different requirements on convergence really make a difference as to whether a question can be reliably answered. There are relativistic problems of inquiry that cannot be reliably solved if scheme-stable convergence is required but that can be solved if only truth-stable convergence is required, and there are problems that cannot be solved if truth-stable convergence is required but that can be solved with unrestricted convergence.

The difficulty of obtaining a reliable method is basically this: Any *fixed* conceptual scheme determines a discovery problem in which there are a number of alternative possible worlds of inquiry. *That* discovery problem might be unsolvable, so if the method stays with the conceptual scheme, it will fail to converge to the correct truth value in that conceptual scheme. But if the discovery problem posed by that conceptual scheme *is* reliably solvable, the investigator must return to that scheme often enough to obtain sufficient data to converge to the correct truth value for the hypothesis. In more vivid terms, deciding when to go along with a scientific revolution is a delicate matter. Given that the goal is to converge to a truth value for some proposition, there are better and worse methods of inquiry. When the number of alternative possible conceptual schemes is finite, there is a universal method, that is, a relativistic discovery procedure that is reliable if any method is reliable. The method is too intricate to consider here, but the philosophical moral is not difficult at all. Even when truth is relative, there are interesting and intricate epistemological norms concerning reliable inference.

CONCLUSION

In the last twenty years there have been an enormous number of careful attempts to give necessary and sufficient conditions for someone to know something. The analyses have almost all been Boolean; that is, a Boolean combination of conditions are offered as necessary and sufficient for knowledge. The inquiry produced no consensus and no firm result, although it did produce several analyses, such as Nozick's, that seem to capture something important about the concept of knowledge, even if they do not provide necessary and sufficient conditions.

An alternative enterprise that received less attention from philosophers has proved more fruitful. That enterprise, the analysis of conditions for reliable inference, was inaugurated by a philosopher, but like many fruitful philosophical ideas, it spread beyond the confines of professional philosophy. Moreover, the investigation of conditions for reliable inference followed a fundamentally different course than the investigation of conditions for knowledge. Rather than insisting that there is one unique correct set of conditions for reliability, researchers entertained a variety of different notions of reliability and investigated the relations among them. And rather than stopping with a statement of one or another conception of reliability, researchers investigated mathematically the properties of methods that are (or are not) reliable in any particular sense.

Review Questions

1. State C. I. Lewis's account of knowledge. What are some problems with the idea of *justified belief*?

2. Give an example of the type of prototypical situation that Gettier uses to refute Lewis's account of knowledge.

3. State Nozick's account of knowledge, and discuss how it circumvents Gettier's objection.

4. Give a definition of "convergence."

5. What is Reichenbach's straight rule of induction? Cite the flaw in Reichenbach's view discussed in the text.

6. Characterize the contrasting rules for conjecture formation proposed by Hempel and Popper. Discuss each with respect to Putnam's criterion for reliability.

7. Explain why any sentence that is logically equivalent to a sentence with a string of universal quantifiers followed by a string of existential quantifiers followed by a formula without quantifiers can be reliably falsified.

Further Reading

Analyses of knowledge and justification

Bonjour, Larry. *The Structure of Empirical Knowledge*. Cambridge: Harvard University Press, 1985.

Chisholm, Roderick. *The Foundations of Knowing*. Brighton: Harvestor Press, 1982.

Dancy, Jonathan. *An Introduction to Contemporary Epistemology*. Oxford: B. Blackwell, 1985.

Dancy, Jonathan, ed. *Perceptual Knowledge*. New York: Oxford University Press, 1988.

Dretske, Fred. *Knowledge and the Flow of Information*. Cambridge: MIT Press, 1981.

Foley, Richard. *The Theory of Epistemic Rationality*. Cambridge: Harvard University Press, 1987.

Goldman, Alan. *Empirical Knowledge*. Berkeley: University of California Press, 1988.

Goldman, Alvin. *Epistemology and Cognition*. Cambridge: Harvard University Press, 1986.

Lehrer, Keith. *Knowledge*. New York: Oxford University Press, 1974.

Lehrer, Keith. *Theory of Knowledge*. Boulder: Westview Press, 1990.

Luper-Foy, Steven. *The Possibility of Knowledge*. Totowa, N.J.: Rowman and Littlefield, 1987.

Lycan, William. *Judgement and Justification*. New York: Cambridge University Press, 1988.

Moser, Paul K. *Knowledge and Evidence*. New York: Cambridge University Press, 1988.

Moser, Paul K., ed. *Empirical Knowledge: Readings in Contemporary Epistemology*. Totowa: Rowman Littlefield, 1986.

Nozick, Robert. *Philosophical Explanations*. Cambridge: Harvard University Press, 1981.

Pollock, John L. *Contemporary Theories of Knowledge*. Totowa: Rowman Littlefield, 1986.

Pollock, John L. *Knowledge and Justification*. Princeton: Princeton University Press, 1974.

Shope, Robert. *The Analysis of Knowing: A Decade of Research*. Princeton: Princeton Univerity Press, 1983.

Swain, Marshall. *Reasons and Knowledge*. Ithaca, N.Y.: Cornell University Press, 1981.

Redundancy and truth
Horwich, Paul. *Truth*. Cambridge: MIT Press, 1990.

Reliability
Glymour, Clark, and Kelly, Kevin. *Logic, Computation, and Discovery*. New York: Cambridge University Press, 1992.

Kahneman, Daniel, Paul Slovic, and Amos Tversky. *Judgement under Uncertainty: Heuristics and Biases*. New York: Cambridge University Press, 1982.

Osherson, Daniel, Michael Stob, and Scott Weinstein. *Systems That Learn*. Cambridge: MIT Press, 1986.

Reichenbach, Hans. *The Theory of Probability*. Berkeley: University of California Press, 1949.

Part III
MINDS

Chapter 11
MIND AND MEANING

INTRODUCTION

One of the fundamental mysteries of philosophy is the place we humans have in nature. Are we completely natural objects subject to the same laws of nature as air and water and apples, or are we special systems whose features—consciousness, deliberation, choice, feeling—are outside of the system of laws that constrain other objects? The sciences of biology and psychology in our time have assumed that we are completely natural objects whose structure and properties can be reduced to physics, chemistry, and computation. Philosophers and logicians helped to create the computational part of this scientific enterprise, while other philosophers have developed a variety of arguments against the very possibility of reducing humans to physical, chemical, and computational systems. In this chapter we will consider the connection of mind and body, focusing on arguments against the possibility of unifying humans with the rest of nature.

Suppose we make a list of some of the kinds of events there are in our everyday world:

- Birthdays
- Elections
- Shopping trips
- Being thirsty
- Seeing chairs
- Seeing autos
- Believing that it is George Washington's birthday
- Collisions
- Eclipses

Birthdays, elections, shopping trips, collisions, and eclipses seem to be public occurrences, while events such as *seeing* chairs or autos or *believing* that it is someone's birthday seem to be private. Private events have to do with a particular person, whoever is doing the seeing or believing. We think of such private events as *mental*. We could also make a list of the kinds of *entities* there are in the world. Again, some of them—cars, chairs, and bathtubs—are public entities, while others—thoughts and desires, hopes and fears—are private entities that we usually think of as mental. The nonmental is not a homogeneous collection. Nonmental events include birthdays, elections, and shopping trips, all of which are social events that could not occur unless appropriate mental events also occurred. Nonmental events also include the decay of uranium atoms, eclipses of the sun, aortic ruptures, and other events that we think of as physical rather than social. Nonmental entities include such physical objects as electrons and refrigerators, but social entities such as nations and political parties are also nonmental.

The division of our world into the mental and the nonmental raises a number of curious questions: What is the basis for the division? That is, what characteristics differentiate the mental from the nonmental? What are the relations between the events, states, entities, and processes of these two different sorts? Are they fundamentally identical in some way, so that when we understand things properly, the distinction disappears? Or if the distinction is genuine, are there causal relations between mental events and processes and nonmental events and processes? Are events of one sort entirely determined by events of the other sort?

Every answer we might give to such questions produces a great many more questions. If, for example, we suppose, as did Bishop Berkeley in the eighteenth century, that nonmental events, entities, and processes do not really exist, then we must ask why, if that is so, it nonetheless *appears* as though there are physical entities whose existence does not depend on thought and whose appearances seem subject to general laws. And, given any answer to that question, another arises: How is the answer, whatever it is, known to be true? Other theories in the philosophy of mind take roughly the same form. An answer to the fundamental questions about the relation between the mental and the nonmental raises further questions about the details of the connection and how, if at all, the fundamental view can explain features of our experience. Other epistemological questions arise concerning the justification for the claims of any theory of the mental and the physical.

In this chapter we will consider some of the general viewpoints about the relations of the mental and the nonmental, and we will focus on special problems about the source of meaning. Then in the two succeeding chapters we will consider the details of some contemporary theories of mind that hold mental states to be intimately connected with computational states.

SOME METAPHYSICAL VIEWS

One view of any entity, whether mental or physical, is provided by the image of a clothesline: any object consists of a substance (the clothesline) to which various properties have been pinned. Although the picture ignores many complexities and qualifications in any philosopher's conception of things, the clothesline view of objects is contained in much of metaphysics from Aristotle to Descartes, and even after. Aristotle considered matter of different kinds as built up by applying different forms to other materials. The bare clothesline in Aristotle's metaphysics is elemental matter. When elemental matter acquires forms (Aristotle sometimes suggests this occurs by mixing the four elements in various proportions), a new substance emerges to which other forms may be attached, and so on. (So if we want to pursue the clothesline metaphor, in Aristotelian metaphysics the clothes on a line may be rolled up and new clothes pinned over them.) Although Aristotle would perfectly well have recognized the distinction between mental events, processes, and entities on the one hand and nonmental events, processes, and entities on the other hand, he did not separate minds and bodies into two different kinds of fundamental substances.

According to Aristotle, the body and the mind (or soul, to use Aristotle's term) are not two different substances. The features of ourselves and others that we call mental are special properties of bodies and could not exist without bodies. Aristotle uses an analogy from geometry: souls and mental features are not like lines and planes, which we think of as kinds of geometrical objects. Souls and mental features are like the geometrical property of being straight, which we think of as a feature of certain lines: "The affections of the soul are inseparable from the material substratum of animal life to which we have seen that such affections, e.g., passion and fear, attach, and have not the same mode of being as a line or a plane."[1]

René Descartes is often credited with introducing into philosophy a metaphysical conception in which there are two distinct kinds of substance, one mental and one physical. It is as though there were two clotheslines and two different sorts of clothes. Clothes of one kind and only that kind, the physical properties, can be pinned on one of the clotheslines, while clothes of the other kind and only that kind, the mental properties, can be pinned on the other clothesline. In the Cartesian view, mental properties of mental substances can have causal relations with physical properties of physical substances, and vice versa. Your intention to move your arm, for example, causes your arm to move, and the alcohol in wine may cause the feeling of dizziness. Both the mental and the physical realms are subject to various regularities or laws. The functioning of the mental has a structure, just as does the functioning of the physical. (Gilbert Ryle, a twentieth-century philosopher who rejected almost all of Descartes' metaphysics, described it this way: the physical world works like clockwork, the mental like "not-clockwork.")

Descartes held that a substance can be characterized as *that which can exist independently of other entities*. Bodies can exist without minds, and, according to Descartes, minds can exist without bodies. In Descartes' terminology, a *mode* of a substance is that which cannot exist unless the substance exists. Descartes held that there are three kinds of substance: God, mental substance, and physical substance, the latter two of which are combined in humans. Unfortunately for the consistency of his views, Descartes also held that the existence of all other things depends on the existence of God: if God did not exist, neither would minds or bodies. Spinoza, applying the Cartesian definitions consistently, concluded that there is but one substance, God, and that the mental and the physical are only different modes of God.

This picture of entities as substances with attached properties was eroded in the eighteenth century, especially by English philosophers. In the seventeenth century John Locke, a friend of Newton and Boyle, found the notion of substance puzzling because substances seem not to be objects of experience: one may see a chair, its color, its shape, feel its weight, and so on, but one has no perception of its substance. Locke nonetheless retained the idea of physical substance, once referring to it as "the something, I know not what, underlying the evident." Early in the eighteenth century George Berkeley, an Anglican bishop, argued that there is no such thing as material or physical substance. There is a mental substance, he maintained, of which each of us is directly aware, and there are mental properties, *ideas*, of which we are also directly aware. But none of us are ever directly aware of anything but ideas and mental substance. We are locked behind a veil of ideas, but there is nothing on the other side of the veil. The notion of material or physical substance is only a confusion of words.

David Hume rejected even the hypothesis of *mental* substance. Recall that Hume held that all ideas, all thoughts, are compounded from the impressions of sensation, whether "inner" sensation or "outer." Hume argued that we have no impression at all of anything corresponding to mental substance. We have current sensations, we have memories, but we have no idea corresponding to a bare entity that is the *self*.

What does it matter whether there is only one substance, some properties of which may be physical and some mental, or whether there are two substances, one mental and one physical, the first taking only physical properties and the second taking only mental properties, or whether there are no substances at all? Among other topics, it matters for the identity of persons.

PERSONAL IDENTITY

Just who you are is a matter of great personal and practical importance. You can mull over the senses in which you are and in which you are not the same person you were five years ago. Legal issues present a context in which the concept of identity is of central importance. Legal proceedings must establish who is *now* the person who did a crime at some earlier time, or who entered into a contract at some earlier time, or who was the person designated at some earlier time to receive an inheritance. In most cases the establishment of identity in legal contexts may present little of conceptual interest, but sometimes legal issues may push our conception of identity to its limits. Is an amnesiac who forgets everything about her past, and must relearn it all, the same person she was before losing her memory? Ought she to be responsible now for harms she did then? If someone suffers a disorder of multiple personalities and one personality is permanently replaced by another, does the person remain identical? It is a lot easier to ask such questions than to see what facts about the world could settle them, but they raise a fundamental philosophical question: What determines the identity of persons through time?

The traditional Western religious answer to the question is that the *soul* determines personal identity. The soul isn't the same as the mind, or consciousness. Rather, it is a kind of marker, an invisible tag, attached to human beings. Captured wild animals are sometimes tagged so that if they are captured again, their identities can be established. The soul serves the same purpose, except that traditionally the soul is more than a marker. One can imagine that two wild bears somehow exchange identification tags, but that wouldn't change the identity of the bears. It is impossible that two people could exchange souls, because the soul necessarily determines the identity of the person.

Evidently, the notion of a soul has some logical resemblance to the notion of a substance: souls, like substances, are what endures through change; souls, like substances, are essential to the thing they constitute. For that very reason, the philosophers who rejected the notion of mental substance would not be satisfied with the notion of soul. The reasons for dissatisfaction are much the same: No one has ever seen or measured a soul, just as no one has ever seen or measured a substance. Instruments that enhance the powers of our senses—telescopes and microscopes— don't reveal souls or substances. There is no scientific phenomenon that requires such things for its explanation.

If the idea of mental substance is given up, the question of personal identity becomes more interesting and more difficult. Consider persons at a given moment as collections of properties located in space-time. I am here now with all of the physical properties and mental properties I have at the moment I am writing this page. I was in Butte, Montana, in 1959, with all of the physical properties and mental properties I had then. What is it about those two collections of properties, one here and now and the other in Butte in 1959, that makes them moments of one and the same person? If there is no such thing as substance that establishes identity and that remains the same through change, what is it that makes for the identity of persons through time? The same kind of question could be posed about objects. If there is no such thing as substance, what makes an object at a moment the same object as that at some other moment?

Two kinds of criteria have arisen for identifying stages of persons as stages of the same person. One emphasizes physical connections between person stages, while the other emphasizes psychological connections between person stages. On one view, what determines that persons at two moments are stages of one and the same person is a physical continuity between the stages: one stage leads to the other by the motion and slow change of matter. On the other view, what determines that persons at two moments are stages of one and the same person is some kind of psychological continuity, as when, for example, the later person stage *remembers being* the earlier person stage. Each of these views must be qualified in various ways to meet obvious difficulties.

Consider first physical continuity. Starting with a wooden boat at a certain moment, we could replace one board of the boat at a time with a new board. After a while a boat stage would be obtained that had none of the original boards, and yet we would naturally think of it as a later stage of the very same boat. Suppose, however, that as the old boards were removed from the boat one by one, they were reassembled into another boat exactly like the first. Then at some moment we would have two boat stages, one made up entirely of new boards and another made up entirely of the old boards in the original boat arranged in the same way. Which of these boats is identical with the original boat? If the criterion is identity of constituents and similarity of arrangements, then it seems the second boat, the one made from the same boards as the original boat, is identical with the original boat. If, however, the criterion for identifying boat stages is the existence of a physically continuous transition from one stage to another, then the conclusion changes. With this criterion we would conclude that the original boat is identical with the boat stage consisting of new boards. Some philosophers suggest that neither boat is identical with the first boat: the existence of the two competitors for the status of being identical with the original boat somehow keeps either of them from being so.

Next consider psychological continuity. We cannot simply say that a later person stage is identical with an earlier person stage if and only if the later stage remembers being the first stage. For one thing, there are earlier stages of me that I do not remember. For another, people can have false memories, as when someone remembers being Napoleon. The first problem is solved readily enough by requiring that between two identical stages there be a sequence of interposed stages such that there is a chain of memories from the first stage to the last. The second problem is more difficult. We might say that it is not enough for one stage to remember being an earlier stage; in addition, the memory must be *correct*. But that requirement seems circular and therefore uninformative: What does it mean to say that a later person stage *correctly* remembers being an earlier person stage, other than that the later person stage is identical with the earlier person stage and remembers having been that stage?

One way to test how these different criteria fit our fundamental conception of what determines identity is to imagine some rather unpleasant experiments. Imagine that there is a machine that can scan and copy every molecule in your body, forming a perfect duplicate of you. Suppose that in the year 2000 you step into the machine and are duplicated. You and your duplicate are rather like the two boats. To make the analogy more complete, you need only imagine that the machine stays with you for a number of years and creates a duplicate of you from the very atoms that you shed over the years. So all of the various views about the identity of boat stages apply equally well to you and your duplicate. Your duplicate has the same memories you have, and so the criteria of *psychological* continuity does not distinguish between the the identity of you$_{now}$ and you$_{2000}$ on the one hand and the identity of you$_{now}$ and your duplicate in 2000 on the other. So we have, at least in imagination, the kind of case about which there seem to be so many conflicting criteria of identity.

Study Question

If some consideration not yet entertained shows that in our usual judgement, you$_{now}$ really are identical with one of the alternatives—you$_{2000}$ or your duplicate—and not the other, that consideration would tell us something about our concept of identity. Suppose that one and only one of you$_{2000}$ and your duplicate made in the year 2000 will thereafter be tortured. You get to choose now which of them it will be. What is your preference, and why?

REDUCTION

After making lists of physical properties and mental properties, one might think that there is some connection between the two. One might guess, for example, that mental properties are simply certain combinations of physical properties and that any entity that has a brain in a certain physical state at a certain moment will therefore also be an entity that has a certain thought or mental state at that moment. Or instead one might guess that physical properties are simply certain combinations of mental properties, as in idealist metaphysics of the kind we found in Kant, Russell, and Carnap. If, however, there are two kinds of substances, one mental and one physical, and the mental kind can have no physical properties and the physical kind can have no mental properties, then any reduction of the mental to the physical or of the physical to the mental seems clearly impossible. Without distinct substances, new possibilities emerge, and many of the most fundamental controversies in Western thought since the seventeenth century have turned on which of these possibilities is correct.

Thomas Hobbes presented a quite different view of mind from other English writers of the seventeenth century. Hobbes held that reasoning and judgement are forms of *computation*. The corpuscles of the body may serve as special counters, like the counters of an abacus. The states of these counters have a symbolic role: they refer to or represent something in the external world. Mind is matter that *functions* in a special way. This view was given a direct endorsement in the eighteenth century by Julien La Mettrie, who claimed that humans should properly be understood as machines. It would follow that mental states, processes, and events are physical aspects of physical systems. Everything mental could be reduced to something physical. The reductive relations would not simply be causal; it wouldn't be, for example, that physical events in the brain *cause* thoughts. Rather, on the reductionist view, special physical events in the brain just *are* thoughts.

The reductionist idea, sometimes called *materialism* or *physicalism*, gained enormous ground with scientific developments in the nineteenth and twentieth centuries: The chemicals of life were found to obey the very same laws as inorganic chemicals. Some animal behavior that seemed purposeful was found to be produced by simple chemical mechanisms. Phototropism in moths, for example, was found to be due to a chemical reaction in the nerve cells, so that when one eye of a moth was blinded, rather than moving toward a light, it would pivot in a circle. Many people supposed that as science progresses, we will find that we are like very complex moths, and that our purposeful, apparently rational, goal-directed behavior is the result of intricate but purposeless mechanisms inside us. Even so, a large philosophical literature has developed arguing that no reduction of the mental to the physical is possible. Let's consider some of the arguments against the possibility.

The Intensional and the Extensional

Franz Brentano, a nineteenth-century philosopher, insisted that a distinguishing mark of mental events is that they have a special sort of content. They are directed at an object or circumstance from a particular *aspect*, and the aspect is crucial. Brentano's thought was forceful but not especially precise, and some twentieth-century philosophers have offered logical revisions of his claim. They depend on some features of logic that are thought to be true of the language of physics but not true of the language of mind.

Let $F(i)$ be a formula in a logical system such as Frege's, where i is the name of an individual. Then from $F(i)$ and $i = k$, it follows deductively that $F(k)$, for any name k. Formal languages with this property are sometimes said to be *extensional*. In an extensional language the truth or falsity of a claim about an object doesn't depend on how the object is named or described. Some parts of ordinary language don't seem to be extensional. Consider, for example, sentences about what someone desires or fears or hopes or believes. It might be true that Sam likes seeing the morning star and false that Sam likes seeing the evening star. But the morning star and the evening star are the very same object, the planet Venus. Phrases such as "likes," "believes," "fears," and so forth are said to create *intensional contexts*. Substitution of names or descriptions for identical objects in intensional contexts can change truth values.

An argument to the conclusion that the mental cannot be reduced to the physical goes like this:

Premise 1: The language of physics is extensional.

Premise 2: The language of mind is intensional.

Premise 3: For the mental to reduce to the physical, all true claims in the language of mind must be entailed by true claims in the language of physics plus definitions.

Premise 4: No addition of definitions to an extensional language can create a language with intensional contexts.

Conclusion: Therefore, the mental cannot be reduced to the physical.

The argument is valid, and the only questions concern the truth of its premises. I will focus on premise 4, although premises 1 and 3 might also be challenged. Assume that we have an extensional language L for stating physics. Let's consider the problem of giving a physical account of the sentence "Sam likes the morning star." If we add to L the predicate "likes," a reduction must find some formula in physical language, call it $\Phi(x, y)$, that holds whenever object x likes object y. But the argument shows that no such equivalence is possible.

"likes(Sam, morning star)"

is true, and

"likes(Sam, evening star)"

is false, even though "morning star = evening star" is true. So whatever Φ is, it would have to satisfy

Φ(Sam, morning star), $\neg\Phi$(Sam, evening star),

and "morning star = evening star." These conditions violate the assumption that the physical language L is extensional.

But suppose that the reduction took a slightly different form. Instead of a two-place predicate "likes," consider a three-place predicate Likes(x, y, z), where z represents a particular description or physical aspect of an object. In the example,

Likes(Sam, Venus, "morning star").

Notice that the third position is taken not by a name of Venus but instead by *a name of a name* of Venus. So it is true that

Likes(Sam, Venus, "morning star")

and false that

Likes(Sam, Venus, "evening star")

and irrelevant that evening star = morning star. Extensionality is satisfied. (In this example, instead of using a linguistic object in the third position of "Likes," we could use an angle, or range of angles, between Sam, Venus, and the Sun.)

Perhaps we can always reduce an intensional language to some extensional language by introducing extra places in predicates. Until there is a proof that this cannot be done, the logical argument against reduction is incomplete.

Functionalism, Physicalism, and the Cartesian Fallacy

Another influential argument against physicalism can be given informally. The argument is that a creature could be in a mental state such as believing or hoping or fearing even if the creature had a very different physical constitution from us. The creature's biology might be based on a silicon chemistry rather than a carbon chemistry, it might use deuterium oxide instead of water, and so forth. But we can at least imagine that such a creature has the same sorts of inner experience we do and the same dispositions to act that we do when we believe or fear or desire something. In such imaginary cases we ought to say that the creature has the corresponding mental states. But since a creature could have the same mental states we do without having the same physical structure we do, mental facts cannot be reduced to physical facts.

In the last thirty years, versions of this argument persuaded some philosophers to think that mental states should be viewed as *functional* states and that functional states are necessarily something quite different from physical states. Functional states are supposed to be causal features or dispositions of a system to produce a certain output from a certain input and to have nothing to do with the material composition of the system. So the imaginary silicon creature could be in the same functional state as a human, even though the two have quite different physical compositions.

The argument has two flaws. One of them is an overly narrow conception of physics, and the other is a common equivocation over the notion of possibility. The first flaw is very simple. Many of the fundamental notions of physics are functional. Consider the fundamental objects of simple mechanics: the lever, the pulley, the inclined plane. What makes something a lever or an inclined plane is a certain function the thing can perform, not its chemical constitution. An inclined plane can be made of ice, of steel, or of wood. The same is true of many other physical notions. Chemical composition is not what makes something a *planet*. So the opposition between physicalism and functionalism is spurious.

The second flaw in the argument is more interesting and more important, because it uses ideas that occur quite frequently in philosophical disputes. It may in fact be among the most common fallacies in philosophical writings about the mind. The first idea is this:

(1) *Imagination* is the test of possibility. Whatever can be consistently imagined is possible.

The argument against physicalism combines this idea with another:

(2) If two properties are identical, they are necessarily identical. In other words, the properties are identical in all possible circumstances.

Principles 1 and 2 provide a spurious strategy for proving that property f cannot be identical with property g: just *imagine* a circumstance in which something has f but not g or a circumstance in which something has g but not f. We have already met principle 1 in Descartes' arguments. The principle is correct if we are talking of *logical* possibility, the sort of possibility we consider when we ask whether a purported proof is valid. But scientific claims (as distinct from proofs) usually involve a narrower conception of possibility, in which principle 1 is false. For example, modern science holds that it is not possible for a massive body to be accelerated from a velocity less than that of light to a velocity greater than that of light, but such an acceleration is certainly *thinkable*. Again, modern science holds that water is the compound of one atom of oxygen and two atoms of hydrogen, but it is certainly imaginable that water is, say, the compound of one atom of oxygen and one atom of hydrogen. Early in the nineteenth century the father of the modern atomic theory, John Dalton, believed that very thing. (The scientific conception of impossibility is undoubtedly vague. It means roughly the following: try as you will with whatever resources, such a thing will never come about; it is a law of nature that it will not come about.) When we consider the question of the identity of the mental and the physical or the reduction of mental properties to physical properties, this second scientific sense of possibility is involved, not the wider sense of logical possibility. To show in this sense that it is possible for creatures with different chemical compositions to be in mental states such as ours, it is not enough to *imagine* creatures who experience as we do but have a different chemical composition. For all we know, it may be a law of nature that no object can have the sort of experience we have unless it has the sort of chemical composition we have.

The moral is that we should not argue about scientific identifications through imaginary cases unless there is good reason to think that the cases imagined could be realized consistently with physical law. Of course, in many cases good reasons will be available, and then there is nothing wrong with arguing by imagination.

Study Questions

1. Find some other examples of scientific identifications of one property or kind with another property or kind.

2. Is principle 2 correct?

WHAT ARE MEANINGS?

Issues about minds are closely connected with issues about meaning. The phenomenon of meaning is of special philosophical interest because meanings seem so central to what it is to be a sentient, rational creature, and yet at the same time the nature of meaning is elusive. Meanings are supposed to be whatever it is one has a hold on when one understands a concept, statement, or rule. One of the things that distinguishes humans from rocks and even from computers is that humans understand concepts, statements, and rules. We grasp meanings. Things without minds don't grasp meanings. Things without minds may behave in ways that can be described by rules, but they don't *apply* rules. A rock doesn't apply the law of gravity when it falls, but a person applies a rule for addition when figuring out the sum of ten numbers. What is it that we grasp when we get the meaning of a rule, a claim, or a word, and what is it to mean something or to understand what something means? We will consider several influential and interesting ways of approaching these questions.

Truth Conditions

Frege's philosophy of language distinguished between the sense and reference of a thought, or as we might say, between the meaning and the truth value of a proposition. Twentieth-century elaborations of Frege's view place the speaker in a system of relations with other speakers and the world and focus on a relation of reference or denotation between thoughts or utterances and objects or features of the world. The views I describe in the next few paragraphs were developed by several philosophers, but most forcefully by Alfred Tarski in the first half of the twentieth century and by others subsequently.

Here is the picture: Names denote particular objects, as "George Bush" denotes George Bush. Predicate terms such as "red," "male," "leader of a nation" denote properties or relationships. So "male" denotes a property that George Bush exemplifies. The relation of denotation determines the conditions for the truth or falsity of claims. The facts determine whether these conditions are met. So, for example, the sentence "George Bush is a male" is true if and only if the object denoted by this use of the term "George Bush" has the property denoted by this use of "male." That is, "George Bush is a male" is true if and only if George Bush is a male. This sort of statement of a condition for the truth of a sentence sounds rather trivial, but if we understand the words in quotes as arbitrary symbols and if we also understand the unquoted words as we ordinarily do, then the statement says something. It gives the condition (in English) for the truth of the quoted sentence. The truth condition only appears trivial because the quoted sentence is already in English. But if it were in French, the truth condition would more clearly provide some information: "George Bush est un mâle" is true if and only if George Bush is a male.

What makes words or phrases denote the particular individuals or properties they do? One standard answer is that thoughts, words, and phrases get their denotations from the causal relations in which speakers find themselves. Our uses of "George Bush" denote George Bush because

George Bush's mother named him "George Bush" and because she told him that his name is "George Bush" and so, through newspapers and television and through talking with other people, we who have never laid eyes on George Bush come to know and use his name. This account is very sensible, but it leaves at least one mystery: What did George Bush's mother do to cause him to be named "George Bush"? Naming someone or something seems to require a certain *intention* on the part of the namer; something had to make it the case that Bush's mother was naming George, rather than naming something else (his crib, for example), and rather than not naming anything at all (as if she had muttered, "(By) George, (I'm) bush(ed)"). We don't as yet have any causal analysis of intending; some philosophers claim we never will.

Whatever constitutes the denoting relation between words and the world, on this view of meaning, what one has when one grasps or understands a concept, rule, or phrase is a knowledge of some aspect of the denoting relation. You understand one sense of the English word "male" because you know that one kind of occurrence of "male" denotes the property of being male. You understand another sense of "male" because you know that another kind of occurrence of "male" denotes the property of being the convex half of a concave-convex coupling device. Similarly, you understand a sentence such as "George Bush is male" because you know the condition for its truth. Clearly, you can know the truth condition for a sentence without knowing whether the sentence is true, or in Frege's terms, you can know the sense of a sentence without knowing its reference.

Many philosophers have complained that the analysis of meaning through truth conditions isn't very illuminating. The analysis tells us that we can know the truth condition for a sentence of our own language only if we already know the meaning of another sentence that looks just like the sentence whose truth condition is being given. The truth condition for "George Bush is male" makes essential use of our understanding of the meaning of "George Bush is male." Truth conditions may provide a good technique for translation from one language to another, but meanings can be acquired even by someone who speaks no language at all. Imagine for a moment trying to teach someone who speaks no language at all, a child, to understand English by giving the person truth conditions for English sentences. Suppose the child is willing and intelligent and learns all of the truth conditions by heart. Even so, the child won't have a glimmer of how to *use* English sentences, and she won't understand their meanings.

About 1960 Willard Van Orman Quine produced an argument against truth-conditional theories of meaning. Quine's argument concluded that if meanings are truth conditions, there are no meanings. Quine's argument began with the case in which a truth conditional analysis of meaning seems most informative: the case of translating sentences in one language into another language. Assume that we are translating the language of a people we know almost nothing about; suppose to start with that we understand their words for affirmation and for denial, but nothing else. Then, Quine claimed, no matter how much we study their behavior, no matter how much evidence we gather about what they say in various circumstances, we will not be able to construct a *unique* translation manual from their language into ours that gives English truth conditions for the sentences of their language. Quine maintained that this sort of "radical translation" always allows alternative translations that are incompatible with one another. For example, Quine argued that if we were to find that the people we are studying seem to apply the word "gavagai" to rabbits, then "gavagai" could be translated as rabbit or equally well as "undetached rabbit part." It must be admitted that Quine's examples of this sort of underdetermination of translation by behavior are not particularly shocking or even interesting. But from this claim, Quine infers that since not even all possible observations of behavior would determine the correct translation, there is therefore no correct translation and no correct set of truth conditions in English for the sentences of the people's language. We should then apply the same conclusion to ourselves, Quine claimed, and conclude that there are no conditions in English that give the requirements for the truth of English sentences.

Study Questions

1. Suppose that a defender of truth conditions as analyses of meaning were to reply that the imaginary case of a child who speaks no language and who memorizes English truth conditions is not really a counterexample to the claim that understanding a language consists in knowing the truth conditions of its sentences. For, the reply continues, the child doesn't *understand* the truth conditions it is taught to memorize, and therefore, even though it knows how to repeat utterances that sound like statements of the truth conditions, the child doesn't really *know the truth conditions*. What do you say in response to this reply?

2. Another objection to the analysis of meaning by truth conditions is that notions of meaning also apply to sentences that aren't declarative. "Close the door!" is a sentence that means something, but it isn't true or false and doesn't have a truth

condition. How might the meanings of imperative sentences be analyzed at least in the spirit (if not the letter) of truth-conditional analyses?

3. "Juliet is the sun" is a metaphor from Shakespeare. Explain some of the difficulties metaphors present for truth-conditional analyses of meaning.

4. Quine's argument seems to require the assumption that nothing can be true of people unless its truth can be determined (at least in principle) from observations of their behavior. This view, championed by Quine's colleague of many years, the psychologist B. F. Skinner, is often called *behaviorism*. What can be said for and against this idea?

Meaning as Use

A quite different approach to meaning was advocated by Ludwig Wittgenstein. Wittgenstein was an Austrian who turned to philosophy while studying engineering in England. He first wrote a celebrated book defending a version of the truth-conditional approach to meaning. In Wittgenstein's early view, simple facts in the world join individuals, properties, and relations, and more complex facts are formed by Boolean combinations of simple facts. The structure of facts is isomorphic to the logical structure of language. A sentence is true if the corresponding facts obtain. Toward midcentury Wittgenstein completely rejected his earlier view and wrote a number of works advocating a different approach to meaning, which has become very influential. Wittgenstein's later writings are notoriously allusive and unsystematic, and his followers and critics have argued at length about what he was saying. The view we will consider mixes Wittgenstein's themes with those of a number of other philosophers.

The idea is this. Understanding a phrase or sentence is knowing how to use it. Knowing how to use a phrase such as "red apple," for example, is knowing that the term applies to paradigm examples of red apples, knowing that it doesn't apply to green figs, being able to make standard inferences in language involving "red apple," and so on. For example, someone who understands the English "red apple" is able to infer that a red apple is a fruit, that red apples are not usually painted red, and that apples grow on trees. There is no single analysis of terms nor a single truth condition for a sentence. Instead, there is a range of applications and nonapplications, contexts where the sentence is appropriate to utter and contexts where it is not, and inferences to be made using a phrase or sentence. This much of Wittgenstein's doctrine seems like good sense, and many philosophers have adopted some version of it. Nevertheless, the view naturally raises many unanswered questions: Are some applications of a word more central to its meaning than others? Are some inferences more important than others? If so, which and why? I won't attempt to answer these questions here.

Another doctrine is associated with Wittgenstein's name, although whether he actually endorsed it is controversial. The doctrine is that there is no such thing as the meaning of any part of language or any act of speech or expression. There are no meanings. Nothing means anything. The argument for this apparently absurd conclusion goes as follows:[2]

Premise 1: Meanings, if anything at all, are *normative.* They constitute partial rules or standards for correct and incorrect uses of language. If someone systematically violates these standards in his use of some phrase, we say that he does not know the meaning of the phrase. If, for example, someone sincerely says "Two plus two is five," we conclude that he does not understand the meanings of his words. Norms are about what *ought or ought not* to happen or to be done. One ought not to say "Two plus two is five." Norms are not about what actually does happen: perhaps some people do say "Two plus two is five," and in any case, everyone sometimes makes errors in addition.

Premise 2: Nothing about what actually exists or about what used to exist entails anything about what *ought* to exist. Hume makes this point in his discussion of morals:

In every system of morality, which I have hitherto met with, I have always remark'd that the author proceeds for some time in the ordinary way of reasoning, and establishes the being of a God, or makes observations concerning human affairs; when of a sudden I am surpriz'd to find, that instead of the usual copulations of propositions, *is,* and *is not,* I meet with no proposition that is not connected with an *ought* or an *ought not.* This change is imperceptible; but is, however, of the last consequence. For as this *ought,* or *ought not,* expresses some new relation or affirmation, 'tis necessary that it shou'd be observ'd and explain'd; and at the same time that a reason should be given, for what seems altogether inconceivable, how this new relation can be a deduction from others, which are entirely different from it.[3]

Premise 3: Therefore, absolutely no statement of any fact about what exists or did exist entails that any usage is erroneous or incorrect in the sense of failing to accord with a norm or standard.

Conclusion: Therefore, absolutely nothing *makes* errors of usage *errors.* Our individual or collective dispositions to use words in a certain way do not themselves entail norms of usage; we as a community just happen to say on particular occasions that some usages of words are incorrect and others are not. But our saying so is a bare fact, and there isn't any property of a speaker, the world, or the speaker's audience that makes a sentence erroneous or otherwise inappropriate. There isn't, in other words, any such thing as a meaning that constitutes a norm or standard of usage.

Almost no one believes the conclusion of this argument. So where is the fallacious inference or the false premise? Many philosophers would reject the inference of (3) from (2), and some would reject (2) altogether. They would say, for example, that one of the things that might exist in the world is a norm or standard at a particular time, and a norm may very well entail that a particular action violates the standard. For example, there is in fact a norm about how "plus" is to be used, and that norm entails which possible uses of "plus" in addition are correct and which are incorrect. The argument overlooks the possibility that meanings are among the things that exist.

Almost everyone would reject the conclusion that nothing means anything, but arguments of this sort can be turned around. From the spirit of Hume's observation that statements about what there is (other than norms) do not imply statements about what ought or ought not to be, the observation that meanings are norms, and the banal conclusion that people really do mean things by their words and thoughts, it seems to follow that the notion of a person cannot be reduced to any structure of physical or functional relations. By the very fact that they mean something by their words and thoughts, persons instantiate norms, and norms are not reducible to physics or to function. We can put this backward argument this way:

1. Meanings are normative.
2. Thoughts have meanings.
3. Nothing physical or functional has normative attributes.
4. Therefore, thoughts are not physical or functional.

Is the possibility of reducing mental phenomena to physical or functional phenomena and structures thus refuted? Let me distinguish among four things, any of which may be connected with the notion of meaning:

1. In use, words may denote objects and properties. Although the physical details of the denoting relation are complex and generally not known to us, of itself, denotation is supposed to be some relation (like floating or

dissolving or being between) that aspects of the world stand in. Whatever denoting may be, there is nothing normative about it.

2. Some utterances may be true, and some false. We may prefer that people speak the truth (sometimes), but because of the denotation relations of their language, whether they do speak the truth or not is a matter of fact, not a matter of norms.

3. There are approvals or disapprovals of usages. You may disapprove of how I use the word "or," which, because I am from Montana, is a little nonstandard. (Like many other Montanans, I would say "Butte *or* Missoula are in Montana," whereas standard English is "Butte *and* Missoula are in Montana." My usage can be understood in this way: pick either one, Butte or Missoula; no matter whether you pick Butte or Missoula, it's in Montana.) Disapproval is a natural attitude, and no reason has been given in the preceding argument to believe that it is impossible to give physical or functional reductions of disapproval.

4. There might conceivably be norms of usage that are distinct from facts of approval and disapproval and also distinct from facts of denotation and truth. Because of what words in fact denote and what the truth values of sentences are, over and above all this, some usages might be *wrong*. In saying that a usage is wrong in this sense, we are not claiming just that what is asserted is not true or just that what is asserted is disapproved of by other speakers of the language. In this sense, a speech act might be logically wrong even though what it asserted is true and even though no one disapproved, or was disposed to disapprove, of the act of speech.

Now the antireductionist argument establishes only that the fourth aspect of meaning cannot be reduced to physics or function. But the fourth aspect seems gratuitous and quite unnecessary for our understanding of the notion of meaning. Suppose that someone did a mathematical calculation and that because of what her mathematical symbols denoted, the outcome of her calculation was false. We would ordinarily say that she made an *error*, a mistake, and that sounds normative. Even if no one else caught her mistake, ever, we would still say that an error was made. But that does not mean that the notion of meaning requires some norm that we now *know* is not a matter of physics or function. When we say that she made an error, we mean that she intended to obtain the true result and did not do so. We do not mean that she failed to abide by some supernatural norm. We can understand the phenomena of meaning very well without the fourth aspect. So the argument that the phenomenon of meaning demonstrates the impossibility of physicalism or functionalism seems inconclusive.

Study Question

Reconsider Boole's difficulty with the fact that people make errors of reasoning.

THE PRIVATE-LANGUAGE ARGUMENT

I began this chapter by contrasting *private* phenomena, the mental, with public phenomena, the nonmental. That very contrast assumes that each of us has features of his or her experience over which he or she has authority. You are the final authority on whether you are in pain and on whether something tastes and looks to you like what you call a tomato. Of course, other people might have very good evidence that you are in pain or, knowing you very well, might be very good judges of whether something tastes and looks to you like what you call a tomato. But were there to be conflicting opinions, your judgements of your private experience are authoritative, and others' judgements defer to yours. Not only does this picture of things seem natural, it also seems to be morally important. If it were not true, a great deal of the notion of individual autonomy would be lost.

That the mental can be private seems to entail that there is a part of language that can be used to name and describe features of experience, and you are the ultimate authority for the correct use of that language. Wittgenstein's most famous argument is that no such language is possible. Some commentators on Wittgenstein have given very lengthy reconstructions of Wittgenstein's argument, but I do not believe these reconstructions clarify it very much or improve on a fairly simple statement of the idea. Here is a version of the argument that is *not* a quotation from Wittgenstein:

Let us agree that by a "private language" we will mean a language used by a person for which she is the sole authority about correct usage. For there to be a language, there must be meanings. Meanings are normative and determine standards for correct and incorrect use. Now a standard, norm, or criterion for anything is something at least possibly distinct from that thing, something against which the thing can, ideally, be measured. The standard for someone's correct usage of a phrase or sentence cannot be just the mere fact that the person used the phrase or sentence. There must be something other than the mere use that provides the standard. But were there such a thing as a private language, the actual use of the speaker of that language would be the standard for use, no matter what the person might say. Hence there can be no private language.

The argument is engaging, and it captures a real tension in the notion of private experience. On the one hand, we think of private experiences as objective, about which someone can be right or wrong in describing. On the other hand, we think of private experiences as like conventions or stipulations in that *whatever* the speaker decides to say of her private experience counts as the truth. We cannot have it both ways.

There are at least two lines of reply, according to which side of the tension one prefers to endorse. One reply is to insist that sometimes a standard and what it is a standard of can be one and the same. A professional baseball umpire once replied to a protest over a called strike, "It ain't nothin' until I call it." And while his remark is not true of pitches in general, it was indeed true of the particular pitch in question. It was the umpire's saying "strike" that made the pitch a strike. The disadvantage of this reply is that it seems to concede that no facts can be reported in a private language that are facts independent of the report.

A second reply to the private-language argument is that a person's authority over his own utterances need not rest simply on the fact that he uttered them. The words of the speaker of a private language denote features of her experience, and in virtue of what that experience really is, the statements of the speaker are true or false. So she could be wrong in what she says. She is the authority about her own usage of her own private language not because she is necessarily infallible but because she is the most reliable judge of correctness. No one else has access to her evidence about what she experiences. This reply allows that it is *imaginable* that circumstances could arise in which you are no longer the authority about usage in your hitherto private language. We could imagine, for example, that neuroscience becomes so detailed and so powerful that by monitoring your brain, it can determine how things appear to you, and that this determination is more reliable than even your own testimony. Some philosophers have accordingly reformulated Wittgenstein's thesis as the claim that there could not exist a *necessarily* private language. But this way of putting the issue equivocates over the notion of possibility in a way we have seen before. In the vague, scientific senses of "possibility" and "necessity," neither Wittgenstein nor anyone else is or has been in a position to know whether the language in which each of us describes his or her own experiences is necessarily private. The reformulated thesis might be this:

there could not exist a language that could not be imagined not to be private. And that reformulated claim may be true, but it has lost interest, since the claim no longer calls into doubt the existence of private experience or individual autonomy.

CONCLUSION

Putting the phenomena of mind together with our understanding of the natural world is possibly the most difficult intellectual challenge to modern thought. The problem has, if anything, been made more difficult by twentieth-century science. On the one hand, through psychological and biological investigations we have come to see ourselves as more like biological machines; on the other hand, through developments in physics we have come to see the physical world as more mysterious and less intelligible. Essential aspects of mental life remain unexplained in physical or functional terms, most central among them the phenomena of consciousness and associated aspects of mental life.

We have considered only a few of the philosophical arguments that aim to show that no unification of the human and mental with the natural and physical is possible. The arguments do not seem decisive. In the next chapters I turn to giving a say to the reductionist, functionalist side. Right or wrong, the results of pursuing the reductionist idea constitute some of the great achievements of twentieth-century philosophy.

Review Questions

1. What are some of the arguments against the possibility of reducing mental states to physical states?

2. Why would the private-language argument, if sound, be important?

3. What are some of the senses of "possibility" that arise in philosophical argument?

4. What is the leading idea of the causal theory of reference and denotation, and what problems present difficulties for the theory?

5. What is Brentano's mark of the mental?

Further Reading

Personal identity
Glover, Jonathan. *I: The Philosophy and Psychology of Personal Identity*. London: Penguin Press, 1988.

Perry, John, ed. *Personal Identity*. Berkeley: University of California Press, 1975.

Rorty, Amélie Oksenberg, ed. *The Identities of Persons*. Berkeley: University of California Press, 1976.

Shoemaker, Sydney, and Richard Swinburne. *Personal Identity*. Oxford: B. Blackwell, 1984.

Vesey, Godfrey. *Personal Identity: A Philosophical Analysis*. Ithaca, N.Y.: Cornell University Press, 1976.

The mental/physical distinction
Brentano, Franz Clemens. *Psychology from an Empirical Standpoint*. New York: Humanities Press, 1973.

McKeon, Richard Peter, ed. *The Basic Works of Aristotle*. New York: Random House, 1941.

Ryle, Gilbert. *The Concept of Mind*. Chicago: University of Chicago Press, 1984.

Meaning
Davidson, Donald. *Essays on Actions and Events*. New York: Oxford University Press, 1980.

Davidson, Donald. *Inquiries into Truth and Interpretation*. New York: Oxford University Press, 1984.

Fodor, Jerry A. *Psychosemantics: The Problem of Meaning in the Philosophy of Mind*. Cambridge: MIT Press, 1987.

Fodor, Jerry A. *A Theory of Content and Other Essays*. Cambridge: MIT Press, 1990.

Hume, David. *A Treatise of Human Nature*. Oxford: Oxford University Press, 1888.

Putnam, Hilary. *Philosophical Papers*. Vols. 1 and 2. New York: Cambridge University Press, 1975.

Tarski, Alfred. *Introduction to Logic and to the Methodology of Deductive Sciences*. New York: Oxford University Press, 1965.

Tarski, Alfred. *Logic, Semantics, Metamathematics: Papers from 1923 to 1938*. 2nd ed. Indianapolis, Ind.: Hackett Publishing Co., 1983.

Wittgenstein
Fogelin, Robert J. *Wittgenstein*. Boston: Routledge and Keagan Paul, 1976.

Holtzman, Steven, and Christopher M. Leich, eds. *Wittgenstein: To Follow a Rule*. Boston: Routledge and Kegan Paul, 1981.

Kripke, Saul A. *Wittgenstein on Rules and Private Language: An Elementary Exposition*. Cambridge: Harvard University Press, 1982.

McGinn, Colin. *Wittgenstein on Meaning*. New York: Oxford University Press, 1984.

Malcolm, Norman. *Nothing Is Hidden: Wittgenstein's Criticism of His Early Thought*. New York: B. Blackwell, 1986.

Wittgenstein, Ludwig. *Philosophical Investigations*. Oxford: B. Blackwell, 1953.

Wittgenstein, Ludwig. *Tractatus Logico-philosophicus*. London: Routldege and Kegan Paul, 1955.

Wright, Crispin. *Wittgenstein on the Foundations of Mathematics*. London: Duckworth, 1980.

Chapter 12

THE COMPUTABLE*

The theory of computation belongs as much to philosophy as to other disciplines. The modern from of computation arose from the application of mathematical logic to philosophical issues concerning the foundations of mathematics. Moreover, at least a rudimentary understanding of the theory of computation is essential to understanding important areas of contemporary philosophical concern, including theories of knowledge and philosophies of mind. Finally, the theory of computation forms an important part of the modern theory of rationality.

Although the word derives from Arabic mathematics, the notion of an *algorithm* seems as ancient as any idea in mathematics. Greek geometers thought of procedures for constructing figures with rule and compass. Thus, in translation, the first proposition of Euclid's elements states a *procedure* for using rule and compass to construct an equilateral triangle on any given line segment in any given plane containing that line segment. But it was in the theory of arithmetic and in algebra that the idea of an algorithm became explicit. Today the teaching of arithmetic in elementary schools consists in large part of the teaching of algorithms for computing simple arithmetic functions: addition, subtraction, multiplication, division (although the availability of cheap electronic calculators may make such skills obsolete). In algebra, much of the focus of research by Arab and then Christian mathematicians was on finding algorithms for the solution of various classes of equations. Thus in algebra we learn algorithms for solving linear equations and for solving systems of linear equations; we learn algorithms for solving quadratic equations and for solving third-degree equations.

In the seventeenth century a remarkable idea began to emerge: thought, any thought, is some form of computation. Thomas Hobbes articulated this idea clearly in the middle of the century. Others who did not take such a view of mentation nonetheless thought of algorithms as means to improve human rational capacities. In the same century Gottfried Leibniz, the great philosopher, mathematician, and diplomat, proposed the development of a kind of *calculus* in which every proposition on any subject could be stated formally and unequivocally and for which an algorithm would determine the truth or falsity of every proposition that could be so stated. Of course, Leibniz did not have such a calculus or any such algorithm, but he envisioned their development as a principal goal of science.

As we will see, the idea of an algorithm is not even yet fully understood, but roughly it means a mechanical or automatic procedure that, at least ideally, will compute something for any of an infinity of different possible cases. If the something is a function, an algorithm will compute the value of the function for any argument over which the function is defined. Such an algorithm is always an algorithm for computing some specific function or other. There might be many ways to compute one and the same function, and so many distinct algorithms that compute one and the same function. You can imagine many different ways to use a telephone book to find someone's phone number; similarly, you can imagine many different algorithms for arithmetic functions. Rather than adding multidigit numbers by forming them in columns and adding the rightmost column and carrying to the left, for example, you could get the same results by starting the additions with the leftmost column and for any column in which the sum is more than nine, backtracking to change the sum in the column to the immediate left.

THE DEVELOPMENT OF COMPUTATION THEORY FROM LOGIC

In the first chapter of this book I briefly discussed Cantor's theory of sets and his arithmetic of infinites. Cantor's mathematical work and the theories that developed from it set off a line of research that led to the modern theory of computation. Some mathematicians, notably Leopold Kronecker, did not believe Cantor's mathematical results, and did not even regard them as real mathematics. Cantor's theory, you will recall, proved the *existence* of certain infinite sets and infinite collections that are, in a well-defined sense, *larger* than the infinity constituted by the natural numbers. Although criticisms of Cantor's work were sometimes clothed in nineteenth-century metaphysical jargon, one theme in the criticisms was this: *The principles of arithmetic are the most certain and sure foundation for mathematics. Any new mathematical theory must be proved consis-*

tent by the methods of arithmetic, and any new mathematical objects or functions should be computable from elementary arithmetic functions. That is, there should be arithmetic algorithms for any such novelties. Kant's philosophy, which gave a special status to arithmetic, provided important support for this view.

At about the same time that the conflict between Cantor and Kronecker developed, Frege had published the first presentation of modern logic. We have already seen that modern logic permits the explicit formulation of nearly every mathematical theory, including number theory, geometry, and set theory. The power of Frege's conception had already been exploited by many mathematicians and philosophers as early as the 1920s. David Hilbert, who ranked among the greatest of mathematicians of the late nineteenth and early twentieth centuries, saw in formal logic a means of meeting Kronecker's objections to set theory and, indeed, a means of reducing the question of the consistency of any mathematical theory to questions of elementary arithmetic.

One of Hilbert's ideas can be derived from a simple reflection on how mathematics is applied in the physical sciences. (It is perhaps relevant that Hilbert was also a great mathematical physicist and, with Einstein, the codiscoverer of the general theory of relativity.) When we apply mathematics, we count things, or assign numbers to things or to states of things. We assign numerical measures to objects when, for example, we weigh them. By counting and assigning measures, we are able to make inferences about things by doing arithmetic.

Consider weighing things on a scale. We do so by adopting some *convention* that correlates states of the scale with numbers. The same number is also correlated with the body we have weighed on the scale. The convention we use may be built into the scale (as with modern chemical scales that have a digital readout) or we may have to mentally assign a number to the state of the scale according to some rule (as with an old-fashioned pan balance). There are lots of different systems by which numbers can be associated with states of the scale: we can measure in grams or ounces or some other unit. The important thing is to use one such system; it doesn't matter which.

When we use a scale and a standard of measurement to assign weights to objects and we weigh first one object and then another on the scale, we use our measurement convention to assign a number to the state of the scale in each case. We call that number the *weight* of the object on the scale. Now the interesting and useful thing about measurement scales is this: we can use arithmetic to determine what the state of the scale will be when, for example, two objects are placed on it. To get the answer we need do only the following: weigh each object separately; add the numbers representing the weights of the two objects; use our measurement convention to infer the state of the scale associated with the number that is the sum. Our measurement practice enables us to represent properties of weights as simple arithmetic relationships.

Hilbert's idea was this: we can associate numbers with the *language of a mathematical theory* in such a way that properties of the mathematical theory, such as its consistency, are represented by arithmetical relationships among numbers associated with parts of the language. *Formal* properties of a theory, such as its consistency, then become equivalent to arithmetical properties of sets of numbers. We could then prove (or disprove) the consistency of a mathematical theory by using nothing but arithmetic. Since no one doubted arithmetic proofs, doubts about the consistency of various mathematical theories, such as set theory, could be resolved. (One important disanalogy with the previous example should be noted. It is an *empirical* fact, established by experiment, that weights are additive: the weight of two objects together is the sum of their individual weights. By assigning numbers to weights, that empirical fact is represented by an arithmetic relation. In contrast, the *consistency* of a theory is a *logical* property, not an empirical property, and one hopes to be able to establish consistency by an a priori proof rather than by experiment.)

When a mathematical theory, set theory, for example, is completely formalized, there is a definite vocabulary of symbols in the language of the theory. Each symbol can be assigned a *natural number* in any arbitrary but mechanically computable way. The sentences of the language of the theory can then also be assigned numbers, because each sentence is just a sequence of vocabulary elements. Suppose, for example, that a formal language had only nine symbols. The rules of the language specify that only certain finite sequences of symbols are well formed. Then we could assign one of the numbers 1, 2, 3, 4, 5, 6, 7, 8, 9 to each of the symbols of the language, and every sentence of the language consisting of a well-formed sequence of symbols would correspond to a finite sequence of nonzero digits. Since every finite sequence of nonzero digits denotes a unique natural number, every sentence of the language would have a corresponding natural number. Similar correspondences can be set up even when the number of symbols is infinite.

If we insist that our formalized languages be constructed so that there is an algorithm to determine whether or not any arbitrary string of vocabulary elements is a well-formed formula, there is some arithmetic algorithm to determine the numbers that correspond to well-formed formulas of the language of the formalized mathematical theory under study.

Let us suppose that when formalized, the mathematical theory we are considering is axiomatizable. The axioms of the theory are then in correspondence with some determinate set of numbers. Since there is an algorithm for determining the axioms of the theory, there is a numerical algorithm for determining the numbers that correspond to the axioms.

A proof, or derivation from the axioms of the formalized theory, according to a proof theory such as Frege's, then corresponds to a finite sequence of numbers. Since, you will recall, one of the requirements of proof theory is that there be an algorithm to determine whether or not any given sequence of formulas is a proof, there will also be a numerical algorithm that decides whether or not a sequence of numbers is the sequence of a proof. The number of the last sentence in a proof is a number of a theorem of whatever theory is being considered.

Definition   A theory is said to be *consistent* if and only if there is no sentence s such that both s and $\neg s$ are theorems of the theory.

Whether or not a specific theory, say set theory, is consistent thus becomes equivalent to a question that is purely about arithmetic: whether there are or are not pairs of sequences of numbers of the appropriate kinds corresponding to a proof of some sentence and its denial, both within the same theory.

If for a formalized theory there exists an algorithm that determines whether or not any given sentence is a theorem of the theory, then it would seem that the spirit of Kronecker's objections would be fully met. One could prove a theory consistent by purely arithmetic means, or as Hilbert put it, by "finitary" means. One could do so by

• formalizing the theory,
• arithmetizing its language,
• proving the existence of a computable number-theoretic function for deciding whether or not an arbitrary sentence is a theorem,
• showing that the function has the property that no sentence and its denial are both theorems of the theory whose consistency is in question.

Hilbert called this program *metamathematics*. It is mathematics done on the *language* of mathematics.

GÖDEL'S THEOREMS

In 1931 a young Viennese logician, Kurt Gödel, proved two theorems that were understood to mean that Hilbert's program as originally conceived could not succeed. Gödel's theorems used a generalization of Cantor's diagonalization strategy. Gödel applied Hilbert's program to arithmetic itself. If the goal of Hilbert's program were to succeed, one could decide the question of the consistency of any axiomatizable theory by using nothing more than arithmetic. So we could in principle formalize the theory of arithmetic itself (as we already did in part in an earlier chapter), and in formalized arithmetic one could represent the sentences of the language of *any* formalized axiomatic theory—represent them as collections of numbers, or special functions on the natural numbers. Then in formal arithmetic one could give a formal proof of the consistency or inconsistency of the formalized theory, whatever it might be.

Gödel proved two extraordinary theorems. The first theorem implies that arithmetic itself cannot be represented as an axiomatizable formalized theory. That requires some explanation. In the nineteenth century Giuseppe Peano had developed an axiomatic system for arithmetic. In their first-order formulation Peano's axioms are infinite in number, but they can be formalized, and they form a set of sentences for which there is an algorithm to determine membership. So Peano's axioms could be the object of arithmetic study, as in Hilbert's program. In fact, one can formalize Peano's axioms for arithmetic and then, in the language of that formal theory, assign a numeral (a term in the language of the theory) to each sentence of that very language. To understand Gödel's first theorem, it is necessary to recall the definition of a complete theory:

Definition   A first-order theory is *complete* if and only if, for every sentence s in the language of the theory, either s is in the theory or $\neg s$ is in the theory.

Gödel's first theorem says the following:

Gödel's theorem   No axiomatizable formal theory true in the natural numbers is complete.

What does this mean? Well, like any other structure, the structure determined by the natural numbers, $\mathcal{N} = [N, +, \times, s, <, =]$, determines a complete theory, call it T, namely the set of all sentences true in the structure $\mathcal{N}$. T includes all of the sentences that are logical consequences of the formalized counterparts of Peano's axioms, but T contains much else besides. Gödel's theorem says something about theory T: it is not axiomatizable. To say that the theory is not axiomatizable is to say something about the *nonexistence of algorithms*. It is to say that there does not exist a possible algorithm that assigns 1 or 0 to sentences so that the set of sentences assigned the value 1 consists of a set of axioms that entail all of the sentences true in the natural numbers (that is, in the structure $[N, +, \times, s, <, =]$), and of no other sentences.

Gödel's theorems actually say more than that the complete theory of arithmetic is not axiomatizable. They say that *there is an algorithm* that, if given as input a finite description of any axiomatizable theory that is true in $\mathcal{N}$ and entails Peano arithmetic, will produce as output a sentence that is true in $\mathcal{N}$ but is not a theorem of the theory.

Why should we care whether the theory of the natural numbers or other complete theories that extend Peano's arithmetic are axiomatizable? For at least two reasons. One is that Hilbert's program supposed that we could axiomatize theories that interest us. Gödel's result says that we can't always do so: the complete theory of the natural numbers is such a theory that cannot be axiomatized. But there is a second philosophical reason why we should care that the theory of the natural numbers cannot be axiomatized. *If a formalized theory cannot be axiomatized, there exists no possible algorithm that will decide for each sentence of the language of the theory whether or not that sentence is in the theory.* For if there were such an algorithm, we could let the set itself of all sentences that the algorithm says are in the theory be the axiomatization of the theory. Actually, something stronger is true. If a theory is not axiomatizable, there is not even an algorithmic means to *list* the theorems of the theory; there is no mechanical procedure that will, every now and then, output some sentence that is a theorem of the theory, never outputting a sentence that is not in the theory, and, for every sentence of the theory, eventually output it. We have no effective means of specifying a theory that cannot be axiomatized.

We all know an algorithm that, for any natural numbers n_1, n_2, and n_3, will determine whether or not $n_1 + n_2 = n_3$. The procedure is just the addition algorithm we learn in elementary school. We know algorithms that will determine the answers to other classes of arithmetic questions, for example, whether or not an arbitrary number is prime. So we might hope that there is an algorithm that will answer *every* question of arithmetic. Such an algorithm would decide the truth or falsity in the natural numbers of any proposition we might choose to put to it. Such an algorithm would be part of the fulfillment of Leibniz's dream. Gödel's theorem says that no such algorithm exists; it is not just that we have not found such an algorithm yet. Rather, *no such algorithm is logically possible.*

The notion of an axiomatizable theory was defined in terms of the notion of an algorithm, or alternatively in terms of a *computable* function (i.e., a function for which there is an algorithm) that assigns the number 1 to formulas that are in an axiom set and the number 0 to formulas that are not in the axiom set. As I have stated it, Gödel's theorem, thus asserts the nonexistence of certain kinds of algorithms; it asserts that certain functions are *not computable.* To prove his claims, Gödel therefore had to characterize the computable functions, and that effort, quite as much as his astonishing theorems, led to the development of computation theory. But rather than describe Gödel's characterizations of the computable functions as *recursive functions*, we will instead consider the characterization provided shortly after by Alan Turing.

Study Questions

1. Gödel's second theorem, also proved in 1931, is this: there is an algorithm that, given a finite description of any consistent, axiomatizable theory, entails formalized Peano arithmetic, outputs a sentence asserting the consistency of the theory, and that sentence cannot be proved in the theory.

Sir Ronald Fisher, the late and distinguished statistician, remarked in connection with the observation that a contradiction implies anything, that Gödel's result ought not to have been a surprise to anyone: "After all, suppose a Ph.D. student came, breathless with excitement, and said, 'Sir, I have *proved* that this system of axioms is free from all contradictions.' You'd say, 'Did you prove it using only those axioms?' He might say, 'Yes, I have here written out a chain of propositions which demonstrate that these axioms are free from all contradiction.' Well, perhaps you'd look at him with mild surprise, and you might say, 'I suppose you know that if this system of axioms did contain a contradiction, you could prove exactly those same propositions.' And so you have the situation that certain propositions which purport to prove the truth, the truth of the theorem, could be equally well demonstrated by the ordinary rigorous processes of deductive reasoning if they were false. And I don't know how much we would give, then, for the chain of theorems which purported to prove that the system of axioms was free from contradictions. It would seem a little absurd to imagine that such a thing was possible."[1] Consider carefully whether this passage is a sound attack on Hilbert's program and on the significance of Gödel's results.

2. An algorithm that lists all of the theorems of a theory does something intuitively less difficult than does an algorithm that, for every sentence, correctly decides whether or not the sentence is a theorem of a theory. Suppose, however, that you had a procedure that lists all the theorems of a theory T and that you had another

procedure that lists all the sentences that are not theorems of that same theory T. Explain how these two listing procedures could be used together to form a procedure that, for every sentence, decides whether or not the sentence is a theorem of T.

TURING MACHINES

Turing conceived of a kind of machine for computing functions, a machine whose operations are so simple that it would be absurd to think that they are in any way mysterious. The idea is that the machine somehow represents a function on the natural numbers, so that if, in a fixed code, you enter the representation of any number or finite sequence of numbers, the machine gives back the value of the function for that number or sequence of numbers. The coding of numbers can be done in many ways. Any number base provides a system of digits whose finite sequences encode all the numbers. We are used to representing numbers in base 10, with 10 digits; but we could just as well represent numbers in base 2 or any other base. Given a finite sequence of digits in some specified base, Turing's machine would compute another sequence of digits, in that base, representing the value of a function for the number input.

The machines Turing conceived can read a square of a tape on which some number has been written (see figure 12.1). The machine has a finite list of instructions that tell the machine, when it is in a particular state reading a particular square of the tape, to erase the digit on the square and write some other digit in its place, or to move to the next square to the left or right on the tape and to change its state. The tape is unbounded; that is, should the machine reach the end of the tape, more tape is always added. The machine starts with its reading and writing device over a blank square of the tape, and all of the squares to one side of the read/write head, say to the left, are blank. A finite number of squares on the other side, to the right, contain symbols representing the input to the machine, and the rest are blank. A computation is carried out with such a machine by starting the machine in its start state. The machine reads a square and does its thing: reading, writing, moving, sometimes to the right, sometimes to the left, changing its internal state as it does its work. Eventually the machine may stop, and when it does, there will be some sequence of symbols written on the tape. That sequence is the output of the machine for the given input.

Behaviorally, a Turing machine can do just three things:

- It can erase a symbol on a square of tape and write another symbol in its place.
- It can move the read/write head one square to the right.
- It can move the read/write head one square to the left.

Internally, the machine can only do one kind of thing: change its state.

Such machines can be physically realized in many ways. The tape could be a magnetic tape or even a section of paper tape; the read/write head of the machine could be a simple optical scanner connected to a printer in one movable unit. The instructions in each state could be implemented by cogs, pulleys, and ropes, by electronic tubes as in early digital computers, or by silicon chips.

There is nothing special about numbers save that certain functions on the numbers form our clearest examples of computable functions. But we know that, given any finite alphabet, the finite sequences of letters from that alphabet, or *words* as they are called, can be systematically coded as numbers, so functions from words to words can be represented as numerical functions. Thus we could just as well have Turing machines that have some finite vocabulary other than a system of digits and that compute functions from words on that vocabulary to words on that vocabulary.

You can think of the instructions, or program, of a Turing machine as a system of annotated points and lines. Represent each distinct state of the machine as a point or node, and draw an arrow from one node to another if some inscription on a tape square will cause the Turing machine when in the first state to go into the second state. Annotate the arrow with the symbol that the machine must read when in the first state to go to the second and with the symbol it writes or the direction in which it moves. Figure 12.1 illustrates a machine that operates on the vocabulary {B, 0, 1}, where B represents a blank square of tape, and that changes every digit to 1.

The machine starts, in state 1, at square 1, which is blank by convention. Then it moves one square to the right and changes to state 2. If the square to the right of square 1 is blank (no input), the machine halts and does nothing further. If that square has a 0, the machine writes a 1 in its place and stays in state 2. If that square has a 1, the machine moves to the right one square and stays in state 2.

To describe the sequence of states of the machine and tape, let the first number represent the number of the state of the machine, let the second number represent the number of the square that the read/write head is

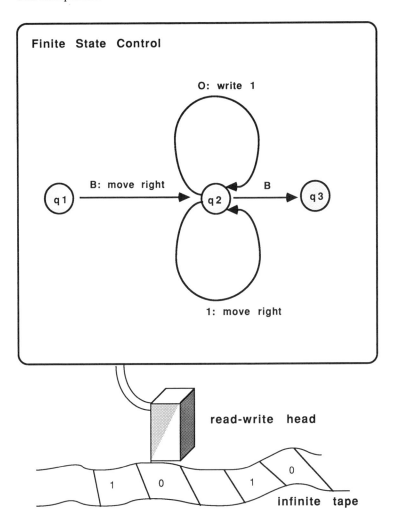

Figure 12.1
A Turing machine

over, counting the square initially underneath the read/write head as 1 and counting positively to the right, and let the remaining sequence of numbers be the sequence of digits on the tape. For example, if the input tape reads B1001, the sequence will be as follows:

1, 1, B1001B
2, 2, B1001B
2, 3, B1001B
2, 3, B1101B
2, 4, B1101B
2, 4, B1111B
2, 5, B1111B
2, 6, B1111B

A Turing machine can be described as a precise mathematical object, specifically as a finite set of 4-tuples of numbers. The first number of such a 4-tuple simply names the state of the machine corresponding to that 4-tuple. (Since the 4-tuples each specify what the machine does when it is reading a square in a certain state, for most machine states and each possible digit that can occur on a square, there will be a distinct 4-tuple.) The second number of the 4-tuple is a digit that can occur on a square, the third number is a digit that can be written on a square or a number representing "move right" or a number representing "move left," and the fourth number is again the number naming a state of the machine. Informally, $\langle n_1 n_2 n_3 n_4 \rangle$ is the instruction "If in state n_1 reading digit n_2, erase n_2 and write n_3, or move one square to the right if $n_3 =$ the special value, or move one square to the left if $n_3 =$ the other special value, and go into state n_4. By convention, we specify that state $n_1 = 1$ is the *start state* of the machine.

We can define the *computation* executed by a Turing machine given by a finite set of 4-tuples as a sequence of *instantaneous states of the machine* in the way illustrated in the previous example. Using the definition of a Turing machine as a finite set of 4-tuples, we can provide a precise inductive definition of a Turing-machine computation, but I leave that as a (difficult) exercise.

Turing proved that there is a single machine that will compute every function that can be computed by any Turing machine. Nowadays such machines are referred to as *universal Turing machines*. The idea is this. Since all Turing machines can be enumerated, we can form some encoding that assigns each Turing machine a number. Then we can design a Turing machine that interprets the first number on its tape as the number of a Turing machine, some conventional sequence of digits following that number as a space marker, and the following number on its tape as the input to the machine represented by the first number on its tape. The universal Turing machine thus simulates the computations that the Turing machine named on its tape would do for the input number on its tape. So there is in a sense one universal algorithm that will do everything any algorithm can do.

Study Questions

1. Write annotated directed graphs representing Turing machines that (a) change all 0s to 1s and erase the last 1, (b) change all 1s to 0s and add a further 0, (c) for some input, never halts.

2. For exercises 1a and 1b, give a trace of the sequence of instantaneous states of your Turing machine for input 1001.

CHURCH'S THESIS

It seems indisputable that any function computed by some Turing machine or other should count as a computable function. Besides Turing machines, there are many other ways in which we could try to model the notion of computation. For example, we could imagine a machine with an unlimited number of registers, in each of which a number can be written. Suppose that we are allowed to write any finite sequence of instructions of any of the following kinds:

$r_i := 0$ (Set the number in the ith register equal to 0.)

$r_i := r_j$ (Set the number in the ith register equal to whatever number is in the jth register.)

$r_i := r_i + 1$ (Set the number in the ith register equal to its successor.)

$goto(i, j, k)$ (If $r_i = r_j$, jump to the kth instruction in the list; otherwise, go to the next instruction.)

A program for such an *unlimited-register machine* (URM) consists of a finite set of instructions. Input is given by numbers in a finite set of the registers, with the convention that any register that does not have a number in it as input is assumed to have the value 0 in it unless given another value in the course of the computation. Output is given by the number in the first register when the machine stops.

A computation by an URM proceeds from the first program line and the initial state of the registers. The registers are changed in accordance with the program line, and a new state of the registers and new program line result (which will be the next program line or possibly some other program line if the present line has a "goto" instruction). Thus, just as with Turing machines, an URM computation can be described as a sequence of finite lists, where each list gives the program line and specifies for each i the value of r_i, the number in the ith (nonempty) register. As with Turing machines, some URMs may never halt for certain inputs.

Theorem   A function is computable by some URM if and only if it is computable by some Turing machine.

The characterization of computable functions as recursive functions, as functions computable by Turing machine, and as URM-computable functions are all equivalent in the sense that exactly the same class of functions satisfies all three descriptions. There are many other characterizations of computable number-theoretic functions. Alonzo Church, who gave one of the very first characterizations of this class of functions (one different from any of those described), formulated the following thesis:

Church's thesis   Computable number-theoretic functions are Turing-computable functions.

Church's thesis is not a mathematical theorem; it is rather in the nature of a proposal. The proposal is that, in view of the coherence of several conceptually very different approaches to characterizing one and the same class of computable functions, in view of the evidence Turing's work provides that the functions in this class are indeed computable by very simple machines, and in view of the fact that every function over the natural numbers that anyone is sure is computable turns out to be Turing computable, we should simply regard the computable functions as those computable by some Turing machine.

Since we know how to reduce functions defined over finite sequences of objects of any specified collection of types to functions over numbers, Church's thesis has broad implications. It is not just about the computability of functions over numbers; it is also about the computability of functions over whatever can be counted or enumerated by a computable one-to-one mapping or coding of objects to natural numbers. Through the device of characteristic functions that assign the value 1 to all members of a set and the value 0 to all members of its complement, the computability of (countable) sets can be reduced to the computability of numerical functions. Since the extensions of properties and relations are sets, the computability of such extensions, if they are countable, is also reduced to the computability of numerical functions.

Church's thesis could be taken more broadly as the claim that whatever can be computed can be reduced to the computation of a recursive function. If the world is in some respects continuous, as our physical theories assume, then we can use physical systems to compute functions defined not just over natural numbers but over the real numbers, or at least the rationals. Again, we might find physical processes that compute characteristic functions for uncountable sets. There have been attempts to characterize the notion of computability for real-valued functions without reducing such computations to computations on the natural numbers.

Hereafter, whenever I talk about the computation of countable objects, I will simply assume that Church's thesis is correct.

RECURSIVE AND RECURSIVELY ENUMERABLE SETS

Any set of numbers (or of objects that can be coded as numbers) can be represented by a function from the objects to $\{0, 1\}$. If S is a set of numbers, then f_S, the *characteristic function of S*, has the value 1 for numbers that are members of S and the value 0 for numbers that are not members of S. The same idea applies to sets of ordered pairs of numbers, to sets of ordered triples, and in general to sets of ordered n-tuples.

If f_S is a Turing computable function, then S is said to be a recursive set. For any recursive set, then, there is an algorithm that will decide for any number (or object coded by numbers or n-tuples of numbers) whether or not it is a member of the set. It is easy to see that a set S is computable if and only if the complement of S, S', is also computable. To prove as much, suppose there is a Turing machine T that computes f_S. Give the output of T as input to a Turing machine that outputs 0 when given 1 as input and outputs 1 when given 0 as input. When run in tandem the two machines represent a procedure for computing $f_{S'}$. Since there is a Turing machine that computes $f_{S'}$, by Church's thesis, S' is recursive.

The union of any finite collection of recursive sets is recursive; similarly the intersection of any finite collection of recursive sets is recursive. Many familiar sets of numbers are recursive. The even numbers are recursive, and therefore so are the odd numbers. The prime numbers are recursive; every finite set is recursive; the set of all natural numbers N is recursive.

Definition Suppose that S is a set for which there is an algorithm that computes a function whose value is 1 for members of S and 0 or undefined for numbers not in S. In that case, S is said to be *recursively enumerable*.

Every recursive set is recursively enumerable. The converse, however, is not true: there are recursively enumerable sets that are not recursive. For example, if we formalize the Peano axioms for arithmetic, then the set of all logical consequences of these axioms is recursively enumerable, but it is not recursive.

If S and its complement S' are both recursively enumerable, they are both recursive. For let T be the Turing machine that computes the value 1 for all and only members of S (but is undefined for all numbers not in S), and let T' be the corresponding machine for the complement set S'. Then run T and T' together. First let T execute a computational step, then T', then T, then T', and so on. Since any number is either in S or S' but not both, one of T or T' must eventually output a 1. Stop when that happens. If T outputs a 1 on input x, then $f_S(x) = 1$ and $f_{S'}(x) = 0$; if T' outputs a 1 on input x, then $f_{S'}(x) = 1$ and $f_S(x) = 0$. So there is a procedure that computes the characteristic functions of S and of S'. Hence again by Church's thesis, S and S' are recursive.

The complement of an recursively enumerable but not recursive set is therefore not recursively enumerable. However, the union and intersection of any two recursively enumerable sets are again recursively enumerable sets.

Sets that are recursively enumerable but not recursive are less familiar than recursive sets. Consider another example. Suppose that we effectively number all Turing machines and give to each recursive function the number of the Turing machine that computes that function. (One and the same function will therefore have an infinity of different numbers assigned to it, since many Turing machines compute the very same function, but given a number, we will be able to effectively determine the function that has that number, since the number will describe a Turing machine that computes the function.) Some of the functions computed by Turing machines will be *partial functions*. That is, the functions will be defined and have a unique value for some arguments but not for other arguments. (Consider the function that maps each natural number n into the first digit of its reciprocal, $1/n$. The function is not defined when $n = 0$.) For some inputs the Turing machines that compute a partial function will eventually stop and give an output, but for other inputs these Turing machines will never halt.

We denote recursive functions by Π_x, where x is the number of a Turing machine that computes the particular recursive function denoted by Π_x. Every partial recursive function has a domain, that is, a set of inputs or arguments for which the function is defined, or equivalently, a set of inputs for which a Turing machine that computes the function halts and gives an output. Since we can number the partial recursive functions, we can also number (or *index*) their domains. We let W_x denote the domain of the partial recursive function Π_x. Consider the set

$\{x : x \text{ is in } W_x\}.$

That set is not recursive, but it is recursively enumerable. Consider the set

$\{x : \Pi_x \text{ is defined for all natural numbers}\}.$

The latter set is not recursive and is not recursively enumerable either.

There are several equivalent characterizations of recursively enumerable sets. One of the most useful is that an recursively enumerable set is the *range of a total recursive function*. I will not prove this equivalence, but its significance should be noted. Suppose that a set has an associated computable function defined over all the natural numbers that will list the members of the set. Then and only then the set is recursively enumerable. Recursively enumerable sets are those that can be generated, or whose members can be listed, algorithmically.

Part of Gödel's achievement was to show that recursive sets can be represented by first-order formulas of number theory. For every recursive set S of numbers, there is a formula $S(x)$ in the first-order language of number theory such that under the natural interpretation of the language in the natural numbers, S is the set of numbers satisfying $S(x)$. Similarly, for every recursive set of n-tuples of numbers, there is a formula of number theory with n free variables satisfied by just that set. If R is a recursively enumerable set of numbers, there is a formula $\exists y S(x, y)$ of number theory such that the extension of $\exists y S(x, y)$ (that is, the set of values of the variable x satisfying the formula) is R and the extension of $S(x, y)$ is a recursive set of ordered pairs of numbers.

Study Questions

1. Using the facts just stated, show that if R is the complement of a recursively enumerable set, there is a formula $\forall y S(x, y)$ of number theory such that the

extension of $\forall y S(x, y)$ is R and the extension of $S(x, y)$ is a recursive set of ordered pairs of numbers.

2. Why is every recursive set recursively enumerable?

DECISION PROBLEMS

Every Turing machine is a finite sequence of 4-tuples. The collection of all *finite* sequences of numbers can be enumerated, and so can be put in one-to-one correspondence with the natural numbers themselves. So if we fix a vocabulary for input and output, the collection of all Turing machines for that alphabet can be enumerated, and in fact the enumeration can be done in a way that is intuitively computable. This is one way to see something interesting about the set of all computable functions: Since, by Church's thesis, the set of computable functions is just the set of functions that can be computed by Turing machines, and since the set of Turing machines is countably infinite, the set of all computable functions over the natural numbers is countably infinite. Since, by Cantor's results, the set of *all* functions on the natural numbers is uncountable infinite, this means that the computable functions form only a tiny fragment of the set of all functions over the natural numbers. And that means something very important: *for many functions and for many sets, properties, and relations for which we wish to have algorithms, it may be that no such algorithms are possible.*

Let's consider an example of an incomputable function. Consider the function $f(m, n)$ that assigns 1 to the pair (m, n) if m is the number of a Turing machine that halts on input n, and assigns 0 otherwise. Is this function computable? I will prove that it is not by a *reductio* argument that is reminiscent of the procedure used in Cantor's diagonalization argument discussed in chapter 1.

Form a infinite table, listing across the top of the table the natural numbers in sequence and listing along the right-hand side of the table the recursive functions (or all of the Turing machines) in sequence. Fill in the table as follows. If the Turing machine Π_i is defined on input number j, put a 1 in row i, column j. If, on the other hand, Π_i is not defined on input number j, put a 0 in row i, column j. The table then looks like the one in figure 12.2.

What the table now records in each row is the *characteristic function* of the domain of the recursive function in that row. The ith row, for example, has an entry of 1 for each member of the set of numbers for which Π_i is

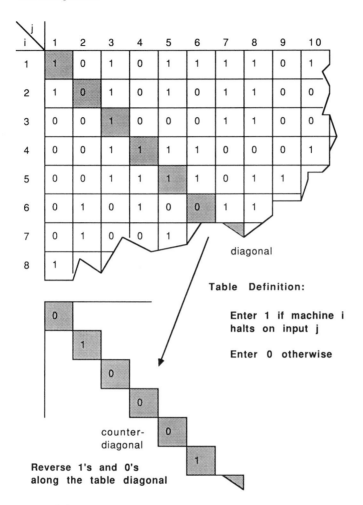

Figure 12.2
Table for the halting function

defined and an entry of 0 for each member of the set of numbers for which Π_i is not defined. In my earlier notation, the set of numbers for which Π_i is defined is W_i, and the set of numbers for which Π_i is not defined is the complement set, $N - W_i$. So, as I said, the ith row of the table simply gives the characteristic function of the set W_i. *Every set that is the domain of a partial recursive function has its characteristic function given by one of the rows of the table.* Hence, if there is a set whose characteristic function is *not* given by one of the rows of the table, that set is not the domain of a partial recursive function. But we know that every recursively enumerable set is the domain of a partial recursive function. Hence, if there is a set whose characteristic function is not given by one of the rows of the table, that set is not recursively enumerable.

Consider the diagonal of the table. If a 1 occurs in the ith row and ith column of the table, then Π_i halts on input i. If a 0 occurs in the ith row and ith column of the table, then Π_i does not halt on input i. So the diagonal of the table is the characteristic function of the set (call it H) of indices of Turing machines that halt when given their own index as input. Now consider what happens if, on the diagonal of the table, we replace each 1 with a 0 and each 0 with a 1. This new counterdiagonal is then the characteristic function of the complement of H (because the characteristic function of the complement of any set S is obtained from the characteristic function of S by interchanging the values of 1 and 0 in f_S). The characteristic function of the complement of H therefore does *not* occur as any of the rows of the table, because where the ith row of the table has a 1 in the ith column, the counterdiagonal has a 0, and where the ith row of the table has a 0, the counterdiagonal has a 1. So the counterdiagonal differs from every row in the table somewhere. Therefore, the counterdiagonal, which is the characteristic function of the complement of H, is not the domain of any recursive function. Hence the complement of H is not recursively enumerable.

The halting problem gives us one example of a function that is not computable. There are many others. Consider the problem of deciding whether an arbitrary first-order formula is valid. A decision procedure for that problem is some algorithm for computing a function that assigns 1 to a formula if and only if it is a valid first-order formula, and 0 otherwise. Clearly there is such a function, but is it a function for which there exists an algorithm? Is it a computable function? The answer is no. *There is no algorithm that will determine for us whether or not an arbitrary first-order formula is valid.* That means also that there is no algorithm that will determine for us whether an arbitrary first-order *argument* is valid, and therefore we cannot have a mechanical procedure that takes as input a finite list of formulas and determines for us whether or not the set consisting of all but the last member of the list entails that last member.

The philosophical consequences of this result, in combination with Church's thesis, are enormous. It means, for example, that the idea of solving all mathematical problems by an algorithm is hopeless. It means that Leibniz's vision of a calculus in which all knowledge can be expressed and its consequences algorithmically obtained must fail. It also means that a rich and difficult question emerges that only makes sense given the fact that first-order validity is not decidable: Which first-order theories are decidable? That is, which sets of sentences have an algorithm that will determine, for any sentence, whether or not it is a consequence of the set. Put another way, since theories are deductively closed collections of sentences, which theories have computable characteristic functions? These questions form what is known in logic as the *decision problem*.

Consider the theory of numbers. Part of what Gödel proved is that the set of theorems of Peano arithmetic is not decidable. Now consider the set of valid Boolean formulas. That set is computable. Consider any first-order theory that is both axiomatizable and complete. The set of sentences in that theory is computable, and the theory is said to be *decidable*. It is easy to see that if a complete, axiomatizable theory is decidable, then for given any sentence in the language of the theory, either that sentence or its denial is in the theory. Since the theory is axiomatizable, there is an algorithm that will decide whether or not a sentence is in an axiom set for the theory. We can also effectively enumerate all finite sequences of sentences in the language and computably determine, for any such sequence, whether or not it is a proof from axioms of the theory. For any sentence in the theory, such a proof will exist. Thus we can computably enumerate all the proofs from axioms of the theory until we find a proof of either a given sentence or its denial. If we find a proof of its denial, our procedure reports that the sentence is not in the theory; if we find a proof of the sentence, our procedure reports that the sentence is in the theory. So while much that we might wish to compute is not computable, many important functions, properties, and relationships are computable. The theory of elementary Euclidean geometry, for example, is axiomatizable and complete, and hence there is an algorithm that will decide, for any sentence in the language of geometry, whether or not the sentence is a theorem of Euclidean geometry.

These examples scarcely touch the intricate structure of the decision problem for first-order theories, a problem that is still an active area of research.

Study Question

Consider any axiomatizable first-order theory T with axiom set A. A sentence S is a theorem of T if and only if there is a proof of S from A. There is an algorithm that effectively lists all of the proofs from A. Explain why the set of theorems of T is recursively enumerable.

WHAT IS A COMPUTATION?

Cognitive psychologists sometimes write programs that they intend to be descriptions of the computational processes in the human brain. They often view the brain as a biological computer from the computations of which human cognitive abilities result. Often the psychologists' programs are intended not only to describe people's behavior but also to describe the very *procedures*, the very program, that people use in performing a cognitive task. Since the "programming language" of the brain must be very different from the LISP or Pascal in which the psychologists' programs are written, the psychologist is tacitly claiming that a program in one computational system describes, or is algorithmically equivalent to, a program in another computational system.

What can such claims mean? We have some idea of what is required for first-order theories to be syntactically equivalent when they are formulated in different formal languages, but what does it mean for two programs to be equivalent when they are in different programming systems? What makes a particular Pascal program equivalent to one LISP program but not to another? Clearly this is a question of fundamental importance for making sense of one of the most interesting applications of the computer. In this section I will try to sketch an answer.

The theory of computability began with two questions that have not been answered: What is a computation? What is an algorithm? Rather than answering either one of those questions, the development of the theory of computation proceeded by providing *specific* computational systems and then characterizing the computable as whatever can be computed in any one of these several systems. But this strategy does not give us any general characterization of a *computational system*, and so it does not give any general characterization of the notion of a computation. Nor does it give us a general account of the the notion of an *algorithm*. Each specific computational system gives us the notion of a *program*—for example, the list of instructions of an URM program or the first number on the input to a universal Turing machine—but we do not have any characterization of when two programs in *different* computational systems, say an URM program and a program on a universal Turing machine, are or are not implementations of one and the same algorithm.

We can get a taste of the variety of alternative computational systems by considering a few examples. The Pascal and LISP programming languages, when implemented on a computing machine, form a computational system. Moreover, they are computational systems capable of computing any recursive function if the machine memory can be increased whenever more is needed.

Consider what can be done with Turing machines. Rather than a Turing machine, which has a single tape on which the input, the intermediate work, and the output must all be done, we could consider a machine designed like a Turing machine but having several tapes: one for input, one for output, and any number for intermediate computations. For any number of tapes k, the class of k-tape Turing machines can compute exactly the Turing-computable functions, that is, the class of functions computable by a one-tape machine. A different sort of computational system is obtained if we introduce probabilities into Turing machines, but the class of computable functions is not thereby expanded.

It should not be thought that every imaginable computational system will be capable of computing the Turing-computable functions. To the contrary, there are many systems that can only compute a more restricted class of functions. For example, consider computational systems called *finite-state automata*. A finite-state automaton looks rather like the graph representing the machine-state transitions of a Turing machine. There are nodes, including a unique, distinguished *initial node*, and a nonempty set of *final nodes*. Each node has a certain number, say k, of arcs from it to other nodes (including possibly to itself), where k is the same number for all nodes and where the k arcs out of a node are given k distinct labels (figure 12.3).

A finite-state automaton executes a computation by taking a finite string of labels as input. The automaton begins in the initial state and then follows the arc with the label corresponding to the first element of the input string, then the arc with label corresponding to the second element

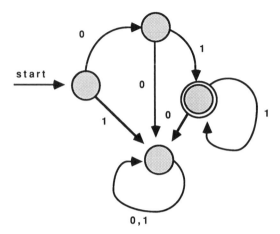

Figure 12.3
A finite-state automaton

of the input string, and so on. The automaton is said to accept the input string *s* if the antomaton ends up in one of its final states. Accepting string *s* is the same as computing a function that assigns 1 to a string if it is accepted and 0 to it otherwise. In representations of finite-state automata a final state is represented by a double ring. There are Turing-computable functions that cannot be computed by any finite-state automaton. The automaton shown will acept any string beginning 01 followed by any finite sequence of 1s. It will not accept any string that begins with 1 or that has two or more occurrences of 0.

Such computational structures as finite-state automata have an important role in representations of problems that humans might have to solve. Consider, for example, the task of making a telescope lens from a glass blank. The blank must be ground, polished, and aluminized to make it into a lens. These actions—grinding, polishing, and aluminizing—each affect the state of the glass. Moreover, to obtain a suitable lens, the operations must be applied in the correct order. If you aluminize the glass, then polish it, then grind it, the result will not be a telescope lens but simply a glass ground to the correct shape. In a problem such as this, the various states of the glass can be represented by nodes of a finite-state automaton, and the alternative actions are each represented by a label (for example, g, p, and a). There is a start state, representing the untreated glass blank, and a final state, representing the desired state achieved when the appropriate sequence of actions is taken. Each node or state has three arcs coming out of it, one arc for each action that could possibly be applied to the glass blank in the state represented by the node.

We can also consider *stochastic finite automata*, in which each label corresponds to a probability function connecting one node with other nodes.

Other computational systems are modeled, at least crudely, on the neural linkages of the brain. For example, *parallel-distributed-processing or connectionist* machines consist of a system of nodes connected by arcs. Each node can be on or off. Except for input nodes, whether a node is on is a stochastic function of the on/off state of the nodes immediately connected to that node. Some of the nodes can record input; that is, the external environment determines whether they are on or off. Other nodes are designated as output nodes, and their final or equilibrium state after the system has been given some input is the output of the system.

Clearly, the range of systems that can intelligibly be called "computational" is very large and diverse; we have no characterization that provides necessary and sufficient conditions for something to be a computational system. Though we have nothing comparable to Church's thesis, we can say something. Many of the computational systems just considered have the following features:

• A finite input vocabulary and a characterization of well-formed strings from this vocabulary.
• A finite output vocabulary and a characterization of well-formed strings from this vocabulary.
• A finite programming vocabulary and a characterization of finite sets of well-formed strings, or programs, from this vocabulary.
• Another finite vocabulary and set of well-formed strings characterizing "instantaneous states" of the computing process—including, for URMs, which instruction line is active and what numbers are in which registers and, for Turing machines, the location of the read/write head, the machine state, and the entries on the tape at a given moment.
• A computable function that takes each pair consisting of a program and an instantaneous state into another instantaneous state. This *transition function* is often tacit, but it is the heart of the matter. In a Turing machine it is the function that executes the machine instruction when the machine is in a specific state in which that instruction applies. In most of our examples, this function is one to one.

• A convention about how strings from the input vocabulary, together with a program, determine an initial instantaneous state.

• An analogous convention giving a computable function from programs and instantaneous states to the output language.

In each case, a *computation* for a program P and input string s is a sequence of instantaneous descriptions. The first member of the sequence is the instantaneous description determined by the input string, the program, and the input convention. Subsequent instantaneous descriptions are determined by the transition function. The final instantaneous description, if there is one, is correlated with an output by the output convention.

For computational systems that have these features, we can roughly say what it is for two programs in different programming systems to be implementations of the same algorithm. Roughly, two programs are algorithmically equivalent if there is a one-to-one (recursive) correspondence between their input languages, between their output languages, and between the languages in which their instantaneous states are described, and for every input s, these correspondences establish a one-to-one correspondence between the instantaneous descriptions of the two systems in the computations for the programs and for s. In the case of probabilistic machines, the one-to-one correspondence between instantaneous state descriptions in computations should preserve the probability measure. That is, the probability of any finite sequence of steps in a computation by one program for a given input should be the same as the probability of the corresponding finite sequence of steps in a computation by the other program for the corresponding input.

Study Questions

1. Describe the set of strings that the finite-state automaton for making a telescopic lens will accept.

2. Describe a finite-state automaton that will accept any input that is a sequence of an even number of 1's, but no other input.

3. Describe a finite-state automaton for making a telescopic lens.

COMPLEXITY

A problem you are given to solve may be easy or hard, depending on your abilities and your knowledge. If you happen already to know the answer to the problem (say you saw the answer sheet), the problem is very easy.

If you do not, solving the problem may require a lot of work. So the intuitive, informal notion we have of the difficulty of a problem makes difficulty a *relation* between persons and tasks; a task is easy or hard not in itself but only *for* some person.

There is an obvious notion of the difficulty of a computational task, a notion that is likewise relational. Suppose, for example, that we have some total function and a Turing machine that can compute that function. If we give a number to the Turing machine as input, we will get an output. In computing the output, the Turing machine will go through a certain number of steps; more exactly, if we write down the sequence of instantaneous descriptions of the Turing machine as it goes through the computation, that sequence will have some definite number of members. We can use that number, whatever it is, as a measure of the effort that the computation requires of the machine. If each step requires the same amount of time, the measure can be thought of as a measure of the time required for the computation.

Evidently, for one and the same input, different Turing machines may require different numbers of steps. Even machines that compute the very same function may differ in the number of computational steps they require. Given any specific Turing machine, we can always form another Turing machine that computes the very same function as the first one but requires more steps for some inputs. In fact, we can always find a machine that requires more steps for *every* input. We simply have to tack on extra initial states and add state transitions that do nothing.

It is easy enough to say roughly how difficult it is for a particular Turing machine to compute its output for a specific input. But can we say something more general? Suppose we have two Turing machines that compute one and the same total function f. Is there some way to *compare* the difficulty they have in computing the function? There is.

For each machine T, we look at how the number of computational steps the machine takes varies with the size of the input given to the machine. Suppose, for example, that we are representing numbers in some base, so each number is represented by a sequence of digits. We can measure the *size* of an input by the number of digits it contains. For any given size, there are only a finite number of possible inputs of that size.

For inputs of size 1, any particular machine T will require a number of computational steps. T might require 10 steps if the input in 0, 15 if the input is 1. Again, for inputs of size 2, T will require a number of computational steps, say 12 for 00, 13 for 10, 15 for 11, and 30 for 01. In principle,

Table 12.1
Numbers of computational steps required by T for various inputs

Input	No. of computational steps required by T
0	10
1	15
00	12
10	13
01	30
11	15

we could make a table listing the possible inputs of each size and the number of computational steps that T requires for each input (table 12.1).

Let's get the pieces straight. We are considering a Turing machine T that computes a function $f(x)$; we have a measure $s(x)$ of the size of inputs; we have a measure $c(T, x)$ of the computational cost for T to compute a value from input x.

Now if we have two different Turing machines, say M and N, each of which computes the same function, we can compare the two functions $c(M, x)$ and $c(N, x)$. It might be, for example, that for every input size, $c(M, x) > c(N, x)$. Or it might be that for all but a finite number of inputs, $c(M, n) > c(N, x)$. Or it might be that $c(N, x)$ is never greater than $c(M, x)$, but $c(M, x) > c(N, x)$ infinitely often. Each of these conditions is distinct, but in each case we would be inclined to say that the computation is more difficult for machine N than for machine M. Of course, it might turn out that none of these conditions obtain and that we can say no more than that for some inputs, M has it easier, and for other inputs, N has it easier.

This measure of computational cost is not very precise. It might be that in a real machine some steps require more time than others; it might be that in a real machine some steps get faster (or slower) if they are repeated. But we have at least a crude way of comparing the time requirements of different machines, and thus of comparing the difficulty they have in computation.

Here is a more difficult issue. We have made some sense of the notion of the difficulty of a problem as a relation between a task and a problem solver. We have even made some sense of the difficulty or complexity for the infinite set of tasks involved in computing a function: each input presents what we might call a problem instance, and the problem as a

Table 12.2
Largest number of steps required by T for various sizes of input

Size of input	Largest no. of steps T requires for input of that size
1	15
2	30

whole is to be able to compute the value of a given function for every input. That task may be more difficult for some Turing machines that compute the function than for others. We have not yet, however, characterized the *intrinsic difficulty* of a problem. We know that some functions are simply not computable, but of computable functions, we still do not have a way to say that some are intrinsically more difficult to compute than others. We have not yet found a way to clarify difficulty as a *property* of computational tasks themselves, rather than as a relation between a problem and a problem solver. We can do so.

For each input size there is an input for which the number of computational steps that T requires is the largest, or at least as large as any other. For inputs of size 1, the biggest value of the number of computational steps T requires for inputs of that size is 15; for inputs of size 2, the largest value is 30. So we can construct another table (table 12.2). And we have a function, call it $W(T, s)$, that measures the computational cost for T of the most difficult input of size s. The function $W(T, s)$ enables us to begin to talk more systematically about the difficulties of computation. In general, $W(T, s)$ will increase as s increases, but not always.

For a given Turing machine, $W(T, s)$ may be quite a ragged function not easy to describe. But we can ask about functions that *bound* $W(T, s)$. That is, we can ask whether a given well-behaved function of s is always greater than $W(T, s)$. For example, we can ask whether the function $g(s) = as + c$, where a and c are constants, is such that $g(s) > W(T, s)$ for all s. If that is true for some a and c, then we say that $W(T, s)$ is *linearly bounded*. Or we might ask whether there is any polynomial function of s, call it $P(s)$, such that for all s, $P(s) > W(T, s)$. If there is, we say that $W(T, s)$ is *polynomially bounded*. Again, we might ask whether there is any exponential function, call it $X(s)$, such that $X(s) > W(T, s)$ for all s. If so, $W(T, s)$ is *exponentially bounded* (see figure 12.4). We also say that T computes the function in *polynomial time* or *exponential time*.

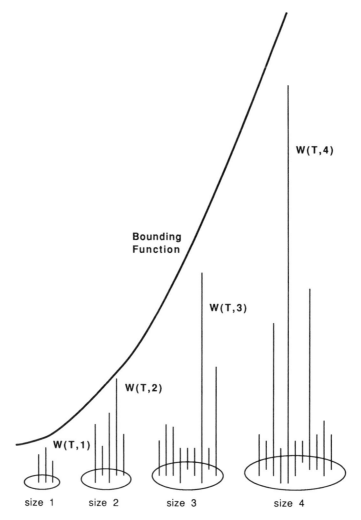

Figure 12.4
Worst-case-complexity bounds

Recall that the issue is whether there is a way to describe how difficult it is to compute a computable function. We are interested in a notion of difficulty that is not a relation between the function to be computed and the machine that computes it but is instead a property of the function itself. We know that if we have a Turing machine that computes a function with a worst-case computational difficulty given by the function $W(T, s)$, we can always build a Turing machine that has a harder time of it. By adding extra steps to T that do nothing useful, we can always find a machine T' such that $W(T, s) < W(T', s)$ for all s. It is easy enough to find a machine that computes a given function in a harder way, but it isn't always easy, or even possible, to find a machine that computes a given function in a sufficiently easy way. *There is, for example, no guarantee that for an arbitrary f we can find a Turing machine such that $W(T, s)$ is polynomially bounded.* Whether or not such a Turing machine exists depends on the function f. Similarly, whether or not there is a Turing machine that computes f such that $W(T, s)$ is exponentially bounded depends on f.

Definition   We say that a computable function is *computable in polynomial time* if there is a Turing machine T that computes f and such that $W(T, s)$ is polynomially bounded.

Definition   We say that a computable function is *computable in exponential time* if there is a Turing machine T that computes f and such that $W(T, s)$ is exponentially bounded.

Clearly, every function computable in polynomial time is also computable in exponential time, but the converse is not true. This classification of computable functions orders them by their intrinsic difficulty.

If a function is computable in exponential but not in polynomial time, we may expect that no Turing machine will offer a feasible means of computing the function. Every Turing machine that computes such a function will require exponentially increasing time for some inputs as the problem instances become larger. We can see what happens with a simple example. Suppose that $W(T, s)$ is of the order of $10s$. Then for the most difficult instances of each size, the time required increases as in table 12.3, or graphically as in figure 12.5.

Are there any interesting computable functions of the exponential class? There are a great many functions whose computation is of enormous practical importance that, *so far as we know*, are in this class. Since our interest here is principally in the theory of rationality, consider an example

Table 12.3
The computational cost for T of inputs of various sizes

s	$W(T, s) = 10^s$
1	10
2	100
3	1,000
4	10,000
5	100,000
6	1,000,000
7	10,000,000
8	100,000,000
9	1,000,000,000

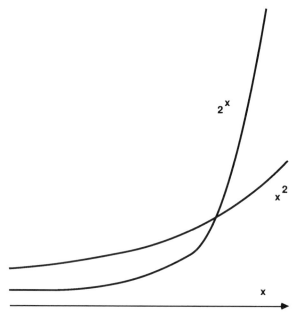

Figure 12.5
Exponential (2^x) and polynomial (x^2) complexity

germane to that theory. We know that there is an algorithm that, given any well-formed Boolean formula p compounded of n variables, will determine whether or not p is made true by any assignment of truth values to the propositional variables in p. In principle, we could implement any such algorithm on a Turing machine. But every known algorithm for this problem requires a number of steps that increases exponentially as n increases.

Something more remarkable is true. Suppose that we fix the number of simple sentences or sentential variables at any number $k > 2$, and suppose that we measure the size of a problem by the length of (that is, the number of symbols occurring in) of a sentential formula. Then every known algorithm that decides the consistency of Boolean formulas (that is, whether or not there exists an assignment of truth values to the variables of a formula that makes the formula true) requires computational time that, in the worst case, increases exponentially with size.

There are thousands of other problems for which every known algorithm is worst-case-exponential (if implemented on a Turing machine). Some of them are quite simple. Recall that a *graph* is any nonempty collection of nodes or vertices, some pairs of which may be connected by lines. A connected pair of vertices is said to be *adjacent*. Consider the following problem: determine for any graph whether or not each of its vertices can be given one of three colors so that no two adjacent vertices have the same color. So far as we know, in the worst case the number of steps any Turing machine will require to solve this problem increases exponentially.

Up to this point I have ignored an important question: What is special about Turing machines? That a function is exponential may be a property of that function, but it isn't a very interesting function if some computational system other than Turing machines can compute the function in polynomial time. What about multitape Turing machines or Turing machines with several read/write heads or URMs or random-access-memory machines, like ordinary computers? The particular computational bound (for the worst case) for a function depends on the class of machines considered. For example, if a function is computed by a two-tape Turing machine with a worst-case time bound $W(T, s)$, then some one-tape Turing machine will compute the same function with a worst-case time bound of $W(T, s)^2$. Moreover, there are functions for which any Turing-machine computation requires (up to a constant times) the square of the time that a two-tape machine requires.

The fact that different kinds of computational systems will have different worst-case bounds for one and the same function suggests that there is no intrinsic measure of the complexity of a function that is independent of the computational system considered. While that is true, it is not as serious as it seems, since some important distinctions do appear to be invariant. For example, whether or not a function is computable in polynomial time seems to be invariant over all familiar computational systems. We can't claim this invariance as a mathematical fact, since we do not know exactly what the class of computational systems includes, but every computational system we know of seems to have this property.

Another important question I have ignored has to do with the focus on the most difficult case in assessing the complexity of a computational task. There are algorithms that are used everyday without difficulty but that are worst-case-exponential. The practical success of these algorithms is due not to the fact that the inputs given to them are small but rather to the fact that the computationally difficult cases of any large size are *very rare*.

Probability and decision theory suggest an alternative way to measure the intrinsic difficulty of computing a function. For a given function f, a given size measure s, and a Turing machine T that computes f, consider the *average number of computational steps that T requires for inputs of size s*.

Definition   Denote the average number of computational steps that T requires for inputs of size s by $E(T, s)$, and call it the *expected complexity* of T for inputs of size s.

$E(T, s)$ can be regarded as a function of s. We can now ask about any computable function f and any function $g(s)$, which may be a linear function, a polynomial function, an exponential function, etc., whether or not there exists a Turing machine such that $E(T, s) < g(s)$. This mathematical apparatus enables us to compare expected computational complexity and worst-case computational complexity for one and the same function. If a function has a very low expected complexity, it may in practice be feasible to compute the function even though its worst-case complexity is very high. In fact, that sometimes turns out to be the case.

Consider again the three-color graph problem discussed earlier. Every known algorithm for deciding the problem is worst-case-exponential. But there is an algorithm for solving the problem that has *constant* expected complexity. The constant is not even very large: 192. What happens is that as the size of the graph increases, the proportion of graphs whose threecolorability is difficult to assess decreases exponentially. While there are always hard cases, they become increasingly rare. Here is another kind of problem where comparisons of worst-case and expected complexity can be surprising. Let me put this one in the form of a puzzle:

Consider the products of the BVD company. BVD (Bank Vaults by Dumbo) makes bank vaults. They make combination locks with as many dials and as many numbers on each dial as the buyer wishes. Their locks don't work in the usual way, however. For a lock with one dial having k settings, for example, the BVD company chooses at random a *subset* of the set of all k settings and fixes the lock so that it will open if and only if the dial is set to a number that is in the chosen subset. All subsets are equally probable. If a lock is preferred that has several dials, say ten of them, the BVD company will consider the set S of all *sequences* $s_1, \ldots, s_{10}$ of dial settings, where the first number is the number of a setting of the first dial, the second that of the second dial, and so on. BVD then chooses a subset of S at random and arranges the lock so that it will open when and only when the dials are set on a sequence in this subset. Again, all subsets are equally probable. BVD advertises, truthfully, that in the worst case the difficulty in cracking its vaults increases exponentially with the number of dials on the vault door. For consider the cases in which the subset that opens the vault consists of a single sequence of dial settings. In those cases, if there are k dial settings and m dials, there are k^m sequences of settings. A safecracker who knows nothing about the combination other than the general procedure by which BVD makes locks cannot do any better than to enumerate all of the possible sequences and try them one after another. In the worst case (worst, that is, for the safecracker), the true combination will be the last one in the enumeration, and so he will have had to try k^m sequences. On the basis of this convincing argument, BVD sold a great many vaults. The Enumeration Boys, a gang of safe-crackers, started specializing in cracking BVD vaults using an enumeration procedure like the one BVD claimed to be worst-case-exponential. They attempted to crack a great many BVD vaults, and they preferred vaults with a large number of dials because these vaults cost more and usually contained more loot than cheaper vaults. On the average, how many combinations (that is, how many trial settings of each dial) did the Enumeration Boys have to test before they found one that opened a BVD vault? The answer is that on the average the Enumeration Boys require no more than two guesses to open a BVD safe!

Review Questions

1. Define the term "algorithm."

2. Describe Hilbert's conception of metamathematics.

3. Discuss the implications of Gödel's theorem.

4. Characterize a Turing machine. Characterize a finite-state automaton.

5. State Church's thesis.

6. Distinguish between recursive and recursively enumerable sets.

7. What is the *characteristic function* of a set?

8. What are some commonly shared characteristics of computational systems?

9. What does it mean for one function to be *bounded* by another?

Further Reading

Computation theory

Davis, Martin, ed. *The Undecidable: Basic Papers on Undecidable Propositions, Unsolvable Problems, and Computable Functions.* Hewlett, N.Y.: Raven Press, 1965.

Jones, Neil D. *Computability Theory: An Introduction.* New York: Academic Press, 1973.

Kronsjo, Lydia. *Algorithms: Their Complexity and Efficiency.* Chichester, N.Y.: Wiley, 1979.

Van Heijenoort, Jean. *From Frege to Gödel: A Source Book in Mathematical Logic, 1879–1931.* Cambridge: Harvard University Press, 1967.

History of computing

Aspray, William. *From Mathematical Constructivity to Computer Science: Turing, Neumann, and the Origins of Computer Science in Mathematical Logic.* Ann Arbor, Mich.: University Microfilms International, 1981.

Aspray, William, ed. *Computing before Computers.* Ames: Iowa State University Press, 1990.

Aspray, William. *John von Neumann and the Origins of Modern Computing.* Cambridge: MIT Press, 1990.

Gardner, Martin. *Logic Machines, Diagrams, and Boolean Algebra.* New York: Dover Publications, 1968.

Goldstine, Herman Heine. *The Computer from Pascal to von Neumann.* Princeton: Princeton University Press, 1972.

Ritchie, David. *The Computer Pioneers: The Making of the Modern Computer.* New York: Simon and Schuster, 1986.

Williams, Michael R. *A History of Computing Technology*. Englewood Cliffs, N.J.: Prentice-Hall, 1985.

Gödel

Gödel, Kurt. *Collected Works*. Ed. Soloman Feferman. New York: Oxford University Press, 1986.

Wang, Hao. *Reflections on Kurt Gödel*. Cambridge: MIT Press, 1987.

Turing

Herken, Rolf, ed. *The Universal Turing Machine: A Half-Century Survey*. Oxford: Oxford University Press, 1988.

Hodges, Andrew. *Alan Turing: The Enigma*. New York: Simon and Schuster, 1983.

Chapter 13

THE COMPUTATIONAL CONCEPT OF MIND

INTRODUCTION

Thomas Hobbes didn't think of computation as an aid to reasoning. Reasoning, he held, *is* computation. Hobbes thought of our brains as composed of particles. The particles somehow serve as counters, as in an abacus, and ideas, or thoughts, are represented as numbers by these counters. When we reason, our brains do arithmetic.

There were no computers when Hobbes wrote, and no theory of computation. Experimental methods had only begun to be applied in the natural sciences, and not at all to questions of psychology. Hobbes's vision could not then constitute a *project* that people could pursue.

The science of psychology developed rapidly in the late nineteenth and early twentieth centuries. In the late nineteenth century a number neuropsychologists and psychiatrists developed the notion that the brain is a kind of machine in which nerve cells function as computational units and in which thoughts and desires are represented by physical states and processes in the brain. Perhaps the most prominent figure in this tradition was Sigmund Freud, whose early psychological work was premised explicitly on such assumptions.

The logical revolution inaugurated by Frege toward the end of the nineteenth century gave Hobbes's vision new support of a different kind. Frege's logic showed how to make theories of many kinds formally explicit, and it led Gödel, Church, and Turing to the modern formal theory of computational procedures. Even before the work of these men, Rudolf Carnap had applied Frege's system to produce an explicit *procedural* theory of cognitive states and features.

Hobbes's conception was remarkably prescient. It is nearly the conception of contemporary cognitive psychology, or "information-processing psychology" as it is sometimes called. The contemporary restatement of the view was developed by many people, but foremost by Allen Newell and Herbert Simon. Today it is a conception endorsed by most people (including psychologists, linguists, philosophers, computer scientists, and engineers) working on the topics vaguely characterized as "cognitive science." It forms a diverse intellectual project that occupies thousands of people. Our task in this chapter is to try to understand that project a little more fully.

THE COMPUTATIONAL CONCEPTION OF MIND

The description of a computational system requires a lot of structure. An input-output "convention" is required, a means for describing instantaneous states of the system, and a "transition function" that determines which states succeed which other states. In any physical realization of a computational system, these various formal structures must be realized by real, physical structures that somehow carry out the tasks formally described in the computational model. Any physical computer that is also to be an actor in the world will require *transducers* that turn physical effects into discrete input. It will require a mechanism (like the Turing machine's tape or the URM's registers) for storing information. It will require some physical means for implementing the transition function: the physical computer will have to make the appropriate states arise after one another. It will require other transducers to turn computational output into action, into motion in the physical world.

The project of cognitive science is to understand us as computational systems of this kind. To get a sense of the difficulty of the task, it may help to indulge your imagination. Suppose that an alien with a sophisticated understanding of conmputation came to study IBM personal computers. The alien, for whatever reasons, can't talk to us or to IBM or read descriptions of IBM computers.

What would the alien find? Well, for one thing, IBM personal computers are pretty much alike physically. For another, IBM computers exhibit a considerable range of different behaviors. The differences are subtle and have to do with what appears on the screen when the keyboard is struck. The alien might reasonably conclude that the keyboard and the screen are transducers, devices that change physical interactions with the environment into computational data structures, or vice versa. On that assumption, if the alien were a pretty good engineer, some idea could be obtained of the input and output conventions of the computational system. But how could the alien explain the enormous differences in the behaviors of different computers?

From a computational point of view, different behavior is to be expected if the many different IBM computers have different programs. So the alien must try to separate the capacities and dispositions of IBM personal computers that are *general* from those that are *specialized* and have to do with the particular programs that have been entered into the various computers.

The cognitive psychologist's task is roughly similar to the alien's. We humans are pretty similar physically. We exhibit a wide range of different patterns of behavior. The psychologist has a fair idea as to which of our organs—eyes and ears and such—are transducers but not a very clear idea at all as to the *code* of the computational inputs produced by physical stimuli or outputs producing physical action. Each human behaves a little differently from every other human because of different physical capacities, but more important, each human behaves a little differently from other humans because of a different history of inputs to the computational system. The psychologist assumes that all of us are born with a program wired into us, as it were; psychologists sometimes call this fundamental computational structure our *functional architecture*. What our innate program does is altered by our experience. In the same way, the IBM personal computer is born with a kind of universal program determined by its computational structure, and it acquires other more specific capacities when other programs, such as an operating system, are entered into it.

From the perspective of cognitive science, then, we are like the androids of science fiction; the only respect in which we are unlike androids is that no one deliberately fashioned us. We arose through natural processes. Not surprisingly, many people do not especially like this view of us. We will consider some of the arguments that have been advanced against it.

THE ARGUMENT OF LUCAS AND PENROSE

A version of the following argument was advanced some years ago by the philosopher James Lucas and has been restated with a slightly different emphasis by Roger Penrose, a distinguished mathematical physicist. Here is the argument in Lucas's own words. (In reading the argument, it may help if you understand "consistent formal system" as "consistent theory" and "provable-in-the-system" as "theorem of the theory.")

Gödel's theorem states that in any consistent system which is strong enough to produce simple arithmetic there are formulae which cannot be proved-in-the-system, but which we can see to be true. Essentially, we consider the formula which says, in effect, "This formula is unprovable-in-the-system." If this formula were provable-in-the-system, we should have a contradiction: for, if it were provable-in-the-system then it would not be unprovable-in-the-system, so that "This formula is unprovable-in-the-system" would be false; equally, if it were provable-in-the-system, then it would not be false, but would be true, since in any consistent system nothing false can be proved-in-the-system, but only truths. So the formula "This formula is unprovable-in-the-system" is not-provable-in-the-system, but unprovable-in-the-system. Further, if the formula "This formula is unprovable-in-the-system" is unprovable-in-the-system, then it is true. . . .

The foregoing argument is very fiddling, and difficult to grasp fully. The whole labor of Gödel's theorem is to show that there is no catch anywhere, and that the result can be established by the most rigorous deduction; it holds for all formal systems which are (i) consistent, (ii) adequate for simple arithmetic, i.e., contain the natural numbers and the operations of addition and multiplication, and it shows that they are incomplete, i.e., contain unprovable, though perfectly meaningful formulae, some of which, moreover, we, standing outside the system, can see to be true.

Gödel's theorem must apply to cybernetical machines, because it is of the essence of being a machine, that it should be a concrete instantiation of a formal system. It follows that given any machine which is consistent and capable of doing simple arithmetic, there is a formula which it is incapable of producing as being true, i.e., the formula is unprovable-in-the-system, but which we can see to be true. It follows that no machine can be a complete or adequate model of the mind, that minds are essentially different from machines.[1]

The crux of Lucas's argument is in the first sentence and the last paragraph. The stuff in between is to remind you of what he is talking about.

Many philosophical arguments that seem to establish something of great importance from assumptions of very little importance give that appearance by confusing the reader. The confusion is often in a "fudge phrase" which has no one exact sense or several exact senses between which the argument equivocates. In Lucas's argument the fudge phrase is "which we can see to be true."

Gödel did not prove that for every consistent formal system adequate for arithmetic, there is a sentence of arithmetic that is not a theorem of the system but that *we can see to be true*. There are no theorems of logic or mathematics about what *we can see to be true*. Gödel might have proved either of two things:

1. For every consistent theory adequate for Peano arithmetic, there *exists* a sentence that is true of the natural numbers but is not a theorem of the theory.

2. There exists an algorithm that, for every consistent theory adequate for Peano arithmetic, finds a sentence that is true of the natural numbers but is not a theorem of the theory. (This is the logically stronger claim.)

The first claim does not at all imply that, given a description of a consistent formal system adequate for arithmetic, *we* have the power to find a truth of arithmetic not entailed by the system. The first claim implies that such a sentence *exists*, not that it can be produced by us or by an algorithm. So if the first claim is what Gödel proved, then Gödel's theorem provides no support for Lucas's assumption that we have the power to locate, for each consistent theory adequate for arithmetic, a truth of arithmetic that the theory does not entail. Hence the first claim provides no support for his conclusion.

If the second claim is true and if, as Lucas says, given any theory adequate for arithmetic, we have the power to find a truth of arithmetic that is not a theorem of that theory, then a machine can do the same thing we can. The machine need only compute the algorithm that Gödel proved to exist.[2] Either way, Gödel's theorem does nothing to support the conclusion that humans are not computationally bounded. (Actually, Gödel proved the second, stronger claim.)

Study Question

Lucas says, "In any consistent system nothing false can be proved-in-the-system, but only truths." By "system" he means a formal first-order theory. Explain why his claim is false.

ARE MENTAL STATES IN THE HEAD?

What, in the computational conception of mind, are mental states? The computational conception says that cognitive capacities are computational capacities and that in exercising those capacities, we are executing a computer program, because we are nature's androids. That of itself says nothing exact about what thoughts are, or wishes or beliefs or any of the mental states that we attribute to ourselves and to others.

One proposal that fits rather naturally with the computational concept of mind is that mental states are *computational states*. Under the computational conception of mind, if we were fully to describe the cognitive structure of a person, we would specify an elaborate computer program, or perhaps a set of programs. Perhaps to each mental state of the person, e.g., to the desire for a pineapple, there would correspond a syntactic or formal feature of instantaneous descriptions of the person's computational system. The person would be in a state of desiring a pineapple whenever the person was also in a computational state that had that feature, whatever it might be.

We know that a computational system, abstractly described, has many possible physical realizations. With Turing machines, for example, we can use paper tape or plastic tape; it makes no difference. A recent article in *Scientific American* (in an April Fools' issue) shows how to make the components of digital central processing and memory units from ropes and pulleys. If features of a computational system that a person realizes characterize mental states, then perhaps the sensible view is that *anything*, any physical system at all, that realizes the same computational system as does a person will have the same mental states. Thus, as Ned Block, a contemporary philosopher, once pointed out, according to functionalism, if all the people in China got out flashlights some dark night and sent signals to one another, perfectly imitating the signals between neurons in a fragment of one person's brain, and if those neural signals in that person's brain constituted an instance of a mental state, then the system consisting of all the people of China flashing signals to one another would also have that mental state.

We already know this view of mental states as *functionalism*. Although it was a creation of philosophers (in fact, the view can be found among Christian philosophers as early as the fifth century A.D.), it corresponds nicely to what some artificial intelligence researchers like to say. John McCarthy, the inventor of LISP, was once asked whether a thermostat has beliefs. His reply was that the thermostat was capable of three beliefs: "Its too cold in here," "Its too hot in here," "Its just about right in here."

Hilary Putnam, who was one of the first to articulate the functionalist view of mental states in computational terms, subsequently produced an argument to show that mental states cannot be computational states. The argument is as follows:

We can consistently imagine that there exists somewhere a planet that is the twin of Earth. Everything happens exactly as on Earth, but with one difference. On this planet water is not H_2O, but something else, maybe deuterium oxide. Anyway, everything happens on Twin Earth as on Earth. So when I want a drink of water, my double on Twin Earth also wants a drink of water. When that happens, we are both in the very same computational state. But are we in the same *mental state*? Arguably not. For our mental states, in this case our wants, have a *content*, which is that some proposition be true. If we want different propositions to be true, then the mental states consisting of those wants must also be different. But the proposition that I want true is not the same as the proposition that my double on Twin Earth wants true when we are in the computational state that he and I both describe as *wanting a drink of water*. For my word "water" denotes H_2O, while my double's word "water" denotes something else. Hence the propositions we want to be true, the circumstances we want realized, are different. Indeed, I might be very unhappy if, instead of a drink of H_2O, I received a drink of whatever my double calls "water." Since the contents of our wants are different, we cannot be in the same mental state. But we are, by assumption, in the same computational state. Therefore, our mental states, my double's and mine, are not identical with our computational states. But if in the actual world mental states are identical with computational states, then in every possible world they must also be identical, because identity is a relation between entities (or properties) that, if true, is necessarily true, and what is necessarily true is true in every possible world.

We might object to this argument at length. Suppose, however, that we grant it and allow that mental states are not, or at least not all, in the head. Mental states are not computational states. Instead, mental states are pairs, consisting of a computational state and a *semantic relation* of some kind. The Twin Earth argument imagines a case where the first element of the pair is the same but the second element is different: features of the computational state denote different properties for me and my double.

It seems a bit mean that some philosophers maintain that this result about mental states constitutes a difficulty for the computational conception of mind (after all, psychologists didn't invent the functionalist doctrine; philosophers did!). The argument goes like this: Psychology is about mental life and its relation to behavior. But mental life consists of a sequence of mental states. Mental states in turn are not features of people's computational states, or of their computational states and behavior. The Twin Earth argument shows that mental states depend on *semantic* features, that is, on relations of denotation between symbols and features of the world, on relations of synonymy, and so on. Semantic relations in turn are at least in part a social creation. What words and phrases denote, which words and phrases are synonymous with each other, and so on, is at least in part (presumably in large part) the result of social practice. Hence the study of mental life cannot be separated from the study of society as a whole, and the idea of a cognitive science that confines its attention to individual behavior and individual computational processes rests on a mistake.

Should cognitive psychologists, faced with this argument, give up their enterprise and start doing sociology? I don't think so. The idea is that each instantiation of a mental state has two parts. One part is an instantiation of a computational or functional state consisting in momentary (or enduring) physical features of someone's brain, while the other part is an instance of a semantic relation between the person, or the physical features of the person's brain that constitute the instantiation of the computational state, and the rest of the world. Cognitive psychology often tries to study the first part, not the second. Why shouldn't it? Every psychologist is embedded in the society as fully as are her subjects. The psychologist knows what words mean and how to use them. Part of the competence of the psychologist is a social facility that does not have to be stated in an explicit theory and is not itself the subject of the psychologist's study. The psychologist, simply by being a member of society, has a practical knowledge of the second part of mental states—the relations of denotation, synonymy, and so forth—in almost every case. Her interest is in discovering the functional architecture of the brain and the rules by which the first parts of mental states succeed one another and interact with behavior. Nothing in the Twin Earth argument shows that there is no such architecture or that there are no such rules or that the psychologist cannot find them.

Study Question

Does the Twin Earth argument assume the Cartesian principle that if one can imagine that *p* then *p* is possible?

THE CHINESE ROOM

Cognitive psychologists and computer scientists interested in artificial intelligence sometimes do the following sort of thing. They find some interesting and complex human capacity that requires intelligence, and they write a computer program that, when executed, *simulates* that activity. The construction of the computer program might take into account, and attempt to be faithful to, human accounts of *how* the capacity is carried out. So one might simulate chess players, or one might simulate the puzzle-solving activities of experts and amateurs, whether at games or at textbook problems; one might even simulate the kind of understanding that people have when they read newspaper articles on various topics. One might, for example, write a program that will read articles on airplane hijackings and answer questions about the articles, questions that require the kind of inferences that we humans make. Or one might write a program that knows what to say and what to expect when ordering in a restaurant. Programs of all of these kinds have been written.

The aim of these simulations is often to attempt to give an explanation of how it is that humans are able to do what they do. The explanation offered is that we do what we do by executing a computer program like the one used in the simulation. Of course, if we execute such a program, it is internal to us, and we may not execute it *deliberately*, although there may be elements of deliberateness, as in problem solving. Some artificial-intelligence workers go on to say that if the computer program correctly describes the procedure that humans follow when they exercise the capacity being simulated, then the computer genuinely has that capacity as well: the computer *understands* or *thinks* or whatever. This view goes quite naturally with functionalism and is even consistent with the view that a mental state is a pair consisting of a computational state and a semantic relation.

John Searle, a philosopher, produced an argument against both of the views in the preceding paragraph. He used as his example programs written by Roger Schank, a computer scientist, designed to simulate reading and understanding a story. Schank's programs could answer reasonable questions about stories they were given on a particular topic. Searle denies (a) that the machine can literally be said to *understand the story and provide answers to questions* and (b) that what the machine and its program do *explains* the human ability to understand the story and answer questions about it.

Searle's objection is not to Schank's programs in particular but to all and any computer programs that, when implemented, are said to understand or to explain human understanding. Searle's argument is in the form of another thought experiment. Suppose that he is locked in a room with a large batch of Chinese writing, which he does not understand, since he does not understand Chinese. After this first batch of Chinese writing (the story), he is given another batch of Chinese script (the questions), and a set of rules, written in English, for producing Chinese script in response to the second batch of Chinese writing, the questions. He can follow the rules, even though he has no idea what the Chinese characters mean, because he can recognize and copy their shapes, and that is all that the rules, written in English, require him to do.

To complicate the story a little bit, imagine that these people also give me stories in English which I understand, and they then ask me questions in English about these stories and I give them back answers in English. Suppose also that after a while I get so good at following the instructions for manipulating the Chinese symbols and the programmers get so good at writing the programs that from the external point of view—that is, from the point of view of somebody outside the room in which I am locked—my answers to the questions are indistinguishable from those of native Chinese speakers. Nobody looking at my answers can tell that I don't speak a word of Chinese.... From the external point of view, from the point of view of someone reading my "answers," the answers to the Chinese questions and the English questions are equally good. But in the Chinese case, unlike the English case, I produce the answers by manipulating uninterpreted formal symbols. As far as the Chinese is concerned, I simply behave like a computer.... For the purposes of the Chinese, I am simply an instantiation of the computer program.[3]

Now Searle claims that it is obvious that he does not *understand* Chinese, even though he is, in this thought experiment, an instantiation of a computer program that behaves as though it understands Chinese. Hence it is false that a system can have mental states and understanding simply by instantiating the right program and exhibiting the right behavior. Furthermore, he claims, these examples give us good reasons to doubt that a computer simulation contributes anything toward explaining understanding.

In the Chinese case, Searle has everything that artificial intelligence can put into him by way of a program, and he understands nothing. In the English case, he understands everything, and there is so far no reason at all to suppose that his understanding has anything to do with computer programs, i.e., with computational operations on purely formally specified elements. As long as the program is defined in terms of computational operations on purely formally defined elements, what the example suggests is that such operations by themselves have no interesting connection with understanding. They are not sufficient conditions, and not the slightest reason has been given to suppose that they are necessary conditions or even that they make a significant contribution to understanding. Notice that the force of the argument is not that different machines can have the same input and output while operating on different formal principles—

that is not the point at all—but rather that whatever purely formal principles you put into the computer will not be sufficient for understanding, since a human will be able to follow the formal principles without understanding anything.

Searle claims that the human brain has special "causal powers" that produce understanding, intentionality, and mental states, and we have no reason to think that any computer executing a program that simulates human behavior has any such powers:

> "Could a machine think?" My own view is that *only* a machine could think, and indeed only very special kinds of machines, namely brains and machines that had the *same causal powers as brains*. And that is the main reason why strong AI has had little to tell us about thinking: it has nothing to tell us about machines. By its own definition it is about programs, and programs are not machines. Whatever else intentionality is, it is a biological phenomenon and it is as likely to be as causally dependent on the specific biochemistry of its origins as lactation, photosynthesis, or any other biological phenomena. No one would suppose that we could produce milk and sugar by running a computer simulation of the formal sequences in lactation and photosynthesis; but where the mind is concerned, many people are willing to believe in such a miracle, because of a deep and abiding dualism: the mind they suppose is a matter of formal processes and is independent of specific material causes in the way that milk and sugar are not.
>
> In defense of this dualism, the hope is often expressed that the brain is a digital computer.... But that is no help. Of course the brain is a digital computer.... The point is that the brain's causal capacity to produce intentionality cannot consist in its instantiating a computer program, since for any program you like it is possible for something to instantiate that program and still not have any mental states. Whatever it is that the brain does to produce intentionality, it cannot consist of instantiating a program, since no program by itself is sufficient for intentionality.[4]

There are several ways to view Searle's argument. In one perspective the argument might be viewed as an instance of the general argument against the reduction of meanings considered in chapter 10. More directly, however, Searle's argument appears to be an instance of the Cartesian fallacy: *I can imagine that p. Therefore, p is possible.* Let us consider this aspect a little more fully.

Searle is surely correct that even if we execute procedures in the process of understanding, not every possible system that executes those same procedures will understand. But no one ever seriously thought differently. An important aspect of many actions is *the time it takes*. A system that executes the very same computational procedures that I carry out in catching a baseball or reading a story or solving a problem but that takes considerably longer than I do to carry out those procedures *does not do what I do*. Nor does a system that carries out the same procedures I do but remarkably faster. Behavioral equivalence implies approximate temporal equivalence. The advocates of machine intelligence never meant (or never should have meant) that a system that takes thousands of years to parse a sentence understands English. The only interesting and plausible thesis for artificial intelligence is that systems that carry out the appropriate formal procedures on symbols that have the appropriate semantic roles, and do so in such a way as to approximate human behavior, understand. To approximate human behavior, the procedures must be executed with sufficient speed.

We can certainly *imagine* that Searle in a locked room can carry out instructions fast enough to simulate a Chinese speaker. But that does not entail that Searle in a locked room can possibly carry out instructions fast enough to simulate a Chinese speaker, and in fact, it seems quite unlikely that Searle could possibly do so. The range of topics over which a Chinese speaker can converse is enormous and unbounded. We can imagine that Searle has a huge set of volumes that list the correspondences between questions and answers in Chinese script (depending, of course, in complicated ways on what exchanges took place previously). Searle can't look them up fast enough to simulate a Chinese speaker. He can't memorize them either, any more than a child could learn English by memorizing all of the well-formed English sentences he might ever meet. If by "instantiating" a program that describes human behavior we mean instantiating it so that it can be executed rapidly enough to simulate human behavior in "real" time, then Searle's implicit claim that any program can be instantiated by having a human manipulate formal symbols seems to be flatly false.

The brain does have special causal powers. But perhaps the question about computation and intentionality is whether the special causal power of the brain is simply the power to compute certain programs rapidly enough. Perhaps nothing save an organic computer can compute the brain's programs rapidly enough to produce human behavior. Or, to the contrary, perhaps other systems, made of silicon and optical fibers or whatever, can. But still, no human trying to execute such a program given as a set of deliberate instructions can.

These considerations don't show that Searle's thesis is false, if his thesis is that computational structure is not the cause of intentionality and understanding and that the biological features that cause intentionality and understanding *merely happen to have* a computational structure, or perhaps even cause or constitute an instance of that computational structure. He could be correct. It might even be the case that there are physically possible systems that compute as we do and as fast as we do, but that don't feel, intend, or understand at all. Nothing has been established on either side.

CHALLENGES OF THE COMPUTATIONAL CONCEPTION OF MIND

We have looked at several arguments that attempt to show that there is something wrong with the very idea of cognitive science as it is now pursued, or something incoherent in the computational conception of mind. None of these arguments succeed, or even come close to succeeding. That does not show that the computational conception of mind is free of troubles. In fact, it has two very different challenges: there are too many possible computational theories of mind, and there are too few. The challenges for the computational theory of mind are not *conceptual*, they don't have to do with some subtle puzzle that has been overlooked. They are *empirical*; they have to do with whether and how the truth about mind can be discovered by observation and experiment.

One can get a sense of how difficult it is to find a computational account of mind by considering what is called the *frame problem*. To illustrate the problem, I will use an example due to the contemporary philosopher Daniel Dennett.

Imagine a robot that must get its spare battery from a room. It enters the room and finds its battery, and a bomb, both on a wagon. So it pulls the wagon from the room. The battery comes along, but so does the bomb. Result: no robot. The robot's problem is that it does not understand the consequences of its actions. It understands that pulling the wagon will bring the battery along, but not that it will bring along any other medium size object resting stably on the wagon. So we might give the robot a complete theory of the consequences of its actions. Let us suppose the theory specifies, for any action the robot might take, all of the circumstances that will change in consequence and all of the circumstances that will not change because of that action. The new robot enters the room and considers whether or not to pull the wagon with the battery (and the bomb) on it from the room. Before acting, it must compute the consequences of the action. One of the consequences is that the Earth will continue to rotate; another is that the stars will continue to shine; 2 plus 2 will still equal 4. The robot computes away until the bomb goes off. The problem with the second robot is that it did not compute the relevant consequences of its actions. So design a third robot that has, in addition to a theory of the consequences of its actions, a theory of relevance. It can tell which consequences are relevant and which consequences are not relevant to its interests. It isn't interested in the fact that the stars continue to shine; it is interested in the fact that if it pulls the wagon, both the battery and the bomb come along. Now the third robot enters the room and starts to compute *relevant consequences* of pulling the wagon out. It computes that a consequence is that the Earth will continue to turn, and that that fact is not relevant to its interests at the moment; it computes that the stars will continue to shine, and that is not relevant; it computes that 2 plus 2 will equal 4, and that is not relevant. And the bomb goes off again.

One moral to this story about the frame problem is about the difficulty of reliable prediction. From limited evidence where we have observed or manipulated physical systems of various kinds, we are able to form theories about the effects of our actions. Infants have a sophisticated capacity to learn enough very quickly about the everyday physical principles governing our world so that by the age of four or so they get around just fine. Scientists have a capacity to predict the effects of policies or actions from observations and experiments. Most of the relevant inferences in these cases have to do somehow with causal relations among events and properties. The question is whether there are general, reliable principles about causal inference that a computational system, whether infant or scientist or digital computer, can use to predict the effects of actions.

Another moral to the story is that to give a computational account of any human capacity, we must explain how it is possible for a computational system to generate and consider only *relevant* hypotheses or consequences. Philosophy has traditionally been concerned with characterizing relevance. Ideas of confirmation, explanation, responsibility, causation, and so on can all be thought of as ideas about particular kinds of relevance. But it is one thing to define or characterize a relevance relation and quite another to show how, from a given *A*, a relevant *B* or all and only the relevant *B*s can be found by a computational process. That is what the computational theory of mind must do. Moreover, it must do it for the kind of computer we appear to be. So finding *any* computational theory that accounts for our behavior is very difficult, and it is fair to say that for really complicated human capacities, we as yet have no such theory. There is, for example, no artificial computational system that will learn a human language from the kind of data available to a child. At the same time, there are too many possible theories of how we do what we do, and it may be that the evidence we have, or normally use, is insufficient to decide among them.

Suppose that we are trying to figure out how an android works, knowing that the android's cognitive behavior is produced by computational processes. We can get lots of copies of basically similar androids, although each android may have a slightly different history than every other android and so will behave slightly differently. We can observe the android's actions, subject it to whatever psychological experiments we please. We can measure the time it takes for the android to do various tasks. Can we discover the truth about how the android works? To see how difficult the task is, let's consider a simpler problem and assume that we (somehow) already have relevant prior knowledge. Suppose that there is a huge box we cannot open; a tape feeds into the box (input) and another tape feeds out of the box (output). The box eats trees, which it internally turns into more tape. Suppose that there is a limitless supply of these boxes and that we know they all have the same program. We know that the box is some kind of Turing machine. Suppose that we know there is a Turing machine inside the box. Can we determine the program of that Turing machine?

The boxes represent a discovery problem. All of the boxes compute the same function. Our task is to determine how they compute it. We can put whatever we want on the input tape to one of the boxes and see what the output is. We can do so for as many inputs as we wish, conjecturing some program at each step. Is there a procedure that will reliably identify the program of the boxes? Not if by "reliably" we mean that for every possible program for the box that computes a total function, when given a sequence of evidence from that function (that is, given argument, value, or input-output pairs for that function, in any order) the procedure eventually conjectures the correct program and conjectures it ever after. Let us say that a procedure *identifies* a collection of programs if it can, in this sense, discover each of them. Recall that a function is *total* if it is defined for every input value. Then if we think of each program as given by a Turing machine, we have the following:

Theorem Let K be the collection of all Turing machines that compute total functions. No computable procedure identifies K.

We need only consider computable procedures, because the very assumption of the computational conception of mind is that we, the would-be discoverers, are computational systems. If we cannot succeed in this rather weak, long-run sense of "function," we cannot succeed in stronger senses either. Success is possible only if we have prior knowledge that will restrict the set of possible programs (in fact, restrict it considerably) or if we have access to some further form of evidence.

Cognitive psychologists have access to additional evidence besides the input-output behavior of people. One thing they can determine in addition is the *time* required to process various inputs and produce an output in response. So the data really consist of a triple: an input, an output, and a real number representing the time required to get the output from the input. Time measurement is more useful if we know a bound on the time required for any computational step. If we know, for example, that the Turing machine inside the box requires *at least* 10^{-3} seconds to carry out the instructions in any state, we can use that information to reduce the number of alternative programs consistent with the data. What we get from the black boxes is input and output data and the time required to produce the output from the input. The time, together with the bound on the time required for each individual computational step, gives us a bound on the number of steps in sequence that the program can have executed in computing the output from the input. We need never conjecture any program that requires (for the input-output data we have already seen) more steps than the bound allows. Clearly, this provides us with a lot of information restricting the alternative Turing-machine programs.

The psychologist's problem is in some ways more difficult than the problem of the android boxes, because the psychologist must also identify what counts as input and output. Consider a psychologist doing research in which subjects are given oral instructions and an example and then are asked to carry out some problem-solving task that requires perception, reasoning, and some mechanical skills. Do the instructions constitute an input to a program instantiated in a subject's brain, and does the subject's consequent behavior constitute the output? Or do the instructions constitute a *mixture* of inputs to several different programs, and the behavior the output of these several distinct programs? Perhaps these programs are not completely distinct, and in the task assigned they interact. The psychologist's task is more difficult than in the case of the android boxes, because the psychologist has to identify the input and the output as well as the program. That task goes hand in hand with determining which human "faculties" are carried out by autonomous programs, which are identical, and which are carried out by programs that interact with one another. Vision, for example, might be carried out by a program in us that interacts with the program that carries out *imagining*; it might be that data structures that arise in the execution of one program have an effect on concurrent (or subsequent) executions of the other program.

I can illustrate this problem simply enough with the android boxes. Suppose that you can examine the input tape and the output tape that results from any android box, but you *don't know* whether the box contains one Turing machine that reads all of the symbols on the input tape and writes all of the symbols on the output tape or whether the box instead contains *several* Turing machines, some of which read and write some of the symbols and others of which read and write other symbols. Indeed, the symbol sets (or vocabularies) for the several Turing machines that might be in the box need not be completely disjoint. The space of possibilities is larger, and the identification problem more difficult.

Actually, the psychologists' problem is even harder. I have assumed throughout that the android box is a Turing machine or a collection of Turing machines. But what if we don't know that? Suppose that the android box can be an instantiation of any computational system whatsoever, so long as it is consistent with certain time bounds. It can be a multitape Turing machine. It can consist of several *nondistinct* Turing machines. They may share tapes or maybe just have some tape squares in common. It may be that some of the Turing machines in the box share symbols and parts of tape, so they can (internally) write over one another. It may be that the state transitions of one are influenced by the instantaneous states of another (two read/write heads can't be over the same square at once, for example). Or the box might contain a URM or a RAM machine or a production system or any of an infinite number of alternative computational systems. The bound on the number of steps that a computation can take between a given input and the output is not of much use in identifying the program inside the box. We know, for example, that if a function is computable by a two-tape Turing machine in time that is proportional to the size of the input, then it is computable by a one-tape Turing machine in time that is proportional to the square of the size of the input. Parallel results hold for three-tape, four-tape, and n-tape Turing machines. So if there is a Turing-machine program that meets the time bounds for given input-output behavior, there is an infinity of different programs (in different programming systems, namely Turing machines with different numbers of tapes) that do so.

The psychologist's task begins to look very hard indeed. Finding a computer program that, when run on a digital computer, simulates a piece of human behavior begins to look like very weak evidence that the program describes just how the human mind executes that behavior. We might begin to think that Searle's skepticism is warranted, but for different reasons than those he gives. There are, however, some reasons for optimism about the possibility of a successful cognitive science.

When people are asked to do a task, they are often able to report *how* they do it. In solving a puzzle or playing a game, one can describe at each moment the move one is considering. Sometimes one can even say *why* a particular move is under consideration. So it is as if we were android boxes that can describe some of their own computational steps. We are able to give away major pieces of our own program. Of course, that sort of information makes the task of finding the program much more feasible.

But perhaps not feasible enough. It might be objected that the parts of our internal program that we are able to articulate are, in a sense, superficial. We can articulate what we can deliberate on. But a lot of our cognitive capacity is not deliberate at all. When you see a sign written in English, you don't deliberately grasp what it says; you can't help yourself. If you are struck by a ball, or bitten by a horse, you may not deliberate the next time a ball or a horse comes by. If you deliberate when you learn a first language, we certainly don't know *how* you deliberate, even in those rare cases (as with Helen Keller) in which a first language is acquired at a comparatively mature age. The ways in which we deliberate seem likelier to be *learned*, and thus to be variable from person to person, than the ways in which we do things without deliberation (or in spite of it). One might reasonably doubt that the strategy of collecting introspective reports of deliberations will provide enough information to enable psychologists to characterize the functional architecture of the mind.

There is something further that can be done: open up the box. It would be a great deal more feasible to figure out how an IBM personal computer works if one could take the computer apart to determine its physical properties and components and how they function. It would be easier to determine how our imaginary android boxes work if we could open the boxes. According to the computational conception of mind, our brains constitute biological computers, and it would seem more feasible to determine our functional architecture if we discover how the pieces of our brains work, how they function in cognition. Much of the work on the physiology of the brain tells us very little about cognition and behavior, but increasingly there are examples of scientific arguments about human capacities that tell us more because in one respect or another they open up the box.

CAN THE COMPUTATIONAL CONCEPTION OF MIND BE WRONG?

I have left out some possibilities. They are not possibilities that will reassure those of us who want humans to have a special place a little outside of nature, but they are possibilities that are quite serious and contrary to the computational conception of mind. That conception has taken form within the confines of Church's thesis. It assumes, at least tacitly, that computation is discrete and limited to Turing-computable functions, and that an appropriate theory of humans is thus a theory of a device for computing Turing-computable functions. But there need be nothing supernatural or mystical in supposing that we are not such a device.

Consider the system of the planets. If you do certain things to that system, you get certain results. If for example, you shoot a space ship off the Earth with a certain thrust, the spaceship will follow a particular trajectory through the planets, depending on where the planets were located when the rocket took off. We can call input and output whatever we choose. If we think of the thrust and mass of the rocket and the positions of the planets as input, and the trajectory of the spaceship as output, this system does not look like a Turing machine, nor does the dependence between input and output look like a recursive function. For one thing, the inputs and outputs are for continuous variables; the functional dependence between input and output is not given by a function on the natural numbers but by a function on systems of real numbers to systems of real numbers. The solar system is a *dynamic system*. Perhaps we are as well, although, of course, a very different dynamic system than the system of the planets. Perhaps the dependencies in our nervous system and between our nervous system and the external world are properly described not by Turing-computable functions but by functions over other number systems besides the natural numbers. Not only is this imaginable, it seems plausible. We could not do physics very well if we confined our physical descriptions to Turing-computable functions. Since we ourselves are physical systems, it would be surprising if we could describe ourselves adequately by Turing-computable functions.

If we are dynamic systems, we may still be computational systems, of course. An instantiation of a Turing machine is a dynamic system that is a computational system as well. So is the computer on which I wrote this book. The point is that, while being dynamic systems, we might have cognitive capacities that are explained not by any computational system we instantiate but instead by the kind of dynamic system we are—just as the behavior of the spaceship after leaving the Earth is explained by the dynamic properties of gravitational systems generally and by the configuration of the solar system in particular.

Perhaps we should generalize the notion of computation and consider the solar system as a kind of computer: you put the rocket in, and the system gives you its trajectory out. So if the mass and thrust of the rocket code any other real-valued quantities and the trajectory of the rocket codes still other real-valued quantities, the solar system serves as a kind of *analog* computer. Considering ourselves as dynamic systems is thus something like considering ourselves as continuous, analog computers. The very idea raises questions about the general characterization of analog computation, about the connections between computation on the real numbers and on the rational numbers, and about the computational properties of various kinds of dynamic systems. Unfortunately, I must leave these issues to more advanced texts.

BOUNDED RATIONALITY

In the first chapters of this book we thought through the implications of a very banal fact: one doesn't always see what is entailed by a sentence, even though one understands it perfectly well. Later, in the discussion of probability, we also considered the implications of the fact that one does not usually simply believe a claim entirely or reject it entirely, but instead one puts some stock in it, gives it some credence, and the confidence one has varies from claim to claim. One result of these inquiries was a theory of meaning and a theory of entailment that together provide a *normative* theory of belief. That theory says what you ought to believe if you wish to believe all and only the necessary consequences of what you believe. These theories were presented as the logic of sentences and the logic of quantifiers, tied together in the theory of the logic of first-order languages. A further result of these inquiries was the theory of subjective probability, understood as a theory about how degrees of belief ought to be distributed.

Each of these theories is, in its way, very tolerant. Neither the logicians nor the Bayesians try to tell us very much about what we ought to believe. Instead, these theories impose *constraints* on our beliefs and partial beliefs.

Logic tells us that *if* we have certain beliefs, we are obliged to have certain other beliefs as well. It doesn't tell us much about which initial beliefs to have or about what to do if our beliefs have consequences that we don't believe. Subjective probability theory tells us constraints on how our degrees of belief should be distributed. It doesn't tell us that any particular proposition must be believed to a particular degree, except, of course, that logical truths must be given a degree of belief of 1 and logical contradictions must be given a degree of belief of 0. Decision theory doesn't tell us what to do; it tells us what to do *given* a specification of our utilities and degrees of belief.

Together these theories constitute the core of the best normative theory we have, the theory of rationality. It would, then, be a shock to discover that the theory does not apply to us and that, as it stands, the theory of rationality gives us no guidance in belief and in action. If, as cognitive science assumes, we reason by computation, that is the conclusion that seems to follow.

Rationality and Computationally Bounded Systems

With a little imagination, many of the things we do can be thought of as determining values of a function. For example, we recognize certain sequences of symbols as grammatical sentences of English, and we recognize certain other sequences as ungrammatical English. In doing so, we can be thought of as determining values for a function, the characteristic function of the set of grammatical English sentences. When we do arithmetic in our heads, or even with the help of a pencil and paper, we can again be thought of as evaluating a function, namely the arithmetic function in question. On any occasion when we are involved in a problem-solving task with a variety of discrete, sequential possible steps, say playing tic-tac-toe or playing chess or carrying out the actions required to make an omelet or to make a telescope lens, we can be thought of as evaluating a function. In these cases the function gives our moves in various positions (in games), or the actions we take at each step in the relevant states (in making an omelet or making a telescope lens).

What functions can we determine or evaluate, and how quickly can we determine or evaluate them? One view, which I will call the computational thesis, is this: *Given any "natural" decomposition of the actions a human can perform and any "natural" description of the selection of a sequence of actions as the evaluation of a function defined on discrete, finite objects and having discrete finite objects as values, all functions that humans evaluate are Turing-computable.* Because of the use of the phrase "natural description," this is quite vague, and it may not be possible to make the thesis a lot more precise. When someone is given, for example, a pair of natural numbers to add together, she produces a number in response. We understand the function she evaluates to be the arithmetic function over the natural numbers. When someone plays chess, we understand the function evaluated to be a function from positions to moves. Of course, when someone makes a move in chess, a lot more happens than simply the making of the move. The player may rub his chin, groan, move his arm in a certain fashion, put the piece down delicately, furrow his brow, wink, change the center of mass of the solar system, and on and on. We ignore all this.

If the computational thesis is true, then the theory of computation describes limitations on our abilities. The theory of computation is not a normative theory; it doesn't tell us what we *ought* to do. But if the computational thesis is true, the theory of computation tells us many things that are beyond our power to do. On that assumption, it is beyond our power to evaluate a function that is not Turing-computable; it is beyond our power to evaluate, in polynomial time, a function that has no polynomial-time algorithm. All the results of the previous chapter about the limits of computability, and many others not described in that chapter, are limits on *us*.

Suppose that people are computationally bounded systems. From this assumption it follows that there are certain things we cannot do. In particular, we cannot evaluate the validity of all deductive arguments in a first-order language if the language contains even a single binary predicate. Furthermore, we cannot determine, for every sentence in such a language, whether or not it is consistent. We cannot determine the set of all theorems of any theory adequate for arithmetic. If, as computational theorists generally believe (but have not yet proved), there is no polynomial-time algorithm that computes the characteristic function for the set of consistent formulas of sentential logic (with three or more atomic sentences), then we cannot determine the consistency of such formulas in polynomial time. Since a nondogmatic probability function must give a probability of 0 only to the inconsistent sentences of the language over which it is defined, it follows that we cannot evaluate a nondogmatic probability function over a first-order language, no matter how much time we take, and we cannot evaluate a nondogmatic probability function over Boolean formulas in polynomial time.

There are further limitations we should expect if we are computationally bounded systems. I have talked about computational complexity in terms of time, but there are also considerations of *space* that arise in computation. Any probability distribution over a set of propositions formed from sentences in a language for sentential logic is determined uniquely by the value of the probability function over the propositions that are conjunctions containing, for each atomic sentence in the language, either that sentence or its negation (but not both). These conjunctions are sometimes called *state descriptions*. If the language has n atomic sentences, there are 2^n different state descriptions. That is, there are 2^n logically nonequivalent sentences of this kind. So if we consider a relatively simple language in which there are only 50 atomic sentences, there are 2^{50} logically distinct state descriptions.

To represent an arbitrary probability distribution, we must specify the value of the probability function for each of the state descriptions. So with 50 atomic sentences, for many probability distributions we must store 2^{50} numbers to represent the entire distribution. Of course, there are particular distributions that can be characterized with many fewer parameters, but in the worst case, the amount of space required to represent a probability distribution increases exponentially with the number of atomic sentences in the language.

We cannot keep 2^{50} parameters in our heads, let alone 2 raised to the power of a few thousand, which is what would be required to represent a probability distribution over a realistic language. So if we can maintain probability distributions in our heads at all (as we must in some form if we are to compute their values), we can do so only for a very limited class of probability distributions. We cannot determine validity, consistency, and logical equivalence for all propositional formulas in time that inceases as a polynomial function of the length of the sentences, and we cannot take extremely long times to make decisions. Therefore, if we must make decisions in realistic time, we cannot be consistent, and we cannot be probabilistically coherent over sentences that are very long. We cannot determine validity, consistency, and logical equivalence for all sentences in a first-order language. For such a language, therefore, there will be cases in which our beliefs are inconsistent and our degrees of belief incoherent.

So we are in the following odd philosophical situation. We have normative theories that tell us what we ought to do, and perhaps we recognize the force of these theories. At the same time, we recognize that it is not in our power to act as the normative theories require. We simply cannot do it, any more than we can jump over the moon. But then, of what force is the normative theory? What is the *point* of a normative theory that tells us that we ought to do things that we cannot possibly do?

One answer is this: The normative theory of rationality imposes constraints on collections of beliefs and degrees of belief. We recognize that those constraints cannot be satisfied *everywhere* in the collection of beliefs and partial beliefs of computationally bounded humans. But they can be satisfied *locally*. The normative theory of rationality tells us what a mistake *is*. When we discover that a particular belief we hold is inconsistent, we can give up that belief. When we discover that a particular subset of probability numbers attached to propositions violate the axioms of probability, we can change some of those degrees of belief until our degrees of belief in *those* propositions no longer violate the axioms of probability. Whenever we find a mistake, we can correct that mistake. Moreover, whenever we find a mistake in our degrees of belief or our beliefs, we *ought* to correct the mistake. We cannot correct all possible mistakes, because we are computationally bounded, but we can correct any mistake we recognize, and we should.

Is this a good answer? Why, exactly, should a computationally bounded agent correct his logical and probabilistic mistakes when he finds them? It cannot be because correcting the mistakes will make the agent perfectly rational. If he is computationally bounded, it won't. Can it be that, by correcting our mistakes, we become, not perfectly rational, but *more* rational? That we move closer to the ideal of rationality? Perhaps, but we don't know what "closer" means. What is it for one inconsistent set of beliefs to be closer to a consistent set of beliefs, or "less inconsistent," than another inconsistent set of beliefs? What does it mean for one distribution of degrees of belief that violates the axioms of probability to be "closer" to a coherent distribution of degrees of belief than is another distribution that also violates the probability axioms? There are as yet few answers to these questions. There is no developed theory of approximate rationality. That does not mean that there could not be a theory of approximate rationality; it means only that no one has fully developed such a theory and given persuasive reasons for it. (In fact, there are scarcely any attempts at such a theory.) So we don't know what it means to get closer to being rational or to increase our degree of rationality.

If we did know what it meant to be a better or worse approximation to rationality, it still might not be the case that we ought to correct our mistakes. It might very well be, for example, that since we are computationally bounded systems, correcting one mistake will only cause us to make another mistake. Perhaps the mistake we make somewhere else by correcting a first mistake is worse than the first mistake itself. Perhaps the policy of correcting our mistakes will make us less rational rather than more. Or perhaps the best thing to do is to correct certain kinds of mistakes and not others. (I, for example, have never become expert in the word-processing system in which this book is written, even though I have written two books and dozens of articles using it. I have not done so because I think that the formatting errors I make are of minor consequence, and on the occasions when they are not, I can get help from others, and also because I think that the time required to become fully expert would cause me to make other mistakes of more consequence in other parts of my professional life. If I am correct in this, is it irrational for me not to correct my formatting mistakes?) The answers to these questions will depend not only on having a theory of approximate rationality but also on our understanding of ourselves, on what science may reveal about the particular limitations we have.

Study Question

Explain why no "computable" probability distribution can assign probability zero to all and only the logically contradictory sentences in a rich first-order language.*

CONCLUSION: ANDROID EPISTEMOLOGY AND ANDROID NORMS

The computational concept of mind is partly the fruit of a long tradition of philosophical work. Cognitive science itself has provided, and continues to provide, a rich source of philosophical issues, problems, and perplexities. The very idea that cognition is computation has prompted attempts at refutation that, if not convincing, are at least interesting. The practice and ambition of cognitive science present an abundance of conceptual problems that have attracted the attention of philosophers, psychologists, and computer scientists. But the richest lode of issues lies in two related questions. First, how can a computationally bounded agent possibly do what humans do? We might regard this question as the fundamental issue of android epistemology. It is remarkably like the kind of question that Kant posed, and it is an a priori question, not an empirical one. It is a question about how computation can be organized so that cognitive competence at least equal to that of humans is possible; it is not the more restricted empirical question about how we humans are *actually* able to do what we do. The issue of android epistemology is typically philosophical.

The other fundamental question posed by cognitive science has to do with normative principles of rationality for computationally bounded agents, in other words, with the principles of android rationality. For a computationally bounded agent, our standard normative theories of rationality do not provide a guide in life, or any set of standards that the agent ought to live up to. In the present state of our understanding of these normative theories, there is not even a good argument that a computationally bounded agent ought to correct particular violations of the norm when those violations are recognized.

Review Questions

1. Paraphrase the argument of Lucas and Penrose that *no machine can be a complete or adequate model of the mind*.

2. What is meant by the term "transducer"?

3. What is *functionalism*, and how does this perspective interpret mental states?

4. Define "functional architecture."

5. In your own words restate Putnam's argument to show that mental states cannot be computational states.

6. Discuss Searle's ideas concerning the intentionality and causal powers of human cognition. How do time constraints on procedures fit into this computational conception of mind?

7. What is a *normative* theory of belief?

8. Discuss some current problems facing the computational conception of mind.

9. State the *computational thesis* presented in this chapter. How is it related to the idea of approximate rationality?

Further Reading

Anderson, John Robert. *The Architecture of Cognition*. Cambridge: Harvard University Press, 1983.

Boden, Margaret A. *Computer Models of Mind: Computational Approaches in Theoretical Psychology*. New York: Cambridge University Press, 1988.

Boden, Margaret A., ed. *The Philosophy of Artificial Intelligence*. New York: Oxford University Press, 1990.

Cummins, Robert. *Meaning and Mental Representation*. Cambridge: MIT Press, 1989.

Cummins, Robert. *The Nature of Psychological Explanation.* Cambridge: MIT Press, 1983.

Dennett, Daniel Clement. *Brainstorms: Philosophical Essays on Mind and Psychology.* Montgomery, Vt.: Bradford Books, 1978.

Dilman, Ilham. *Mind, Brain, and Behavior: Discussions of B. F. Skinner and J. R. Searle.* New York: Routledge, 1988.

Fodor, Jerry A. *The Language of Thought.* New York: Crowell, 1975.

Fodor, Jerry A. *Modularity of Mind: An Essay on Faculty Psychology.* Cambridge: MIT Press, 1983.

Fodor, Jerry A. *Psychosemantics: The Problem of Meaning in the Philosophy of Mind.* Cambridge: MIT Press, 1987.

Fodor, Jerry A. *A Theory of Content and Other Essays.* Cambridge: MIT Press, 1990.

Haugeland, John. *Artificial Intelligence: The Very Idea.* Cambridge: MIT Press, 1985.

Haugeland, John. *Mind Design: Philosophy, Psychology, Artificial Intelligence.* Cambridge: MIT Press, 1981.

Hilbert, David, and Wilhelm Ackerman. *Principles of Mathematical Logic.* New York: Chelsea Publishing Co., 1950.

Irvine, A. D., ed. *Physicalism in Mathematics.* Boston: Kluwer Academic Publishers, 1990.

Lanczos, Cornelius. *Space through the Ages: The Evolution of Geometrical Ideas from Pythagoras to Hilbert and Einstein.* New York: Academic Press, 1973.

Lycan, William G., ed. *Mind and Cognition: A Reader.* Cambridge: B. Blackwell, 1990.

McClellan, James L., David E. Rumelhart, and the PDP Research Group. *Parallel Distributed Processing: Explorations in the Microstructure of Cognition.* Vol. 1, *Foundations.* Vol. 2, *Psychological and Biological Models.* Cambridge: MIT Press, 1986.

Newell, Allen. *Unified Theories of Cognition.* Cambridge: Harvard University Press, 1990.

Newell, Allen, and Herb Simon. *Human Problem-Solving.* Englewood Cliffs, N.J.: Prentice-Hall, 1972.

Penrose, Roger. *The Emperor's New Mind: Concerning Computers, Minds, and the Laws of Physics.* New York: Oxford University Press, 1989.

Posner, Michael I., ed. *Foundations of Cognitive Science.* Cambridge: MIT Press, 1989.

Pylyshyn, Zenon W. *Computation and Cognition: Toward a Foundation for Cognitive Science*. Cambridge: MIT Press, 1984.

Pylyshyn, Zenon W., ed. *Perspectives on the Computer Revolution*. Englewood Cliffs, N.J.: Prentice-Hall, 1970.

Pylyshyn, Zenon W., ed. *The Robot's Dilemma: The Frame Problem in Artificial Intelligence*. Norwood, N.J.: Ablex, 1987.

Reid, Constance, and Herman Weyl. *Hilbert*. New York: Springer-Verlag, 1970.

Searle, John R. *Minds, Brains, and Science*. Cambridge: Harvard University Press, 1984.

Sieg, Wilfried, ed. *Acting and Reflecting: The Interdisciplinary Turn in Philosophy*. Boston: Kluwer Academic Publishers, 1990.

Simon, Herbert Alexander. *Models of Bounded Rationality*. Cambridge: MIT Press, 1982.

Simon, Herbert Alexander. *The Sciences of the Artificial*. Cambridge: MIT Press, 1969.

Slezak, Peter, and W. R. Albury, eds. *Computers, Brains, and Minds: Essays in Cognitive Science*. Boston: Kluwer Academic Publishers, 1989.

Stich, Stephen P. *The Fragmentation of Reason: Preface to a Pragmatic Theory of Cognitive Evaluation*. Cambridge: MIT Press, 1990.

Stich, Stephen P. *From Folk Psychology to Cognitive Science: The Case against Belief*. Cambridge: MIT Press, 1983.

Stich, Stephen P., ed. *Innate Ideas*. Berkeley: University of California Press, 1975.

Woodfield, Andrew. *Thought and Object: Essays on Intentionality*. New York: Oxford University Press, 1982.

Part IV

CONCLUSION

Chapter 14

THE ENTERPRISE OF PHILOSOPHY

A philosopher is someone who has no laboratory, performs no experiments, usually collects little data of any kind, has no resources except the knowledge others have provided together with her own perspicacity and powers of reasoning. With so little, the philosopher nonetheless claims to be engaged in an enterprise that furthers human understanding. The claim may seem unlikely, but in many cases it is nonetheless true. How can that be? Part of the reason, of course, is that the world is always full of foolishness, and anyone with a mind to can try to further understanding by debunking silly claims and projects. But philosophers claim to do more than that. How can they?

While philosophy is an a priori enterprise, it is not really separated from empirical knowledge, or at least it should not be. Great philosophical inquiry has always been informed by empirical understanding of nature and ourselves, and by mathematical knowledge. The problems of bounded rationality illustrate the point. But that is still only a fragment of the answer. The better part is that a great deal of what we need to understand our world, ourselves, and other creatures, actual or possible, involves thinking through the implications of fundamental concepts and assumptions.

The chapters in this book have considered some of the background of philosophical thought that led to branches of contemporary knowledge, including mathematical logic, computer science, cognitive psychology, artificial intelligence, and statistics. There are other subjects, such as economics, for which the philosophical tradition has been equally important but that we have not considered at all. Even for the subjects we have considered, only a few of the more prominent contributions of philosophy have been described. Other pieces of philosophical work have been of real importance to the sciences, and still other works of great importance are in the making. A few examples, chosen simply because I know of them, can serve as illustrations.

Some years ago Donald Davidson and Patrick Suppes carried out empirical studies of how people actually make decisions. Davidson later gave fascinating, nontechnical accounts of familiar human phenomena, such as weakness of will, by supposing that each of us has an internal decision-theoretic framework. Suppes, among many other things, helped to develop the mathematical theory of psychological measurement. The best philosophical work on the foundations of physics has formed a part of physics itself. For example, David Malament at the University of Chicago and John Earman at the University of Pittsburgh have made interesting contributions to our understanding of the structure and implications of modern space-time theories. In recent years the mathematical structure of reliable inference has been pursued by Scott Weinstein, a logician and philosopher, in collaboration with Michael Stob, a mathematician, and Daniel Osherson, a psychologist; and also by Kevin Kelly, a young philosopher and logician at Carnegie-Mellon University. Some of the most interesting present work on causal inference and prediction is being carried out by Peter Spirtes, a philosopher and computer scientist. The project of investigating how probabilistic and decision-theoretic norms may be adapted to agents whose rationality is bounded in one way or another has been pursued by Teddy Seidenfeld, a philosopher-statistician, and in a quite different way by Brian Skyrms, a philosopher at the University of California at Irvine. There are too many philosophers to name who have contributed and continue to contribute to the development of logical systems for representing formal aspects of our theories of belief, obligation, and necessity. Still others, such as Donald Nute at the University of Georgia, John Pollock at the University of Arizona, and Wilfried Sieg at Carnegie-Mellon have worked in different ways toward developing logical systems for computationally bounded systems.

What makes any of this and other contemporary work *philosophy* rather than statistics, physics, economics, computer science, or something else? One thing that marks philosophical work is the attempt to make sense of entire enterprises that on reflection seem profoundly puzzling or obscure in some fundamental respect. That, for example, is part of what distinguishes the work of such philosophers as Jerry Fodor, Daniel Dennett, and Paul and Patricia Churchland, who have worked for decades to clarify the enterprise of cognitive science. It is also what distinguishes some of the best philosophical work on the foundations of physics. There is no reason, of course, why the philosophical business of making sense of an enterprise must be done by professional philosophers. Zenon Pylysyn is a psychologist who has given a great deal of thought to how to make sense of the idea of a computational theory of mind, and more physicists than philosophers have worried about the interpretation of quantum mechanics.

Another mark of philosophical work is that, while addressing a discipline, it deliberately and self-consciously violates the assumptions of that discipline, not from ignorance or incompetence but for good reason. Thus Seidenfeld's work denies some of the axioms of the usual theory of probability to better represent the human situation, or simply in the interest of working out a possible case.

A third mark of philosophical thought is that it brings to bear rational standards that may, for accidental reasons, be ignored within a discipline. John Rawls's work on the theory of justice, for example, provided a decision-theoretic realization of ideals of fairness to argue for constraints on political and economic institutions in a way that was rather foreign to economics and political science. Again, Spirtes's work applies to causal inference the standards of reliability that statisticians have used for other sorts of inference problems but have failed to apply to the problem of determining causes.

Finally, philosophical work has its peculiar motives: it asks who we are and how we stand in the world, how it is possible for there to be creatures like us, what we can and cannot know, and how we can best conduct our lives.

These marks are the good effects of considering the history of philosophical perplexity, theory, and argument, free from the conventions of any particular contemporary scientific discipline but informed nonetheless by scientific and mathematical knowledge.

NOTES

Chapter 1

1. From Euclid, *The Thirteen Books of Euclid's Elements*, trans. Thomas Heath (New York: Dover, 1956).

2. From J. Hick, *The Existence of God* (New York: Macmillan, 1964), pp. 25–26.

3. S. Cahn, ed., *Classics of Western Philosophy* (Indianapolis: Hackett, 1977), p. 296.

4. Ibid., p. 297.

5. Ibid., p. 416.

Chapter 3

1. A. Edwards, *Pascal's Arithmetic Triangle* (New York: Oxford University Press, 1987), p. 20.

2. Thomas Hobbes, *De Corpore*, chap. 1, in *English Works*, ed. Molesworth (1839), reprinted in *Body, Man and Citizen* (New York: Collier, 1962), pp. 24–26.

3. *Rules for the Direction of the Mind*, in *The Philosophical Works of Descartes*, ed. E. Haldane and G. Ross (New York: Cambridge University Press, 1970), vol. 1, p. 3.

4. Ibid., p. 9.

5. Ibid., p. 7.

6. Ibid., p. 8.

7. "Objections and Replies," in *Philosophical Works of Descartes*, vol. 2, pp. 41–42.

8. *Principles of Philosophy*, in *Philosophical Works of Descartes*, vol. 1, pp. 224–225.

9. "Objections and Replies," in *Philosophical Works of Descartes*, vol. 2, pp. 34–35.

10. Ibid., p. 158. Descartes response will be found in the same work on p. 216.

11. *Philosophical Works of Descartes*, vol. 2, p. 45.

12. *Leibniz Logical Papers*, trans. and ed. G. Parkinson (New York: Oxford University Press 1966), p. 93.

Chapter 4

1. G. Boole, *The Laws of Thought* (New York: Dover, 1951), p. 42.

2. A directed graph would be better, but the use of undirected graphs is standard.

3. Boole actually used the rule $1 + 1 = 0$, so we would now call the algebra he described *Mod 2 arithmetic*.

4. Boole, *Laws of Thought*, pp. 181–182.

5. Ibid., pp. 407–408.

Chapter 6

1. The system is taken, with minor modifications, from H. Enderton, *A Mathematical Introduction to Logic* (New York: Academic Press, 1972).

Chapter 7

1. Isaac Newton, *Newton's Principia*, Motte's translation revised by F. Cajori (Berkeley: University of California Press, 1946), p. 12.

2. Ibid., p. 21.

3. Ibid., pp. 398–400.

4. G. Grube, *Plato: Five Dialogues* (Indianapolis: Hackett, 1981).

5. Sextus Empiricus, *Outlines of Pyrrhonism*, trans. R. Bury (Cambridge: Harvard University Press, 1935), p. 283.

6. D. Hume, *An Enquiry Concerning Human Understanding*, in S. Cahn, ed., *Classics of Western Philosophy*, p. 707.

7. Ibid., p. 711.

8. Ibid., p. 712.

9. Ibid., p. 715.

10. Ibid., p. 715.

11. *Meditations on First Philosophy*, trans. D. Cress (Indianapolis: Hackett, 1980), p. 60.

Chapter 8

1. From S. Cahn, ed., *Classics of Western Philosophy*, p. 795.

2. S. Stigler, *The History of Statistics* (Cambridge: Harvard University Press, 1986), pp. 65–66.

3. Hume, *Enquiry Concerning Human Understanding*, in S. Cahn, ed., *Classics of Western Philosophy*, p. 726.

4. Thomas Bayes, "An Essay towards Solving a Problem in the Doctrine of Chances," *Philosophical Transactions of the Royal Society of London* 1764:376.

5. Ibid., p. 373.

6. Ibid, p. 380.

Chapter 9

1. *Metaphysical Foundations of Natural Science*, trans. J. Ellington (Indianpolis: Bobbs-Merrill, 1970), pp. 104–105.

2. Perhaps because primitivism emphasizes social authority rather than the autonomy of individuals and because it denegrates rationality and inquiries into the claims of knowledge, primitivism has an ugly record of political associations: Heidegger was a prominent and active Nazi. Merleau-Ponty wrote a book-length defense of Stalin's crimes and purges. Several leaders of the Khmer Rouge, including Pol Pot, who are reported to be collectively responsible for killing more than a million Cambodians, studied primitivist philosophy in Paris after World War II. After his death it was discovered that Paul de Mann, late professor of French literature at Yale and prominent champion of primitivist approaches to literature, had been an anti-Semitic journalist in Europe during World War II. Clearly no one needs be a primitivist philosopher to have rotten political views (Michael Dummett, one of Frege's present-day interpreters, claims that Frege was an anti-Semite), but it seems to help.

Chapter 10

1. Edmund Gettier, "Is Justified True Belief Knowledge?" *Analysis* 23:121–123

2. Nozick sometimes requires only that if p were not true, one would not believe p.

3. Edith Hamilton and Huntington Cairns, eds., *Plato: The Collected Dialogues* (Princeton: Princeton University Press, 1963), pp. 381–382.

Chapter 11

1. Aristotle, *De Anima* (On the Soul), trans. J. Smith, in *The Basic Works of Aristotle*, ed. R. McKeon (New York: Random House, 1941), p. 538.

2. The argument given is based loosely on Saul Kripke's reconstruction of Wittgenstein. See Kripke, *Wittgenstein on Rules and Private Language* (Cambridge: Harvard University Press, 1982).

3. David Hume, *A Treatise of Human Nature* (Oxford: Oxford University Press, 1888), p. 469.

Chapter 12

1. Ronald Fisher, *Smoking: The Cancer Controversy* (Edinburgh: Oliver and Boyd, 1959), p. 46.

Chapter 13

1. J. R. Lucas, "Minds, Machines, and Gödel," in Alan Ross Anderson, ed., *Minds and Machines* (Englewood Cliffs, N.J.: Prentice-Hall, 1964), pp. 43–44.

2. Those who have read the previous chapter will notice that this step assumes Church's thesis. So one way to view Lucas's argument is that it is just an unsubstantiated denial of Church's thesis.

3. J. Searle, *Minds, Brains, and Science* (Cambridge: Harvard University Press, 1984), p. 37.

4. Ibid., p. 42.

INDEX

Absolute space, 172
Accidental properties, 40
Achilles paradox, 22
Algebra, 86, 100
 atoms of, 198
 Boolean, 102 f.
 product, 198
Algorithm, 301, 305, 307, 320, 323
 equivalent, 326
Analog computer, 358
Analysis (method of), 69, 72, 117
Anselm, 16 f., 20
Aquinas, Thomas, 19 f., 22
Argument,
 invalid, 6
 sound, 6
 transcendental, 225, 228
 valid, 6
Aristotle, 19, chap. 2, 66, 67, 72, 74,
 81, 95, 100, 115, 137, 167, 277
Arithmetic, 302
Arithmetization (of syntax), 305
Artificial intelligence, 57 f.
Attribute, 38, 84
Augustine, 78
Austin, John, 241
Automaton, finite-state, 323
Axiomatic method, 44
Axiomatic system, 11
Axiomatic theory, incomplete, 88
Axiomatizability, 305, 306, 322

Bacon, Francis, 65, 66, 115, 168, 180,
 182

inductive method of, 168 f.
Bayes, Thomas, 204, 205, 206 f., 213,
 217
Belief, degrees of, 359
Berkeley, George, 117, 180, 186, 278
Bernoulli, Jacob, 195, 196, 200, 202
Bernoulli trials, 195 f.
Bernoulli's rule, 198 f.
Bernoulli's theorem, 203 f.
Binomial coefficient, 82, 83
Binomial distribution, 200 f., 204
Binomial theorem, 81 f.
Boethius, 69
Bohr, Niels, 135, 136, 138
Boole, George, 89, 95 f., 120, 130
Bounded rationality, 358 f.
Boyle, Robert, 278
Brentano, Franz, 283

Camus, Albert, 242
Cantor, Georg, 27 f., 302, 303
 diagonalization strategy of, 306
Cardinality, defined, 26
Carnap, Rudolf, 228 f., 234, 235, 282
Cartesian fallacy, 285 f., 349
Cartesian principle, 346
Cartesian product, 143
Causality, 227
Cause, 41 f., 171
 efficient, 41
 final, 42
 formal, 41
 material, 41
Chinese room argument, 346 f.